How You Can Use
INFLATION
to Beat the
IRS

WARNER BOOK

How You Can Use INFLATION to Beat the IRS

All the legal ways to keep your money for yourself and your family . . . without getting in trouble with the IRS

B. Ray Anderson

Introduction by Howard J. Ruff

WARNER BOOKS

A Warner Communications Company

This Warner Books Edition is published by arrangement with Harper & Row Publishers, Inc., 10 East 53rd Street, New York, N.Y. 10022.

Warner Books, Inc., 75 Rockefeller Plaza, New York, N.Y. 10019.

Ⓦ A Warner Communications Company

Printed in the United States of America

First printing: February 1982

10 9 8 7 6 5 4 3 2 1

Library of Congress Cataloging in Publication Data

Anderson, B. Ray (Billie Ray), 1933–
  How you can use inflation to beat the IRS.

  Bibliography: p.
  Includes index.
  1. Income tax—United States—Effect of inflation.
HJ4652.A872   1982   343.7304   81-13093
ISBN 0-446-37126-2   AACR2

Dedication

**To Margaret, my wife—who believes in me
and still has enough ''pioneer spirit'' to think
our real success in life is yet to come.**

Contents

Acknowledgments

So many people have in so many ways contributed to the development and publication of this book, and I would like to express my special thanks to each of them. To Joyce Stauffer, a true friend and faithful legal assistant, who kept my office intact while I put the book together; to Glen Hoggan, a book publisher who first suggested it could be done; to Howard J. Ruff, who had enough faith in my tax talents to entrust me with his "people" and who worked out the creative "inflation indexing" gold clause strategies in chapter 4; to Ron Wright, who created the land banking ideas in chapter 16; to Steve Skabelund, McKay Johnson, Wil Reiser, Gillette Edmunds, Ron Boyer, Marc Bouret, Dave Brown, Dave Nearon and a host of other tax technicians who gave their assistance on much of the material in the book; to Nancy Crawford, my editor; and to Erik Sandberg-Diment, a talented and helpful writer.

DEAR READER:

The most devastating impact on your financial security and that of your family is the double whammy of *inflation* and the *progressive tax rates* imposed by our federal government. Millions of hard-working Americans labor for years to gain some measure of financial security for themselves and their families only to find that what they thought was a very nice nest egg has been totally destroyed by these two debilitating forces.

No one can afford to underestimate inflation. Not only will it be here for several more years; it's probably going to get even worse. Actually, inflation has been silently and insidiously eating away at our money for years, but we didn't realize the gravity of the situation until just recently. My own father, for example, who began working as a railroader for the Union Pacific Railroad Company in southwestern Wyoming in 1922, was enticed by the promise of increased income and a retirement program supported by the Railroad Retirement Act. He was led to believe that this program would provide adequately for his wife and support his children if he happened to die early. His whole life was tied to this promise of financial security. Yet, when he died at the age of 68, after forty-five years of faithful service and just three years after his retirement, his widow received a pension of only $250 a month. Not enough to pay the rent, let alone support herself. No one in 1922 could foresee that the amount of money my mother now receives, which is equal to my father's monthly wage in the early days of his railroad service, would become only a token payment in our present economy. *Inflation can destroy your life's work and wreak havoc with the financial and emotional security of those you love.*

There is also a progressive tax rate dilemma in this country. Simply stated, it means the more money you earn or save, the higher the rate of taxes you will have to pay on your income and on the property you and your family own. In other words, as you earn more, you get to keep proportionately less. Our onerous tax laws are slowly but surely destroying the incentive of millions of decent American workers who resent forfeiting the fruits of their labor to taxes they feel are imposed by an increasingly out-of-touch, hopelessly morassed governmental bureaucracy. True, tax protest programs and tax reforms are now underway in many states. And President Reagan was successful in pushing through Congress the Economic Recovery Tax Act of 1981 (ERTA), which includes a tax cut of some $22 billion beginning in 1981. But this new bill is not going to make a significant difference because it won't begin to make a dent in what the individual taxpayer pays the IRS each year.

The question that faces you is: What can you do to keep your money *now*, while you wait for the government to get its act together?

I have written this book to give you the answer, or, more accurately, the *answers*. Because there *are* many ways—all of them 100% legal—in which you can beat both inflation and the IRS. In fact, **you can actually use inflation to beat the IRS,** as the title of this book promises. Turn to page 1 and begin reading. You'll see how you can do it.

I have also written this book because I know that many of you who feel frustrated by the never-ending battle to keep up with inflation and taxes also feel confused about where to turn for help. Each year dozens of books are published that promise to tell you how to invest in exotic schemes to conquer inflation or how to set up a Swiss bank account to protect your money from the IRS. Tax-evasion schemes dupe thousands of unsuspecting Americans every year. And yet when people turn to their lawyers and accountants for honest advice, they find that some of the most highly paid professionals don't know the remedy.

The information in this book represents a synthesis of the best legal and inflation/tax planning advice available. It reflects not only federal laws governing taxes, but summarizes state laws as well. It recommends inflation-proof investments and financial strategies that are the result of nearly two decades of helping to solve the inflation and tax problems of hundreds of clients in many states. It also reflects my experience as a tax attorney, authorized to practice before the U.S. Tax Court, and as a Certified Tax Specialist. In addition, I have been an attorney for the Internal Revenue Service, which gives me the advantage of knowing how the IRS thinks, what they're up to, and exactly when and where they are likely to crack down on the taxpayer.

I have used the strategies in this book to protect my own income and property and to keep it for myself, my wife, and my seven children. **Some 80 percent of the families in this country urgently need to use them, too.**

I encourage you to take decisive and immediate action to reduce your taxes, keep more of your money now so you can transfer it tax-free later, and allow whole tax dollars to work for you. If you do, you will be more secure now and for the rest of your life. If you don't, inflation and the IRS will not only continue to drain you of your money, they'll also be your principal heirs.

Good luck!

B. Ray Anderson
November 1981
New York

Introduction

B. Ray (Bill) Anderson is my attorney and does my estate planning. I can think of no higher recommendation of a man's expertise and services than to pay him good money for them. I pay Bill good money because he is the best there is.

For several years I have known him as church associate, estate planner, personal attorney, corporate counsel, neighbor, seminar co-speaker, and fishing buddy.

In 1978, we at *The Ruff Times* developed the broad outlines of a concept for using inflation and "hard money" to beat the tax man. I had concluded that even if my recommendations to buy gold, silver, real estate, and diamonds should result in big profits, beating inflation by a whole lot, the odds were that by the time capital gains taxes and estate taxes (at the time of death) had been paid, all of our "beat-inflation" gains would have been poured down the rat hole of taxation. I found that people who worried about beating a 15 percent inflation rate were ignoring the problems of a 50 percent income tax rate, a 28 percent capital gains tax rate, and ruinous estate taxes, which seemed to me to be a case of closing the front door of the barn while the horses sauntered out the back.

Bill and I put our heads together and came up with a detailed program to help our clients actually benefit from the inflationary spiral, consistent with Will Rogers' advice to "invest in inflation, it's the only thing that's going up," while escaping taxation—legally. My job was to lead the offensive team—to teach people to make investments that would increase in value faster than their money was losing purchasing power. Bill was to run the defense to make sure that the money did not leak out the tax back door.

The concepts that Bill has developed are unique. Most financial planners are into "tax shelters" and "deferred taxation," but grossly underestimate the impact of inflation on an estate because they consistently underestimate the future inflation rate. Traditional estate planning seems to be based on the assumption that inflation will continue at manageable, and predictable, and acceptable levels. I don't believe that will be the case and neither does Bill. The strategies which he has developed are based on the assumption that inflation will continue and, in fact, increase. The principles embodied in this book are very similar to those of judo. You use your opponent's own strength to defeat him. We are using the strength of inflation to defeat inflation's impact.

Bill Anderson is honest, pragmatic, practical, cool-headed, and professional in the best sense of the word, and both he and the principles and strategies in this book have my unqualified endorsement.

I know very few people that I would entrust with my life but Bill is one of them.

One word of caution. If this book becomes the bestseller that it deserves to be and lots of people begin utilizing these strategies, the IRS will probably counterattack to plug up the holes. This book is only one salvo in an ongoing battle between the citizens who feel they deserve to keep the fruits of their labors and pass them on to the next generation and a rapacious government with a life of its own which is turning to more and more repressive police-state methods to finance its needs, even in the face of the growing tax revolt its methods are creating. This is war, but the spirit of this book is that this war should be fought openly and within the rules. There is a growing band of tax protestors who believe that we should refuse to pay taxes, using various devices such as forming your own church or refusing to fill out your 1040 form, claiming their Fifth Amendment rights. Neither Bill nor I is prepared to abandon and confront the system. There are ample ways, within the rules established by the system, to defeat that system, and it is to those methods this book is dedicated.

History records that any nation which does not pass its values and its wealth on to the next generation is only a generation or two away from dissolution. This book, if widely enough read, could be the salvation of the American free-enterprise economic system and the capital that makes it work.

—Howard J. Ruff

How You Can Use
INFLATION
to Beat the IRS

1

Yes, You Really Can!

Anyone may so arrange his affairs that his taxes shall be as low as possible; he is not bound to choose that pattern which best pays the Treasury. Everyone does it, rich and poor alike, and all do right; for nobody owes any public duty to pay more than the law demands.

—Judge Learned Hand

Today's collapsing economy is a great battlefield where the armies of inflation and ever-increasing taxes are warring with your money. Right now, these forces of monetary destruction are engaged in a colossal pincers movement, crushing your hard-earned income in their jaws.

This is war. And if you're going to fight, you need a battle plan. A plan that will turn these enemies of your money against each other. A plan that will leave them fighting only each other, while your money escapes to the safety of the sidelines where it can grow and prosper. A plan that will work the year around, not just in April, to fend off the IRS's grasping hands. That plan is *creative tax avoidance*—which actually uses inflation to increase your real assets dramatically, at the same time cutting them off from the IRS.

Creative tax avoidance, and how to use it to keep your money for your family and yourself and away from the dual ravages of inflation and the IRS, is what this book is all about.

NO, IT'S NOT ILLEGAL

Tax *evasion*, not paying taxes owed—that's illegal. But tax *avoidance*, reducing your tax bill or even eliminating it through some careful paperwork, is not only legal, it's actually encouraged by the Congress of the United States. Every time you take a deduction or an exemption or a credit on your income-tax return, you avoid paying tax money that you would otherwise owe. Avoiding, not evading—that's the legal way.

For the most part, the deductions you now take are the ones everyone else takes. That's not the way to do it. You need the creative tax-advantaged plans in this book, the perfectly legal yet little-known ways to keep the tax man from touching your dollars for decades. After that, he's welcome to what's left of his share. Given the current inflation, it will be next to nothing.

Ordinary tax avoidance is simply not enough anymore. That $1,000 personal deduction you are presently allowed every year when filing your income-tax return has barely gone up from the original $600 deemed necessary for a year's expenses during the Civil War. That's like living in a world where hamburgers are still supposed to cost a nickel. The best that can be said for taking the common income-tax deductions is that they keep you on a par with the rest of the taxpaying public—at a level where you fall further behind your goals and dreams every year because of inflation.

You need to avoid taxes the way the wealthy have always done it. In years past, these lesser-known means simply didn't make sense for anyone but the rich. Now, however, inflation is changing all that. You may not feel rich. But the IRS is beginning to treat you as if you were. Your income goes up, your income-tax bracket goes up, and the tax man's share goes up most of all. It's known as *bracket creep*. And your escalation up the tax brackets goes faster with each upward ratcheting of inflation. At best it's taxflation. At worst it's tax robbery.

TAXFLATION IS GOING TO GET YOU IF YOU DON'T WATCH OUT

Consider a man who earned a yearly salary of $10,000 in 1979. After taxes, his income was $9,017. Then suppose that for 1980 he received a 14.5-percent raise. A $10,000-a-year salary may not be much these days, but a nearly 15-percent raise used to be something to write home about. However, look at what happened to that $1,450 raise. His federal income tax went up by $261. The Social Security tax went up $89. The state income tax went up, too, but let's be generous and leave that out of the depressing picture. Subtracting the income and Social Security taxes, he ended up with a gain of $1,100 over his previous take-home pay of $9,017. That's $10,117 he took home in 1980.

But the 1981 inflation, at this revised writing, looked as if it would reduce the purchasing power of the 1980 dollar to 87 cents at best. However, even that conservatively estimated 13-cents-per-dollar inflation loss equaled a loss of $1,315 in purchasing power for this employee. **The 14.5 percent raise ended up as a 2.4 percent cut in pay.** Look at the following tables to see, first, what inflation is going to do to *your* future earnings. If you think consumer prices are rising fast, you don't know the half of it—the tax increases that accompany inflation are rarely publicized. But figures compiled by the Washington-based Tax Foundation show that taxes climbed 13 percent in 1978–79, while prices rose 9 percent. For the period from 1975 to 1979, taxes rose 65 percent, more than double the 30-percent rise in prices for the same period. The indexing provisions of the Economic Recovery Tax Act of 1981 are designed to eliminate this vexing problem. This boon, however, will not help anyone until the 1985 tax year. And, of course, there's no guarantee that indexing is here to stay. What Congress giveth, Congress can taketh away.

KEEPING PACE WITH INFLATION AND PROGRESSIVE INCOME TAXES

Prices doubled due to inflation in the past seven years. To keep up, you need to more than double your income, because your tax burden will outpace your income growth.

If you had this income in **1980***	You will need at least *this* income in **1987** to maintain the same standard of living, if inflation continues at the same rate	You will need at least *this* income in **1994**, if the tendency continues 7 more years
$10,000	$22,000	$51,500
$20,000	$48,000	$122,000
$40,000	$97,000	$265,000
$50,000	$122,500	$327,000
$100,000	$249,500	$670,500

The actual result will probably be even worse than this, as it does not take into account state and local taxes, Social Security taxes, or any taxes other than U.S. income taxes.

*Figures assume no indexing and are for a married taxpayer filing a joint return showing two dependent children. Tax rates for 1980 are those in effect in 1979–1980; 1984–1985 rates are used for 1987 and 1994. All figures are rounded to the nearest $500.

INTERACTION OF INFLATION AND PROGRESSIVE TAX RATES

Assuming your before-tax income keeps pace with inflation each year, note that *your after-tax income will decline even when adjusted for inflation because you are moving into higher tax brackets.*

1980 Income Before Tax* $	1980 Income After Tax $	1985 Inflation Adjusted After Tax $
5,000	4,693	4,106
10,000	9,009	8,489
15,000	12,833	12,298
20,000	16,503	15,824
25,000	19,963	19,080
30,000	23,462	22,173
35,000	26,795	25,059
50,000	35,594	33,385
100,000	58,774	60,298

*This table assumes Social Security taxes of 6.13 percent up to a maximum of $25,900 income for 1981 and a 6.7 percent tax on an assumed maximum of $35,000 for 1984, a married taxpayer with two dependent children, 12 percent annual inflation, income from all sources, and a 23 percent cumulative income tax reduction between 1981 and 1984, and no further changes in the income tax laws.

If you have a gross income of $20,000 and you receive a 12 percent annual raise to keep up with inflation, your marginal tax rate (that's the top rate) could go from 21 percent in 1980 to 33 percent by 1984.

BRACKET CREEP

Current Income $	1980 Tax Rate	1984 Tax Rate
5,000	0	14
10,000	16%	18
20,000	21%	33
30,000	32%	38

This table does not give the effect of Social Security taxes. But note that the figures show significant bracket creep for middle income taxpayers in the face of the Economic Recovery Tax Act of 1981, which was supposed to eliminate this problem.

Where inflation is horrendous, taxflation is completely out of hand. But it needn't be out of *your* hands. You can do something about it—**cut your tax bill by 20 or 30 percent now!** You have nothing to lose, and a lot of dollars to gain. It's certainly more profitable than waiting for the government to do it for you.

For instance, in mid-October 1980, as I was writing the original edition of this book, the two presidential candidates announced their customary preelection vote-getting tax cuts. If elected, Carter said he would cut taxes by a total of $27.6 billion. If elected, Reagan said he would cut taxes by $22 billion. And the Senate Finance Committee, not wanting to be left out of the happy hour, was shooting for an overall tax cut of $39 billion. Even if taxes are cut a full $39 billion, bracket creep and inflated taxes are projected to *increase* govennment revenues by over $50 billion. Some tax cut!

With all this chicanery, taxes are becoming a very emotional issue. Add the double whammy of inflation, and the financial situation of most Americans becomes urgent.

YOU'RE WORTH A LOT MORE THAN YOU THINK

The fact is, you are worth considerably more than you realize. And a large part of your worth is directly due to the skyrocketing inflation of the last five years. But the *next* five years are probably going to be even *more* inflationary, increasing your worth even more.

Today, any family that owns a home (including mortgage insurance), two cars, a couple of bicycles, and the other accouterments of family life is probably worth over a quarter of a million dollars.

To quote from an October 13, 1980, *Wall Street Journal* editorial entitled "All in the Family":

> There was a time in this country when only the rich worried about estate taxes, and they were usually rich enough and smart enough to hire lawyers skillful in helping them avoid such levies. But as with so much else, inflation has changed all that. *A $300,000 estate is no longer out of the ordinary;* almost any viable farm in the Midwest can be worth more than that, not to mention service stations, machine shops, restaurants or any number of other enterprises that individuals own and operate. . . . Which, of course, has meant that many heirs to family businesses have found that they have had little alternative but to sell their holdings to pay estate taxes. [Italics mine.]

The Economic Recovery Tax Act of 1981 has significantly diminished the adverse impact of estate taxes; however, inflation may well reduce the benefits created by the new tax bill.

The only way to avoid this predicament is to set up, right now, a long-term

inflation tax plan using shelters. Tax shelters are no longer for the rich alone. As San Francisco attorney Paul J. Sax put it in *The Tax Lawyer* magazine, when he was noting the effect of inflation, "tax shelters have become more mid-American every year." The tax man is after everybody's hide—and he'll get yours, too, if you fail to set up a long-range tax avoidance plan for your current income and the future growth of your assets.

ESTATE PLANNING MEANS YOU LIVE BETTER *NOW!*

Before we go any further, let's once and for all dispel an old notion—that estate planning means death and dying. It's true that over the years the word estate has somehow come to mean what you leave behind when you die. But actually, it refers simply to the ownership or interest you have in land or property, just as the "estate" of some English nobleman does. There is no law that says you can't profit from your estate while you're hale and hearty. Quite the contrary.

In today's high-inflation, high-taxation times, a well-planned estate means a better life for you *now*. Why? Because it lets you keep, for your own enjoyment and use, money that would otherwise feed the bottomless coffers in Washington.

WHAT THE IRS KNOWS CAN HURT YOU

The IRS knows most people simply avoid estate planning. For this very reason, even though Auntie ERTA raises the amount of estate over the next few years exempt from gift and estate tax, **the IRS has left some of the most fertile areas for tax avoidance in estate planning untouched.** Instead, it has focused its attention on eliminating liberal tax rules in other areas. The IRS has limited manpower, and it will send its fire strike force wherever the tax barricade seems weakest and most likely to collapse under the aggrieved taxpayers' assault. Because so few people are willing to avail themselves of the tax benefits that estate planning provides—perhaps because they are unaware of the potential profit such financial finesse can bring them right now, or perhaps because they are put off by the word *estate*—this area of tax remains relatively unmolested by the IRS. That is to say, it is ripe for creative tax avoidance that lets you profit from inflation. This is why you will find that estate planning, which in this case really means inflation tax planning, is one of your crucial inflation/tax avoidance tools in this book.

THE WORSE INFLATION GETS, THE BETTER OFF YOU'LL BE

Central to your strategy in beating the double whammy of inflation and taxes is to not think about them with despair. Although inflation may seem hopelessly destructive to your income by all ordinary standards, what you need to do is to get off the beaten track of today's standard financial planning. Once you realize that the kind of inflation this country is presently subjected to by a printing-press-happy government actually offers you *unique opportunities to make substantial profits*, you're well on the way to making—and keeping—more money than ever before.

The truth is, if you can save whole dollars—that is, before-tax dollars—and pyramid these year after year, tax-free, then the higher the rate of inflation, the better off you are financially.

Suppose, for instance, that inflation is running at 10 percent. And suppose you put away $1,000 for ten years where the tax man can't get at it. At the end of ten years, you'll end up with $2,594. And your gain will be even more impressive if you make investments that actually *outpace inflation*, as I will show you how to do in this book. Then your money will have the explosive growth of tax-free dollars fueled by inflation *plus* the extra earnings from investments whose profitability far exceeds the rate of inflation.

After ten years, if inflation hits 20 percent, you'll have $6,192 to invest creatively in inflation-indexed assets. And should inflation reach 30 percent—which is not unlikely for the 1980s—your $1,000 would, in ten years, become an astounding tax-free $13,786. That's almost as good as owning a gold mine (and actually owning part of a gold mine can be very fruitful too, as you'll see).

But now suppose that the tax man were to take his cut every year of the ten years you invested your $1,000. Instead of $13,786, even with a 30-percent inflation rate, you'd have only $4,046. That's $9,740 you, with some help from inflation, can beat the tax man out of. And while the IRS is bound to get its share somewhere down the line, even if it's twenty or thirty years from now, you'll be paying only a nickel on the dollar or less — because that's all the dollar will be worth.

Meanwhile, even if your original $1,000 and all the additional money it has earned is locked away where the tax man can't touch it, I'll show you how you can use it—any way you want to—including how to use it to make *more* tax-free dollars. With creative tax avoidance, your dollars will multiply faster than rabbits, leaving the IRS wondering how to get its share. But the IRS won't be able to get a cent because everything you're going to do is 100-percent legal.

WHY THIS BOOK IS DIFFERENT

This book does not deal with simplistic illegalities such as sneaking your assets abroad to evade taxes. If you want to know how to do that, pick up any of the numerous volumes available on how to pack your suitcase with cash and fly to Europe by way of a short drive to Canada first. All I'm going to say about it is that it's illegal. And although it may make you feel like a big international operator, why not take on a really big challenge: beating the IRS on its home turf—legally? It *can* be done, and done with style.

This is not just another book about how to increase your deductions. You can pick up a wheelbarrow full of those at the book store any April.

Nor is this a do-it-yourself book with snap-out forms. The IRS is staffed with pros. I know. I worked there. In order to fence with the IRS, you need pros on your team as well.

This book is not just one more in the endless flood of repetitious volumes on how to stay ahead of inflation. There is a major problem with all those tomes telling you how to invest in gold, or how to make a million in real estate, or how diamonds are your best friend—namely, the money you gain goes to the IRS. What I'm going to show you is how to prevent that from happening by actually using inflation to keep the IRS from getting at the money you earn from now on.

This book will open a whole new world of sophisticated tax avoidance for you. It will explain all the unfamiliar legal rules of the tax game. Because if you don't know the rules, you can't begin to win.

TAXFLATION STRATEGIES THAT WORK

Knowing the rules isn't enough, however. The rules only provide the framework for you to work within. To make your moves, you need strategies—strategies that work in any economic climate, but strategies that really work best when inflation is flogging you along. You see, most IRS rules were written for noninflationary times. And even ERTA hasn't adjusted all these rules to the inflation that spiraled up in the seventies.

Playing by the old rules, but utilizing the new strategies I'm going to show you, you can actually use inflation to leverage your savings, piling pretax dollar upon pretax dollar while the tax man stands by empty-handed. Right now, inflation is offering you a unique opportunity to make more tax-free money than you could ever make before. And the higher inflation goes, the more you'll stay ahead, because you'll be keeping every cent inflation gives you. Those who don't follow the new strategies for the eighties will be the ones burdened by the ever-increasing taxes.

For instance, **did you know there's a strategy that allows you to sell your property, invest the money to keep up with inflation, pay no taxes—and get a tax deduction to boot?** After you pass away, the money goes to charity. So the plan is practical mostly for people with no children or direct heirs. But you don't have to use this strategy for all your money. And there are other strategies for other special situations.

There are tax-advantaged strategies for children, for the elderly, for the single person, for the small business. There are even phony strategies — there's a whole chapter of those, just to show you where people step off the straight and narrow into the tax court's arms.

One facet of your inflation strategy is the basic economic law that inflation transfers money from creditors to debtors. With a little sophisticated planning, you can turn yourself and the members of your family into debtors. Now I realize this doesn't sound particularly clever, much less sophisticated. Spending oneself rich is not a new concept. Nor is it the one I recommend.

What you want to do is to turn the members of your family into debtors by selling them your assets in return for their long-term IOUs. Don't worry about the fact that your children have no money with which to buy your own assets for what, in effect, are your own IOUs. If it sounds like a shell game or three-card monte, well, it is. But it's legal, and the only loser is the IRS.

And neither you nor your family will have to pay any gift tax or estate tax on the value of the assets transferred by inflation after the sale. The capital gains tax can be deferred until years later or even until after you die. Even the tax you have to pay on the interest income you receive from the IOUs will be depreciated.

The trick is to win one of your opponents, inflation, over to your side. Then have it join you in your attack on your other antagonist, the tax man.

WHO CAN USE THIS BOOK?

This is truly a tax-saving book for everyone. It's a book for anyone who has a family. At the same time, it's a book for confirmed bachelors, single working women, divorced persons, widows and widowers, and for the elderly, who may now be alone in the world. It's a book for *anyone*, married or single, who would like to pay less taxes and who is worried about what inflation is doing to destroy his or her purchasing power. You don't have to be rich to profit from this book. All you need is an income, whether it's $15,000 a year or $215,000 a year—of which the government lets you keep less than 100 percent—and some kind of property. It can be any kind of property: your own home or apartment, a farm, an office building, gold coins, stamps, stocks, a closely held corporation, a promising new business venture, a professional practice, or even just a valuable idea—anything that is subject to appreciation and taxation. It's a fascinating fact of financial life that inflation shifts income and wealth, silently and efficiently, from creditors to debtors.

Of course, sometimes you can't avoid becoming a creditor. The sale of a business, the sale of a home where you have to take back a mortgage because the banks close their windows—such situations require it. Even when you must become a creditor, however, there's still a way to prevent inflation from robbing you. Check the gold clause in chapter 4, Inflation Indexing. But don't stop there. Check out every detail of inflation indexing, and apply it wherever you possibly can in your financial game plan. It's the only real way to increase your purchasing power instead of adding empty, inflation-riddled zeros to the bottom line.

So come on and learn the rules that let you win the taxflation game.

THE TAXFLATION FIGHTER'S STRATEGY

$ Set up your finances so that you're using whole pretax dollars rather than the shredded leftovers the IRS now lets you keep. This tactic has the net effect of letting inflation build up your assets.

$ Use tax shelters and tax-deferment techniques to convert your ordinarily highly taxed earnings into the much lower-taxed capital gains.

$ Defer taxes in general so that you can pay the IRS with inflation-ravaged dollars that will be worth less years from now.

$ Inflation-index not only your assets but any interest you earn as well.

$ Transfer the future growth of your assets to your family while keeping full control—plus all the income—yourself.

$ Index your pension and build tax-exempt wealth for your retirement.

$ Reduce the future taxes on existing assets by taking advantage of giving programs.

$ Take advantage of the Internal Revenue Code exemption of certain assets from taxation, to create more tax-exempt wealth.

$ Discover the wonderful world of tax-advantaged trusts.

$ Learn how to clone multiple taxpayers in lower tax brackets to shoulder your money and lift the tax burden off your back.

$ Map out an overall taxflation fighting plan.

MONEY MEANS A LOT—BUT NOT BY ITSELF

And that brings up one last point that needs to be made before you, I, and inflation tackle the IRS in earnest. In order for you to have a successful financial plan, if you're married, you need a family plan as well. Too many "heads of households" tend to leave out the rest of the heads when it comes to the long-range planning that is going to affect and influence the whole family—the future of civilization, one might say, without being melodramatic.

A recent study of the San Francisco flower children of the sixties showed that what they were running away from at home was not a lack of money in their families but a lack of values. Their parents meant nothing to them, and the children felt they meant nothing to their parents. Money bought everything but communication and shared lives. So they left their homes to find others with whom to share their lives.

When it comes to creating, retaining, and eventually transferring your assets, your success will not benefit our society unless you transfer your family values with them. Walter Lippmann said, many years ago, that "what enables men to know more than their ancestors is that they start with a knowledge of what their ancestors have already learned." This knowledge includes the technology of our society as a whole, but most of all it includes our social values.

I personally believe very strongly that any asset-building program should include a focus, first, on the values of the family and, second, on your fellow man. Responsibility for the future is one just tax of society not to be avoided.

2

Inflation—Here Today and Tomorrow

Tis the Night before Xmas, and all through the nation
Your bonus means nothing because of inflation.
—*MAD.* JANUARY 1975

Just about everyone knows the story of Germany's hyperinflation during the early 1920s. It's become legendary how you ordered a cup of coffee for 5,000 marks and ended up with a bill for 8,000 marks by the time you finished drinking it, and how people took wheelbarrows to work in order to cart home their pay. Loaves of bread cost 500,000 marks, then a million marks, then a billion. At the height of that now-historic inflation, a postage stamp cost 90 billion marks, a newspaper 200 billion marks.

Describing the German hyperinflation is certainly a catchy and apropos way to gain a worried public's attention. There is, however, something the soothsaying economists and the news commentators always leave out of the story, and that's the fact that, at the time, the income tax in Germany was almost nonexistent. Also, no one ever seems to bother telling how it all ended.

An understanding of both these neglected points is crucial to your financial survival today. For they are the reason why the current worldwide inflation is different—and why, this time around, the story may well not have an end. In today's world, the end of Germany's hyperinflation would seem even more bizarre than the inflation itself.

On November 15, 1923, with inflation running at 300,000 percent a year, the German government announced that inflation would officially end on November 16. *And it did!*

For a number of years after that, inflation in Germany hovered at around zero percent. Just as importantly, the drop in Germany's gross national product during 1924, the year following the unprecedented pronouncement, was only 10 percent.

Now don't get your hopes up. It's not going to happen here. The United States had a drop close to 10 percent in its 1980 gross national product. Meanwhile President Carter, who announced that he would end inflation when it was a horrendous 6 percent, has helped to raise it to 10 or 15 percent or even more, depending on how and when you look at the statistics. Current economic statistical theory may well be part of the problem, in fact. It certainly adds to it.

Consider, for instance, the speculations of the late Arthur Okun, certainly one of the premier economists during the inception of the current inflation and a man whose influence on American economics was tremendous. Applying a formula Okun devised, Roy Webb, writing in the Federal Reserve Bank of Richmond's *Economic Review*, determined that in order to eliminate a 300,000-percent inflation rate, Germany should have had a 50-percent drop in the GNP. A 50-percent drop a year for six hundred years, to be precise. Luckily for the Germans, they didn't have the new math.

HOW GERMANY STOPPED INFLATION

What Germany did have was a government whose words the people believed. German government officials had misunderstood the real cause of their hyperinflation, according to Thomas M. Humphrey, again writing in the *Economic Review*. "But they at least had not lied to the public about the policy rule they were following at the time. On the contrary, throughout the inflationary episode the authorities candidly acknowledged that their main policy objective was to accommodate inflation with sufficient monetary growth to overcome inflation-induced shortages of money and to stabilize the real value of the money stock." Dr. Rudolf Havenstein, president of the Reichsbank (the German equivalent of the Federal Reserve), "even boasted of the installation of new high-speed currency printing presses that would enable money growth to keep up with skyrocketing prices."

Compare such governmental candor with the barrage of false platitudes recently emanating from a Washington of Abscams and Watergates, and you can see why we wonder what's going to happen next. How do you believe in a government that ends up citing itself for false financial advertising? As of this writing, the Federal Trade Commission had just accused the Treasury Department of "unfair and deceptive" advertising practices in promoting those old inflationary ripoffs, savings bonds! The difference is the German people were confident that their government was going to stop inflation when it said it would. And it did.

Of course, truth in government (no matter how refreshing), if temporary, is not enough to stop inflation. A plan is needed—one that's not only believed but gets to the heart of the problem. One that works.

The German anti-inflation plan was amazingly simple. First, all the zeros on bank notes were crossed out. A new Rentenmark, equal in value to one prein-flation gold mark, was issued. One new one replaced one trillion old ones. (That's one for 1,000,000,000,000.) Psychologically, inflation was licked. Buying a kilo of hamburger for one mark felt right. It made sense. Buying a kilo of hamburger for 1,000,000,000,000 marks didn't.

But what kept the hamburger from going to 1,000 marks the very next day? Ah, that's where the not-so-subtle concept of discipline comes in. The government threw out their new high-speed money presses. The Rentenmark was backed by real assets—not gold, Germany still being in a financial vise from World War I, but something just as valuable—land. Germany actually pledged its mines, farms, and forests as backing for the new currency.

You can't make more land, so the government established a fixed upper limit on the number of Rentenmarks that could be issued. The government went a step further. It directed the Reichsbank to stop issuing Treasury bills. That meant funny money couldn't be created by the German equivalent of the Federal Reserve. The very government itself was not allowed to borrow unless it could put up hard assets as collateral.

Even taxes were levied in proportion to something of real value, in this case gold. You paid less, but when you did pay you paid in something the government was actually entitled to spend.

As a final step—and now you'll see why in our wildest dreams this country could never stop inflation in the same manner—the German government eliminated budget deficits almost entirely. That meant biting the bullet by simply cutting out such transfer payments as unemployment compensation for striking workers. It also meant reducing the government payroll by paring away waste, duplication, and inefficiency.

Well, you've heard that plan often enough in past presidential elections. The only difference is that for some inexplicable reason the German government officials actually carried out the plan. And the people actually supported them.

WHY THERE'S NO STOPPING INFLATION TODAY

Forget for a moment about whether or not the people of this country can believe in their government's attempts to halt inflation. Merely look at what would have to be done to stop inflation in this country. Balancing the budget, slowing the printing presses to the point where we would have only as much money as the country's production actually warrants, backing the currency with real assets—of course it couldn't be done.

Can you imagine stopping unemployment insurance, food stamps, and welfare payments for workers on strike in this country? Note that I said *on strike*. Not unemployed. The people without jobs are on unemployment compensation. Consider just those on strike. And then add the unemployment figures, the food stamp expenditures. . . . Of course it all couldn't be done.

The fact is that transfer payments—where the government taxes people and then gives the money back to the people in one way or another—have become one of the largest forces in modern-day economics. Over the past fifteen years transfer payments, ranging from Social Security to veterans' benefits to Medicare to food stamps and child-nutrition programs, have risen from $39 billion a year to almost $300 billion a year. They now account for 50 percent of all federal expenditures—mostly in the wrong way. That is, money is just changing hands. No new jobs are created, no capital is accumulated, nothing productive occurs to boost the economy. True, there is some benefit in that the recipients of this money spend it boosting consumer sales. But an economy that's kept afloat with buying instead of building is a cancerous inflationary economy feeding on itself.

Let's take Social Security, for instance. Without going into the very valid debate over whether participation in the Social Security program should be mandatory or voluntary, Social Security is a prime example of putting the political cart before the economic jackass. As a bona fide retirement program, it could be immensely beneficial to the nation generally as well as to retirees. Instead, it's a billion-dollar drain on the economy. Why?

Because it's not funded. The money is not actually put aside as the employee works. The current income of the Social Security plan is used to pay out current obligations.

Meanwhile, the government has mandated that companies in the private sector must begin funding their pension plans. That's to be lauded. Even so, the unfunded pension-plan fund obligations of the hundred largest private companies in the country rose 14 percent in 1979 alone. Profits rose 22 percent the same year, one may add. But then consider the profit decline the companies entered in 1980. Do you get the picture of what's developing?

For example, the unfunded legal obligation of Bethlehem Steel's pension fund equals 46 percent of its total net worth. As for Chrysler, its future debt represents 66 percent of its total net worth. And then there's Lockheed. Remember when the government decided to bail it out? Are you curious about Lockheed's unfunded pension obligation? Well, it's 117 percent of Lockheed's total net worth. In other words, if the company sold everything it owned, right down to the boardroom table, it still couldn't pay its pension obligation. Oh, well, the government, the bail-out king, will take care of things.

Of course, all the while the government is busy bailing out the private pension funds, it has its own exploding Social Security deficit to worry about. Talk about printing money to fuel the fires of inflation. . . .

ONE WAY THE GOVERNMENT COULD PUT A BRAKE ON INFLATION

Now rewrite the scenario. The government begins to build up a true, functioning Social Security fund, just as it is requiring the private sector to do. Obviously a debt as large as the current one can't be funded overnight. So let's say 10 percent of revenue goes into the fund the first year. Then—since this project won't be cheap—in four years, after the next election, let's say, to make the politicians' life a little more bearable, it goes to 20 percent, and so on.

The exact scenario itself is not important; its details would be open to much debate. What counts is the result. After a few decades, what we're talking about is hundreds of billions of dollars that have been saved and are being held in trust by the government. Hundreds of billions of dollars that must be invested in order to earn a fair return. That investment, in turn, creates thousands and thousands of new jobs.

In case there are any politicians in power out there reading this book, the concept involved is called savings. And it's what kept the economy growing from the country's founding until the 1960s, when spending became the byword in fiscal management.

Judicious paring and prudent restructuring may be politically acceptable if accompanied by a lot of purposeful education. But severe cuts in the transfer programs would be political suicide, with well-meaning individuals and special-interest groups alike throughout the nation proclaiming that anyone attempting to put the house in order is greedy, inhuman, racist, or whatever else at the time signifies someone not of the most liberal Keynesian economic persuasion.

From a truly objective point of view, however, it's no longer a matter of dividing up the pie more equitably. What this nation is doing—and much of the rest of the Western world as well—is going ahead and devouring the pie.

Starting with the filling, now working on the crust, we are faced with the prospect that soon there will be little but the pan left. No one is really speculating on where we go from there.

Not meaning to sound like an alarmist, I hasten to add that, wherever we go, it will probably not be the end of the world, though it may be the end of the economic universe as we know it. As George Santayana once remarked, "Civilization is perhaps approaching one of those long winters that overtake it from time to time."

THE WONDERFUL IDEA THAT FAILED

The fact is that the rise in transfer payments in this country since 1965 has worked just the way it wasn't supposed to. Politicians of both liberal and conservative bent expected that the purchasing of votes by the simple expediency of giving money away in transfer payments would be a one-time thing. Programs to set up jobs, for instance, would simply wither away once their purpose had been accomplished. But, of course, they didn't wither away, any more than the politicians did.

Indeed, the benefiting constituency of this largesse had become so powerful by 1980 that at the time both President Carter and then-presidential candidate Ronald Reagan pledged not to tamper with the current setup. They had to make this promise, or they could just save their campaign funds and sit home in front of the fire. Of course, they both took the mandatory-balanced-budget and government-restraint-in-spending pledges as well.

At one level, the transfer programs seem to have been very effective. The number of poor families, according to the Census Bureau figures, dropped from 12 percent in 1965 to 4 percent in 1980. Even more impressively, the number of elderly households living in poverty decreased from 35 percent to 4 percent over the same period of time. That ought to be enough to make even Scrooge feel beneficent—until he finally sees the Spirit of Poverty Yet to Come.

Unfortunately, most economists have discovered that transfer payments as they are now structured discourage people from working—and from saving. Indeed, the Institute for Research on Poverty at the University of Wisconsin established that without the massive, continuing infusion of government benefits, the number of households below the poverty line today would be the same as it was in 1965. The country as a whole is spending more, much more, while earning the same amount and—this point is *crucial*—with no real improvement in the nation's economic situation whatsoever. Overall, people are better off, yes—but they're working less. They're saving less. Less savings means less capital investment, which in turn means less work available. We have become a nation of grasshoppers, and the winter of our discontent is not far off.

POSITIVE TAXATION COULD HAVE HELPED

Using creative taxation to encourage saving and yield real jobs over the same fifteen-year period would undoubtedly have cost just as much. But by now we would have had some real national benefits as well, including a stronger economy, more jobs, and a higher standard of living for all. And even though the Economic Recovery Tax Act of 1981 was passed as a solid effort to encourage business expansion, it may be a case of too little too late. Maybe someday we will finally realize the old truism that there's no such thing as a free lunch.

Meanwhile we are living with a situation in which inflation has been condoned—nay, sponsored—by the government, not in the forthright if naive manner of the Weimar Republic but in a coldly calculated way, to retain power—transfer payments buy votes. The problem is that by now inflation has become a political necessity in this country. Understanding and remembering this point is going to be decisive in your financial survival and that of your family. For what you must do is learn to use inflation to beat the tax man insofar as is humanly—and legally—possible. As you will see in the later chapters of this book, there's much more you can do than you may realize.

HYPERINFLATION COMING? NO SUCH LUCK

Besides preparing for a future in which inflation is the norm rather than the exception, you have to structure your affairs knowing that the inflation you face is not going to spiral as far as hyperinflation—that is, inflation running consistently over 100 percent and even up to several thousand percent a year. And, as contradictory as this might sound, the want of a future hyperinflation on the horizon may be one of the worst facets of the economic cancer we call inflation today, because it means there's little hope for a blowoff and a chance to start over, and thus it calls for an untoward acceptance of the state of things as they are.

The psychological role played by accepting inflation at its face value is not to be underrated. After all, the Latin word *credere* means "to believe"—and guess what the origin of our word *credit* is. Belief in a country's currency, and in the credit it represents, is central to the day-to-day transactions of that country's populace. It is trust in the money's intrinsic worth that greases the wheels of commerce, not money itself.

Take another look at that familiar example of post-World War I Germany. By 1922 citizens across the land were getting rid of money. They were using anything tangible they could get their hands on—diamonds, gold, real estate, even bric-a-brac, furniture, and cases of soap, anything but money—as a storehouse of value. Prostitution flourished, snorting cocaine was the "in" way to get high, and everywhere in the cities cabarets and fashionable shops catered to the nouveau riche and the wealthy foreigners, whose "real" money bought more with each upward lurch of inflation. Sound familiar?

If the parallel is so strong, why then can't we count on inflation playing out its inevitable blowoff into hyperinflation? The phenomenon is, after all, strictly an anomaly. During most of recorded history, inflation has reared its head only on rare occasions. When the Romans debased their currency, when the New World's gold flooded the Old World with money—such monetary excess, unlike war, is only a sometime happening in our past. In the entire century preceding World War I, there were only one or two serious outbreaks of this economic disease, the one hitting closest to our pocketbooks being the Civil War–induced inflation. Even the South American countries, stereotypes of inflation-battered economies, led reasonably stable economic lives until early in this century.

The reason inflation has trampled our pocketbooks for so long and can be expected to do so for many a year to come is not the OPEC oil price explosion, as so many politicians in search of a scapegoat would have it, though the jump in petroleum prices hasn't helped matters, of course. No, **it's a matter of inflation's having been institutionalized.**

Deficit spending is an accepted governmental truth. (Try deficit spending for a few years, and you'll wonder how people in their right minds can accept such a theory. About the only way for a family to make any headway under such circumstances is to adopt counterfeiting as a profession, which is, of course, exactly how the government is presently operating.)

Worse than that, inflation has become official policy. It's built into the economic system. Those uncancellable transfer payments, massive construction boondoggles, and other government expenditures escalate with inflation *automatically*. When the consumer price index goes up, so do benefits. The inflationary tiger is chasing its tail, while Uncle Sam stands in the middle of the circle explaining why it will stop soon.

In fact, **the government needs inflation to fight inflation—and recession.** The opposite of inflation is deflation—not recession or depression, though that's what many of today's economic promulgations would seem to have you believe. Even the recent history of simultaneous inflation and recession during the mid-seventies somehow hasn't altered this fallacy in many people's minds.

True, in an economy as dependent as ours on government spending, inflation can help relieve the pain of recession itself. For as inflation continues, the government doles out more money in transfer payments. You can fault it for botching its job. But at least it's trying to take care of its own. This it can do because as inflation increases, so does the government's take from taxes, not only in nominal terms but in real percentages. And that is why *the government now needs continuous inflation*. I'm not saying it's all a conscious plot on the part of elected officials. But just think of all the retreating that various members of Congress started to do after ERTA threatened to put some fiscal sanity into our fiscal system. The bottom line is that various escalators and other monetary mechanisms have been set into action during the last couple of decades, and they're still now simply running themselves. Among these mechanisms is *tax inflation*, or taxflation, as I like to call this double whammy to your finances.

3

The Financial Double Whammy—
Galloping Inflation and Ever-Increasing Taxes

Heads they win; tails you lose.

—OLD AMERICAN FOLK SAYING

If inflation is a historical aberration, taxes are the financial bedrock of civilization. They've been around in one form or another since the first tribesman was picked as boss. Cicero called them "the sinews of the State." But this state is becoming muscle-bound beyond recognition.

Consider the federal income tax alone. It's less than seventy years old as I write this. And the first half of its life was spent in relatively harmless slumber, taking a little money here and a little there, mostly from people who hardly noticed it was missing. It might have been considered a reasonable tax at its inception, which occurred when the Sixteenth Amendment to the Constitution was ratified on February 3, 1913.

Simply and to the point, the amendment stated, "The Congress shall have power to lay and collect taxes on income from whatever source derived, without apportionment among the several states, and without regard to any census or enumeration." Proponents argued that the tax would never go above 3 percent of any citizen's income. Unfortunately, they failed to write that argument into the amendment. Today, if you're an average American, you pay twelve times as much.

In all, taxes consume 45 percent of the average income. That's tallying up the income tax plus the other *direct* taxes, such as Social Security, sales tax, unemployment compensation tax, gasoline tax, property tax, entertainment tax, liquor tax, vault tax, estate tax, and a host of others.

Add to this a 7.5-percent annual inflation rate, slightly less than that which produced a ten-year increase of 113 percent in the decade just past, and the purchasing power of your after-tax 55-percent share of your money is cut in half in less than ten years. A projected 10-percent annual inflation for the eighties is probably underestimating matters.

THE TAX MULTIPLIER

Then, of course, there are the *indirect* taxes, incessantly gnawing away at your income. If you were to plug in a computer to calculate the effect of indirect taxation on your finances, it would not be surprising to see it spew forth a **grand-total tax figure of 60 to 70 percent of your earnings.**

Think about it for a minute. There's a tax multiplier effect whose cumulative result is that on some goods—cigarettes and gasoline particularly come to mind—the taxes represent more than half the cost. Bread—a more basic commodity than that is hard to find—falls victim to taxation almost as high. The farmer pays a property tax on farmland and storage buildings and a gasoline tax on fuel for the equipment. The grain company pays the same taxes. So do the transportation companies. So does the baker. So does the store. Add them all together and the motto of modern economics becomes Let Them Eat Taxes.

Is it beginning to seem a minor miracle that you have any after-tax money left at all? Let's look at the picture more closely.

If you as a married taxpayer with a family of three additional dependents earned $10,000 in 1970, you needed an income of $22,552 in 1980 just to keep your family finances on an equal keel. The $12,552 increase merely kept you at the economic level where you were before. You didn't really get ahead financially even though you earned more in dollars, because every additional cent went either to inflation or to the increased taxes levied because you were now earning more. Your extra income didn't add one single item you wouldn't have been able to purchase back in 1970, not even a quarter candy bar.

By 1990, assuming inflation and tax rates equivalent to those in 1981, you would need to earn $55,941 just to live at the same standard you did in 1970—for $10,000!

The higher your income bracket, the worse the monetary future looks. To keep pace, a $200,000 income in 1970 needs to rise to $118,689 by 1990. A $40,000 1970 income must be pulled up to almost a quarter of a million dollars.

Consider the past decade alone. For a family of four with one breadwinner earning $19,751 gross pay in 1970, the actual spendable income was $12,643. What happened to the rest? Well, $3,176 went to direct federal taxes. Inflation over the preceding decade, from 1960 to 1970, chewed up another $3,932 in purchasing power. Inflation was slightly ahead of taxes, but the two were relatively neck and neck when it came to picking your pocket.

Now look at the column for 1979, the last column on the Inflation chart. You needed to earn $37,531 in order to retain that same $12,643 in real spendable income. Federal taxes took $7,453 this time. Inflation—well, it took the lion's share, $17,435, almost 150 percent of what you were allowed to keep. One last example of inflation—and the government's use of it—is the long-term bonds issued by the U.S. Treasury. The Treasury is now selling debt instruments that will become due in the year 2010. By then, with a 10-percent annual inflation, these will be worth less than a penny on the dollar in today's terms. Some investment!

BUT HARD-ASSET INVESTMENTS KEEP UP WITH INFLATION— DON'T THEY?

Inflation brings with it not only a wage-price spiral, government controls in one form or another, and a sharp increase in unemployment, but also a steady rise in the value of many hard assets, the ones which, unlike printing-press money, are limited by nature in their amounts—gold, silver, precious stones, oil, real estate, and similar commodities that are normally purchased with the government's printing-press money. These assets will become more valuable with each inflationary day, as scores of current books have already pointed out. What these volumes usually fail to mention, however, is that when it comes to transferring this real wealth to your children, to the next generation, it really ends up being transferred to the government and various government officials, not your heirs. How?

The reason is the federal estate and gift tax. These taxes are graduated; rates begin at 18 percent and escalate to a high of 70 percent in 1981 (reduced to a maximum of 50 percent after 1984). Thus they become more and more confiscatory with every twist in the inflationary spiral. If the current rate of inflation continues, more than half of this country's middle-income taxpayers may well be in the 40-percent estate tax bracket in another twenty years.

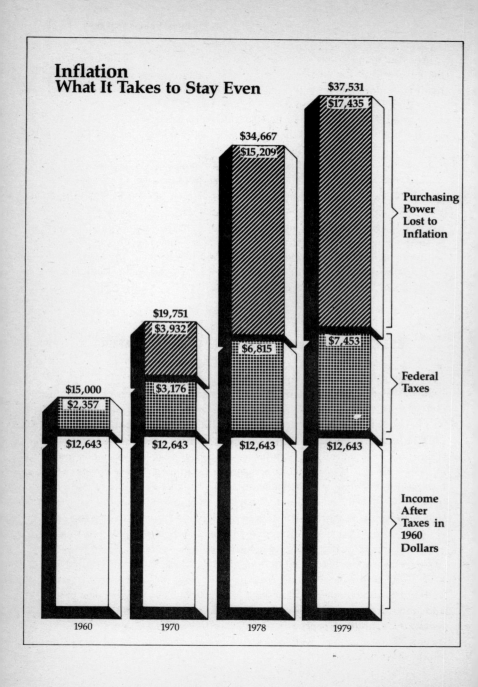

Inflation
What It Takes to Stay Even

Purchasing Power Lost to Inflation

Federal Taxes

Income After Taxes in 1960 Dollars

1960 — $15,000 / $2,357 / $12,643

1970 — $19,751 / $3,932 / $3,176 / $12,643

1978 — $34,667 / $15,209 / $6,815 / $12,643

1979 — $37,531 / $17,435 / $7,453 / $12,643

Are you going to do something about it, or will you just sit there and let the government and inflation take it all? If you're ready to fight, you're ready for inflation-indexing.

KEEPING PACE WITH INFLATION AND ESTATE TAXES

If you had an estate of *this* amount in 1970	You would have to have an estate of *this* amount to leave the same buying power to your heirs in 1980	And *this* amount, if inflation continues at the same rate in 1990
$100,000	$225,000	$565,000
$150,000	$335,000	$835,000
$200,000	$455,000	$1,100,000
$300,000	$685,000	$1,650,000
$500,000	$1,165,000	$2,860,000

*This table assumes 112.9-percent inflation from 1980 to 1990, the same as existed from 1970 to 1980. Figures are rounded to the nearest $5,000 interval.

Now let's see exactly what the tax will be on the increased value of assets which, of course, will result in reducing the amount of assets to be transferred to your heirs.

Value of Estate in 1980	Federal Estate Tax	Value of Estate in 1990	Federal Estate Tax	Tax on Increase (Taxflation)
$ 225,000	$ 15,800	$ 565,000	—0—	—0—
335,000	52,700	835,000	88,650	35,950
455,000	93,500	1,100,000	194,000	100,500
685,000	177,250	1,650,000	430,500	253,250
1,165,000	366,450	2,860,000	1,013,000	646,550

This chart assumes a single taxpayer who would transfer his or her estate in 1981 or later. It does not give credit for state death taxes, but it does reflect the 1981 tax cuts by increasing the amount of estate exempt from estate taxes to $600,000 by 1987.

If you used the tax-avoidance plans in this book, you *could* transfer the increased value of your estate between 1980 and 1990 *tax-free*. That is, *you could avoid paying the tax on inflation (right-hand column)*.

4

Inflation Indexing:
The Key to Your Financial Survival

The greatest of all gifts is the power to estimate things at their true worth.

—La Rochefoucauld

Inflation indexing is on the way to becoming the most important financial tool of the decade. Actually, in a minor way, this means of keeping up with inflation already is an important tool for millions of people.

For example, Social Security payments have been indexed to the Consumer Price Index, or CPI. As the cost of living measured by the CPI goes up, so do the Social Security payments. Retirement benefits for the military as well as for members of the more powerful unions have been indexed in the same way. But most of the focus of inflation indexing has been on the elderly who live on fixed incomes which are being destroyed by inflation.

For the great majority of middle-income Americans, whose day-to-day living standards are sliding rapidly downhill, raises and improvements in fringe benefits simply haven't kept up with inflation. As to their savings, they're actually being consumed. For every $1,000 put in the bank, the average American will withdraw $300-400 in buying power ten years later—maybe $500-$600 if he or she decides to spend it in five years rather than continue the foolishness of saving under these circumstances. No wonder the economy is collapsing into itself as if it were a big black hole.

Bond investments, once the prudent man's choice, have become the laughingstock of Wall Street. With their fixed interest rates, bonds plunged in value as overall interest rates shot up. Yet there is a way to actually inflation-index a bond portfolio, as you will soon discover.

Stocks are up—but they're really down. With the Dow Jones average at 1,000, the average is actually 350 measured in the purchasing power of 1960s dollars. Some gain! Again, inflation-indexed stocks do actually exist. Not stocks that rise because of some spectacular development—these are always around in any market. Try to pick them consistently. As *Forbes'* famous Dart Board Portfolio proves, in the long run even a dart board is better than many of the choices made by professional stock advisers.

About the only thing most Americans have that is keeping up with inflation is their home. Sell that, and they have to buy a new one at a higher price. There's a gain in their net worth, but not much else, unless they wait more than eighteen months to buy the new house, in which case they're entitled to pay a hefty income tax on their gain as well.

As to selling a business, or some other asset they've built up over the years, either they're hit with a huge tax on the "profit"—which is probably half due to inflation, and thus illusory—or they must string out the payments for fifteen years or so to lower the IRS's take. If they can get 10, 11, or even 12 percent on the money while it's owed them, maybe that's not such a bad idea, you say; it should keep them ahead of inflation? Well, let me tell you a story.

Recently, a man decided, for various personal reasons, to sell his company. Among other things, he wanted to travel and see the world. His dream was justly deserved. After all, he'd worked hard for three decades to build up his business.

The price he asked for it was $200,000, a reasonable amount for the company involved, and a buyer was soon found. The seller discussed the deal with his lawyer, stressing the need to minimize taxes. Considering the importance of minimizing taxes in the transaction, the lawyer decided that the seller should accept no down payment but instead receive payment in monthly installments of $2,216.41, including interest at 10 percent. At the time, 10 percent was a quite acceptable interest figure for such a purchase, what with the prime rate at about 8 percent and Treasury bills yielding about 6 percent. There would be 168 payments over a total of fourteen years. And a large part of each year's total payment of $26,596.92 would be taxed at the lower capital-gains rate rather than as ordinary income, effectively answering the seller's major concern—income tax.

REDUCING INCOME TAX THE WRONG WAY
LETS INFLATION EAT UP THE PROFITS

The only thing wrong with this plan was that income tax wasn't the seller's major problem at all. Oh, it was a problem all right. But too many people focus exclusively on the tax implications of their business, and this man was one of them. *Inflation*, not taxes, is going to destroy the value of his life work. Yet there's no need for such a tragedy.

Looking at the situation more closely, we discover that the seller actually became a lender. And if there's one thing you can't afford to be in inflationary times, it's a lender—unless you inflation-index your loan. What happened was that after seven years, or halfway through the installment payments, the outstanding debt to the seller was $133,509.15.

Over the same period of time, the cost of just living, the cost of goods and services, doubled. The dollar lost 50 percent of its value. Today, what is actually owed the seller, in terms of buying power, is $66,754.58. The following two tables give a telling breakdown of what inflation would cost you as a lender in a similar situation.

INFLATION LOSS OF PRINCIPAL ON $40,000 SECOND MORTGAGE AFTER SEVEN YEARS

	10%	15%	20%	25%	30%	50%
Rate of Inflation						
Purchasing Power Loss	20,868	27,177	31,611	34,661	36,706	39,687
Percent of Purchasing Power Lost	52%	68%	79%	87%	92%	99%
Future Value of Mortgage Remaining after Seven Years	19,132	12,823	8,389	5,339	3,294	313

INFLATION LOSS OF PRINCIPAL ON $40,000 SECOND MORTGAGE AFTER SEVEN YEARS

(10% Interest—$4,000/year—30% tax bracket)

Rate of Inflation	10%	15%	20%	25%	30%	50%
Year 1	1,600	1,800	2,000	2,200	2,400	3,200
Year 2	1,960	2,310	2,640	2,950	3,240	4,200
Year 3	2,284	2,743	3,152	3,512	3,828	4,700
Year 4	2,576	3,112	3,562	3,934	4,240	4,950
Year 5	2,838	3,425	3,889	4,251	4,528	5,075
Year 6	3,074	3,691*	4,151*	4,488*	4,729*	5,137
Year 7	3,287	3,917*	4,361*	4,666*	4,871*	5,169
Total of Inflation Loss and Tax Cost to Lender on $28,000 Interest	17,619	20,998	23,755	26,001	27,836	32,431
Percent of Interest Income Lost to Taxes and Inflation	63%	75%	85%	93%	99%	115%

*Cost greater than income due to fixed nature of tax cost.

To see how the borrower gains, look at the third table. With 15-percent inflation, which is well within the range that can be expected during the next decade, a 10-percent loan ends up costing only 2.5 percent a year. At 30-percent inflation—which we hope will not befall us, though it's far from impossible—the loan is actually free. Above that, the borrower begins to make a profit on the loan.

YEARLY COST TO BORROWER OF $40,000 SECOND MORTGAGE AFTER INFLATION AND TAX BENEFIT

(10% Interest—$4,000/year—30% tax bracket)						
Rate of inflation	10%	15%	20%	25%	30%	50%
Year 1	2,400	2,200	2,000	1,800	1,600	800
Year 2	2,040	1,690	1,360	1,050	760	*(200)
Year 3	1,716	1,257	848	488	172	*(700)
Year 4	1,424	888	438	66	*(240)	*(950)
Year 5	1,162	575	*(111)	*(251)	*(528)	*(1,075)
Year 6	926	309	*(151)	*(488)	*(729)	*(1,137)
Year 7	713	82	*(361)	*(666)	*(871)	*(1,169)
Net Interest Cost to Borrower After Inflation and Tax Benefit	10,381	7,001	4,023	1,999	164	(4,431)
Average True Interest Rate Paid per Year by Borrower	3.7%	2.5%	1.4%	.7%	—	—

*Represents negative expense—or income—due to tax benefits of interest expense.

PROFITING FROM BORROWED MONEY

Whenever inflation exceeds three times the cost of a loan, the income-tax deductions allowed by the IRS actually guarantee that you'll make money by borrowing it. "But that's a pretty high ratio," you say. "It will never happen."

Nonetheless, it did happen, in 1980. There were plenty of people who had 6-percent mortgages that carried over from the early sixties. When inflation hit 18 percent, they were making money on every dollar they spent to pay off those mortgages. And that was above and beyond the appreciation of the property itself, where the really spectacular you-couldn't-miss-it profit lay at every turn of events.

So how do lenders harness this beneficent inflation? By hitching up their loans to it. Businesses in high-inflation nations have always found a way to have their sales tied to the rise. Consumers, too, have pegged much of their money to inflation. As I've said, inflation indexing is not a new concept.

However, in this country, outside of the government and, recently, some trade unions, the concept of inflation indexing has never been accepted.

Actually, it's never been tried. After all, if you as a seller were to say that you wanted your sale price tied to inflation, your potential buyer would most likely go elsewhere, muttering, "I won't do that."

THE LATEST GAME IN FINANCE

But suddenly, in 1980, the whole American world of finance changed. Inflation indexing was in, at least among the cognoscenti. The funny thing is, even as this vast change swept through the economy, no one really made much of an issue of it. It was almost as if inflation indexing didn't exist. No one uses the word even yet. But people are using the concept, to keep their money growing.

Look at the stock market, for instance. Sunshine Mining Company recently came out with an 8.5-percent silver-indexed bond. The whole $30,000,000 issue is indexed to the fluctuating value of silver—the $1,000 principal of the bond is, I should say, not the interest. Still, it makes a complete turnaround for American bonds, the backing being appreciating rather than depreciating assets.

One wonders if perhaps there was something symbolic about the fact that these bonds were issued on the IRS's favorite day, April 15. In some ways, it's really too easy to shrug off such coincidences. I remember wondering why, when the U.S. government decided to plunge the dollar into chaos by removing its gold backing, it chose April Fool's Day, of all occasions, to do so. Years later it became obvious.

Now, even though only the principal of Sunshine Mining's bond is inflation-indexed, if you look at the following table you can readily see what happened between the time the bond was issued and the writing of this chapter. Each $1,000 invested in the Sunshine Mining bond was now worth $1,410. Inflation chewed up $60 or so of purchasing power, leaving a $350 gain in capital. A similarly yielding issue of AT&T, already discounted to 78½, or $785, by high inflation and high interest rates on April 15, fell even further to 73½, or $735, by October 7. For every $1,000 AT&T bond you bought at a bargain price of $785, you actually *lost* about $50 of your capital on the investment *plus* another $40 in buying power due to inflation.

The score, then? The inflation-indexed bond gained about $350. The nonindexed bond lost about $90. That's a $440 difference in six months

INFLATION INDEXING FOR BONDS

	Company	Yield in Percent	Year Due	Price April 23, 1980	Price October 7, 1980
INFLATION-INDEXED BOND	Sunshine	8½	1995	102	141
FIXED-VALUE BONDS	AT&T	8⅝	2007	78½	73½
	ARCO	8	1984	89¾	88¾
	GMA	8	1993	76½	70⅝
	Merck	7⅞	1985	85¼	84¼

between an inflation-indexed bond and a fixed-value bond. You would have earned interest income on both bonds as well, which is why I say "about." But in the case of an indexed asset, the interest may actually be a minor consideration in your financial planning, though it too can play an important role in certain circumstances.

Indexing interest is not a new phenomenon. Banks have used it for years—to squeeze extra dollars out of their loans. They benefit. You don't. Typically, these indexed loans have been granted to businesses, and thus they have affected consumers and savers only indirectly, by raising the cost of goods and feeding inflation. Now, however, the consumer is being made a major target, and the banks are about to score a direct hit.

INFLATION-INDEXED MORTGAGES

The variable-rate mortgage has just gotten a toehold in the $900-billion homeowner's loan market. That happened in 1980. But sweeping changes are following with amazing rapidity. At the end of 1980, the Federal Home Loan Bank proposed two new types of homeowner's loans. Named SAM and GPAM, these newer loans should offer good opportunities for financial planning if you're an investor.

As a borrower, of course, you'll find they're simply another pair of thumbscrews from the government's torture chamber. But from an investor's point of view, both the SAM and the GPAM mortgages offer the potential for *asset indexing*. The value of the mortgage, and your investment, will be coupled to one of the most rapidly appreciating of commodities—houses. As the homes rise in value because of inflation, your capital invested, particularly in SAM mortgages, rises right along with them.

GPAM stands for Graduated Payment Adjustable Mortgage. This type of mortgage offers an initially low series of payments that increase in amount as time goes by. The interest rates are allowed to rise and fall with the prime rate, assuring the banks— and you, if you happen to be investing in second mortgages or trust deeds—a solid profit. A most unique feature is that as soon as the first payment is made, the unpaid principal *increases*. The early payments do not even cover the interest expenses, and so the leftover interest each month is added onto the principal. The principal actually keeps on increasing for several years. The home buyer with a thirty-year $50,000 mortgage at 13 percent, for instance, actually owes the bank $55,000 at the end of six years.

The GPAM plan is one only a government completely bent on continuing inflation could conceive. Still, if you can't beat 'em, investing in the in-flation-indexed GPAM instruments when they become available as listed mortgage pass-through securities is one way to inflation-index your money.

SAM stands for Shared Appreciation Mortgage. The mortgage lender shares in the appreciation of the home for which he or she lends the money. Any banker proposing such a thing even three years ago would have risked being immediately tarred and feathered by every consumer group in the country. The fact is, the concept is so alien to even the thrift institution savings banks, savings and loans, and others that serve primarily the mortgage market bankers themselves that they're probably pinching each other to see if they're dreaming. They're not.

On a limited basis, SAM mortgages are already being offered in several areas, including Florida, Washington D.C., and Colorado, by the Advanced Mortgage Corporation, an affiliate of Oppenheimer Company. They've been besieged by inquiries from house hunters and investors alike. The reason? When mortgage rates were running 12 percent, the rate for a SAM, if you could get one, was 8 percent.

Let's compare. For an $85,000 house with a 10-percent down payment, a 12-percent mortgage would entail monthly payments of $787. A SAM would cost $562 a month. The savings to the borrower would be $225 a month, which could very well spell the difference between being able to afford the house and not being able to meet the payments.

Now let's look at the lender's viewpoint, since this is the position you should be in when it comes to inflation indexing. Assuming the house appreciates 10 percent a year, it will be worth $182,200 after eight years. Suppose the borrower then decides to sell and move. The gross profit from selling the house is $97,200. But the borrower has to split this profit with the mortgage holder, who gets a full third, or $32,400. Of course, the mortgage holder has also earned 8-percent interest, over the years, and has the original $76,500 capital back.

The investor's yield is actually 12 percent, the same as the yield he would have received if he'd lent the money under a conventional mortgage. The big difference is that the $32,400 is capital gains, not ordinary income. That means a much lower income tax due, the tax being imposed on capital gains rather than ordinary gain.

"The whole idea supposes inflation will continue," as Jerome Grossman, vice-president of Oppenheimer and originator of its SAM program, says in a *Forbes* magazine interview. And right now it's pretty hard to imagine any alternative. "But even if it doesn't," Grossman points out, "and interest rates drop, an 8-percent investment may then look pretty good."

THE RIGHT SHIFT

Shifting indexed profits from ordinary income to the lower-taxed capital gains is one of the key moves in using inflation to beat the IRS at its own game. And the move can be made successfully only during inflation. Basically, as long as inflation doesn't go hyper, the higher the inflation rate, the greater your profit, and the less the IRS gets in terms of a percentage.

Capital indexing simply means your capital is invested in things such as farms, homes, and equipment that will increase in value with inflation. It can be effectively used in many ways. But the most profitable results occur when you combine it with a trust or some other tax-deferred plan. Under those circumstances, often you can sell the asset at a gain, paying a minimum tax—or no tax at all, in some instances—and reinvest your enlarged capital.

For instance, Sunshine Mining bonds are redeemable at the company's discretion on sixty days' notice whenever the indexed principal amount of each $1,000 bond has remained above $2,000 for thirty days. If that happens—and it's very likely the bonds will do just that, and well before their actual due date—you'll end up with a $1,000 capital gain on each bond you bought.

If you were to hold those bonds as part of your regular portfolio, the capital-gains tax on the $1,000 profit per bond would become due immediately on their redemption or sale. If you're in the higher tax brackets, you could be left with as little as $600. On the other hand, if you kept that same investment in one of the numerous tax-sheltered forms covered in this book, you'd probably pay a minimal tax of, say, $100. In any event, you'll be able to *reindex*—that is, reinvest in another inflation-indexed asset—at least $1,600. If the money is sheltered through a trust arrangement whereby your children are liable for the taxes due, for example, you'll have about $1,900 to reindex.

THE HIGHER THE INFLATION RATE, THE MORE MONEY YOU GET TO KEEP

Look at the table on tax-sheltered investing. The numbers have been oversimplified by not separating the money taxable as capital gains from that taxable as interest. If I'd followed the more accurate but much more complicated procedure, the results would have been even more dramatic.

The first column of the chart indicates a 10-percent inflation. With an initial unsheltered $1,000 investment, you end up with $1,276.29 after five years and $1,628.89 after ten years. With a tax-sheltered investment, on the other hand, you end up with $1,610.51 after five years, if inflation is running at 10 percent, and $2,593.75 after ten years. Now, if inflation were to average 20 percent over that same period, which is all too likely, the five-year figure for the tax-sheltered investment would be $2,488.32; the ten-year figure $6,191.74. At 30-percent inflation, you would have $13,785.85 at the end of ten years. That's $12,159.96 more than the $1,628.89 you'd have with a 10-percent inflation and a shelterless investment.

The higher inflation goes, the more money you can keep for yourself and away from the IRS.

Inflation really can help you beat the IRS. If you are in a 50-percent tax bracket, at a 30-percent inflation rate, your tax-sheltered money will earn *4 times as much* as an unsheltered investment over a ten-year period. At only 10-percent inflation, your tax-sheltered investment doesn't even earn twice as much as the unsheltered investment. If you are in a lower tax bracket, your extra earnings would be a little less but still very dramatic.

If you play your capital right, then, the higher the rate of inflation, the more you get and the less, proportionately, the IRS takes. Oh, I know, it looks too good to be true. And it may not be true for long. Once the IRS becomes aware of its future collection problems, the laws may well change. But if

ADVANTAGES OF TAX-SHELTERED INVESTING

Number of Years for which Investment Is Held	Inflation Rate					
	10%		20%		30%	
	Unsheltered Investment	Tax-Sheltered Investment	Unsheltered Investment	Tax-Sheltered Investment	Unsheltered Investment	Tax-Sheltered Investment
0	$1,000.00	$1,000.00	$1,000.00	$1,000.00	$1,000.00	$1,000.00
1	1,050.00	1,100.00	1,100.00	1,200.00	1,150.00	1,300.00
2	1,102.50	1,210.00	1,210.00	1,440.00	1,322.50	1,690.00
3	1,157.63	1,331.00	1,331.00	1,728.00	1,520.88	2,197.00
4	1,215.51	1,464.10	1,464.10	2,073.60	1,749.01	2,856.10
5	1,276.29	1,610.51	1,610.51	2,488.32	2,011.36	3,712.93
6	1,340.10	1,771.56	1,771.56	2,985.98	2,313.06	4,826.81
7	1,407.11	1,948.72	1,948.72	3,583.18	2,660.02	6,274.85
8	1,477.47	2,143.59	2,143.59	4,299.82	3,059.02	8,157.31
9	1,551.34	2,357.95	2,357.95	5,159.78	3,517.87	10,604.50
10	1,628.89	2,593.75	2,593.75	6,191.74	4,045.55	13,785.85

you act now, the money belonging to you and your family should be untouchable by the time the IRS changes the rules. Even if the government gets desperate enough to stop inflation somehow, you'll be ahead of the game until it manages actually to pull off that herculean task. And if that miraculous day does come, your sheltered investments will still outperform the tax man, if to a less spectacular degree.

NEW INFLATION-INDEXED INVESTMENTS FOR THE 1980s

"But Sunshine Mining is a special case," you may say—and correctly so. The Sunshine Mining bonds are the first of a whole new breed of financial instruments for the inflationary eighties offered by your stockbroker. SAMs are here too, as I've mentioned, and while not every company has the kind of easily indexed assets a silver-mining company has, the oil companies provide a wonderful potential example. How about bonds backed by barrels of oil? Would you buy them? Can you think of anyone who wouldn't? There are copper companies and numerous other hard money commodity producers whose situation would lend itself admirably to inflation indexing. Then again, there's no need to limit it to the obvious candidates. Real-estate holding companies could issue bonds indexed in a way similar to that used for the SAM mortgages.

The possibilities go on and on. And they will probably materialize. But, of course, once almost everyone is sailing along on the same course, then it's apt to be time for your investments to take a new tack. There are bound to be some major collisions once the harbor gets crowded.

INFLATION-INDEXING INTEREST

On the interest inflation-indexing front, a lot more has developed already than in capital indexing. It all started a number of years ago—in 1974, to be exact—when First National City Bank issued its floating-rate notes due in 1989. The interest on these notes is based on three-month Treasury bills and is reset twice a year. Their yield is 1 percent above the T-bills' discounted rate as averaged over the preceding period.

In a sense, these bonds were the precursors of money funds, whose current rise to the top of the investment hit parade is due precisely to their floating interest rates, which at least follow the general interest trends, if they don't always exceed the rate of inflation itself.

Other floating-rate investments are also available. And Landmark Bancshares Corporation, a bank holding company in St. Louis, has just issued a preferred stock with the dividend pegged to the Chase Manhattan Bank prime rate. Now the maximum rate is 13¼ percent, so if the prime hits 21½ percent again, you'll be out in the cold by 8¼ percent. On the positive side, however, there's also a floor rate, a guaranteed minimum 9 percent. Then, too, there's a kicker, in that the preferred stock can be converted into common stock, which gives your investment a chance to participate in an inflation-instigated rise in the stock market if that should occur.

The possibilities for inflation-indexing your investments will certainly increase as inflation continues. But until most everything becomes indexed, which it probably will, you'll need to look around, and you'll need to do some extra planning.

A CONTRACT IS WHAT YOU MAKE IT

Let's go back for a moment to the original example at the beginning of this chapter, and look at it from the viewpoint of inflation indexing. The businessman was selling his company for $200,000, you remember. But the asset could equally well have been a $100,000 bookstore or a $50,000 summer house.

The first thing to be aware of is that almost anything is possible in a contract. There's no such thing as, for instance, "the bookstore contract" or "the contract for selling a business." The terms of any transaction are developed by the particular parties involved. One of the parties may say, "that can't be done," really meaning, "I don't want to do it." In other words, one party is not motivated enough to deal with the terms the other party is asking. Motivation is the single most dominant factor in a contract negotiation. If a seller is highly motivated to sell, the buyer will get a better deal, and vice versa.

Now when either party to a transaction is on a plane of high motivation, the chances for a creative or unorthodox deal are much greater. And that's the situation really needed for inflation indexing. It's still an oddball deal, you see. Most people haven't heard of it. So they feel uncomfortable with it. They feel they can't cope with it.

Then again, the concept of a SAM mortgage wouldn't have gotten to even the conversation stage ten years ago. Yet today someone like Robert A. Beck, chairman of Prudential, which, like all insurance companies, made fixed-return investments for decades, can say, "Regardless of whether the government brings inflation under control or not, we have shifted our emphasis to equity arrangements. In this environment we simply cannot afford to go by the old rules." Neither can you.

So not only can the buyer of that $200,000 business or what-have-you argue the terms of the sale, but any seller who expects to survive financially will have to make some kind of inflation-indexed agreement—or find another buyer. Now, given a little thought, neither of these alternatives is as difficult to achieve as it may seem, because while inflation indexing favors the seller, there are other terms to the sale agreement which can be made more favorable to the buyer, simply because the seller is protected from loss due to inflation.

Consider the example where the mortgage buyer was offered an 8-percent mortgage instead of a 12-percent one, in exchange for the inflation-indexing addition of an equity kicker. What if the seller of that business had offered to accept 6 percent or even 5 percent when the prime was 12 percent? He'd have been offering a deal the buyer couldn't refuse.

Yet considering that the seller was shifting the gain from the ordinary-income tax level to the lower capital-gains tax level, he could hardly have failed to come out ahead, unless inflation dropped to 4 or 5 percent—and that's about as likely as the return of the nickel candy bar.

Just as with a SAM mortgage, the seller hedges against inflation. The buyer gets a lower current interest and hopes to cover for inflation out of the business's rising prices and profits. Everybody is happy.

PICKING THE RIGHT INDEX

What's the best index to use when linking up with inflation? That's a question probably passing through your mind about now. And it's a fair enough question, though the answer is not that straightforward—besides which, much depends on your own personal preferences. But let's look at two basic possibilities that should cover most situations.

Probably the easiest index to use, and the one most readily acceptable to a buyer, is the Consumer Price Index (CPI). It's already widely used in labor contracts and leases.

Let's take for an example the seller of a $35,000 boat. The buyer is having difficulty getting a bank loan because, although the boat is in magnificent condition, it's over ten years old. And let's suppose, for the purposes of this example, that the seller would like to stretch the buyer's payments out over three years. The payments due would be $10,000 on June 1, 1982, $10,000 on June 1, 1983, and a final installment of $15,000 on June 1, 1984. Since this is only an example and I'm trying to keep it clear and simple, let's leave out the interest, the negotiation of which is, in any case, up to the seller.

If the installments were to be tied to the Consumer Price Index, the contract provisions between the parties might read as follows:

The indexing adjustment for each installment due on June 1 shall be the final Consumer Price Index increase established for the prior calendar year, which is prepared annually, usually during the month of January or February.

The amount due on the following June 1 (beginning June 1, 1982) shall be adjusted by the relevant Consumer Price Index percentage. For example, the principal amount to be paid on June 1, 1982, is $10,000, and if the Consumer Price Index adjustment for the calendar year 1981 is finally determined to be 10%, then the principal payment due on June 1, 1982 will be $11,000.

For subsequent years, the index adjustment will be the sum of the Consumer Price Index adjustment for the prior two or three years, as the case may be. For example, if the amount to be paid on June 1, 1983, is $10,000, and the CPI adjustment for the calendar year 1981 is 10% and that for the year 1982 is also 10%, then the amount to be paid on June 1, 1983, will be adjusted to $12,000.

The CPI increase to be used for any payments which are prepaid

> prior to the indicated payment date shall be the last quarterly CPI adjustment percentage which shall have been announced by the U.S. Bureau of Labor Statistics. The adjustment formula shall be similar to the formula already prescribed for the annual installment.

Now we must consider that the Consumer Price Index is a little bit less than an accurate barometer in the minds of many people. The latest example of improvements in the index is the sudden first-time inclusion, just before the 1980 elections, of car dealers' end-of-year discounts. This new entry had inflation declining 0.2 percent for the month rather than increasing 0.4 percent for the month. Oh, well, it's only a 0.6 percent difference. That's barely more than 7 percent on an annual basis. And chances are that kind of adjustment won't occur for at least another—well, let's say four years.

A BETTER INDEX TO HITCH YOUR CAPITAL TO

So some people aren't enamored of the CPI as an index. What they'd really like to use is that estimable commodity which has been a storehouse of value almost since the beginning of time—namely, gold. Now, as you may or may not know, gold clauses were outlawed in 1933 along with just about everything else golden except wedding bands.

In 1973 and 1974, respectively, Public Laws 93-110 and 93-373 were passed, returning to Americans the right to purchase, hold, buy, sell, and otherwise deal in gold. But this right was not extended to a gold-value clause, meaning one used to denote the intent of contracting parties to relate the payment of obligations to the value of gold and *not the gold itself.*

However, on October 28, 1977, President Carter signed into law HR 5675, making contracts calling for payment in gold, or in dollars measured in gold, enforceable in court. Once more the inflation-hedging gold-value clause was legal. As Senator Jesse Helms, prime mover behind the bill, put it, "For those who believe that gold is a better store of value than dollars, it provides a means of investing with minimum risks from inflation. For those who wish to raise capital, it may provide a means of obtaining lower interest rates. For example, a utility company may wish to sell bonds for a new plant. If people were promised that they would receive back their capital as measured in the market value of gold at maturity, the bonds might be sold at a lower interest rate than would otherwise be obtainable."

Other authorities believe the real effect of the legislation will involve not gold but rather the multiple-currency contract. Multiple-currency contracts have always been legal overseas, and in this decade they have sprouted whenever the dollar has been depressed.

The new law makes it permissible for anyone to index a contract, be it for a $35,000 boat or a $200,00 business transaction, to:

1. The *gold clause*, by which gold, either in coins or by weight, is established as the material instrument of payment;
2. The *gold-asset clause*, by which gold is taken simply as the currency of reckoning—that is, the means of calculating the sum due—and payment is made in U.S currency;
3. The *foreign-money clause*, by which the currency of another country faithful to the gold standard is adopted as the currency, either for payment or, more frequently, for computing the sum due.

Since the early 1960s, reserve paper currencies, such as U.S. Federal Reserve notes and pounds sterling, have been seriously devalued, and recently the dollar has fallen sharply against almost every major European currency. This development can only help to enforce the confidence in gold, which, in turn, will no doubt increase the use of gold clauses.

HOW THE GOLD CLAUSE WORKS

Let's say someone makes a ten-year loan of $10,000 at 9-percent annual interest. A regular non-gold-clause-indexed loan at the same time might earn as much as 15 percent. That 6-percent saving to the borrower is what you offer in return for acceptance of your gold clause.

To peg the capital to gold, the contract would require the payment of an escalated, or perhaps deescalated, amount in dollars, reflecting the index price of gold. The amount payable at the end of the ten years would then be $10,000 plus or minus any adjustment made for the price of gold. Of course, the contract need not specify that the principal payment at the end of the ten-year period be reduced if the adjustment happens to be downward, nor would the lender be inclined to seek this choice.

The actual price of gold referred to in the contract could be either that fixed by the U.S. Treasury or the free-market price on the London, Zurich, or New York gold markets, and the price determination could be made either the day before the contract payment date or as an average over some defined period of time.

Suppose, for example, the price of gold at the time two parties enter into a loan contract is $453.50 an ounce (as it was on October 9, 1981, London Spot, second fixing). The stipulated $10,000 would purchase 22.05 ounces of gold. Now suppose the free-market price of gold the day before the contract payment date is $544.22 an ounce. It would then take $12,000 to purchase 22.05 ounces of gold. So the borrower would owe this sum or its equivalent in gold. If the contract also provided for adjustment in the event that gold dropped in value (although, as I've noted, this provision is unlikely), and the price of gold were $362.81 an ounce at the contract payment date, then the borrower would repay only $8,000.

So why on earth would any borrower accept a gold clause in a contract with you if you're going to profit so much from inflation? There are two reasons. First of all, there are plenty of people who still believe inflation is a temporary phenomenon. When you are making that $10,000 loan and the marketplace is asking 15 percent for the same loan you're offering at 9 percent, it looks like a terrific deal to these people.

Secondly, even if the borrower feels that inflation will continue, he or she can hedge the bet by buying a futures contract in gold. A futures contract requires putting up only 10 percent of the gold's worth. So with $1,000 of the loan, the borrower buys $10,000 worth of gold futures. If gold goes through the roof, the borrower makes as much as, or in some cases even more than, the extra money owed you due to inflation.

THE USURY PROBLEM

The contract could also peg the interest payments to gold or gold value. But this might open a whole new can of worms because of various state usury laws. A finding of usury might invalidate the contract or even permit the borrower to repudiate the debt.

However, if usury laws at first glance seem to present a potential problem, consider this fact: any gold-based increase in the amount of the interest payments made by the borrower is due to long-term capital-gain increase and should be deemed an increase in capital, not in interest income. So the usury laws do not apply.

INCOME TAX SAVINGS USING A GOLD CLAUSE

Compare the tax result in the following situations. Assume both A and B are in the 50-percent tax bracket. Each makes a before-tax profit of $7,500 on the following transactions. Only their tax results are different.

Situation #1

A agrees to lend a friend $25,000 at 15 percent interest for two years. Interest is payable in full at the end of the two-year period. At that time, A's friend repays him the $25,000 principal and $7,500 interest. *Tax result.* The interest is taxable to A as ordinary income at A's 50-percent tax rate. A owes $3,750 in taxes on the transaction, and has a total of $28,750 for reinvestment. His annual average net return after taxes is 7.5 percent.

Situation #2

B agrees to lend a friend $25,000 at 9 percent simple interest for two years and his friend agrees to repay the principal in gold-indexed dollars at the end of the two years. On the date of the agreement, gold is selling for $600 an ounce. The principal amount thus represents 41.67 oz. of gold. At the end of the two-year period, the friend pays B $4,500 in interest. Gold is then selling at $672 an ounce. The friend is thus repaying B the equivalent of 41.67 oz. of gold, or $28,000, at the repayment date.
Tax result. The interest is taxable to B as ordinary income at B's 50-percent tax rate. B owes $2,250 in taxes on the interest. It is assumed that the principal gain of $3,000 is a long-term capital gain. B only pays $600 in taxes on this gain.

B's total tax obligation is $2,850 compared with A's total tax obligation of $3,750 and he has a total $29,650 for reinvestment. B's annual average net return after taxes is 9.3 percent.

Where interest is properly a factor and it is payable in gold-value dollars, there's still a valid defense against charges of usury. A contract provision could simply require the payment of interest in gold-value dollars, whether the price of gold went up or down. The contract then would not include a usurious interest rate.

Generally, intent is the mainspring of the usury controversy. A clear, concise statement in the contract regarding the intentions of the con-tracting parties greatly reduces the chances of a usury dispute's occurring.

Usury laws apply only to contracts between private parties, and, as a rule, they cannot be enforced in the case of a corporation. So if you really want to index interest as well as capital, the surest way to go may be the corporate route—even if it means you require the borrower to create a corporation exclusively for the purpose of paying off the loan. It costs only a few hundred dollars to create a single-purpose corporation. However, various state corporate taxes and fees then enter the picture, and all of them must be balanced against the possible gains before a sound decision can be made. As additional loan protection for a seller, the owner or owners of the debt-paying corporation could be made personally responsible for guaran-teeing the payments.

MAKING IT UNIFORM

A last consideration when dealing with gold clauses is the so-called Uniform Commercial Code. The jurisdiction of this uniform legislation is on a state-by-state basis. Negotiable instruments, such as bank drafts, checks, certificates of deposit, and notes, must conform to UCC 3-106 Sum Certain, a statute which, as its name implies, stipulates that an instrument's promise to pay must specify a certain sum. The computation of this sum "must be one which can be made from the instrument itself without reference to any outside source."

The Uniform Negotiable Instruments Law, on the other hand, states that the negotiable character of an instrument will not be affected by the designation of a "particular kind of current money in which payment is to be made." A clear analogy under this clause would be an instrument payable in foreign currency, declared by the code to be a promise to pay a "sum certain" in money.

Specifically, UCC 3-107(2) states:

A promise or order to pay a sum stated in a foreign currency is for a sum certain in money and, unless a different medium of payment is specified in the instrument, *may be satisfied by payment of that number of dollars which the stated foreign currency will purchase at the buying site rate for that currency on the day on which the instrument is payable or, if payable on demand, on the day of demand.* [Italics mine.]

It is believed that gold clauses fall into this category.

Nevertheless, while it's not absolutely necessary, you might consider using a non-negotiable note. See, for example, the samples in Appendix B.

TAX CONSEQUENCES OF THE GOLD CLAUSE

The decision of the Internal Revenue Service on whether to tax any increase in your capital because of gold-clause gains as ordinary income or to tax it as capital gains is not fully predictable. Accordingly, in a large transaction, a private-letter ruling from the IRS might be desirable for all parties concerned. At the present time, my opinion is that the IRS is likely to view the underlying transaction as being the determining factor. For instance, if the gain on the transaction would normally be taxed as ordinary income, the change in value will also be taxed as an ordinary gain. If, however, the transaction would normally be taxed as a long-term capital gain, then the dollar increase would be taxed as an additional long-term capital gain. Adjustments to the interest payable on a loan or in a sale transaction would probably be taxed as ordinary income.

STARTING OVER

An existing contract can be renegotiated and adjusted by the insertion of a gold clause if both parties agree. However, the other provisions of the contract must be carefully scrutinized in order to determine if the addition of the gold clause requires the adjustment and rewriting of other clauses.

SAMPLE GOLD CLAUSES

The typical American gold clause in contracts executed prior to 1933 provided that the borrower would pay a certain number of dollars "in gold coin of the United States of the standard of weight and fineness existing on" the date of the contract. This clause also implied a promise to pay the equivalent value in currency if gold coin became unavailable for payment.

There were many variations on the gold clause, the gold-value clause, and the foreign-money clause. Some clauses, instead of specifying a date on which the value of gold was to be indexed, merely noted that it should be "of the *present* standard weight and fineness" [italics mine]. Another common variant was to put "or equal to" before the words "the standard of weight and fineness." Yet a third variation was to add at the end of those words the phrase "or the equivalent thereof." And a fourth common form read "in the United States gold coin of the present standard weight and fineness or equivalent currency, at the option of the holder."

Since gold coins may be of numismatic value, a modern gold clause might delete all reference to coin and simply refer to a given weight of gold bullion of a specified fineness as a measure of the obligation.

In Appendix B you'll find sample gold clauses constructed to meet present legal considerations. However, it would be impossible to take into consideration in these samples all the potentially relevant factors, pertinent laws, and issues of public policy that must affect their use in any particular given circumstances. They are included in the book only as guides. If you're considering using a gold-value or gold-index clause, consult a lawyer.

5

Look Before You Leap

Our plans miscarry because they have no aim. When a man does not know what harbor he is making for, no wind is the right wind.

—SENECA

Rigidly planned lives rarely work any better than rigidly planned economies do. But far too many people operate without any long-term goals or objectives at all. As long as you know where you and your family are going, you can successfully modify what you do if circumstances change. Drifting along from day to day, on the other hand, is an ineffectual way to live, in almost every way. But it can be a particular disaster financially. **During inflationary times, the lack of long-range planning is equivalent to destroying your future.**

It is not my intent to help you plan your career, the specifics of your children's education, or your retirement. But these goals, and most others, are tied to your financial future. So let's look at what you have—which may surprise you. And where you're going—which shouldn't.

DO YOU KNOW HOW MUCH YOU'RE *REALLY* WORTH?

Amazingly enough, most people really have little idea of what they are worth. Oh, they're aware of the mortgage payments due, the amount of their paycheck, and how much their real estate tax runs a year. If you're more sophisticated than the average person, you may know the status of your pension plan, how much has been vested, what your monthly payments are, and whether there's an inflation-escalation clause for those payments. That puts you one up on most individuals. Even the self-employed I've talked to often don't know exactly what's in their own Keogh plans until they go and check.

Certainly, determining your exact net worth can be time-consuming. Yet not only is it essential for any kind of long-range planning, but in these inflationary days the bottom line may amaze you—pleasantly.

One of the best times to figure out your net worth is during the period before April 15 when you are dredging up old financial records in preparation for the annual IRS fencing match. Since you'll be going through most of your records then in any case, additional work will be minimized. And since you're now preparing a long-range defense against future IRS confiscation, you may feel better than usual about your annual battle.

Getting all the details down and organized may well be something only the head of the household can do. If so, something is wrong. Acquaintance with the financial facts should be a family responsibility these days, even if there is only one breadwinner. Husbands, particularly, tend to leave the house and go off to build their fortunes, never explaining their financial quest to their wives. Often there's very little in the way of good records, and sometimes nobody knows what they've been doing. The following true story illustrates forcefully this failure of communication and its sometimes awesome results.

There was a man in San Francisco who had a modest house. He gave his wife a modest allowance each week to run it, buy the groceries, clothe the family, and pay the rent. She had to be rather frugal to make ends meet.

And then the man went off and invested heavily in real estate and development around the city. She didn't know what he was doing; there was no communication between them on financial matters. She knew only that he made enough money to give her a $250-a-week allowance.

Years later, the man had a heart attack and died. His widow eventually got a call from a trust officer of one of the major California banks informing her that the bank was the executor of her husband's estate and that the will was going to be presented for probate. He wanted to meet with her to decide what kind of a widow's allowance she needed.

The trust officer asked this rather elderly woman to come down to his office, and there he proceeded to explain to her what a widow's allowance was. It was an interim allowance, a monthly sum paid to support her until the estate was finally settled. It didn't mean this was all she was going to get, he assured her, but since the bank was going to administer and manage the estate as trustee for her benefit, it should be enough to tide her over each month until a more permanent trust figure was determined. So the trust officer looked at her and asked, "Would ten thousand dollars a month be sufficient?"

Well, you can appreciate her surprise. Aghast, she protested that the estate could never afford that.

The trust officer replied, "Oh, yes, it could. You know, you're worth eighteen million dollars." At that she was so upset she had a stroke in his office, went into a coma, and never regained consciousness.

I've always wondered what happened when these two, husband and wife, met in the spirit world, and she confronted him with his lack of disclosure. But the point is made. Neglect in communication on financial matters between husband and wife and other family members can be a tremendous problem.

Obviously, not all financial decisions can be made "by committee." In fact, most of them may not be executable in such a manner. Nor, in all probability, should they be. But if your spouse and older children, along with anyone who may be part of your future estate, are unaware of how things stand, and where things are physically, great losses can occur, thwarting your entire plan and netting the IRS and inflation far more than their fair share of the goods. This can happen not just at your death; it can also happen during your lifetime, while you're still hale and hearty and expecting to profit personally from your careful planning.

Single persons, too, need to let others know of their financial plans and how to execute them. Single individuals need to address themselves to different facets of the problem, as you will see later. But address them they must. The best-laid plans of mice and men will go awry on occasion. However, if they're not implemented at all, they most certainly will go awry.

YOUR IRS INFLATION ATTACK PLAN

In Appendix A you will find a complete questionnaire to help you formulate your IRS/inflation attack plan. While it may seem formidable in length, it has been carefully designed to make it as effortless as possible to fill out. It covers all possible financial situations. **Filling out this form is absolutely essential.**

COMPLETE AND CANDID INFORMATION

When it comes to divulging financial information, people are by nature reticent, and with good cause. What with all the information files modern data processing is generating, privacy is rapidly becoming a precious lost right. And the government's past record of legal flip-flops doesn't exactly reassure one on this matter. Remember the sudden 1933 mandate to relinquish all private gold, at a price of $22 an ounce, and the subsequent revaluation of that very same gold to $35 an ounce for the government's benefit? Sad to say, the public's trust in those leading our country today may well be at an all-time low.

Remember, however, not all the information you are compiling will go beyond you, your family, and your attorney, who is bound by client/attorney confidentiality not to divulge anything. Of course, you yourself have to be able to live with and trust that attorney. In chapter 24 I'll show you how to pick—so that they are right for you—not only an attorney but trustees and other people you might need to further your financial goals.

Meanwhile, let's get on with compiling the information necessary to reshape your future so you can profit from the inflationary decades ahead. A complete and detailed disclosure of the history and nature of each asset and liability you have is absolutely essential, for acting on insufficient or improper information forces both you and your planners to shoot from the hip. If you fail to take all the facts—facts that may at first seem irrelevant—into account, you increase your chances of making decisions which, under certain circumstances, could prove worthless or, even worse, costly to your financial security.

An attorney once went through a lengthy estate-planning session with a client. The client named all his children by the present marriage, those by a previous marriage, previous spouses, and their children. Afterward, double-checking the obvious, the attorney asked, "Are these all of your children?" "Yes," was the reply, and so would it have remained had not the client, relaxing over a cup of coffee, added, "Of course, there was another son. He left home at seventeen and has never bothered to contact me, so I don't consider him my son anymore."

But the law does. This is the stuff around which mystery novels are written. The long-lost and forgotten heir returns to make his claim on the past. If it was the client's intent to cut the son off without a cent, then not mentioning his existence was a crucial mistake. Fortunately for him, the error was rectified. For failure to mention the son's name in his will would have made the son a "pretermitted heir"—that is, an heir whose name has been inadvertently omitted from the will. In the case of a family with, say, three surviving children including the errant one, the errant child could end up inheriting a third of the estate *specifically because he was not mentioned in the will.* If the wish was to make sure the son did not share in the inheritance, then he had to be specifically referred to in the last will and testament as disinherited.

Trusts, to be truly effective, may need to be even more encompassing. And, believe me, if you've never thought of establishing a trust, you will have your eyes open by the time you finish this book.

KEEPING EVERYONE INFORMED

In my own case, I've established a revocable living trust with myself as present trustee, or estate manager, and my wife as successor trustee. Together, we've thought through and discussed how that trust is to be operated to the best benefit of the family should I die. Not only did I candidly fill my wife in on all the basic information when I first set up the trust, but every six months or so I give her a *written* memorandum updating my business dealings. I do so more frequently if a radical change has occurred in our finances.

A yearly update is usually sufficient for most families. But make it written. Memory is far from perfect; many people have difficulty recalling such common details as a wedding anniversary date, license plate number, or date when the final payment on the car is due. Make a written financial update at least once a year.

My wife and I have also talked over whom she should contact about our different investments if I die. Whom to trust. Whom not to trust. In short, we've made a dry run in case she becomes trustee.

We've discussed who should be trustee if we both die, and we've decided we don't want that person to also be the guardian for our minor children. We've chosen the guardians and discussed the details and potential problems of our estate with them.

There are many other aspects we've covered as well in planning the management of our estate, things that you'll need to discuss and decide. For instance, in 1977 I established a different trust, an irrevocable trust for the benefit of my children. But in setting it up I also planned for other contingencies. I named, as *income* beneficiaries of that trust, not only my children, but my nieces and nephews, my brother and my sister, my wife's brother and sister, and both my parents and those of my wife. I did this not with the intent of having money from the trust go to them, but simply to give me flexibility in the future. Adding their names took up a few lines on a piece of paper. It didn't obligate me or the trust to anything. All it did was to make the people named permissible income distributors. In plain English, the trustee *may* distribute money to them. He doesn't have to.

The principal beneficiaries of that trust remain my children. Income, however, can also be distributed to other beneficiaries. Certain of my nieces and nephews who are minor children, for example, can earn $1,000 passive income a year with no income-tax consequences and the trustee, who is independent of the family, can distribute income to those children on or before June 30 (the end of the trust year) each year.

In this way I can allow those young people to have some economic benefits from the trust. And yet it's no tax burden on anyone, because they're not earners at this point.

I also have a mother living who is an income beneficiary of the trust. If she were to need income, the trustee could distribute $1,000 or more each year to her with very minimal income-tax consequences since she is retired and in a much lower tax bracket than I am. This works out far better for both of us than my sending her money that has flowed through my income-tax return.

Both these examples point up why complete information is so necessary to your planning. If those children were not named in the trust, if my mother were not named, the ploys wouldn't work. Whether we're speaking in terms of hundreds of dollars, thousands of dollars, or millions, all the nitty-gritty details and possibilities have to be worked out in advance.

Those two examples I've drawn also indicate one of the many ways a trust can be used during your prime. Death is not a necessary factor in the creative manipulation of trust assets to bypass the IRS in battling inflation.

PICKY, PICKY, PICKY

There are numerous other questions in Appendix A you might think unimportant. They aren't. Fill in everything you possibly can, no matter how insignificant it may seem to you at the time. Attorneys and other financial advisers are usually paid by the hour. The better prepared you are for their queries, the less money you'll have to spend. Also, of course, details avoid assumptions.

You'll note in the questionnaire a request for the source of the money used to buy the family assets and for details concerning any property agreement made with a spouse before or during marriage. An agreement is an agreement. Right? One doesn't have to spell it out all over again. Right? Dead wrong.

In community-property states (Arizona, California, Idaho, Louisiana, Nevada, New Mexico, Texas, and Washington), an attorney may assume that all the property under consideration is owned one half by each spouse. Yet that may not be the case, because special contracts to the contrary may have been drawn up previously.

The same situation can arise in a separate-property state, where the assumption might be that the husband's earnings generated all the assets when, in fact, inheritances and other income used to purchase property were actually passed through the wife. If she never had an income-generating job, that false assumption would be very easy to make.

Why is all this so important? Because planning with half the facts can cause horrendous distortions in the intended results. For instance, many financial advisers work on the theory of estate equalization, where each party owns half the total assets. If who legally owns what is not defined accurately, the 50-50 split obviously becomes a matter of chance, not of design.

So when you get to the question "How are the assets titled?" don't skip over it, saying, "They're ours." As romantic and selfless as that answer may sound, you could be playing yourselves right into a higher tax bracket. Don't use guesswork, either, when completing this section. Consult the physical deeds and copy the wording precisely. Better yet, make copies and attach them to the questionnaire. It may sound like more paperwork than you're accustomed to doing, but most of it you'll do only once. And, if you want to look at it from a strictly monetary point of view, your efforts could be saving you the equivalent of several thousand dollars per hour—tax-free. That kind of pay is hard to come by these days and well worth the effort.

The same principle holds true for life-insurance policies. Attach copies to the form. The expression "Some documents are so complicated they require the services of a Philadelphia lawyer to understand" may well have originated with insurance policies.

As you go down the questionnaire, filling in liabilities, business interests, domicile, and so on, you'll find that you will have several blank spots. Don't worry. Remember that the form is geared to be as all-inclusive as possible. So there are sections to be completed by those who are self-employed, those who own a small business, those concerned with surviving a massive breakdown in society, those who refuse to think about such an occurrence, and even those who feel that 1980 was the world's worst year and everything is going to get better from now on.

The point is, any ultimate financial plan has to be geared to your specific philosophy and life-style. This is what taking personal inventory and projecting goals is all about—to define yourself, for yourself and for your advisers. But be sure that anything you can fill in, no matter how remotely applicable you feel it may be, is in fact filled in.

LOOKING FORWARD—THE WHAT IFS?

Once the facts are all in, you need to add the hypotheticals, the "what ifs" of the future in terms of your specific present and long-range financial goals. Look at your family situation. Is there someone who has special future financial needs? A handicapped child, for instance? You should also note that **inflation/tax planning is best done from a total family perspective.**

Personal attitudes play a key role in defining the objectives of your estate. Do you feel that your heirs should have complete and free use of the assets immediately? Or do you think, knowing your children, it would be better for them to have merely the use of the earnings, rather than the principal, at least for a number of years? What would be the attitude of your children upon suddenly being endowed with a lump-sum payment? Would they run out and buy a $35,000 Porsche? Or would their expenditures be more judicious? Only you know your family well enough to answer questions like that.

From a psychological viewpoint, many parents find it undesirable to transfer the ownership of assets to the children before they themselves die, even when it would mean substantial tax savings. Their feeling is that the loss of financial control could put them at the mercy of their children in case of personal financial reversals. This might or might not be true. But it's the feeling that counts. Even in the cold numerical world of taxation, emotion is a crucial factor to be reckoned with.

In such situations it is possible, through corporate and trust devices as well as through family partnerships, for the parents to retain continuing control even when the assets and some of the income are transferred to the benefit of others. Indeed, as you will see, it's possible in some cases for the parents to continue adding value, tax-free, to the transferred assets.

The payout objective is central to inflation tax planning. But it is not an isolated objective. For instance, a sizable donation to a favorite charity may actually lead to the retention of more after-tax money for your estate than would be available without the contribution. All your objectives must be considered as interacting. Too much emphasis on one can destroy the effectiveness of the others as well as detract from its own potential. This is why, as important as tax avoidance is to each and every one of us, we must consider how, once tax avoidance in and of itself becomes the only objective of an estate, the transfer objectives of that estate may be jeopardized. When all your assets and objectives are mapped out, you'll need to weigh each means of achieving those objectives against its tax consequences to determine which routes your estate should take.

Protection for your spouse, children, and other dependents seems a self-evident objective of an estate. Yet it often requires more than a minimum of planning to avoid the problems that can occur during the traumatic transition period that follows a death in the family. Distraught survivors are often prey to financial scavengers, the IRS, and even well-meaning friends and relatives. Even a person of the most sound judgment and character may let decision-making take its own course during periods of severe emotional stress. To avoid such a potentially disastrous situation, special provisions should be made in advance to cover questions about the funeral, insurance, and the like, and to assure an uninterrupted flow of funds without the grieving parties having to make major decisions during this difficult period.

Another problem that sometimes arises is that while you may wish to treat, say, each of two children equally, their circumstances may not permit it unless you plan around those circumstances carefully. Consider a $500,000 estate to be divided equally between two sons, John and Ray. Let's say John is thirty-two and successfully practicing medicine. He has an income of over $70,000 a year. Ray is every bit as hard-working and intelligent but Ray is twenty-three and still in graduate school. His earnings are minimal. Ray's share of the estate could be distributed to him directly without being destroyed by taxation. John's share on the other hand, would be pulverized by the IRS were it to be distributed outright. It would be a double disaster, taking its licks from both John's income tax and your estate tax.

One solution would be to leave John's share in a trust and give the trustee discretion to distribute the income to John, his wife, or their children. Then the taxes could be effectively reduced by spreading the benefits among the beneficiaries in lower tax brackets. Alternatively, should there be unexpected financial reversals in John's life, the trustee could make the income available to him. Meanwhile the trust would keep earning money year after year.

SOLVING PROBLEMS BEFORE THEY ARISE

There are solutions to most estate problems. But those solutions can be found only if all the information is available when the active planning is done. To be considered are such factors as estate liquidity, potential investment income, business continuity, guardians, and trustees. But don't minimize such nonfinancial matters as family friction, actual or potential. People often name one of their own children as executor or trustee. The children have always gotten along well, they reason, so it should cause no problems. Suddenly, however, conflict erupts. One offspring feels neglected, not necessarily financially, since his share of the estate may be as great or greater than that of his sibling. But the old "My parents don't trust me" syndrome suddenly appears.

The psychological variables in your family and your own vision of the future are things only you can express. Your assets and liabilities can be determined by anyone with access to your papers—and will so be determined by the IRS and court cohorts unless you do it first, in the manner best for you and your family.

The more information you can present to your planners, the more imaginative they can be. I'm reminded here of a case that occurred in the state of Kentucky a few years ago. A widow had a very large estate, about $3 million. She had one son, who was only recently married. There were no grandchildren. And, as often happens, this wealthy woman did not like her daughter-in-law. As time went on, her dislike grew. She wouldn't even acknowledge her daughter-in-law's real name, referring to her, among her friends, as "what's-her-name." Eventually she decided to change her will to bypass her son and the hated daughter-in-law and leave all her property to her grandchildren, if any should materialize. If there were none, she would leave all her possessions to her favorite charity, a church.

Well, at the time she changed the will, she had a terminal illness. She hadn't long to live. And the son and daughter-in-law had no children. Somehow they found out what the mother had done in the new will. And they were desperate.

They didn't want to lose the estate, they had no children, and they figured that, what with the gestation period of nine months, they didn't have time to have a child of their own.

They checked with their county adoption agencies and found that there would probably be a six-month waiting period before an adoption could be completed, and they were afraid the mother would die within that period.

They then consulted an estate-planning attorney. He advised the husband, the mother's son, to adopt his wife, under the adult adoption statute of the state of Kentucky, because no waiting period was involved in this procedure.

So the wife became the daughter, or the granddaughter of the mother, in that new, incestuous relationship.

Well, the mother didn't know about that arrangement, and when she died, the question that consumed the trial court's time and eventually worked its way up to the Supreme Court of the state of Kentucky was, Who should receive the money? The granddaughter, who was really the daughter-in-law? Or the church? The Supreme Court of the state of Kentucky decreed that the adoption was lawful and awarded all the estate to "what's-her-name."

One author, writing about this case in a law review article, commented that the result was not surprising in a state that gave so much emphasis to the raising of Thoroughbreds. And the sequel to the story is that "what's-her-name" divorced her husband and lived happily ever after.

All your information gathering is preparatory to actually tailoring a tax-avoidance plan specifically to your assets and needs. Once you have the input at your fingertips, turn the problem around and look at it another way. You want to keep what you own, and you want to make it grow. But you want to do this by playing by the little known, and even more seldom used, IRS rules. So take a look at those rules. Familiarize yourself with them. Do it now. Don't procrastinate and leave the IRS as your principal heir.

6

Federal Estate and Gift Taxes— The Government Takes, and Takes, and Takes

It is the part of a good shepherd to shear his flock, not to flay it.

—TIBERIUS

If you think taxes are bad when you're alive, it's lucky you won't be around to see what the tax man can do to your estate, particularly if your will was made years ago, before inflation revalued your assets. But your heirs will not only see it, they'll feel it—right through the pocketbook—unless you plan your counterattack now. Plan it so that you, as well as your heirs, will benefit in the coming years.

Your estate includes everything you own, and a well-planned estate is an ongoing entity that can benefit you while you're alive as much as it benefits your beneficiaries later. But in order for you to use trusts and other tax-avoidance ideas to battle inflation and the IRS, you have to do two things. The first is to keep your estate from reaching unnecessary taxable proportions by **freezing its worth now.** The second is to **define your opponent's strength.** Remember, this is war, the war over your capital. Misjudging your opponent can only lead to defeat.

In order to map out your battle plan, you need to know what the on-coming taxes are, and to whom and what they apply. Now, this knowledge isn't totally necessary. With your personal-property inventory and goals clearly defined, as discussed in chapter 5, you can skip to the actual in-flation-conquering chapters of the book, such as 11, Estate Freezing; 12, How You Can Create Tax-Exempt Wealth; and 17, The Ultimate Tax Shelter—and do a pretty good job of presenting what you want to an at-torney. However, if you do that, you'll probably come back to this chapter, if for no other reason than curiosity. In any case, it will give you a better overall picture of the terrain on which today's tax battles are fought. So read on.

THE PRIVILEGE TAX

The federal estate and gift taxes are excise taxes imposed on your privilege of transferring property during life or at death. That's no more than a fancy way of saying that you might not be able to take it with you, but the government's going to make sure you can't give it away either. The word *excise*, incidentally, comes from the Old French word *assise*, meaning "to seat," not, as one might linguistically assume, from the Latin *excisus*, meaning "removed by cutting." Realistically, the Latin term would seem more apropos.

An estate tax is not the same as an inheritance tax. An inheritance tax is paid by the beneficiary on the share of the estate that is received. It usually allows for certain exemptions, depending on the beneficiary's relationship to the person who died, the decedent. An estate tax, on the other hand, is based on the total value of the estate *before* it is distributed. No special exemptions are provided for close relatives, other than a wife—not even for children, unless you design your estate to accommodate them.

The federal government imposes the estate tax. Several states have estate or inheritance taxes as well. Check Appendix H for the complete details of your state's income and death taxes. Also, if you're contemplating retiring in a state different from the one in which you now live, you may wish to use the state-by-state comparison in this appendix in your planning.

Neither the federal government nor the states had either of these taxes until World War I, and many countries still manage very well without dealing this final ignominious blow to a hard-working life. Take Austria, for instance. Even though it is a "socialist" state, it has no inheritance tax at all—no capital-gains tax either, for that matter—and incredibly low real-estate taxes. What it does have is a steep sales tax. But even the socialist government there still feels that once you earn your money, you are entitled to keep it, or spend it, as you choose. Of course, the high tax on spending and no tax on saving have led to a great deal of capital accumulation and a prosperous economy capped by a solid, gold-backed international currency. But let's get back to your own watered-down dollars, inflation, and estate taxes.

Prior to January 1, 1977, the federal estate tax and the federal gift tax were two distinct taxes, with separate rate structures and different rates. Many provisions of law required that property on which gift taxes might have been paid prior to one's death still be included in one's gross estate.

Now one would naturally expect a gift tax to be more unlike an estate tax than an inheritance tax is. Separating the two seems perfectly logical. Unfortunately, the legislators' logic in Washington runs toward simplification by complication. The gift-tax rates and the estate-tax rates are now one and the same. During the 1976 tax reform, they were unified, and a unified credit was authorized to reduce your taxes. At the same time, a tax range of 18 to 70 perecnt was established.

The Economic Recovery Tax Act of 1981 made further changes in the estate and gift tax laws. While the important changes will be discussed in greater detail later on, some of the major revisions should be noted here. First, the law increases, by 1987, the size of a tax-exempt estate to $600,000. Second, all property transferred to a surviving spouse passes tax-free. That is, the new law provides an unlimited marital deduction for both estate and gift taxes. Third, the amount you can give away without incurring any gift taxes was raised from $3,000 to $10,000 per beneficiary.

TAX CREDITS ARE BETTER THAN DEDUCTIONS

There's a crucial difference between a credit and a deduction when it comes to determining the taxes you have to pay. An estate-tax deduction is *subtracted* from the gross estate, whereas a credit is *applied* directly to the taxes owed.

Let's take a hypothetical case. The taxable estate of a single person at death is $750,000. Looking at the table of the unified tax rates for estate and gift taxes, you will see that the gross tax is $248,300. Now, if the person dies in 1982, the estate is allowed a tax credit of $62,800. When the credit is subtracted from the gross tax, the net tax payable is $185,500.

Under the unified gift and estate tax rate schedule, a single rate is applied to the cumulative value of all adjusted taxable gifts you make during your lifetime *plus* all the transfers made at your death.

Actually, the unified transfer tax does reduce the government's take on small estates. Estates with a net value of $225,000 or less won't be liable for estate taxes in 1982. The problem is that anyone who owns a house and some other property will probably find that inflation has boosted his or her total estate to a higher figure than that. The larger estate means—you guessed it—a larger estate tax.

UNIFIED ESTATE AND GIFT TAX RATES FOR U.S. RESIDENTS AND CITIZENS

UNIFIED TAX RATE SCHEDULE

If the amount is:		Tentative Tax* Is:		On Excess
From	To	Tax	+%	Over
$ 0	$ 10,000	0	18	0
$ 10,000	20,000	$ 1,800	20	$ 10,000
20,000	40,000	3,800	22	20,000
40,000	60,000	8,200	24	40,000
60,000	80,000	13,000	26	60,000
80,000	100,000	18,200	28	80,000
100,000	150,000	23,800	30	100,000
150,000	250,000	38,800	32	150,000
250,000	500,000	70,800	34	250,000
500,000	750,000	155,800	37	500,000
750,000	1,000,000	248,300	39	750,000
1,000,000	1,250,000	345,800	41	1,000,000
1,250,000	1,500,000	448,300	43	1,250,000
1,500,000	2,000,000	555,800	45	1,500,000
2,000,000	2,500,000	780,800	49	2,000,000
**2,500,000	3,000,000	1,025,800	53	2,500,000
3,000,000	3,500,000	1,290,800	57	3,000,000
3,500,000	4,000,000	1,575,800	61	3,500,000
4,000,000	4,500,000	1,880,800	65	4,000,000
4,500,000	5,000,000	2,205,800	69	4,500,000
5,000,000	—	2,550,800	70	5,000,000

*The tentative tax applies to the sum of (a) the amount of the taxable estate and (b) the amount of the taxable gifts made by the decedent after 1976 other than gifts includable in the gross estate.

**After 1984 the tax rate on amounts greater than $2.5 million will be $1,025,800 plus 50 percent of the excess over $2.5 million.

UNIFIED CREDIT

Year	Amount of Credit	Amount of Exemption Equivalent
1981	$47,000	$175,625
1982	62,800	225,000
1983	79,300	275,000
1984	96,300	325,000
1985	121,800	400,000
1986	155,800	500,000
1987	192,800	600,000

GIFT TAXES

After December 31, 1981, you can give $10,000 a year to as many people as you want without incurring any federal tax. Prior to 1982, even the $3,000 annual exclusion was a residual boon for middle-sized estates, those over $500,000 but well below the multi-million-dollar range associated with the wealthy. Let's see how it worked.

Suppose you have four children and nine grandchildren. Giving away $3,000 to each of them would equal $39,000 a year in presents. Now suppose you have an estate worth $500,000. Such an estate is in the 34-percent tax bracket (in 1981), which means that the $39,000 given away will reduce your final tax bill by $13,260. Since the $3,000 is an annual exclusion, you can do the same thing again next year, and again your tax bill will be reduced by $13,260. You can keep this up indefinitely—until your estate runs out of money, of course.

Modification of the gift-tax rules has eliminated the gifts-in-contemplation-of-death problems of the old law—by simply removing them from consideration. The Economic Recovery Tax Act of 1981 provides that the appreciated value of gifts made within 3 years will not be included in your taxable estate. Under the old law (as it was prior to 1977), when you made a gift and died within three years, the government could say, "Aha, your reason for making the gift was that you were thinking about estate-tax planning, so we're going to tax it anyway." The estate then had the burden of proving that the gift was given at a time when the donor had no reason whatsoever to suspect that death was imminent.

One particular case points up rather well the bizarre convolutions to which this presumption sometimes led. There was a man in the Midwest who had a large farm. He was widowed, and his son, also single, lived with him. The man's accountant and attorney advised him, "Look, make a gift, get the property out of your estate because the gift-tax rate is 25 percent lower that the estate-tax rate. You'll save $100,000, and that's a pretty strong lifetime motive for making the gift." So the father gave the family farm to his son.

Then his accountant said, "Now look, you've got to stay alive three years. We know you've got this serious illness, and because of your health, it's going to be hard to establish a lifetime motive. If you don't live three years, they could tax your estate as though you passed title at the time of death."

One morning two years, eleven months, and twenty-nine days later, the father had a heart attack and died while eating breakfast. And the son thought, Oh, my gosh, we missed the three years! So he took his father's body out to the meat cooler and kept it on ice for three or four days, until after the three-year period had expired. He then placed it back at the breakfast table and called the county coroner.

An autopsy revealed something in the stomach, a certain kind of berry that doesn't keep, which the father had apparently eaten for breakfast on the day of his real death. That aroused suspicion and the county coroner's report led to an investigation.

Eventually, the case came before the tax court on the question of when the father died. And even though the son would never agree or confess that his father had died within the three-year period, the court found that the evidence showed otherwise and taxed the property in the father's estate.

In view of the IRS's line of reasoning, what we, as tax and estate attorneys, used to do was to build the record for a client so that if he died, we'd have evidence to prove that he had made a gift for what you'd call lifetime reasons, such as wanting to transfer the use and enjoyment of his property to his child or some other beneficiary recipient.

If the gift was a sizable one, often we'd have the person get a medical checkup so that, if the gift was questioned by the IRS, the doctor's records would show that the person felt good and had no reason to believe he was going to die in the near future. We had him write letters to his children telling them about how he'd just finished climbing a mountain or running a marathon—anything that said, in effect, "Hey, I feel great, I'm in good health, don't worry about me, my motive isn't the thought of death."

THERE MAY BE MORE TO YOUR ESTATE
THAN YOU REALIZE

So there you are, faced with the two transfer taxes, estate and gift—or one, if you prefer, now that they are unified. What exactly will the IRS tax? "Your estate" is the obvious answer. But the actual definition of what constitutes that estate may not be so obvious. And it is a definition you must understand before you can find effective ways to reduce the onerous tax burden.

One common misconception is that your estate is limited to property covered by your will. Nothing could be further from the truth. That much is obvious when you consider all the intestates—that is, people who die without a will. But if leaving possessions out of a will because of predeath transfers—gifts you gave before dying—or merely failing to include the properties in the will automatically exempted them from taxation, this book need not have been written. On the other hand, predeath transfers *may* remove property from a taxable estate. And, under certain circumstances, lack of inclusion in your last will and testament *can* cause property to escape taxation. That's why you're reading this book, and why you'll profit from it.

For now, without going into the fancy footwork you'll need to learn to salvage the rewards of your hard work from the IRS, let's deal with the simple, basic fact that **your taxable estate includes all the property owned by you, or in which you have an interest, and the tax due on your estate is based on the combined value of all this property.** Of course, how it is evaluated is open to interpretation and manipulation, with the outcome in either your favor or the IRS's, depending on the methods chosen.

"What if I have a small vacation home in the Bahamas? Or Switzerland?" you ask. "Surely that's not included in my estate?" Wrong. Until July 1, 1964, the gross estate, the total value of the estate before any deductions, credits, or settlement expenses are taken, did not, in fact, include real property located outside the United States. Now, however, under the amended law, it does in some cases, even when the estate must also pay overseas taxes.

Note that this bit of noose tightening on your assets occurred about the time the United States decided to demonetize by removing the silver from its coins. Every time the government makes a financial mistake, it's the taxpayer who pays.

When it comes to taxes, your estate isn't limited to property owned. Your gross estate can include other assets in which you are deemed to have an interest substantially equivalent to ownership—control over how the property is to be handed out would be an example of such an interest—even though you may not be legally entitled to a share of that property. Most of these nonowned assets are tied to predeath transfers.

RETAINED LIFE USE

The question whether a nonowned asset should be included in your estate for tax purposes revolves around power—not the IRS's, but yours. For instance, a retained life interest—anything you own or could control—in any form, even if it only absolves you from an obligation, is treated by the tax laws as if you still actually owned the property at the time of your death. Consider the following example.

A father created an irrevocable trust for his two children, appointing as trustee a totally independent, nonrelated friend. Any income from the trust was to be used to help pay the children's medical, clothing, and school bills as well as to fund an educational year abroad during their senior year in high school. After the children reached the age of eighteen, the income from the trust's interest was to continue for the rest of their lives, with no restrictions.

The father died when his children were twelve and seventeen years old. The entire value of the trust immediately became part of his taxable estate. Why? The father had no control over the trust, nor did he derive any personal benefits from it. So why the ruling in favor of the tax? Because the trust was used to pay expenses such as the children's medical bills, expenses for which the father was legally responsible, and hence was considered an implied life use.

Let's take an example from the other side of the coin. A husband deeded a house free and clear, with no encumbrances, to his wife. He continued to live in it. Five years later he died. The value of the house was *not* pulled into his estate for tax purposes, even though he lived there all along. Why not? Because there was no implicit agreement that the husband might live in the house.

On the other hand, if the father had given the house to one of his children and continued to live there, even without a written agreement permitting him to do so, the full value of the house would probably have been taxed in the father's estate at death.

As you can see from these examples, dealing with our money-collecting bureaucracy is fraught with difficulties. Normal logic doesn't work. The IRS regulations are interpreted, for the most part, on the basis of past event and past procedure. For instance, the decision on the house that was given away to the wife, in the example just given, is the Gutchess case ruling of 1966. Before that date, the house might have been included in the estate. Then again, it might not have been. It would have all depended on whether or not the executor took the case to court and whether or not the court's decision turned out to be the same as the one on the Gutchess estate.

Tax laws are constantly changing, the one small certainty amid the flux being that the changes are rarely to the taxpayer's benefit. Also, while some rulings are retroactive, these are in the minority. So the sooner you implement the tax-avoidance devices detailed in this book, the better your future tax situation is apt to be.

THE RIGHT TO CHANGE YOUR MIND
ABOUT WHO GETS WHAT AND WHEN

Another instance of a nonowned asset which is drawn back into, or recaptured by, the estate is the **irrevocable transfer**, in which the future recipient of the property can be changed. In plain English, it's your right to change your mind about who gets what and when. Here again, it's control that counts. Let's say you set up a trust with the income going to your wife for the rest of her life. The principal eventually goes to your son. Acting as trustee, you retain the right to channel the capital to your daughter instead, in case a major change in your son's circumstances, such as chronic disease, should occur. That's fine for your family, not so fine for your estate. While there's no way you can get the money back, the fact that you exercise some control—no matter that it's over such a financially minor matter as choosing between two family members to act in a tragic situation—means that the total trust is counted in establishing the worth of your estate.

RETAINING A REVERSIONARY INTEREST

Yet another giveaway that the IRS does not recognize for estate purposes is a transfer made contingent on the recipient's outliving you. Again, it's not necessary for you to be able to get the money or other property back. What is necessary is simply the chance, however remote, that it may revert to you—hence the legal term *reversionary interest*.

Let's say you draw up another trust. This time the income is payable to your wife for life and the remainder is to go to your son upon your wife's death—unless you're still alive, in which case it reverts to you. Since your son can't get the money unless he lives longer than you do, the trust's value is counted as part of your estate, even if you never collect a cent.

In this instance, however, not the total estate is recaptured. Instead, a fraction of the property's value, related to the value of your wife's estate, is included in your estate. Actually, to be more specific, the rule is that if the decedent's reversionary interest the moment before death exceeds 5 percent of the value of the trust property, the value of the property less the value of the wife's outstanding estate is includable in the decedent's gross estate. No, don't bother to read that sentence again. File it for reference, if you will. But the point is, the more you know about your own estate, the *simpler* you can make a trust. And as long as all bases are covered, the simpler the better. Complexity fattens lawyers unnecessarily.

ANNUITIES

Annuities, those fixed-payment contracts guaranteeing you an income during your retirement, are another financial tool some people believe won't be included in their estate. That's not necessarily true. However, it is true that some annuities are less includable than others. With foresight, it is possible to use annuities for your own and your family's future security without inviting the tax man to share in the money through your estate.

The trick is to persuade your employer to pay for an annuity as part of your retirement package. A *qualified* annuity purchased by the employer or by an employee's trust, and forming part of a *qualified* pension, stock bonus, or profit-sharing plan, will *not* be included in your estate. The key word is *qualified*, which in this case means simply that it has a stamp of approval from the IRS.

If *you* make a contribution to such a qualified plan, however, everything changes. A proportion of the benefits, based on the percentage you paid in, will be included in your estate.

A detailed discussion of how and when to use annuities and other qualified retirement-plan proceeds on an inheritance-tax-free basis is in chapter 17, The Ultimate Tax Shelter. I mention annuities here simply by way of illustrating the ambiguities surrounding the tax laws and their common interpretation—and by way of warning. There is, after all, a right way and a wrong way, a productive and a counterproductive way, to do almost everything.

JOINT TENANCY

Your gross estate includes the entire value of any property held jointly at the time of your death by you and anyone else with a right of survivorship. That's the general rule, but there are two exceptions. First, any portion of that property which was acquired by the other joint owner for full and adequate consideration (that is, money or money's worth) or by bequest or gift from a third party and your estate has the burden of proving that the other joint owner acquired this interest for consideration or by bequest or gift.

Look out for the tax trap here. It has ensnared many well-meaning people who have transferred title to property into joint tenancy with a son or daughter thinking that only half of the property will be subject to federal estate tax. This is simply not the case unless it can be shown that the surviving joint tenant contributed to the purchase or acquisition of the property from independent funds.

The second exception is for *qualified joint interests*. After 1981, only one half of the value of any property held in joint tenancy is included in your estate, if you and your spouse hold the property (1) as tenants by the entirety, or (2) as joint tenants with rights of survivorship. Who actually paid for the property is immaterial so long as the only other joint tenant is your spouse. (Tenant in this case refers to actual ownership. The fact that your children live with you, or even that you rent out a room to a college student, doesn't make them tenants for estate purposes.)

Note, however, that when the surviving spouse passes away, 100 percent of the value will still be held in his or her taxable estate. More importantly, the surviving spouse will not be able to take advantage of the usual step-up in basis. Take, for example, a couple whose principal asset is a house worth $220,000 that cost $80,000 several years ago. If he dies and the property is held in joint tenancy, only one half of its value will be included in his gross estate. The rub is that basis can be increased only by the amount included in his gross estate. Thus, if the wife sells the home, she will have $70,000 in taxable gains. (Basis = $40,000 + 110,000.) If the property was titled solely in the husband's name, there would be no taxable gains, and no estate taxes would be due in 1982 or later.

If you should pass away before December 31, 1981, however, a different set of rules would apply under the old law. In that case, the value included in the estate of the first spouse to die will be half the total value of the joint tenancy property if it constitutes a qualified joint interest created after December 31, 1976.

Before the enactment of the Economic Recovery Tax Act of 1981, you and your spouse would not only have to hold the property as joint tenants or in a similar arrangement known as tenants by the entirety, but the joint tenancy would also have to meet the following criteria:

(1) created by you or your spouse or both,
(2) a completed gift, if the joint tenancy is in personal property, and
(3) treated as a taxable gift when the joint interest was created, if the interest is in real property.

Because the joint interest must be created by one or both spouses, a joint tenancy inherited by both spouses would not be a qualified joint interest, since it was not actually created by the spouses.

If property held in joint tenancy is determined to be a qualified joint interest, the value included in the gross estate will be half the value of the qualified joint interest. A contribution by the surviving joint owner need not be proven.

The Economic Recovery Tax Act of 1981 greatly simplified the requirements. The Act provides that as long as you and your spouse hold the property as tenants in the entirety or as joint tenants (but only if you and your wife are the only joint tenants), the property will qualify as a qualified joint interest. ERTA also provides that there will be no gift taxes payable upon the creation of the joint tenancy or tenancy by the entirety.

However, the qualified joint interest rule applies only to spouses. Don't count on the benefits provided by the qualified joint interest rule unless your co-joint tenant is your spouse—a child, parent, or friend simply doesn't qualify.

For example, let's say A, B, and C each put up $10,000 to buy a tract of land and that costs $30,000, and the deed states that they are joint tenants with rights of survivorship. Unless they can prove that $30,000 came from their separate funds, the entire fair market value of the tract will be included in A's gross estate, assuming he dies first. Then, if B passes away, all of the property's value will be included in his gross estate; when C dies the entire value is again included—and taxed—in his estate. Failing to prove that A, B, and C each put up $10,000 would mean that the same property would be taxed three times, once in each estate! Thus each estate must have the evidence to prove that it indeed owned only part of the joint property, and that no ongoing gift was involved.

TAX TROUBLES WITH JOINT TENANCY

With joint tenancy you may pay more taxes. A married couple could have an estate of $1,200,000 in 1987 which, with the proper planning, would incur no death tax payable to the federal government. By proper planning I mean marital trust wills or a revocable living trust, coupled with a good gifting program. You would not achieve the same result by a simple will or by keeping the property in joint tenancy.

Now let's take a bigger 1987 example, a husband and wife with an estate of $1,500,000. If they used trust planning effectively, at their deaths their entire estate could pass to the heirs with a federal estate tax of about $86,400. In comparison, joint tenancy by itself could cause the estate to pay a federal estate tax as high as $298,600.

Let's look more closely at some common joint-tenancy situations. Suppose a person owns some property which he or she decides to put into joint tenancy with a child—a common arrangement. A father, let's say, has a favorite son. The father buys a piece of real estate, and the title reads, "John Jones, the father, and Fred Jones, the son, as joint tenants." Now whether or not the father intended to make a gift to his son, and whether or not he filed a gift tax return and paid the gift tax, when the father dies, 100 percent of that property will be taxed in his estate, simply because he was the one who originally put up the money, the one who contributed the property to the joint tenancy.

It's a kind of joint-tenancy trap, you see. If you intend to have your son inherit your property when you die, and you want to do it through joint tenancy, that's fine. Your property will pass—free of probate—to the surviving joint tenant. But the entire fair market value of the property at your death will be subject to estate tax, because you put up the contribution.

OTHER PROBLEMS WITH JOINT TENANCY

Joint tenancy can create traps other than taxes. Once you put property into joint tenancy, especially if the property is real estate, you can't sell it without the approval of the other joint tenant. I had a case here in

California not too long ago that reinforces this point.

My client, an elderly woman, single, about seventy years old, had one major asset, a house in California worth approximately $200,000. She had fallen and broken her hip, and she was going into the hospital for an operation. But she was worried about her chances of surviving the operation.

Now this woman has a nephew in northern California whom she wanted at that time to be the beneficiary of her estate. So she went to an escrow company for advice and the suggestion made to her was, "Why don't you put the title in joint tenancy with your nephew? Then if you die on the operating table he'll receive and inherit the property."

That sounded good to her, so that's what she did. Then she went through the operation—successfully.

After convalescing for about three weeks, however, she had a change of heart and went back to the escrow company requesting that they get the title to her property back from her nephew.

Accordingly, the title escrow officer prepared a quit-claim deed and mailed it to the nephew, asking him to please sign it so that his aunt could clear the title and once again have it in her own name.

Human nature being what it is, you've probably already guessed what the nephew's response was. He said, "Go fly a kite. I'm not going to sign a quit-claim deed."

Well, that put a lien on the property. The nephew had a vested equity ownership and his aunt couldn't do anything about it. She couldn't even sell the house without her nephew's approval.

We ended up filing a suit, naming the escrow company as defendant for practicing law, among other things. But the woman was so overwrought from the emotional stress all this had caused that she died before the case came to trial. And the nephew ended up with the house.

The entire predicament *could have been avoided* if the woman had put the title of her property in a trust that she could personally revoke. It would then have passed to the nephew at her death, free of probate, the estate tax would have been the same, and she wouldn't have had the highly significant problem of attempting to clear the title.

There are very few instances in planning, in my opinion, where joint tenancy is the answer. I know it's a very common arrangement between spouses, especially in a state like California. All real-estate offices and most escrow companies tend automatically to put the title in joint tenancy when a couple buys a house. But for the most part there are simply too many problems, both legal and tax-related, with joint tenancy. Revocable trusts, which share with joint tenancy the advantage of avoiding probate, are preferable in most cases.

LIFE INSURANCE

Life-insurance proceeds all too often end up in a taxable estate, though there's no reason for this to occur. Here again, as in the case of the revocable transfer, the tax problem arises because of a retained right. When you take out life insurance naming someone else as beneficiary, even though neither you nor your estate is ever going to profit monetarily, it is common for you to retain the right to change beneficiaries. As tenuous as your rights in the policy may seem, the mere fact that you can choose a different beneficiary means that you still exercise control over the policy. Hypothetically, you see, you could make yourself the beneficiary by naming your estate as the recipient of the insurance funds. So, just to be safe, the IRS includes the value of the policy in your gross estate.

The way around the problem is to relinquish all rights in the policy. In the case of family insurance planning, the solution may be to have the wife own the life-insurance policy on her husband, and have him own the policy on her. Then if the husband dies, the proceeds of the insurance on him go to the wife *free and clear of all taxes,* and vice versa. An even better solution, in many family situations, may be to use an irrevocable life-insurance trust, or ancestor trust, described in chapter 12.

THE CRUCIAL ROLE OF CROSS INSURANCE

For now, let's look at why a cross-insurance plan plays a crucial role in your financial strategy. All too often a wife is not insured. After all, she may not "work," in the sense of bringing home a paycheck. Well, as any widower with a family will tell you, this is a big mistake. Taking care of the children and the house can be a full-time job. The expense of hiring help in the form of baby-sitters, house cleaners, and so on can strain the budget of an otherwise financially secure family. It can be a burden particularly during the period of grief and adjustment following the wife's death.

Thanks to the new unlimited marital deduction, even if the proceeds of a policy on your life are included in your gross estate, the proceeds will pass to your spouse completely tax-free.

However, if your spouse is not your sole beneficiary, or if your estate plan calls for an intervivos trust for your spouse so that his or her assets will pass tax-free on the second death, the traditional cross-ownership arrangement can be most important. Under this approach, separate checking accounts should be used to pay the different life insurance premiums. Each spouse must own and pay for the life insurance on the other. And establishing that the money paying for the policy is actually earned or otherwise belongs to the payer is crucial.

"But," you say, "my wife doesn't currently earn an independent salary. How can she pay for life insurance—much less her half of the mortgage—with money she doesn't have?" The answer is simple. Give it to her. Instead of paying the premiums yourself, give her the money to pay them. But make it a recognized and irrevocable gift each January with no strings attached, for her to spend as she feels led.

POWERS OF APPOINTMENT

A common provision in many wills specifies that the testator does not exercise any powers of appointment he or she may have. That's so *general* powers of appointment created *prior* to October 21, 1942 which you may not even be aware of don't end up in your estate.

A general power of appointment is one in which the holder of the power has the right to pass his interest in the property on to anyone, including his estate or his creditors. By contrast, a *special* power of appointment, which does not create a tax problem, is one in which the holder can appoint his interest in the property only to specified individuals.

For most of us, the fictional long-lost uncle with millions to give away and no one closer than his nephew or niece to give it to remains just that: fiction. Still, however remote the possibility of such an inheritance might be, your estate must be protected against it—not against the sudden influx of money per se, of course, but against the taxes that might be due on money you might be deemed by the IRS to control, even though you might never actually see a cent of it.

Consider the hoped-for lost uncle. Let's say sometime prior to 1942 he gave you the right or power to redirect his trust assets from his son, the designated beneficiary of his $2 million vineyards on the slopes of Grinzing outside of Vienna, to you or your heirs and you were unaware of the implication of the power given to you. Suppose your uncle dies this year. Your own $500,000 estate suddenly becomes worth $2.5 million—for tax purposes only. You or your heirs may never actually receive any of your uncle's estate.

Now, if you were to die without exercising the power of appointment your uncle gave you, your estate has a fundamental problem—how to pay the taxes due on a $2.5 million estate. With your estate consisting of only $500,000, the taxes you owe will literally wipe out your estate unless your executor can collect the money for the excess taxes from your cousin. The odds of your ending up in this predicament may be one to a million, but a three-line clause in your will eliminating your exercise of the power of appointment could spell the difference between a smoothly settled estate and a decade of trouble. The odds on dying in a plane crash are even higher—but you buy flight insurance, don't you?

If a general power of appointment was created for you *after* October 21, 1942, the property subject to the power of appointment will be taxed as part of your gross estate *whether or not you exercise that power.*

YOUR ESTATE IS WORTH LESS THAN IT REALLY IS— FOR TAX PURPOSES

The question of what your estate is worth seems at first to have an obvious ready answer. It's worth whatever you could sell the property for plus any available cash from bank accounts, insurance policies, and the like. And that's more or less the way it stands for tax purposes—but not entirely.

In most circumstances, the assets are accounted for on the basis of fair market value—fair market value being defined, somewhat obtusely, as "the price at which the property would change hands between a willing buyer and a willing seller, neither being under compulsion to buy or sell and both having reasonable knowledge of all pertinent and relevant facts pertaining to the property to be purchased and sold." Now obviously it cannot be in the capacity of this book to determine the value of all conceivable property in an estate. An actual valuation is up to the executor of a particular estate. And, in any case, most of your assets should be outside the estate for tax purposes—a fact you should be thoroughly convinced of by the time you finish reading this volume. Still, knowing some of the basic rules of valuing a gross estate may help you choose which assets to relocate from your potential estate to trusts.

Stocks quoted over the counter on a bid/asked basis may be harder to average if they are traded only sporadically. The real difficulty, however, lies in assessing lettered stock, stock that the SEC does not allow to be freely traded, and shares in closely held corporations, those with only a few shareholders and with no public market for the shares. A minority stockholder in a closely held corporation, for instance, exercises very little control. Often, there is an exceedingly limited market for the stock. It might be possible to argue that such stock is, in fact, worth quite a bit less than the fair market value assigned to it. The same situation could occur at the opposite end of the spectrum if the deceased held a very large position in a major company. The sale of such a block of equity could depress prices overall, so the stock would be worth less than normal fair value. Then again, in either of these cases, the stock should probably be in a trust rather than your estate (more on that in chapter 21, The Closely Held Business).

An executor or trustee may elect to use the alternate valuation method, which allows the assessment of property included in an estate to be based upon values established six months from the date of death rather than at the time of death. Such a choice doesn't change the basic rules covering what property is to be included for federal estate tax. It's a relief provision that dates from the Depression, and it can be particularly effective in fair-valuing equity shares during periods of wide price swings on the stock exchanges. Basically, it provides a cushioning effect for individuals who die during a period of general—or personal—economic downturn.

Special valuation rules for farms and business real property are provided for under the Tax Reform Act of 1976, further amended by the Economic Recovery Tax Act of 1981. The general rule is that all assets must be valued at fair market value—which means the highest and best use of the property. If real property devoted to farming or to closely held business use is included in your gross estate, it *may* be valued on the basis of its worth as a farm or its value in the closely held business rather than, for example, its value for subdivision purposes, which might be the property's highest or best use. However, the special-use valuation procedure cannot be employed to reduce the gross estate by more than $750,000 for estates of those who die in 1983 and thereafter. If the year of death is 1982, the reduction is limited to $700,000; if 1981, $600,000.

In order to qualify for this special valuation, five requirements must be met. First, the real property in question must be used as a farm or in a closely held business (qualified use) on the date of the decedent's death. Second, the decedent or a member of his family must "materially participate" in the farm or business for an aggregate of five out of the eight years before the date the decedent retired, became disabled, or died—whichever event came first. Whether one has "materially participated" in the farm or business is a question of (1) how much actual labor the person performed. and (2) whether the person participated in management decisions. In the case of a surviving spouse who acquires the property, however, the new law provides that instead of material participation, "active management" will satisfy the second requirement. Active management means the making of business decisions other than daily operating decisions, and thus requires less activity than actual material participation.

The next two requirements deal with the size of the farm or business in relationship to the rest of the gross estate. The third requirement states that at least 50 percent of the value of the gross estate must be attributable to real or personal property that was being used for a qualified use, and that amount of property must end up in the hands of a qualified heir (either by purchase or inheritance). Under the fourth requirement, at least 25 percent of the gross estate must be attributable to the real estate in question.

Finally, the fifth requirement states (in general terms) that the qualified heir who receives the land cannot sell it to anyone outside the family, he must use the property for a qualified use, and during a period of ten years he or a member of his family must materially participate in the operation of the farm or business. Failure to meet this last requirement will trigger a "recapture tax" representing the taxes not paid originally because the estate benefited from the special valuation rules.

TAKE EVERY DEDUCTION YOU CAN

After setting the pins up according to the tax man's rules comes the time for making sure he doesn't score a strike on your estate. As with your income tax, taking every permissible deduction makes the difference between paying only what you absolutely must and giving the government a free handout—from your pocket.

Actually this part of your task is fairly routine. Most executors take the deductions for administrative expenses, funeral expenses, claims against the estate, mortgages, and other indebtedness, as well as transfers or gifts to public, charitable, and religious organizations.

An additional deduction for which any competent executor will apply whenever he can is the marital deduction. This is a financial facet of an estate with which you should be familiar for planning purposes. It may contribute to your peace of mind.

THE MARITAL DEDUCTION

Much more common, and offering great tax-planning and tax saving opportunities, the marital deduction allows an estate to make a tax-free transfer of 100 percent of the gross estate to a surviving spouse. The only requirements for this deduction are that you are married, that your spouse survives your death, and that you pass away after December 31, 1981.

Under the old law, the marital deduction was limited to $250,000 or one half of the gross estate, whichever was larger. Seizing on this opportunity to reduce estate taxes, many people drafted their wills or trusts to obtain the largest possible marital deduction. This was usually done by making a bequest to the surviving spouse in terms of a formula specifically geared to the ceiling of $250,000 or one half of the gross estate.

Now, what does the new law mean to you if you already have a will or trust? That depends. Maybe you really want your spouse to get all of the property. In that case you should amend your trust or will to take advantage of the new law. On the other hand, if you intend to limit the amount of property passing to your spouse, there's a good chance the new law won't apply and you should leave your will or trust as it is now. But you should definitely have your will or trust reviewed; otherwise, part of your property could unintentionally go to the wrong people, or your estate could pay extra taxes.

The purpose of the marital deduction was to put separate-property states on the same footing with community-property states, such as California and Texas. In community-property states, the surviving spouse already owns half of most of the property accumulated during a marriage, so only half of such property is taxable when his or her spouse dies.

Even in community-property states, however, the marital deduction available before 1982 was very important, particularly to medium-sized estates with total community property in the $250,000 to $450,000 range. Remember, the entire $250,000 marital deduction could be taken, even if it was greater than half the total community estate. For example, in the case of a total community estate of $400,000, the marital deduction would cut the taxable estate of a deceased spouse to only $150,000. However, the federal tax due—$138,800 is less than the $47,000 unified tax credit (see table earlier in chapter). So the federal estate tax is eliminated entirely.

Total Community Estate	$400,000
Estate of deceased spouse	200,000
Additional deduction (allowed by marital deduction: $250,000 less $200,000 = $50,000)	50,000
Taxable estate	$150,000

In an example with larger figures, the results may not be quite as impressive. A $700,000 separate property estate permits a $350,000 marital deduction. (For simplicity's sake, I'll leave out the settlement costs, which usually run about 10 percent of the total estate, as you'll note I did in the previous example.) Subtracting the $350,000 deduction from the gross estate leaves a taxable estate of $350,000, on which the gross taxes due would be $104,800.* Applying the unified tax credit again reduces the actual taxes due to $57,800. That's almost $60,000 that the government gets. However, as you will see later in this book, if you used the right strategy, for example estate freezing, to prevent your taxable estate from reaching such proportions in the first place, you could avoid paying the $60,000 tax and keep the money for your family.

Before leaving the marital deduction for greener pastures, you should take note of one serious shortcoming it has besides its relative ineffectuality in relieving the tax burdens of larger estates. When the surviving spouse in a marriage dies, there is no longer a marital deduction for the estate to avail itself of. A lot of money that should have gone to the children, other relatives, or charitable and religious organizations ends up instead in the government's coffers.

For example, assume for a moment that our hypothetical $700,000 separate property estate had again, through inflation and income, reached the dollar value that it had when the second spouse died. Now the IRS really gets its cut. The present $700,000 estate is liable for $229,800 in taxes less the $47,000 unified credit, or $182,800. Who do you think could use that $182,800 more, the family of the deceased or the government?

Besides the federal tax due, there are also administrative expenses, probate fees, and state taxes to be paid out of the estate. These factors

---

*This example and all other examples in the book are computed without any credit for state death taxes and without any credit for taxes on prior transfers.

combined could easily lead to a situation in which the family homestead has to be sold in order to meet the tax obligations.

THE MARITAL-DEDUCTION TRUST

There is a simple, trusty remedy to the inherent shortcomings of an outright inheritance, however. It's called, not surprisingly, the marital-deduction trust, and it merely involves dividing the estate into two separate trusts, a marital trust and a unified credit trust.* When either the husband or the wife dies, the survivor has control over the assets in the marital trust. The unified credit trust can be held in reserve for the children or for charitable objectives. However, the surviving spouse has lifelong rights not only to the income earned by the unified credit trust, but to any portion of the principal necessary to provide for his or her support or maintenance. In other words, the money is accessible whenever needed.

Suppose we're dealing with an estate of $950,000. When the first spouse dies in 1987, the estate is divided into two halves—one for the spouse and one for the children. There are no estate taxes because the spouse's half is covered by the unlimited marital deduction, and the taxes on the half going to the kids are less than the unified credit. Then, even if the spouse's half were to increase due to inflation, there would not be any taxes on her estate of $600,000 or less. Without a trust, the entire estate could pass tax-free to the spouse, but there will be at least $133,500 in taxes on the second death.

The marital deduction, as you might surmise, is considered at least one reason for some couples to marry. I once had an elderly client whose total assets were about $750,000 who steadfastly refused to marry the woman he was living with. They wanted to spend the rest of their lives together, and the man wanted to leave his entire estate to her if she survived him. There was no question of protecting his property in case their relationship dissolved, since that could have been done with an antenuptial agreement before their marriage. They simply, as a matter of principle, did not want to be married.

I explained without marriage the federal estate tax imposed at his death would be about $150,000, roughly 20 percent of his estate. If he were married, on the other hand, the federal tax on his estate would be zero.

My client was impressed. But he had one more hurdle for me to overcome. He didn't think his woman friend would be able to look after the property as well as he did, and he wanted some strong management im-

*The amount passing tax-free thanks to the unified credit is placed in this trust. In 1987, for example, an estate of $600,000 is tax-exempt, so in that year, $600,000 would be placed in the unified credit trust.

posed upon her. The question was, could he have both his management and a marital deduction if he were to marry? The answer was yes, he could. I explained how, in order to qualify for a marital deduction, his property did not have to be given outright to his surviving spouse. It could be placed in a marital deduction trust and a third party could be named trustee to manage the trust for the benefit of the widow, provided that she was given a life use of the property and the right to decide, up until her death, where the remaining value of the marital-trust property would go. As will be explained in chapter 8, this last power is called a general power of appointment. My client and his friend liked the idea and were married.

A trust can be—indeed, should be—tailored to your particular circumstances. It can reflect your wishes and concerns, as this story shows. With reference to the strictly monetary advantages, there is a general rule of thumb for the cutoff point at which you should stop thinking about the marital deduction plain and simple and start thinking about the unified credit trust. The cutoff point for a marital deduction is an estate value of $600,000 in 1987 and thereafter. Above that, the advantages of the unified credit trust begin to take effect, and they increase rapidly with the escalation in the value of the estate.

NEW RULES FOR THE MARITAL DEDUCTION TRUST

Another important change brought about by Auntie ERTA is that, beginning in 1982, certain "terminable interests" will qualify for the marital deduction. Suppose, for instance, you have a sizeable estate and want to leave it to *your* designated heirs—children, grandchildren, etc. But on an interim basis, you want your surviving spouse to have the economic use of the estate. In other words, you want to give your spouse the income from the estate and generally be supported in the manner now accustomed. Under the old law (still in effect through 1981), in order for at least one half of your separate estate to escape tax when you die, your spouse had to be given the income from the estate half during her life and the right, either during life or at death, to decide where that portion of your estate was to be ultimately distributed. Now, under the *new* tax law, in order to qualify for the marital deduction the surviving spouse does *not* have to be given the power of disposition. Beginning in 1982, you can direct that any designated portion of your estate will go into an irrevocable trust at death which provides your surviving spouse with the income and other benefits from your estate in trust. And you can designate where the estate will go following the spouse's death. As long as the property is part of the spouse's taxable estate,

The Marital Deduction Trust

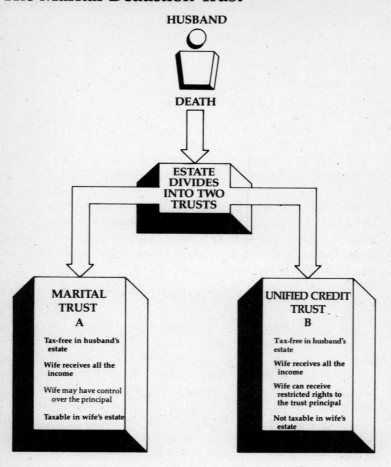

HUSBAND

DEATH

ESTATE DIVIDES INTO TWO TRUSTS

MARITAL TRUST

A

Tax-free in husband's estate

Wife receives all the income

Wife may have control over the principal

Taxable in wife's estate

UNIFIED CREDIT TRUST

B

Tax-free in husband's estate

Wife receives all the income

Wife can receive restricted rights to the trust principal

Not taxable in wife's estate

This trust arrangement is ideal for the typical family where the husband's earnings are primarily responsible for building the estate. A different Marital Deduction Trust arrangement can be created when the wife has an estate equal to or greater than the husband's.

the property will qualify for the marital deduction. *The result—none of your estate so designated will be taxed at your death.*

In order to qualify for the marital deduction, an interest that terminates at the surviving spouse's death must meet the following requirements. First, all of the income for a specific portion thereof must be payable at least annually and must go only to the surviving spouse, for his or her life. The income interest must not be cut off by an event other than the spouse's death. Second, if there is a power to give away part of the principal during the spouse's lifetime, that power may be exercised only in favor of the surviving spouse. No one else can receive part of the principal. Third, the personal representative of the decedent must make an election to qualify the interest for the marital deduction, and by making the election, the fair market value of the property will be included in the gross estate of the surviving spouse.

HOW TO FREEZE TAXES OUT OF YOUR ESTATE

The key to minimizing estate taxes is not to let your estate reach unnecessary taxable proportions in the first place. You can achieve this by freezing your estate, developing programs which create assets exempt from estate taxes, and by siphoning off extra money into various tax-sheltered trusts. Now trusts won't do your bidding unless they are very carefully planned. There are probably as many bad trusts and tax shelters around today as there are good ones. But when it comes to using inflation to minimize taxes, there are definitely right roads to take.

In essence, what they and most other legally defensible tax-freezing programs do is to take the current value of your assets and define them at their present worth for future tax purposes. Any growth in the assets' value from the date of freezing becomes taxed in different ways or to different people—always at a more favorable rate. With the inflationary eighties pumping up the value of real assets as never before, a larger dollar amount than ever before can be tax deferred or tax transferred. Inflation has made tax avoidance one of the most profitable financial games in town. One you can't afford not to play if you want to survive. However, before guiding your assets through the wonderful world of legal tax avoidance, let's deal in the next chapters with two very important planning concepts—how to avoid probate, and the great benefits of the revocable living trust.

7

Probate, the Costly Game

Probate is the most expensive undertaking establishment in the world.

—FIORELLO H. LA GUARDIA

Probate is the legal certification of your will by the state and its assurance that your wishes will be carried out after your death. It's an ancient legal concept inherited from medieval days, and about as apropos to today's estate as chain mail and the mace are to modern warfare. Wielding its broad ax, probate can actually lop off a major part of your estate.

The right of probate was first appropriated by the ecclesiastical courts of England during the Middle Ages, when they had jurisdiction over the succession of all personal property—personal property being opposed to real estate, which only the church and royalty could own at the time. These courts were to supervise the proceedings initiated to make sure that the property actually belonged to the deceased and that it actually went to the person intended.

From the outset, the system was flawed by excessive costs, fees, and downright fraud against the estate. Still, it was an improvement over the estate-settlement practices of earlier, primitive tribes, in which all property, be it implements or living slaves, was often destroyed upon the death of the owner. Actually the word *destroyed* is a conceptual interpretation of our own times. Frequently the property was buried along with the deceased, so that this wealth might be taken to the next world.

A testament in those days was quite distinct from a will, and remained so for some time to come. That's why in all those old British whodunits, when everyone sat around the solicitor's office waiting for the announcement as to who actually inherited the murdered millionaire's estate, the document involved was always "the last will *and* testament." The will disposed of real property, or real estate. The testament disposed of everything else.

The secular courts of England always maintained the right of probate over real property. And by 1857, the probate power over personal property was also in the hands of these courts. Thus the processing of will and testament became combined into one simplified operation, and the fees devolved to the worldly legal profession as well, rather than to the church. The secular courts set up in nineteenth-century America dealt with both types of property from the outset, but always at a state level and, one might add, usually with more hanky-panky.

There is no federal jurisdiction over probate in this country. Each state has its own probate court, though it may not go by that name. For instance, in New York probate passes through the surrogate court and in New Jersey through the orphan's court. Each state has its own regulations, fees, and other complications. Many states have already adopted the Uniform Probate Code in an attempt to streamline the currently unwieldy probate system. However, even this Code does not allow for sufficient flexibility of investment and continuity of management. The only consistency to be found in the probate process nationwide is that it's one of the most profitable aspects of the legal profession.

Now you might think it strange that I as an attorney would speak out against my own profession. And I'm not really doing so. My criticism is directed only to certain lawyers who abuse it. These lawyers put all their clients through the costly process of probate, regardless of the client's wishes or whether or not probate is more advantageous to their estates than an alternative, such as a revocable living trust. These lawyers are more interested in how much money the probate process will make them in fees than in how beneficial it is to their clients. The probate process is simply much too readily abused, on top of which it may take so long that the time delays also can add considerable expense and shrink the estate in these inflationary times.

Historically, the advantage of having an estate proceed through probate has been the fact that a court will supervise the settlement and assist in making sure the wishes of the decedent are complied with. But while this purpose cannot be faulted, in practice there are other—better—ways to accomplish the same thing. **A living trust naming someone trustworthy as the successor trustee is the best example.** The proponents of probate often protest that a lay trustee can misuse his or her broad powers and misinterpret the distribution or investment provisions of the trust, causing unintended results. True, no trustee should proceed without at least some supervision from a qualified trust lawyer. The red tape of processing an estate is not totally eliminated by the use of a revocable living trust. But it can be substantially reduced without the court's having supervisory power in the settlement.

THE TIME AND INFLEXIBILITY PROBLEMS OF PROBATE

The two most serious disadvantages of the probate process are 1) that the investment powers of an executor may be limited during the course of the settlement and 2) that most probate courts are inflexible when it comes to restructuring the estate's investments to make them more profitable in a highly inflationary, constantly shifting market. Even when a court order permitting such investment adjustments can be obtained, many executors are reluctant to seek such an order simply because of the extra work it involves. As a result, all too often, the assets under probate are simply dumped into non-inflation-proof investments and allowed to waste away. Let me give you an example.

I'm the attorney for one of the heirs of a man who died two and a half years ago in California. There are lawsuits going on between the wife, whom I represent, and certain of the children, and there are a lot of problems. But it may all be for naught, because the assets of the estate at the time the man died were all held in tax-free municipal bonds of a questionable character.

Now the estate taxes are based on the value of those bonds—with the tax by law computed on the value of the estate either at the time of death or six months later. There's no other alternative for valuation purposes. Meanwhile, because the bank trustee has never bothered to take the initiative in trying to alter the estate's investments, its assets are shrinking.

We began with an $800,000 estate. We are paying taxes on an $800,000 estate. But when the dust has settled and the distribution finally takes place, it may be a $400,000 estate—all because, in this particular situation, court permission is required to alter the investments, and the bank has not made any effort to do so. The bank, in my judgment, has not served the best interests of the heirs. It has just sat for two and a half years, making no effort to put the estate's assets into higher yielding, more inflation-proof investments, even though inflation was reducing the estate's value day by day.

You may be wondering, along about now, why this case has dragged on for two and a half years anyway. There are a number of reasons for the inevitable—and sometimes interminable—delays in probate proceedings. One of these is the legal requirement that all tax liens be eliminated and all taxes paid before the estate is settled. Another is that creditors must be given the opportunity to file their claims and have them litigated if they are denied by the estate's executor. Then, too, assets may need to be sold in order to raise the cash with which to pay the death taxes, and the sale must make its way through a statutory maze before it can be confirmed by the court.

The federal estate tax is not due until nine months following the date of death, and this deadline establishes at least one target date for closing the estate. Publication of the notice to creditors will generally take between four and six months, and this establishes a target date for settling an estate where a federal tax return is not required. But a target date does not assure a bull's-eye. The total term for settling an estate requiring a federal estate tax return can easily be a year or more.

The experience of probate can be traumatic and may have the effect of deepening and prolonging the devastation and emptiness caused by the death of, say, a spouse. Even if someone other than the surviving spouse is named as the executor of the estate, the widow or widower must often rely on a court-imposed allowance for support during the period of the settlement. **This is a major argument for using a living trust. It reduces the delays and complexities of settling an estate considerably. The transition is often much easier and more flexible. There's simply more continuity and less frustration than in probate administration.**

Some proponents of the probate system argue that proceeding through probate is the only way to cut off creditors' claims. In other words, it's the only procedure which requires that all creditors submit a claim within a certain period fixed by law, at the end of which they are forever barred from asserting that claim against the estate or the heirs. This is important, of course, and it's one great advantage of the probate system. There is no comparable publication statute in most states for an estate's being settled through a revocable living trust.

However, the right to use the publication statute cannot be equated with a concomitant obligation to have a full probate of all the assets. The benefits of the publication statute can be obtained simply by probating one small asset and letting the rest pass through a living trust. Whenever I go through a post-mortem interview with a surviving spouse or other heirs to determine and establish what is needed to settle an estate where all assets are in a living trust, one of the first questions I ask is whether there is any possibility of any claims, contingent or otherwise, being filed against either the decedent or the surviving spouse. Then I carefully review the liabilities, existing or potential, and decide whether it is advisable to have a small probate in order to cut off those claims. If the decedent was a physician, dentist, lawyer, or any other person against whom contingent claims such as malpractice suits from professional practice might show up at a significant later date, I always recommend a probate of some minimum asset in order to have the umbrella protection of the publication statute and cut off all creditor's claims. It is simply a matter of good practice and good judgment.

THE COST PROBLEM OF PROBATE

Probate costs can consist of statutory and extraordinary commissions paid to an executor or estate administrator and statutory and extraordinary fees paid to the attorney representing the executor or the estate administrator. In some states, such as California, the fees are fixed by law. In other states the fees are set by discretion of the judge, and these fees may be substantially higher. In all states the executor and/or attorney may be entitled to extraordinary compensation if services out of the ordinary are rendered, and the amount of such compensation is totally within the discretion of the court to approve. Items for which extraordinary fees might be charged include the preparation of federal estate-tax returns, a complicated valuation of the estate's assets, the sale of assets, the defense of a contested will or heirship, and the like.

In addition, to a lesser degree, there are such court-related costs as filing fees, publication fees, appraisal fees, fees incurred in accounting and tax work, and fees incurred in the selling of assets. Certain of these miscellaneous fees would also be required in settling an estate with a living trust, of course.

In many states the statutory or customary fees to which the executor or estate administrator is entitled are the same as the fees payable to the estate attorney. In states where fees or commissions are established by law, the payment of such compensation is usually based on the actual estate accounted for, which might include income received during the administration period.

COMPARISON PROBATE FEES FOR FIVE STATES

AMOUNT OF ESTATE	EXECUTOR'S COMMISSION	ATTORNEY FEES	TOTAL COMMISSION AND FEES
1. California			
$ 50,000	$ 1,650	$ 1,650	$ 3,300
100,000	3,150	3,150	6,300
250,000	6,150	6,150	12,300
500,000	11,150	11,150	22,300
1,000,000	21,150	21,150	42,300
2. Florida			
$ 50,000			
100,000			
250,000	Reasonable fees (RF), exact amount undeterminable		
500,000			
1,000,000			
3. Nevada			
$ 50,000	$ 1,120	RF	$ 1,120 + RF
100,000	2,120	RF	2,120 + RF
250,000	4,720	RF	4,720 + RF
500,000	10,120	RF	10,120 + RF
1,000,000	20,120	RF	20,120 + RF
4. New York			
$ 50,000	$ 1,875	RF	$ 1,875 + RF
100,000	3,625	RF	3,625 + RF
250,000	8,375	RF	8,375 + RF
500,000	13,875	RF	13,875 + RF
1,000,000	23,875	RF	23,875 + RF
5. Texas			
$ 50,000	$ 2,500	RF	$ 2,500 + RF
100,000	5,000	RF	5,000 + RF
250,000	12,500	RF	12,500 + RF
500,000	25,000	RF	25,000 + RF
1,000,000	50,000	RF	50,000 + RF

**COMPARISON OF CALIFORNIA PROBATE FEES
WITH SAVINGS IN FEES
USING A LIVING TRUST**

Estate Size	Probate Combined Fees and Commissions*	Living Trust Typical Attorney's Fees on Death of Trustor†	Savings with Living Trust†
$ 150,000	$ 8,300	$ 2,075	$ 6,225
200,000	10,300	2,575	7,725
300,000	14,300	3,575	10,725
400,000	18,300	4,575	13,725
500,000	22,300	5,575	16,725
600,000	26,300	6,575	19,725
700,000	30,300	7,575	22,725
800,000	34,300	8,575	25,725
900,000	38,300	9,575	28,725
1,000,000	42,300	10,575	31,725

* Combination of attorney's fees and executor's commissions. This amount would be reduced by as much as one half if the executor waives compensation.

† The current typical charge for trust settlements upon the death of a trustor or co-trustor. There is no guarantee that this fee will remain constant. The savings assumes that had the property not passed under a living trust, an executor's commission and attorney's fee would have been paid upon the entire amount.

THE PRIVACY PROBLEM OF PROBATE

Yet another disadvantage associated with probate has to do with the publicity generated by a court-supervised settlement. As with all court proceedings, the documents filed in a probate proceeding are matters of public record, and anyone can review the file. Usually that file will contain an inventory of all the assets of the estate, including an appraisal or evaluation of those assets. So you could go over to your courthouse and ask to see the estate file on, say, the man next door who's been dead for six months. You'd know the inventory of assets, you'd know the opinion on the value of the assets—his whole financial life would be laid bare. That's one apprehension some people understandably have about proceeding through probate. Probate is not a private settlement. It's a quite public settlement.

COMPUTING PROBATE FEES FOR FIVE STATES

1. California

Total of executor's commissions and attorney's fees:

If the estate is:	The total commissions and fees are:
0– $15,000	8%
$15,001– $100,000	$1,200 plus 6% of excess over $15,000
$100,001–$1,000,000	$6,300 plus 4% of excess over $100,000
Over $1,000,000	$42,300 plus 2% of excess over $1,000,000

2. Florida

Florida has no set fee schedule for executor's or attorney's fees. Florida law merely allows the payment of reasonable fee for services rendered by personal representatives, executors, attorneys, accountants, and other agents of the estate.

3. Nevada

Executors are allowed commissions as follows:

If the estate is:	The commission allowed is:
0–$1,000	6%
$1,001–$5,000	$60 plus 4% of the excess over $1,000
Over $5,000	$220 plus 2% of the excess over $5,000

Attorney and others employed by the estate are allowed reasonable compensation for their services. These fees are charged *in addition to* the executor's commissions.

4. New York

Executors are allowed commissions as follows:

If the estate is:	The commission allowed is:
0– $25,000	4%
$25,001–$150,000	$1,000 plus 3½% of the excess over $25,000
$150,000–$300,000	$5,375 plus 3% of the excess over $150,000
Over $300,000	$9,875 plus 2% of the excess over $300,000

Attorneys and others employed by the estate are allowed reasonable compensation for their services. These fees are charged *in addition to* the executor's commissions.

5. Texas

Texas allows the executor or personal representative a commission of 5% of the estate. Texas also allows reasonable attorney's fees and other fees for those performing services for the estate. These fees are charged *in addition to* the executor's commission.

DOUBLE-TROUBLE PROBATE

One final complication of probate has to do with the location of the property of a decedent in another state which requires an "ancillary" or secondary probate. Some states do not permit a resident of another state to serve as executor. For example, if someone dies in Arizona and the will appoints a resident of California as executor or trustee, that "foreigner" may serve, although the appointment might complicate probate proceedings. On the other hand, if a person dies in Wyoming, a California resident may not serve as the only executor of the estate. For a state-by-state breakdown of foreign executor and trustee regulations, see Appendix C.

SUMMING UP THE PROBLEMS OF PROBATE

We've been collecting a lot of reasons to avoid probate here. Let's tick off the major ones:

1. You can minimize estate-settlement expenses and substantially reduce attorney's fees.
2. Probate may take a lot more time than you've anticipated.
3. If you wish to keep the settlement of an estate private, not turn it into a public affair, then probate is not for you.
4. Inflation may severely reduce the "real" value of the estate where local probate law restricts the kind of investments which can be held or makes it difficult to change investments.

In the next chapter, I am going to lead you by the hand to the conclusion that a revocable living trust will cost you less and be much more flexible. With a revocable living trust, the attorney's fees are negotiable, and they can be less than half those of probate. After all, if you cut the red tape in half, you should be able to cut the expenses in half. Then, too, a private settlement reduces the amount of time it takes to convey the estate, meanwhile giving you more flexibility of investment.

JOINT TENANCY—A COUPLE OF HEADACHES

First, there's another way to avoid probate that I should mention, and that is to put all of your property into joint tenancy. Now there are a lot of problems with joint tenancy—I've already shown you a few of them—and personally I don't recommend it except for some small estates. But you should be familiar with its provisions.

Somehow the idea that joint tenancy is an alternative to a will has taken hold in many people's minds. What's mine is thine and never the tax man's. It's not true. To see why, let's explore joint tenancy.

Joint tenancy is perhaps the most widely used form of property holding there is, and yet it's one of the forms least understood. Basically, of course, it's an arrangement whereby two or more people take title to a property. There's nothing that says these individuals must be related. They can be, but their relationship is irrelevant to the question of ownership.

What is significant, however, is the right-of-survivorship position the property is put into by this arrangement. If you have property in joint tenancy, its future ownership is out of your hands. No matter whom you might want to pass the property on to, it goes to the surviving tenant. There's no getting around the fact. This survivorship arrangement transcends all others, *including a will.*

On the positive side, since jointly owned property does not pass on through your will, it escapes probate—this is an advantage often stressed by those maintaining joint ownership. It's a valid point, as are several others one could bring up. But the potential complications of joint ownership outweigh its benefits for most families. Let's look at the overall picture.

By avoiding probate, joint tenancy maintains privacy. Unlike an estate under probate, where proceedings are open to public inspection, property held jointly normally passes to the surviving tenant without publicity.

Joint tenancy is also convenient and time-saving. A joint bank account, for instance, is readily accessible to either party. This can be a particular blessing in case of an emergency. In addition, a joint account as a vehicle for avoiding probate requires an absolute minimum of planning as compared with other methods of achieving this goal.

Protection from creditors, while a distant objective for most people, can be another positive feature of joint tenancy. In some states creditors cannot attach jointly owned property when one joint tenant dies.

There is also a potential savings in state inheritance taxes, depending on where you live. Some states have a lower rate schedule for joint tenancy property passing on to the surviving spouse.

Now that joint tenancy is beginning to look better and better to you, let's look at some of its drawbacks.

First of all, there's the major consideration of losing control over your property, not necessarily after you die but while you're still living and in need of it. Take, for example, a house held in joint tenancy with your wife. Divorce is an all too common occurrence today, and should you be involved in one, your joint tenancy would leave you with an undivided interest in a property you would be unable to sell until all marital matters were settled. It's more than a case of who gets what. It's a case of having one of your principal assets frozen. **There's no way to obtain a clear title to sell a house in joint tenancy unless all parties of the tenancy agree to the sale.** Yet in divorce proceedings agreements are rare. The value of your home could be declining sharply because of economic circumstances beyond your control, and yet, even as you watched it happen, and even though selling the house would be in the best interests of both of you, there might be nothing you could do about it.

You also can't reduce the second tax. **Joint tenancy means there is no way for the surviving spouse's estate to avoid paying estate tax on the value of the whole house.**

Joint tenancy problems produced by family discord need not be limited to divorce situations. A similar situation can arise when an individual places property in joint tenancy with his or her oldest child. "My son's a good boy" is the way the reasoning goes. And that may well be the case. The boy may act responsibly. Then again, he may not. Or his siblings may feel he doesn't.

This type of arrangement not only fosters family discord, it's likely to foster higher inheritance taxes as well. In states which impose an inheritance tax, the tax will usually be greater if the property is distributed through joint tenancy than if it is passed on through a will.

Another tax problem arises if a noncontributing joint tenant dies first. Consider a certain Mr. and Mrs. J. T. Proper. Mr. Proper, the sole breadwinner in the family, places the homestead in joint tenancy with his wife, thus assuring her the ownership of the house without problems should he die. Instead, Mrs. Proper dies first. Now he, in effect, inherits his own property. And while he will be able to avoid federal estate taxes, he could well end up paying a state inheritance tax on his own property!

Then there's the matter of the gift tax. No gift tax is due on the creation of a joint tenancy in real property between husband and wife. In other words, husbands and wives are allowed to exchange gifts of any value tax-free. However, **a gift tax is levied on property owned jointly outside of the marriage relationship** itself, even though the arrangement may be between family members. A joint tenancy between father and son, for instance, can create a gift-tax liability.

Remember, too, that joint tenancy is not limited to real estate. Stocks, bonds, and other securities placed in joint tenancy will result immediately in a gift, for tax purposes, of half their value.

Bank accounts on the other hand, have a slightly different status. In their case, the joint tenancy with anyone besides a spouse will not be considered a taxable gift until the noncontributing partner withdraws funds.

Stop and look at that sentence for a minute. If you have a joint checking account with your daughter, every time she makes out a check to the milkman or the diaper service or the grocery store, you are in effect handing over a gift that may be taxable. It's no big deal if she keeps the tally under $10,000 a year. Above that amount, you actually have to pay a gift tax on those household expenditures.

If you're still breathing after that last statement, you may be ready to switch out of joint tenancy before the day is through. Don't do it so precipitously. It's entirely possible that terminating a joint tenancy will result in yet another unnecessary gift-tax obligation. So consult an attorney. But read the next chapter first.

8

The Best Way to Avoid Probate—
Revocable Living Trusts

*The great family trusts are like underground rivers in a barren
countryside, the only signs of whose existence are the green fields
they make fertile in unexpected places.*

—ANTHONY SAMPSON

**The solution to almost all the problems of joint tenancy and probate can be
found in a revocable living trust.** Living, or *inter vivos*, trusts actually
predate the legal concept of inheritance. Thus the solution actually
predates the problems it now solves.

LIVING TRUSTS—A HISTORICAL PERSPECTIVE

Historically, living trusts are older than wills. When kings and emperors
began losing their superior rights, under which real property reverted to the
ruler upon the death of the property owner, the sale or exchange of land
became a possibility. Often, since the notion of inheritance had not yet
acquired legal significance, land was transferred to a middleman *inter
vivos*—the literal Latin meaning is "between the living"—with the
stipulation that the original owner could use the property throughout life.
At that point it might again be transferred, this time perhaps, on the
previous instructions of the deceased, to another family member. Truly an
exchange between living persons, this *inter vivos* arrangement, common in
ancient Japan and China as well as the Roman empire, bypassed the spirit
world.

During the fifth century B.C., living trusts were so common in Rome that
there even evolved a vague precursor of our probate specialist called
familiae emptor, a buyer of family property. It wasn't until the first century

A.D. that the same society developed the concept of the testamentary distribution of property.

Both concepts, that of the will and that of the living trust, vanished in the abyss of the early Middle Ages, and Roman law was not rediscovered in Europe again until the fifteenth century. Trusts then once more became acceptable, and since that time they have been recurrent, profitable—and relatively unknown except to a few wealthy families. Now all that has changed.

The revocable living trust is becoming increasingly popular as a tool useful to the average taxpayer. To give credit where credit is due, this commendable trend toward utilizing living trusts in estate planning has been brought about in part by Norman Dacey's book *How to Avoid Probate*. Essentially a do-it-yourself kit with tear-out forms, the volume advocates the living trust as an answer to every estate-planning problem—which unfortunately it is not. Economically we may all be chained slaves rowing away in the government galley of state, but we're all still individual slaves, with individual problems to confront. The indiscriminate use of form documents (such as those found in Mr. Dacey's book) for sophisticated estate planning is a dangerous practice. It is doubly so in an inflationary time, when mistakes are easily compounded. Without built-in flexibility, for instance, a trust can become locked into investments that simply don't match the rate of inflation.

The content of a trust is plainly as important as the trust itself. Your objectives must be considered carefully if the instruments of your estate are to reflect your wishes and choices. In addition, the laws governing the operation of a trust vary from state to state. A tear-out form designed to fit every person's objectives, all the laws of every state, and each and every Internal Revenue Code consideration simply does not and cannot exist. Forms given in a book should always be considered samples, to be used just for educational and illustrative purposes. Only at the hands of a skilled tax and trust attorney can such sample forms be properly tailored to your specific situation and your needs.

FOUR KEYS TO SETTING UP A LIVING TRUST

1. A living trust must be established within the legal framework of the state in which it is located.

2. It must abide by state laws under which it is governed.
3. It must conform to the prevailing Internal Revenue Code laws governing estate taxes and the pertinent state laws governing inheritance taxes.
4. It must also use the proper legal language with precision. However, for a trust to be set up at all, you need to know what you want it for. So let's talk about revocable living trusts and what they can do.

THE LANGUAGE OF TRUSTS

The person who creates a living trust is called the *grantor*, or *trustor*, while the person or institution named to manage the trust and handle its assets is the *trustee*. The *beneficiaries* of a trust are those who are named to receive its economic and residual benefits. Someone who is to receive income from the trust would be called an *income beneficiary*, whereas the person designated to receive the principal of the trust, when it is distributed, is the *principal beneficiary*.

BE YOUR OWN TRUSTEE

Although many bank trust officers say you can't be your own trustee, don't believe it! There is no imperative tax reason why the trustee of a revocable trust should be a bank institution. It is not uncommon for the trustor, the trustee, and the beneficiary to be one and the same person. I've heard it said that this type of arrangement causes a merger of titles, and consequently termination of the trust, but research has proved that not to be the case. Most states will consider a trust valid under law so long as it is the *intent* of the grantor to create a valid trust. In other words, you can act as the trustee of your own trust.

To enable you to do that, however, an antimerger clause should be included in the original trust. The merger in question is not to be confused with the Wall Street kind, and the clause is not to keep some conglomerate from offering to merge your trust into their potpourri of companies. Rather, it's a legal device to prevent anyone from construing your conduct when you act in the capacity of a trustee as an attempt to merge the trust with yourself.

Look at it this way. A trust is a separate entity. A living trust with you as both trustee and beneficiary is, to all intents and purposes, your financial clone. Matters could get mighty confusing if these clones did not keep to separate rooms, as it were.

For your reference, an antimerger clause, in proper legalese, typically reads:

> The trust created hereby shall not terminate or be held to have terminated upon any theory of merger based on the fact that the same persons are, by the terms of this instrument, made sole beneficiaries and Trustee of said trust; and said beneficiaries are expressly given the right and privilege to participate in the property and business and the profits, dividends, earnings, and increase thereof, without regard to the relation as Trustee which such beneficiaries may bear to said trust.

Revocable living trusts embodying such a clause are established for numerous reasons, including the fact that most people are, with good reason, simply not willing to turn all their affairs over to a bank or other party. The point is, **you can keep control.** You don't have to give control to a third party.

The particular reason why a trust is set up, in fact, does much to shape the form that trust takes, the substantive language of one trust differing greatly from that of another. High on the list of factors differentiating the various trusts is whether or not the grantor is married.

TRUSTS AND THE MARRIED TAXPAYER

The language and direction of trusts for married couples are usually quite different from those for single people. Typically, a husband and wife, acting together as co-grantors, create a trust naming themselves, or perhaps one of them, as trustee. Or one of them may create the trust individually.

During the time both the husband and wife are living, the trust is revocable and amendable. What happens when one of them dies?

In a community-property state, when one of the co-grantors dies, the trust is usually divided into two trusts, labeled Trust A and Trust B. Trust A contains the surviving spouse's half interest in the community estate. Trust B contains the decedent's half and becomes irrevocable. But the amounts going into the two trusts can vary under the rules explained on page 83. In a separate-property state, if, say, the husband is the grantor of the trust, when he dies this trust is also divided. Trust B contains the unified credit equivalent amount and becomes irrevocable when he dies. Trust A can contain the balance of the estate and qualify for a marital deduction.

In either case, the surviving spouse can act as trustee of both trusts. He or she has unlimited use of the income, and at least the principal, of Trust A. The survivor might also have a general power of appointment and designate where the property will pass at his or her death. But now Auntie ERTA allows the first spouse to make that designation and still have a marital deduction.

Remember that the assets in Trust A are not subject to estate tax when the first spouse dies, because if they are community property, they belong to the surviving spouse, and if they are separate property, they qualify for a marital deduction. Trust B, on the other hand, is subject to estate tax when the grantor or the first spouse, as the case may be, dies. It will pass free of additional estate tax, however, upon the death of the survivor, or life beneficiary, provided it complies with certain regulations of the Internal Revenue Code.

As life beneficiary, the surviving spouse can be entitled to use all the income from Trust B as needed. He or she can also be given the power to use the principal of this trust to provide for care, support, and maintenance if Trust A has been substantially depleted.

Let's look at a $700,000 estate owned equally by a husband and wife in 1987. The first chart shows the federal estate tax incurred where the estate is held in joint tenancy; the same tax is applied in the case of a simple will. The second chart shows the same estate put in an AB living trust, one which is divided into two trusts, Trust A and Trust B, when the grantor dies. As you can see when you compare the figures, by simply moving the lines on the estate organization chart, estate taxes have been eliminated—for a tax saving of $19,000. The savings in 1984, given the smaller unified credit, would be at least $117,000.

Now you should note that if the assets of Trust B at the time of the husband's death exceed $600,000, the equivalent exemption allowed, there would probably be some estate tax due on Trust B. If Trust A exceeds $600,000 at the wife's death, there may be some tax due on Trust A. In this case, however, no matter how large Trust B has become by that time, there should be no tax due on it. In any event, at least $19,000 will be saved by using the living trust, and in some cases the tax savings will be much more.

Federal Estate Tax Result If Property Is Held in Joint Tenancy or Passes Under a Simple Will

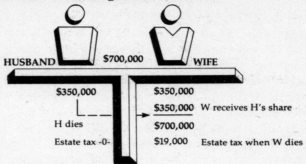

HUSBAND $700,000 WIFE

$350,000	$350,000
	$350,000 W receives H's share
H dies	$700,000
Estate tax -0-	$19,000 Estate tax when W dies

Federal Estate Tax Result with the Use of a Living Trust

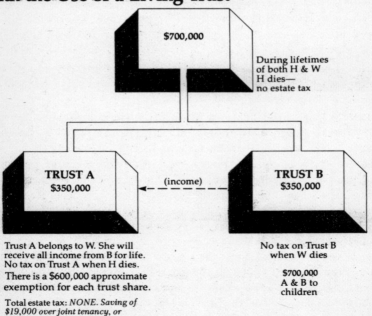

$700,000

During lifetimes of both H & W
H dies—
no estate tax

TRUST A $350,000 (income) **TRUST B** $350,000

Trust A belongs to W. She will receive all income from B for life. No tax on Trust A when H dies. There is a $600,000 approximate exemption for each trust share.

Total estate tax: *NONE. Saving of $19,000 over joint tenancy, or reciprocal "simple will."*

No tax on Trust B when W dies

$700,000 A & B to children

The tables show you the comparative tax results you can expect on estates ranging from $600,000 to $2 million—by using simple wills or joint tenancy (Plan A) or tax savings trusts (Plan B).

ILLUSTRATION OF FEDERAL TAXATION OVER TWO TRANSFERS

PLAN A
Surviving Spouse Inherits Outright

Value of Property	Federal Estate Tax on Death of first spouse	Federal Estate Tax on Death of second spouse	Total Federal Estate Tax
$ 200,000	—	0	0
300,000	—	0	0
400,000	—	0	0
500,000	—	0	0
600,000	—	0	0
700,000	—	19,000	19,000
800,000	—	52,000	52,000
900,000	—	86,400	86,400
1,000,000	—	119,800	119,800
1,100,000	—	155,200	155,200
1,200,000	—	189,800	189,800
1,300,000	—	225,400	225,400
1,400,000	—	262,000	262,000
1,500,000	—	298,600	298,600
1,600,000	—	337,200	337,200
1,700,000	—	375,000	375,000
1,800,000	—	412,000	412,000
1,900,000	—	450,000	450,000
2,000,000	—	488,400	488,400

ASSUMPTIONS:
1. Estates are of citizens and residents dying after 1986.
2. Surviving spouse inherits outright.
3. The property can be either community or separate property.
4. Federal Estate Tax is computed with full state death tax credit.

PLAN B
SURVIVING SPOUSE INHERITS IN TAX-SAVING TRUST

Value of Property	Federal Estate Tax on Death of first spouse	Federal Estate Tax on Death of second spouse	Total Federal Estate Tax	Tax Savings Plan B
$ 200,000	—	0	0	0
300,000	—	0	0	0
400,000	—	0	0	0
500,000	—	0	0	0
600,000	—	0	0	0
700,000	—	0	0	19,000
800,000	—	0	0	52,200
900,000	—	0	0	86,400
1,000,000	—	0	0	119,800
1,100,000	—	0	0	155,200
1,200,000	—	0	0	189,800
1,300,000	—	19,000	19,000	206,400
1,400,000	—	52,200	52,200	209,800
1,500,000	—	86,400	86,400	212,200
1,600,000	—	119,800	119,800	217,400
1,700,000	—	155,200	155,200	219,800
1,800,000	—	189,800	189,800	223,000
1,900,000	—	225,400	225,400	225,200
2,000,000	—	262,000	262,000	226,400

ASSUMPTIONS:
1. Estates are of citizens and residents dying after 1986.
2. Up to $600,000 passes into a non-marital deduction trust on the death of the first spouse. The balance passes into marital deduction trust.
3. Surviving spouse does not have a general power to appoint property placed in either trust.
4. The property can be either community or separate property.
5. Federal Estate Tax is computed with full state death tax credit.

THE LIVING TRUST CAN BE A SUBSTITUTE FOR A GUARDIAN OR CONSERVATOR

One major advantage of living trusts not often given full consideration is that if you become incompetent to manage your estate, a guardian or conservator, who takes care of the estate for you, need not be appointed by the court. When court proceedings are necessary, all your affairs become matters of public record, and they continue to remain matters of public record throughout your incompetency. In a community-property state, if a competent husband is appointed guardian for his wife, his affairs may *also* become public, possibly to his detriment in business situations. Court procedures can be expensive as well. It costs hundreds of dollars in legal fees to set up a conservatorship or guardianship, and it costs even more to manage one over the years. In addition, the court may well require that the guardian or conservator, even if that person is the husband or wife of the incompetent, purchase a fidelity bond from an insurance company to protect the estate against any mismanagement.

With a funded living trust, none of this is necessary. If you become incompetent to handle your own affairs, a successor trustee named in the trust agreement can step into the trusteeship to make the investments, pay the bills, and the like—wholly without court proceedings. There's no public record. There's no bond, provided the trust waives it. There are no annual legal fees incurred by required court records.

OWNING REAL ESTATE IN MORE THAN ONE STATE

Yet another advantage of using a living trust—a financial advantage which transcends the question of estate-tax savings—concerns the ownership of real property in more than one state. When you die, the procedure by which title to a parcel of real property can be passed to your heirs is governed by the laws of the state in which the property is located, regardless of your residence at death.

For example, if you live in Florida and own real estate in Nevada, the Nevada laws must be consulted to determine how title to the property can validly be transferred to your heirs. Where the title is held in your name alone and your last will and testament is the document under which title can be lawfully passed, you will need another (ancillary) probate in Nevada. But since your lawyer, in this hypothetical case, is apt to be a Florida resident licensed to practice law only in Florida, the executor of your estate will have to hire another lawyer in Nevada to accomplish the second probate. That will entail additional costs, probably lengthen the amount of time it takes to settle the estate, and generally complicate matters for everyone concerned.

If you own real estate in five states, it may be necessary to have five probates and five lawyers. Besides that, some states will not permit an out-of-state executor to act within their boundaries. If the executor of your estate happens to be your surviving wife or one of your sons who also resides in Florida and the state where you hold real estate does not permit a Florida resident to act as executor, it will be necessary to have, not only a lawyer in the other state, but some person or institution of that state to act as executor as well, thus doubling the subsidiary costs.

If you have real estate in more than one state, a living trust becomes a very important tool indeed. For by having the title to the real estate transferred to you as trustee of your revocable trust, you can empower the trustee named to succeed you to pass title to that real estate at your death with a minimum of red tape. And the trustee will not be required to retain an attorney in the state where the property is situated, because there would be no court-supervised settlement.

TRUSTS AND THE SINGLE TAXPAYER

Trusts can play a very special role in securing the future of a single person. **A trust can be used to mitigate the problems facing a single person who becomes incapacitated.** In such circumstances, the assets of even a small estate in the $30,000 to $40,000 range profit by being converted into a living trust.

Consider an elderly person who has been disabled by a crippling heart attack, a stroke, or some other infirmity. Another member of the family is then usually confronted with the time-consuming and costly task of petitioning the court to become guardian or conservator of the incapacitated person's assets.

Not only does this lengthy procedure require the services of an attorney, but it usually entails an annual presentation to the court of the accounting records of the guardianship or conservatorship as well. In addition, the court usually limits the investment options for the assets, which means that the disabled individual's savings may be drawing 5-percent interest in a bank account while the money market and other very prudent investments are yielding 15 percent and inflation is running even higher. The incapacitated person is thus actually forced by the court to expend capital rather than living off the interest. This isn't a hypothetical financial situation, incidentally. It's exactly what happened to money in inflation-riddled 1980.

A revocable living trust would solve all these problems plus eliminate the red tape of probate in case of death. Now, for an older person—even more for a younger person who becomes incapacitated to some degree—relinquishing control over one's own affairs can be a psychologically very difficult proposition and understandably so. After all, when one has worked hard all one's life, relinquishing control of the fruits of that labor before one is fully incapacitated is like admitting that life is nearly over.

But in fact there is no need to relinquish control. What needs to be accomplished is simply the setting in motion—and the earlier in one's life, the better—of the proper machinery to effect a smooth, calm change in money managers in the event of a truly debilitating illness. This means setting up a revocable living trust with more than one trustee, whose powers should be coextensive—that is, the same in scope and duration.

Then if you, as the originating trustee, become disabled, the additional trustee can take over immediately, with no transition problems. Up to that point, however, you, as the trust's originator, have complete control, including the right to terminate the trust if you become apprehensive about the second trustee's doing as expected.

The United States, despite the accumulation of massive powers by the federal government, is still just that—a united group of states together forming a nation. Perhaps nowhere is this more obvious than in the different state statutes dealing with inheritance, death taxes, and estate management. One problem arising from this often confronts the elderly when they move their residence to balmier climes, leaving children and family in other states. Because of the variation in state laws, the children may not be allowed to serve as executors or trustees of their parents' wills. Although some states absolutely bar "foreign" trustees, including those of living trusts as well as those of wills, a living trust can usually circumvent the out-of-state-trustee problem. (Check Appendix C for a state-by-state breakdown of the legal restrictions on trusteeships.)

TRUSTS AND THE FUTURE OF YOUR MINOR CHILDREN

No matter how small the estate, it is absolutely essential that all parents of minor children create a trust. It can be either a living trust or a testamentary trust that continues for the benefit of the children at the death of both parents. Which of these trusts you use will depend primarily on your personal family circumstances. But without one or the other, your children's future could be a washout.

Look at what happens without a trust. Let's take as our example a family with three minor children, sixteen, eleven, and six years old. The parents are both killed in a car accident, leaving an estate, including life insurance, of $300,000 after death taxes. If the parents die intestate—that is to say, without a will—or even if there is a will stating that on their joint death all their assets are to be distributed on an equal basis to the children, the scenario in most states will be as follows.

The $300,000 will most likely be placed in three separate blocked bank accounts by the judge presiding over the estate. Now consider the fate of the six-year-old child's $100,000. With an annual inflation rate of 10 to 15 percent, the dollar shrinks by 50 percent every five to six years. How much real value will be left in the estate twelve years from now when the child comes of age and the funds can finally be invested in something more able to keep up with inflation than a savings account?

The future I've just sketched is actually a best-case scenario. It assumes that the couple has mortgage insurance on their home. Otherwise, the house will probably have to be sold before the property can be equitably divided, adding more trauma to a very difficult situation for the children. The proceeds will then remain in blocked accounts until the beneficiaries reach the legal age—which is eighteen in most states—with the same inflationary results as in the previous example.

Dying intestate, or without a will, usually means that no guardian has been chosen for the children. When this happens, the court will appoint one—who may be insensitive to your children's special needs.

Prior to the distribution of the money as each of the children in turn becomes eighteen, whenever the guardian requires funds for their care, the attorney who is handling the estate must be consulted. Then a petition detailing the financial need must be filed with the court. A hearing will be held, and if the need is deemed appropriate, an order will be conveyed to the bank, instructing it to release the funds. The process will be repeated as often as funds are needed. It's really something only a red-tape lover could be enthusiastic about.

WHEN YOUR CHILD COMES OF AGE

Still another problem arises when the children reach the age of eighteen. Consider the sixteen-year-old, who will come into $100,000 in cold cash—all at once—within two years. I realize there are exceptionally responsible eighteen-year-olds in this country who possess the maturity and patience to regard such a windfall with an eye to the future. Still, realistically speaking, such individuals are the exception rather than the rule. Think of any three eighteen-year-olds you know. How would they react to a bonanza like that?

The creation of a trust for the benefit of the children solves these three potential problems: (1) certain erosion of your estate by inflation, (2) time-consuming and frustrating court petitions, and (3) turning over the financial responsibility of managing capital to someone perhaps too young to deal with it.

A trustee whom you have appointed in a revocable living trust can be given full discretionary powers to invest the estate funds in something other than blocked savings accounts so that presumably, if you choose the trustee wisely, the investment will keep up with the inflationary rise. Also, the trustee can be given full power and discretion to distribute as much of the income and/or principal as may be required for the health, care, education, and other special needs of the children until they reach the age at which you as parents choose to have the funds distributed to them. Perhaps half of a child's share might be distributed at the age of twenty-five and the balance at age thirty. For those interested in fostering their children's education or professional training, such an arrangement would ensure that funds would be available through undergraduate and graduate school. Then, too, this arrangement would protect a spendthrift child against personal misfortune. For instance, if the child was involved in an automobile accident and became liable for injuries resulting in a judgment well above the amount covered by the automobile insurance, the creditors, under the terms of a spendthrift provision in the trust, could not reach the funds.

Trustee charges from a bank usually run three-quarters of one percent per year of the estate's total value for servicing a trust. Private individuals usually do it free as a service to friends.

HAVE YOU NAMED A GUARDIAN?

Naming a guardian for your minor children, the individual or couple whom you would choose to raise your children, and who would be responsible for their care and support until they reached legal age, is not something that should be left to chance or to the devices of the court. If parents say nothing, the judge will usually call the surviving family members together and ask them to mutually agree on a choice. He will also seek the help of a probation department or county counseling organization in appointing the guardian.

Guardianship, even though your choice may be named in your last will and testament, is never a settled matter until approved by the appropriate judge, and that approval is given on the basis of a consideration of all the relevant circumstances in existence at the time of your death. If you think it possible that the court might choose someone other than the guardian designated in your will—for whatever reason—I'd recommend that you prepare a handwritten, dated, and signed memorandum explaining in depth all the reasons why you've chosen the person you've named, as well as all the reasons why you have not selected any other people you think might seek the guardianship. Such a memorandum can give a judge valuable insight into your personal philosophy of raising children, and it might make a significant difference in a case where the judge might otherwise be persuaded that your choice, as designated by your will, is not a tenable one.

To illustrate, a young couple with strong religious convictions had two minor children. They had often discussed what would happen if they were to die, and they had decided that they would want the wife's aunt, a charming unmarried woman in her fifties who loved the children, to raise them, because she had the same religious affiliation. The only other living relatives were a brother and sister-in-law of the husband, who were much younger than the aunt and who had minor children about the same age as those of the parents we're discussing, but who attended another church.

The husband and wife died in a plane accident, leaving no will designating a guardian, and no other information as to their choice of a guardian in the event of their untimely death. The judge received petitions both from the wife's unmarried aunt and from the husband's brother and sister-in-law and for obvious reasons chose the latter. Had the parents put their wishes in writing, in depth and detail, along with the reasons for those wishes, the judge's decision might have been different.

Guesswork, yours and that of others, is a hazardous way to provide for your children's future. Errors in judgment can be so easily introduced by the omission not only of facts but of your real desires—and so easily avoided by mapping out the direction and route you want your estate to take. This is particularly true in the more complicated estate situations that sometimes arise. Let's take another example, one which illustrates such a situation.

SEGREGATING ASSETS

Segregating assets is a highly useful function of a living trust. Let's say a wealthy widow considering remarriage is worried about the future of her children, or perhaps her grandchildren. She wants her money to go to them, but she is afraid that her assets will become commingled with those of her future husband, who has his own offspring to worry about. Simply by placing her assets in a trust, she can have complete control over and use of the assets during her lifetime. Yet the children or grandchildren as ultimate beneficiaries would be shielded from any accidental commingling of the mother's and the stepfather's estates.

SKIPPING ISN'T WHAT IT USED TO BE

One of the basic family wealth builders used by the super-rich almost from the inception of the trust concept is the generation-skipping trust. This form of estate building requires the same forethought and bountiful belief in a distant future as that which a gardener maintains when he plants a row of oak seedlings. The trees will not come into their prime for centuries. Then again, that's the only way to grow the mighty oak.

In a generation-skipping trust, parents leave their property at death in trust for their children. The children receive a life use of the property, but not the property itself. That is to say, they may use all or part of the trust's earnings, but not the principal. The principal is not distributed until the trust designates that the grandchildren are ready to receive it.

In the past, it was not unusual for such trusts to skip several generations, growing and growing as behemoths of financial power, accumulating wealth and multiplying it many times over by the postponement, and in some cases even the elimination, of transfer taxes. Prior to the Tax Reform

Act of 1976, the only limitation placed on such trusts in most states was the rule that the trust must end sometime. Remember, a trust may be as much a legal entity as you or I, but it's not entitled to immortality. The trust has to terminate not later than twenty-one years following the death of all the named beneficiaries of the trust who were living when that trust was established.

The law adds a $250,000 second-generation exclusion as a small pacifier. Given a million-dollar estate and two children, a trust can be established distributing to them the income from the capital for life. The principal is then distributed to their children—or, in other words, the grantor's grandchildren. The full estate is liable to estate tax at the grantor's death. But at the death of each child of the grantor, $250,000 would be exempt from the tax. Fortunately, Congress does not appear to be very happy with this law. The effective date has been postponed until January 1, 1983, and in the meantime Congress may amend the law to simplify its mechanics.

THE TAX MAN GETS HIS

Revocable trusts can help minimize estate taxes. When it comes to income tax, however, you need more tools in order to whittle down Uncle Sam's take. You'll find a broad spectrum of these tools to choose from in the second half of this book.

Your income-tax liabilities for a revocable living trust come under the heading of grantor trusts in Sections 671-677 of the Internal Revenue Code. If you're curious, you can look it up. If you just want to know your responsibility under this section, it can be summed up simply by saying that all items of income, deductions, and credits are applied directly to the trust grantor's personal tax base.

However, the trust is a separate tax-reporting entity. As such it must file a separate informational income-tax return. Now it's true that all earnings and deductions are reported on your income-tax return as if no trust actually existed. But don't let logic fool you. The trust still needs to fill in its very own clone form every year, the 1041 (see sample). As you can see, complying with this rule is not an arduous task, merely a minor annoyance.

Attached to the annual 1041 form for your trust should be the following statement, giving the trust name, the identification number, and the name of the grantor or grantors:

Form **1041**

Department of the Treasury
Internal Revenue Service

U.S. Fiduciary Income Tax Return

for the calendar year 1980 or fiscal year

beginning ...., 1980, and ending ...., 19......

1980

Check applicable box(es):
- ☐ Estate ($600 exemption)
- ☑ Testamentary trust
- ☑ Inter vivos trust
- ☐ Simple trust ($300)
- ☐ Complex trust ($100)
- ☐ Complex trust ($300)
- ☑ Grantor type trust
- ☐ Family estate type trust
- ☐ Pooled income fund

Name of estate or trust ("Grantor type" trusts, see instruction J.)
Taxpayer Family Trust

Name and title of fiduciary
John Q. Taxpayer, Trustee

Address of fiduciary (number and street)
1924 Tice Valley Blvd.

City, State, and ZIP code
Walnut Creek, California 94595

Employer identification number
94-0000000

Nonexempt charitable and split-interest trusts check applicable boxes (See instruction Q.):
- ☐ Described in section 4947(a)(1)
- ☐ Not treated as a private foundation by reason of sec. 509(a) (1), (2) or (3)
- ☐ Described in section 4947(a)(2)

Has the fiduciary's name and/or address changed? ☐ Yes ☐ No. Final return? ☐ Yes ☐ No.

Income	1 Dividends (Enter full amount before exclusion) **(Attach schedule if over $400)**	1	
	2 Interest (Attach schedule if over $400)	2	
	3 Income from partnerships and name and E.I. No.	3	
	4 Income from other estates and trusts and name and E.I. No.	4	
	5 Gross rents and royalties (Attach schedule if over $400)	5	
	6 Net business and farm income or (loss) **(Attach Schedules C and F (Form 1040))**	6	
	7 Capital gain or (loss) **(Attach Schedule D (Form 1041))**	7	
	8 Ordinary gain or (loss) **(Attach Form 4797)**	8	
	9 Other income (Attach schedule of income and list by payer if over $400)	9	
	10 Total income (add lines 1 to 9, inclusive)	10	
Deductions	11 Interest	11	
	12 Taxes	12	
	13 Fiduciary's portion of depreciation (Schedule A) and depletion. Explain depl	13	
	14 Charitable deduction (from line 56)	14	
	15 Fiduciary fees	15	
	16 Attorney, accountant, and return preparer fees	16	
	17 Other deductions (List on a separate sheet ...ch)	17	
	18 Total (add lines 11 to 17, inclu	18	
	19 Subtract line 18 from line 10 (Complex ...a estates enter this amount on line 57; simple trusts, see instr. O.)	19	
	20 Distributions deduction (fro... ...) **(Attach Schedule K-1 (Form 1041))**	20	
	21 Adjustment of dividend...	21	
	22 Estate tax deducti...on computation)	22	
	23 Long-term capital ...n deduction from Schedule D (Form 1041)	23	
	24 Exemption (If final return, see instruction M.)	24	
	25 Total (add lines 20 to 24, inclusive)	25	
	26 Taxable income of fiduciary (subtract line 25 from line 19)	26	
Computation of Tax	27 Tax on amount on line 26 (See tax rate schedule)	27	
	28 If alternative tax is applicable, enter the tax from Schedule D (Form 1041)	28	
	29 Fiduciary's share of foreign tax credit (Attach Form 1116)	29	
	30 Fiduciary's share of investment credit (Attach Form 3468)	30	
	31 a WIN credit ▶ ; b Jobs credit ▶ ; c Total ▶	31	
	32 Total (add lines 29 to 31, inclusive)	32	
	33 Balance (subtract line 32 from 27 or 28, whichever is applicable)	33	
	34 Tax from recomputing fiduciary's share of prior year investment credit **(Attach Form 4255)**	34	
	35 Minimum tax **(Attach Form 4626)**	35	
	36 Total (add lines 33 to 35, inclusive)	36	
	37 Other credits; see instruction 37	37	
	38 Federal income tax: a Previously paid ▶ ; b Withheld ▶ ; c Total ▶	38	
	39 Total (add lines 37 and 38)	39	
	40 Balance of tax due (subtract line 39 from line 36) (See instruction H.)	40	
	41 Overpayment (subtract line 36 from line 39)	41	

SEE STATEMENT ATTACHED

Please Sign Here

Under penalties of perjury, I declare that I have examined this return, including accompanying schedules and statements; and to the best of my knowledge and belief it is true, correct, and complete. Declaration of preparer (other than fiduciary) is based on all information of which preparer has any knowledge.

Signature of fiduciary or officer representing fiduciary .... Date ....

Paid Preparer's Information

Preparer's signature ▶	Date	Preparer's social security no. ▶	Check if self-employed ▶ ☐
Firm's name (or yours, if self-employed), address and ZIP code ▶	E.I. No. ▶	
	Date ▶	

The [TAXPAYER FAMILY TRUST], I.D. No. [00-0000000]is a Grantor Trust within the meaning of Sections 671 through 677 of the Internal Revenue Code of 1954 as amended, and the regulations promulgated under such sections. Accordingly, all items of income, deductions or credits, are treated as owned by the trust grantor and are reported on the income tax return (Form 1040) filed by [JOHN Q. TAXPAYER] under Social Security Number [000-00-0000], and [MARY TAXPAYER] under Social Security Number [000-00-0000].

Note: it is very likely that in 1981 a new proposed IRS regulation will take effect. This regulation will eliminate the filing of a 1041 for all grantor trusts. Check with your accountant.

HOW TO FUND YOUR OWN REVOCABLE LIVING TRUST

The question probably nagging at the back of your mind by now is, If trusts have so many benefits, how do I go about starting one? Is it expensive and complicated? Well, yes, it can be, but it doesn't have to be—if you have all the information ready. Fill out the questionnaire in the back of the book and meet with an attorney who specializes in taxes and estate planning. First, however, always ask what the fees will be, and make sure much of the total bill will be tax deductible, of course.

To create a living trust, essentially all you do is transfer property to the trustee. You transfer the property by an arrangement with the trustee, who is yourself, your wife, or both of you. The property is to be held by the trustee for the use of the beneficiaries specifically named in the trust agreement. Oh, I know, it sounds crazy. It seems as if you're simply transferring property to yourself. Well, it *is* crazy.

Crazy like a fox. You may be playing by some obtuse rules, but on careful inspection they really do make sound financial sense. The trust becomes your financial clone. It's distinct, but not really different. No one is trying to hide anything, merely separating properties legally. The left hand certainly knows what the right hand is doing. They're passing assets back and forth without letting the estate tax get between them.

Now, in order to secure the trust's existence, the assets must be actually transferred through a legal retitling of the property. For instance, to use that old stalwart example from the IRS, John Q. Taxpayer and his wife Mary Taxpayer create a living trust on January 1, 1981. John Q. is made trustee. Then the various documents of *all* the assets transferred to the trust must be retitled to read "John Q. Taxpayer, trustee, The Taxpayer Family Trust, established January 1, 1981." It has a nice ring to it, doesn't it, that "established 1981"? It lends a bit of credence and solidity to the whole thing in everyone's mind. But it's also crucial. Retitling is the process by which you actually transfer the assets to the trust. If a deed to a house, for instance, still says, "John Q. Taxpayer" on it, no matter what your trust papers say, that house is not included in the trust. Examples of title transfers for you to peruse are in Appendix D.

What can actually be put into a living trust? Just about anything of value, from your home to real estate to savings accounts, limited partnerships, jewelry, furniture, and the family horse. Don't laugh. When it comes to beating the IRS, a little horse sense comes in very handy.

Some assets need a bit of special attention when they are placed in trust. For instance, while a trust may contain both community property and separate property belonging to either spouse, the assets must be labeled to indicate who owns what. Typically, and with amazing simplicity, a trust provision might authorize the designation SPH (for Separate Property Husband) on title documents referring to separate property belonging to the husband. That would leave SPW (Separate Property Wife) for the wife's property and CP for community property. You see, the execution of a trust really can be basically uncomplicated.

But there are antiques, works of art, silver, jewelry, and hosts of other assets that have no title. How are they transferred to a trust? Again, it's easy. You create a title for them, specifically for the trust. Describe each item in reasonable detail and draw up an assignment for the assets. The grantor of the living trust will be the person whose name is on the title of the trust.

If the trustee you choose is someone other than the owner of the assets, your declaration should state that the owner has assigned these assets to the trustee. The reason for this assignment is to assure that these assets are included as part of the trust. Unless they are specifically mentioned, they might be considered part of your probatable estate.

FLOWER BONDS FOR TAX POWER

Certain U.S. government bonds have a specific application in estate planning. However, by design, they necessarily have certain restrictions as well. There's an old story about an attorney called to the hospital when one of his clients, elderly and rich, had a severe heart attack. On arriving and finding the patient unconscious, the attorney let out a quiet, frustrated, "Oh, no, I forgot the flowers," and swung around to exit again.

"No need to worry about that," the nurse soothed. "He isn't aware of a thing."

"My problem exactly," replied the departing attorney. He then went to the telephone in the hospital lobby. Calling up his client's stockbroker, and using his power of attorney, the lawyer ordered a million dollars' worth of flowers.

The flowers in question were not of the horticultural variety, of course. They were *flower bonds*, a somewhat obscure debt instrument no longer issued by the government. However, there are still a considerable number of these low-yielding issues around.

The interest on flower bonds is terribly uncompetitive, frankly. For instance, the 3.5-percent flower bonds due in November of 1998 sell at 75 (100 is the face value), for a yield of 5.56 percent—this at a time when money funds are paying around 14 percent and even T-bills are bringing in close to 12.

Now, who on earth would choose a 5.5-percent yield over 14 percent? An estate executor, that's who, for these bonds have one unique attribute which makes them highly desirable for estate purposes when there is estate tax due: **Flower bonds are accepted at face value in paying this estate tax.** Take those 3.5-percent November 1998 bonds, for instance. Every $750 worth of those bonds can be used by the estate to pay $1,000 worth of taxes. That's a 25-percent saving. Let me put it another way. If the bonds are held for one year before the person's death, their actual yield is 30.56 percent. Now that beats inflation.

For the attorney in the story just told, however, they were not a good idea. The bonds must be owned before death. He didn't order his flowers in time for the funeral—the ceremony originating the bond's descriptive name.

Flower bonds may be owned by the trustee of a revocable living trust. The only requirement besides that of predeath ownership is that the trust instrument actually authorize the trustee to pay all or part of the estate tax with these specific bonds.

Returning one last time to the bouquet of problems our attorney picked by not ordering his bonds on time, it's important to note that even if his client had lived on for several months more, the lawyer's purchase of the bonds may not have been valid. The Bureau of Public Debt takes the position that an estate may not use flower bonds at face value in paying federal estate taxes if the bonds were purchased through a power of attorney while the deceased was unconscious or incompetent. The bonds in the story I've related were not redeemed at par by the Treasury Department, which decided that the unconscious individual was not really the owner of the bonds at the time of his death.

PUTTING YOUR PROFESSIONAL CORPORATION
STOCK IN TRUST

Shares of stock in a professional corporation are another asset that can cause trust problems if not handled with care. Such shares may be held only by another corporation or individual licensed in the same profession. For instance, if a doctor's practice is a professional corporation, a trust may not hold shares in that corporation unless it is also a licensed doctor—an unlikely possibility, considering a trust's inability to practice medicine.

One solution to this problem which I have used effectively is to make the licensed person sole trustee of a revocable living trust containing a special provision in the trust document stating that the trustee may hold title to assets without using the term *trustee* or disclosing that he is holding title as a trustee. You will remember the discussion earlier in this chapter on the importance of actually transferring the title of all assets to the trust's name. In this instance, the trust actually holds title, but, because of the special provision, this fact need not be disclosed.

To support the special power written into the trust, the professional person could sign a separate declaration, to be held with the original trust instrument, stating that he or she does indeed hold title to the professional corporation stock as the trustee under the trust.

Following the original trustee's death, the successor trustee, who need not be licensed, would be able to act as continuing trustee without probate. Using the declaration, the successor trustee could liquidate or sell the corporate assets as necessary. The professional license board would not, in my opinion, be likely to have any interest in such a nonprobate disposition of the property. At this stage, after all, the orginal trustee would be dead. Revoking the license would have no consequential effect.

I had a case recently that demonstrates the time advantage offered by having assets pass through a living trust rather than through probate. It involved an orthodontist. Now an orthodontist's practice loses its value very rapidly if the orthodontist dies. People need to have their braces adjusted every week or two. They can't wait six months or a year for someone to pick up the practice.

The orthodontist in this case died unexpectedly of a heart attack while jogging. However, his wife, who was not licensed, was successor trustee, and the practice was sold in two weeks. Had the practice passed through probate, the extra time involved would have reduced the sale price of the practice by at least $20,000 simply because so many patients had gone elsewhere.

PUTTING SUBCHAPTER S CORPORATION STOCK IN TRUST

Subchapter S stock of small corporations, the type often associated with closely held corporations, actually come out ahead, at least for estate purposes, in the Economic Recovery Tax Act of 1981. Effective in 1982, the new law increases the number and types of trusts that can legally hold Subchapter S corporation stock. Up to the end of 1981, only grantor trusts, stock-voting trusts, and certain testamentary trusts are eligible shareholders. In the case of a grantor trust, shareholder status is continued for at least sixty days following the grantor's death. If all the trust's assets are includable in the grantor's estate, the sixty-day period is extended to two years.

In 1982 two additional trusts will become eligible shareholders of Subchapter S corporation stock. First are those trusts where someone besides the grantor is deemed to be the owner because he has the power to give the principal or the income to himself. The sixty-day or two-year continuation of shareholder status, following the death of the deemed owner, also applies to this kind of trust. Second are "qualified Subchapter S trusts." To qualify, a trust may have only one income beneficiary at a time, all of the income must be distributed, and the income beneficiary must elect to be treated as the trust's owner.

PUTTING PARTNERSHIP INTERESTS IN TRUST

Partnership interest may be a particularly tricky asset to transfer into a trust. Many partnership agreements specify that the interest of the partnership may not be transferred without first offering that interest to the other partners. At the very least, no transfer may occur without the consent of the other partners.

Under such stipulations, the transfer of partnership interest into a revocable trust, even when the original partner is designated as sole trustee, may be a breach of the partnership agreement, resulting in lawsuits as well as the trust's losing many of the rights which a partner may have. The problem is solved by amending the Partnership agreement—with the approval of the other partners, of course—to show the substitution of a new partner, as discussed in chapter 21, The Closely Held Business.

CAN YOU USE KEOGH PLANS AND IRAs IN LIVING TRUSTS?

Can I assign the proceeds of my Keogh plan or Individual Retirement Account to a revocable living trust?" How often have I heard that question. The answer is a simple yes. Qualified pension plans and profit-sharing plans may also be included.

The proceeds of these plans would not pass through probate if they were made payable to a named beneficiary other than the estate of the participant. They can be totally exempted from federal estate taxes. To further extend the estate tax savings, the proceeds can be made payable to the successor trustee of Trust B (the marital trust) over a period of two years as long as the trustee is under the following written instructions:

> Anything else herein to the contrary notwithstanding, the Trustee shall not pay any debts or expenses or any estate or inheritance taxes, or satisfy any creditors' claims, if any, from funds or property received as an annuity payment or distribution under a trust forming part of a pension, stock bonus, or profit-sharing plan meeting the requirements of Section 401 (a) of the Internal Revenue Code of 1954 as amended, or under a retirement annuity contract purchased pursuant to a plan described in Section 403 (a) payment or distribution is designated to any trust contained in this Trust Agreement.

And now, with all these assets covered by your living trust, you may well ask, "Is a will still necessary?" The answer is emphatically *yes!*

9

Do You Still Need a Will?

Let's choose executors and talk of wills:
And yet not so, for what can we bequeath
Save our deposed bodies to the ground?

—SHAKESPEARE

Shakespeare was speaking more in metaphorical than in literal terms, at a time when most people had few possessions to pass on after their death. Money was important, but to the few, not the many. For the majority, life was a day-to-day affair far simpler than our own passage through time. The valuable part of Everyman's estate was not physical. It was the values, the attitudes, the knowledge he passed on to his offspring.

Today these facets of life are far too readily passed over. However, the fact that you are reading this book indicates that you are in a very important minority. You want to prepare for your future and that of your family—in a way, even for the future of our society, because by passing on in the best possible way, not only your assets but your values, you are helping to shape our country for the generations to come.

THE INTRACTABLE CASE OF THE INTESTATE

Chances are you will not achieve these goals if you die intestate. Now, dying intestate does not mean dying without a will. It means dying without a *valid* will, one that the courts will recognize, one that will dispose of your property as you wish after death. In wills as in other things, there is a matter of the right one for the job.

Some form of will is a necessity for everyone. It's simply not possible to anticipate and exempt from probate every last asset that might be part of your estate. Consider someone who has a heart attack upon discovering that he's just won a million-dollar lottery. Or consider the more likely possibility of an accident. Let's say every item you possess, right down to your collection of Indian-head pennies, has been catalogued and transferred to revocable living trusts. You're walking out of a restaurant, on top of the world after a sumptuous business lunch, when suddenly a car mounts the sidewalk and runs you over.

Your estate sues and collects hefty damages, which obviously pass through probate. But what would you have done with the money? Whom would you have wanted to have it?

Minor children are a particularly important consideration in circumstances as sad as these. If one parent dies, no one will argue the fact that the surviving parent will continue as head of the family. But what if, instead of setting off after a business lunch, you had been walking out of that restaurant arm in arm with your wife on the way to the theater? The probate court will choose a guardian, one who might well be quite contrary to your desires—had you expressed them.

"No problem," you say. "I've named a guardian for my child in my living trust." Wrong. You have named the successor trustee, or guardian of your child's *property*. You also need a guardian for your child as a *person*. For that you need a will.

Over the centuries, the legal rights of people were extended from the right to dispose of personal property as they wished to the right to dispose of real property as they wished. However, that right was never actually extended to disposing of their offspring as they wished—though disposing is obviously less than the ideal word in this instance. And the failure of personal legal control over this situation can probably be traced to the concept—and dilemma—of slavery. For any individual to be able to treat another person as property is, to all intents and purposes, slavery.

Nevertheless, protection against slaveholding brings up the conflicting problem that even when you specifically name a guardian in your will, the courts need not abide by your wishes. Guardianship, we said, falls under the jurisdiction of the state rather than the federal court system, so there are many variations on the theme. One consistent point, however, is that an orphaned child is a ward of the court. You have no absolute right to name a guardian. You have only the right to request a specific guardian. The court reserves the right of final judgment.

Chances are that if your wishes are reasonable, they will be honored. But if those wishes are not part of your will, your children will be taking pot luck.

There is an actual case which particularly demonstrates the financial consequences to the children of parents dying intestate. A husband and wife, recently married, were both killed in a multi-car collision. The husband's separate estate was worth $3 million. The wife had an estate of negligible value. Neither had a valid last will and testament.

The husband and wife were each survived by two adult children from previous marriages, and the question which eventually consumed much of the court's time was, Who inherits the $3 million estate?

Under the California statute, the question could be answered only after a factual determination of who really died first. Most states have a similar arrangement. If the wife died first, then the husband's two children would receive the entire estate. If the husband died first, his surviving wife would receive a third of his estate ($1 million) and his surviving children the balance ($2 million). The wife's two children would then inherit the $1 million from their mother, now dead.

As you can imagine, the factual determination was very difficult. Much evidence favored the finding that they died simultaneously. Under the Uniform Simultaneous Death Act, however, such a conclusion would require a distribution of the estates of both husband and wife as though each had survived the other. The result would be the same as if the wife died first.

After long and expensive litigation, the court finally concluded there was some evidence that the wife survived her husband by "moments," and her children inherited a third of her husband's estate—a third of what was left after extensive legal fees, court costs, and, of course, taxes. Much of the expense could have been avoided had the man and his wife had properly drafted wills and a living trust.

Creditors against the estate are another reason for having a will. Claims against an estate may show up a long time after a person's death. This is particularly true for professional people such as doctors, dentists, engineers, and other individuals with professional practices where unexpected liabilities may suddenly appear.

As I pointed out in chapter 7, the publication status of probate is an effective way to terminate all claims against the estate. That is to say, with the legal publication of your death, and the notice to all creditors that attends the probate process, all future credit action is invalidated. The creditors, once given notice that they have only so much time to step forward with their claims, have no further recourse.

In cases where creditors' claims might arise, I always recommend leaving some small asset out of the family trust and letting it pass through probate by means of a will. The will adds the umbrella protection of publication to all the other benefits.

By now the old idea that only the wealthy need wills should be thoroughly quashed. Yet, according to a recent survey, only 19 percent of people of voting age or older have wills. Make sure you're part of that 19 percent.

HOLOGRAPHIC WILLS

A will is not just a will, of course. There are variations in both their physical and legal characteristics. But before we look at these features, let's run through some of the basic legalese embodied in wills.

The person making the will is called a *testator* if male, a *testatrix* if female. The person named to take charge of the assets, paying outstanding bills and settling the overall estate, is the *executor*. If the testator fails to name an executor, the court will do so, and call him an *administrator* instead. In the case of personal property, a recipient of the will's distribution is called a *legatee*. In the case of real property, a recipient is referred to as a *devisee*.

Physically, representing a carryover from bygone days, there is the holographic will—still accepted in nineteen states.* The holographic will is essentially a handwritten letter delineating the disposition of assets, all written, dated, and signed by the testator. It's the classic mystery-story will that no one knows about, found hidden in the dictionary under *d* for *death*, or the one in the front-page newspaper story about an impoverished elderly lady who lived on bread in a fifth-floor walk-up apartment with twenty-six cats. She left $263,240 behind in $20 bills and scribbled on the back of a greasy envelope, "Being of sound mind and body, I, Edith Katz, leave all

*Arizona, Arkansas, California, Iowa, Kentucky, Louisiana, Mississippi, Montana, Nevada, North Carolina, North Dakota, Oklahoma, South Dakota, Tennessee, Texas, Utah, Virginia, West Virginia, and Wyoming.

my earthly belongings to the ASPCA in exchange for the perpetual care of my beloved cats upon my death." It's also trouble.

Ambiguous language, along with other ambiguities, has been the source of much litigation over holographic wills. Consider the forthright "I leave my home and all the contents therein to my daughter. The balance of my estate I bequeath to my niece." The writer of this apparently clear statement dies. He has $30,000 worth of stock besides the house and its contents. But he kept the stock certificates in the house. Who gets them? Are they part of the house's "contents" or part of the "balance of the estate"? The only certainty in what originally seemed to be an obvious case is attorneys' fees.

Let's try a different example, one in which a farmer drew up a holographic will, took it to town, and had the postmaster witness it. That seems a sensible and perfectly prudent thing to do. Legal documents certainly can't be harmed by a witness's signature, can they?

Well, in the case of wills, once a holographic will is witnessed, its whole character changes. It becomes an *attested will*. An attested will, even if it's handwritten, must be completed with all the formality and phraseology we normally associate with such an instrument. The witnessing of a holographic will may very well negate it.

Attested wills were always handwritten, of course, before the invention of the typewriter. Today, almost without exception, they are typewritten. The primary requisites of this kind of will are that the testator's signature and mental capacity to act responsibly both be attested by at least two witnesses. Some states require three witnesses, and the procedure for acting as a witness also varies from state to state. All states, however, prohibit beneficiaries or fiduciaries of the will from acting as witnesses.

Strange though it may seem, most states do not require the dating of wills. In fact, only two states—Louisiana and Michigan—require all wills to be dated. Even when it's not required, however, dating is certainly desirable. Where there are several wills drawn up by the same person, the one dated last is usually the one accepted for probate. In the case of two undated wills, choosing between them not only could be difficult but might run quite opposite to the writer's real wishes.

FIVE COMMON TYPES OF WILLS

The legal characteristics of wills vary with their purpose. The documents range all the way from simple wills, which merely dispose of the assets and pay the tax man, to pour-over wills, where the assets of the estate are removed from public record.

1. A simple will is a nontrust will with uncomplicated provisions. Besides nominating an executor, the essential provisions of a simple will are concerned with distributing the estate's assets. The provisions may be general, like one, for instnce, which lets me leave "all of my property of every kind, nature, and wherever located, both real and personal, to my spouse . . . ." Or they may be specific ones such as "I hereby leave my gold watch to my son James Warren."

A simple will is simply for very simple estates. It should probably play no role in your estate planning. A simple will may not even be adequate to fulfill the publication purpose, which is your primary concern once you have established the appropriate trusts.

2. A contingent trust will is a simple will with a little fillip added, and it is applicable to modest estates where there is some significant amount of life insurance on the life of either the husband or the wife and where there are minor children. There are contingency provisions in the will stating that if the primary beneficiary is deceased as well as the testator, the whole estate, or at least most of it, is to be passed on to a specific trustee. This trustee is then put under the obligation to hold the estate's property for the benefit of the minor children, or possibly spendthrift children. The funds do not have to be released when the children come of age. You can specify that they receive the interest from the property, or that it be used for their education and the like, while the actual principal is not to be handed over until they reach the age of twenty-five, thirty, or ninety-nine, for that matter.

A contingent trust, once it becomes operative after you die, usually continues for its whole duration under probate-court supervision. The decision as to whom you choose as trustee in this situation will hinge primarily on the ability of the potential trustee to manage the assets according to your wishes. Cost may be another factor. Many people's first thought is to name a bank as trustee, but a bank is usually the most expensive choice you can make. The cost of using a trustworthy friend instead is lower. And a friend may well be a more effective trustee in the case of a small estate, which is where this type of will can be most useful. In the case of a larger estate, there are better alternatives than a contingent trust will for distributing assets.

3. The marital-trust will is an exercise in federal death-tax avoidance paralleling the living marital-deduction trust. It accomplishes the same purposes *except* that it does not avoid probate. Thus it's more an item of historical interest than it is a practical tool—in most cases. The simple fact is that, when it comes to wills, there are always special situations, as there are in estates as a whole, which negate the general rules. While I tend to recommend the marital-deduction trust for my clients along with a pour-over will (see the fifth type of will), occasionally the marital-trust will presents superior opportunities.

4. The election will is a variant of the marital-trust will. In it, a surviving spouse is required to make certain decisions. You might say it's a multiple-choice will, one with certain options left open. The blanks allow some adjustments to be made in the estate to compensate for changing tax situations or other unforeseeable circumstances.

For example, in a case where a husband dies, leaving his wife all but the amount passing tax-free thanks to the unified credit, an election will might specify that she be given either a life interest in the rest of the estate or the opportunity to purchase that life interest. She would buy it with assets she received tax-free thanks to the unlimited marital deduction.

Such a purchase is usually made through a third trust. The wife then has a life interest in the whole estate again, and its entirety may be passed on to a third party upon her death. This ploy might be a commendable plan of action in a situation where the husband is concerned about the amount of the total estate which, upon his wife's subsequent death, will pass to her heirs. The election purchase reduces that amount.

Another situation where this ploy is useful is the one where the taxpayer chooses to use inflation to save taxes with a purchase program. For example, a husband has an estate of $750,000 and dies in 1985. If he leaves one half of the estate to his wife as a marital deduction, the basis for computing the tax on his wife's subsequent death will be the $375,000 as appreciated. Suppose her estate has grown to $750,000. Under current law, the taxes when she dies could be as high as $55,500. Let's assume, however, that shortly after the death of her husband, the wife is given the option of purchasing a life interest in the other half of the estate, and she pays for it with the transfer of money from her $375,000 share. The price for her purchase will depend on her age and life expectancy. In other words, it will be an actuarial determination. For the purpose of our example, let's value the life-estate purchase at $75,000. The wife, then, transfers $75,000 of her $375,000 to a third living trust, which will not be taxed in her estate when she dies. If she puts into the third trust those assets with the greatest inflation potential, she can use inflation to reduce taxes. The result—the value of the wife's estate will be not $750,000 but will be reduced to $600,000 or less; and at that level, no taxes would be due on her death either.

5. The pour-over will is the single most important type of will for the well-

planned estate. It is set up to provide sufficient assets to cover any potential outstanding obligations of the estate. The remainder of the estate is placed in appropriate trusts.

The principal provision of a pour-over will is the one giving the money to the trustee to cover outstanding estate obligations. Any assets left over at the conclusion of the estate settlement then "pour" into a trust.

The trust provisions are not part of the will, and the trust into which the assets pour is not a matter of open record. The money simply runs out of a predesigned hole in the will. As far as the public is concerned, it vanishes.

In all the foregoing examples I have assumed that the couples live in a separate-property state and that the husband (usually the main bread-winner) dies before his wife does. Of course, the opportunities for estate planning are equally valid in community-property states and in cases where the wife dies first.

By now you should begin to feel that you have the basic "legalese" to begin to plan realistically and knowledgeably for your future and that of your family. With trusts and wills both mapped out to serve your goals, you will find there's one more consideration to take into account before completing these documents, and that's cutting out inflation's extra tax burden. This, as you will see, is like cutting out the middleman—and it's just as profitable.

10

How to Inflation-Proof Trusts and Wills

Does the road wind up-hill all the way? Yes, to the very end.
—CHRISTINA GEORGINA ROSSETTI

Every clause in a will and a trust should reflect inflation planning. There nothing to lose by it, and all of inflation's profits to gain. In the extremely unlikely event that inflation were to come to a halt, these clauses would not affect the will or the trust negatively. After all, you would have determined the future direction of your assets according to what you felt should be done with them. Adding the inflation provisions will merely protect these goals, not change them.

Remember, when you can divert assets with the greatest inflation potential to trusts which will not be taxed at the death of your spouse and therefore will pass tax-free to your children or other heirs, you are using inflation to save taxes and beat the IRS at its own game.

THE PROFITS OF AVOIDING OWNERSHIP

Consider a valuable painting. Should you die, you would like the picture to remain in your family for their enjoyment. First and foremost, you would like your wife to have it. But when she passes on, you would like your daughter, who used to stand and stare up at the mist-covered landscape with fascination on the rainy days of her childhood, to have it.

Traditionally, your painting would have passed through the estate by means of a simple bequest in your will. Today, with the rapid appreciation in value of such assets as works of art and jewelry, giving them away outright can be very expensive. Take a simple two-ounce gold brooch set with a single one-carat diamond—an heirloom, let's say, from your grandmother. Ten years ago, it might have sold for $700 or $800 on the value of the gold and the diamond alone. Today it's probably worth close to $10,000. If gold and diamonds keep up this dizzying pace of appreciation, which is altogether likely, that same brooch may well be worth $20,000 by 1990. Now if you were to die, your estate would pay taxes on that $10,000. If your wife were then to die in 1990, her estate would pay taxes on the $20,000. The government would have taken its cut on $30,000 before the next generation even got the brooch.

As to the little girl, now grown, who loved the painting, who can guess how much the government would scrape off the top of the canvas before she finally got it. Select paintings can rise in value even more than precious metals and stones do. The appreciation of works of art may be less predictable, but the end results of that appreciation can be more destructive.

The solution to the tax problem presented by rapidly appreciating assets, then, is to give all such assets to a trust which will not be included in the survivor's estate, yet which will allow the survivor to use the assets during his or her lifetime.

Either a living trust or a testamentary trust set up in the will can be used, the gift being given either specifically to the trust or to the executor or trustee, who then has the power to place the assets in the trust, or not, as desired.

The latter alternative is often the more desirable one, because it gives the executor or trustee the opportunity to evaluate both spouses' estates before any actual transfers are made. Where the two estates don't appear to have a double tax problem, the executor or trustee can give the items outright to the survivors. Where taxes are a concern, or might become one, a bypass trust can be activated.

This bypass trust, which allows the assets to bypass the estate, should explicitly state that the survivors can use the assets for life without rental payments. Otherwise the trustee may be forced to charge rent. The trust should also be required to pay all taxes, insurance, and other expenses through the independent trustee, while at the same time prohibiting the trustee, unless the trustee and the survivor are one and the same, from selling the assets without the consent of the survivors.

A sample clause covering these points and more might read as follows:

> My wife shall have the right during her lifetime to use the jewelry and works of art included in the trust estate. She shall also have the right to occupy any property of the trust estate that was

being used by us as our principal residence at the time of my death. The Trustee in his discretion may pay out of income of the trust estate all real and personal property taxes and insurance premiums, maintenance, and other expenses relating to jewelry, works of art, and the residence. The Trustee shall not be liable to any beneficiary of this trust for losses resulting from the use of such property by my wife and shall not sell any of such property during my wife's lifetime without the consent of my wife or the consent of the guardian or conservator of her estate.

THE FIXED-SUM DILEMMA

Bequests of fixed sums of money and other specific assets also present problems. A gift of $100,000, for instance, may seem significant now, but by the date of death it may provide much less buying power. A hundred shares of stock in the family business bequeathed to an only son and $250,000 bequeathed to an only daughter may be equal gifts at the time a will is drawn up but completely unfair by the time they are inherited, either because both the dollar and the business have become worthless or because the business has prospered but the dollar hasn't. The solution here is to **tie gifts to the fluctuating value of your estate.**

In order to equalize the value of your gifts, you might consider making them fractional shares of your estate. Let's see how such a division would work in the case of the only son and only daughter. Half the estate would go to the son and half to the daughter, with the son's bequest to be first satisfied out of family stock at fair market value and the daughter's bequest to be first satisfied out of cash. The difference in value between the two gifts, if any, could then be equalized by the value of other assets in the estate. Such an arrangement would provide both son and daughter with equal buying power at the time of their father's death.

Again, a simple clause inserted in the will can make all the difference between an equitable distribution and a really unfair one brought about by a factor out of your control—namely, inflation. Here's such a remedial clause:

> The sum of [$20,000] is based on the trust monetary values. If there is a decrease in the monetary purchasing power between the date my Will/Trust is executed and the date of my death as measured by the United States Department of Labor's Consumer Price Index—

the U.S. all-items index, where 1967 equals 100—the bequest to my son/daughter shall be increased to an amount that shall have the purchasing power at the date of my death which is equal to the above-specified amount in the month my Will/Trust is executed.

Cash gifts can also be indexed to gold, foreign currency, or other desired measures of value. In addition, to protect the value of the gifts, you can specify that they pay interest at a chosen rate during the estate's administration or the period of the trust's settlement. Many states already require interest on cash gifts during administration. But the rates specified when the laws were made are far too low to protect the gifts' true worth in these inflationary times.

LIMITING BEQUESTS

Ceilings can also be applied to bequests. Usually these maximums are represented by percentages of the estate. What you should note particularly is that inflation adjustments can be made *down* as well as *up* when it comes to distributing assets, although such clauses are not common. A suggested form for such a clause would be as follows:

If the gift of [$20,000] to [my daughter] is less than [20] or more than [30] percent of the gross value of my probate/trust estate as of the date of my death, based on the initial and supplemental inventories and appraisements filed in probate/trust estate, the gift shall be increased or decreased to equal [25] percent of the value of my probate/trust estate as aforesaid.

A crucial condition of all fluctuating specific bequests is that they must be capable of accurate valuation. Such valuation is to be made either at death, if given by will, or at the start of the trust, if given by means of an inter vivos, or living, trust.

DESCRIBING ASSETS IN PERCENTS
IS BETTER THAN DOLLARS

The type of marital-deduction clause used is also significant in inflation-proofing your will or trust. Should the surviving spouse's share of the property be described in actual dollar values? Or should it be expressed as a percentage of the total estate? Given a $700,000 estate, would it be better to give the surviving spouse $350,000 or 50 percent when setting up marital and residuary trusts?

That may seem to be a rather inane question, considering that 50 percent of the estate *is* $350,000. But remember, when it comes to dealing with the IRS, you are dealing in technicalities. If a true pecuniary clause, one that specifies the legacy in dollars, is used, then the surviving spouse's half does not share in any gain or loss of assets during the time it takes for the estate to be settled. With a fractional clause it does, whether the widow or widower needs the money or not.

It may be advantageous in many cases to force all asset appreciation into the residuary or unified credit equivalent trust. Remember that the marital trust is subject to estate tax once the surviving spouse dies. The residency trust is not. If a dollars-and-cents definition of assets, rather than percentages, is used in setting up the trusts, the taxes on the marital trust are apt to be lower once the second spouse dies. Any appreciating assets will be primarily in the now-larger residuary trust, which passes on to the children or heirs without estate taxes.

To fully utilize the benefits from using the pecuniary formula, the trustee or executor of the estate should be given the discretion to choose which assets will be used to fund the marital deduction. Slow-appreciating assets can thus be separated from the movers and shakers and each placed in the most appropriate trust.

REMOVING LIFE INSURANCE
FROM YOUR TAXABLE ESTATE

Usually you want to keep life insurance and other liquid assets out of a taxable estate. This is commonly done by means of life-insurance trusts and other similar trusts. These trusts prevent insurance and other such assets from being added onto a decedent's taxable estate and taxed at its highest rate.

If, however, the estate has no other sources of cash, such trust arrangements may cause liquidity problems. Cash must be made available to pay taxes and administrative expenses. The trick is to make liquid assets available to pay taxes and expenses without also making them includable in the taxable estate.

The solution lies in authorizing the trustee of the insurance trust to buy estate assets or to lend the estate cash, and then authorizing the executor or trustee of the estate to sell estate assets and to borrow from the life insurance trust. This quite legitimate sleight-of-hand will make cash available but prevent the insurance from being includable in the estate, as long as neither party is *required* to use these liquid assets for the payment of estate taxes and expenses. For added liquidity, the trust or will could allow loans from and purchases by individuals like widows and children who can be direct beneficiaries of the life insurance.

Another asset which the trust or will should prevent from being used for the payment of estate taxes is qualified employee benefits. Otherwise the benefits may lose their estate-tax exemption.

THE EXECUTOR'S RESPONSIBILITY

The executor is responsible for administering the estate's assets from the date of death until distribution. This period may be as long as a year or more, during which interval inflation and other economic conditions can destroy the value of the assets. The executor should be given license to handle—with good judgment, of course—all the contingencies that might arise.

In many states an executor can invest only in conservative assets such as government bonds and savings accounts unless a will specifies otherwise. So the executor should be specifically empowered to operate the decedent's business, continue with investment strategies, and otherwise manage the estate with great flexibility. These problems are solved routinely by using a living trust as your principal estate-planning tool.

THE POWERS OF THE TRUSTEE

Since most trusts are in existence for many years, the trustee should also be given broad powers to deal with all the economic conditions which might arise. As a rule, a trustee is required to give equal emphasis to current income and the future appreciation of trust assets. This requirement may be inappropriate in an inflationary economy, where many non-income-producing assets keep pace with inflation better than the income-producing assets do.

The remedy is to allow the trustee to invest in such non-income-producing assets as gold, vacant land, or stock which pays no dividends. It may also be desirable to define the trustee's duty as being the obligation to invest for total return rather than for equal weight between income and appreciation. A marital-deduction trust generally must pay income if the deduction is not to be lost. When the surviving spouse has the power to direct investment into income-producing assets or to take assets in lieu of income, however, this requirement is met.

Many trustees, given very broad discretionary powers, will still invest only in conservative stocks and bonds. Corporate trustees are particularly apt to do so. You, as the testator, should consider giving the investment powers over your trust to a trustee whose investment philosophy agrees with your own and giving the administrative powers to a corporate trustee. This kind of apportionment will combine aggressive investment with professional accounting and distribution and is likely to result in a more balanced and ultimately profitable administration of your estate.

A trustee's power to distribute the assets of a trust should take into account both the beneficiaries' needs and the trust income. Traditionally, trusts have been inflexible in this regard. Fixed amounts of income have been paid to predetermined beneficiaries until their death, and then the principal has gone to others. This is appropriate when the grantor does not trust the discretion of the trustee. Yet such a distribution scheme often results in large income payments to beneficiaries who don't need the income but who pay a high tax rate on it. Meanwhile, other beneficiaries who do need income, and who are in low tax brackets, receive nothing but a remainder interest from the residual trust when it is finally distributed, long after they have become established in their businesses or professions.

A trustee's discretion can be almost unlimited, without any tax effect, if that trustee is a nonbeneficiary and otherwise independent. This discretion can include the power to pay income or principal or not to pay anything, based on the various beneficiaries' needs. Where equality among the beneficiaries is important, the assets can be divided into separate trusts, one for each beneficiary, and discretion can be given for each trust, without crossovers. That is to say, the assets of one trust cannot be added to another. Any discretionary instrument should clearly state the purpose or purposes for which discretion is given, such as the goal of balancing trust income and beneficiary need.

THE BENEFICIARY'S TRUST POWERS

A beneficiary may have certain limited powers over trust assets without incurring adverse estate-tax consequences. For example, the right to withdraw annually 5 percent of the trust's value or $5,000, whichever is larger, is a special power which will not cause the entire trust value to be taxed for estate purposes. Such a special power allows the beneficiary to take care of his or her own needs during rocky economic or personal times. A beneficary may also receive trust assets based on his or her support, maintenance, health, or educational needs. In addition, the benificiary can be empowered to require that payments be made to others, so long as he or she gains no direct or indirect benefit from those payments. All three powers may be given to the same beneficiary.

It is important to examine each and every statement of a will or a trust as it is drawn up and ask yourself what effect inflation may have on that provision. Many alternatives will be rejected because of impracticality or other overriding concerns. But knowingly eliminating alternatives will produce more effective estate planning than will ignoring the continuing presence of inflation in your future estate.

CODICILS AND AMENDMENTS

The last word on wills is codicils. It is not necessary to rewrite a will if you want to make changes in it. A codicil, a document modifying the terms of the will and written after the signing of the original will, can be added at any time, although it must be executed as carefully and formally as the will itself.

Trusts, too, may be changed. If a trust is properly structured in the first place, amending it is no more complicated than altering a will is.

So don't use the excuse, "I'm not exactly sure how I want to dispose of my estate yet," to put off having a will drawn up. Wills reflect ongoing desires and can be changed. Estates themselves, on the other hand, should be frozen—frozen to keep the tax man and inflation out.

11

Estate Freezing—The Tax Buck Stops Here

> Taking it all in all, I find it is more trouble to watch after money
> than to get it.
>
> —MONTAIGNE

Once you have a general estate plan organized, it's time for your all-out attack on inflation. To do battle is an absolute necessity, not only because of inflation's debilitating effect on your dollars, but even more because of the escalating nature of the unified estate and gift tax (see table in chapter 6). Considering the massive increase in the value of assets due to inflation alone, it's not unusual for this transfer tax on assets passing from one generation to the next to increase approximately 100 percent every seven years. The assets don't necessarily double. But the taxes do.

By necessity, then, your attack on inflation requires a two-pronged plan. One direction of attack is to **index all the possible present and future assets of your estate to inflation itself.** By doing so selectively, you should be able to actually increase your assets at a greater rate than inflation. I'll show you how to use some little-known tax shelters for this purpose in chapter 16.

FREEZING YOUR ESTATE

But profiting from inflation is not enough if the IRS is going to take the profit and part of the original assets as well. The second direction of your attack is to freeze the assets of your estate. You need to know how to freeze your estate so that any increase in asset value goes to your family rather than to the government. Usually this means establishing trusts or family partnerships so that you can have use of the assets and at the same time make sure that all of the assets' appreciation due to inflation passes on to your beneficiaries without any estate taxes.

(Note: Your temptation may be to skip this chapter and proceed straight

to the one on tax-sheltered investments, which may appear to offer you much more immediate benefits. Well, I sympathize with that temptation. Indulge it if you wish, but do come back to join me here after you've perused the tax shelters. There's a wealth of tax-saving ideas in this section. Even if the benefits of trusts take longer to accrue than simple tax shelters, the trusts' end results in dollar terms can be staggering. And the sooner you begin, the more impressive the gain.)

Let's consider a farmer who has four or five hundred acres of land in the Midwest that is appreciating rapidly. Or an entrepreneur launching a business which just might become a very valuable entity in a decade. Or an investor with a coin collection that looks like it's going to double or triple or even quadruple because of scarcity and inflation. The time for these people to transfer some or all of the ownership of their assets to the next generation is not once the assets have become really valuable but *now*, before they do. **All the increase in value can then remain untaxed for decades.** An asset need not be transferred in its entirety, and there are several ways for you to retain effective control and use of it while at the same time, for the most part, cutting out that tax man.

AN ESTATE FREEZING PLAN THAT'S TOO SIMPLE TO WORK ANYMORE

The most straightforward technique for estate freezing is simply to give your assets away at their current valuation. Any increase in their value will be taxed to the recipient.

Like all simple schemes, however, at least when it comes to taxes, this one has serious drawbacks, not the least of which is that old bugaboo of estate planners, the Tax Reform Act of 1976. Prior to its taking effect, gifts were taxed at a lower rate than the same assets transferred at the time of death. This is no longer true. Thus the biggest benefit has been removed.

Even under the old tax plan, there were serious drawbacks to the scheme. The gift tax, though lower than the estate tax, was due immediately after the gift was bestowed. You had annual exclusions and lifetime exemptions, of course, on some money. But you didn't have enough of those for a sizable transfer of money.

A second drawback of the old tax plan, and perhaps the more important one, was the loss of control. We all want to avoid taxes wherever possible, but for many people, giving up the control of their assets may be too much of a price to pay. After all, one works hard to build up assets. To enjoy the fruits of one's labor only by proxy is frustrating at best.

There *are* ways to use the tax laws about giving very creatively and profitably, and I'll cover these in chapters 13 and 19, Lifetime Giving and Charitable Giving. For now, however, suffice it to note again that, except when you're dealing in cash, one of the crucial necessities in transferring for tax purposes is determining the actual dollar value of the property to be transferred. This is the central point around which the concept of estate freezing revolves, one that is open to much fruitful manipulation.

WHEN YOU CALL THE SHOTS

Value is what you make it. The Internal Revenue Code breaks down the tax consequences of a completed transaction on the basis of the fair market value of the property involved. Certain extra liabilities may be incurred if the transaction is not *at arm's length*—if you're dealing with yourself or your family in what is essentially a sham transaction to avoid taxes.

In some cases, however, the arm's-length posture can become arm-in-arm without negative tax consequences, since you may determine who evaluates an asset. In such cases, the taxpayer wins because you can select the actual asset value from within what is considered to be a range of acceptable fair market values. And the value the marketplace might put on an asset can vary widely. Go to an auction sometime and watch. A pair of candlesticks you think is worth $50 can go for $10 or for $100. All three values are acceptable and real. When you're talking in terms of land or buildings or other more valuable assets, the difference in valuation and its importance in tax avoidance become much more obvious, as you'll see.

A man came to my office a couple of weeks before I wrote this book. He had a lot of farmland—2,000 acres—in Texas. I asked what the property was worth and he replied that it was worth about $400 an acre. So I asked what he meant by "about."

"Well," he said, "maybe it's worth five hundred dollars an acre."

Do you realize the difference in death taxes just raising the value of that land $100 an acre entails? We figured that, in this instance, if that land were suddenly to become worth only $50 more an acre, it would cost $39,000 more in death taxes when he died.

Now this man's life-style isn't going to change if his land goes up $50 an acre. He's the kind of guy who wants to keep farming in the family. He wants to keep operating this 2,000-acre dairy farm for his children. The amount of income being produced by that land, based on its value, is very, very small; he's probably getting a less-than-1-percent return. So, from a return point of view, he isn't getting much. But the significant thing is that the land just might suddenly double, triple, or even quadruple in value, and then the death taxes could be astronomical.

We are talking, then, about a tax on inflation, not a tax on true increase in value. And the problem facing my Texas client is the same one confronting anyone who owns a parcel of land, however small, or improved real estate with a building on it, or almost anything else that is going to grow and inflate in value.

What you really want to be able to do is to transfer wealth to the next generation while at the same time retaining the economic use of it. In other words, you want to control it, if that is possible. But you want to do so in such a way that you can, if you choose, shift some of the income-tax burden to the shoulders of the next generation. In effect, you want to pass—in a lawful manner, and in a manner which will stand up to IRS attack—more than meets the eye.

THE INSTALLMENT SALE

Let's talk about another farm, a hypothetical one this time. Let's say our hypothetical taxpayer has a family farm worth somewhere between $500,000 and $1 million. He doesn't really know for sure what it's worth. And he's concerned about his children's being financially able to take over the farm someday. Chances are that estate taxes would force them to sell the land, particularly if only one of his four children decided to go into farming. To prevent estate taxes from forcing that sale, the farmer needs to freeze his estate.

As a first step toward freezing his estate, he should have his property evaluated by an outside appraiser. Of course, appraisals can vary widely. Obviously, the true value of the property is what a willing buyer would pay for it if the man were willing to sell and neither one of them was under any compulsion. But a simple, objective appraisal will give the man a valuation for his family farm.

Let's say the farmer gets two different evaluations from two different appraisers. One comes in with an estimate of $800,000 and the other comes in at $500,000. Which appraisal is more advantageous to the man in terms of his taxes? The answer is obviously the $500,000 appraisal because it means less taxes.

The next step in estate freezing here is for the man to sell his farm to his children for $500,000. If he doesn't particularly want to deal with all four children, the best thing for him to do is to create a special kind of irrevocable trust—by an irrevocable trust I mean one that cannot be altered, changed, or amended—naming his four children as beneficiaries. The advantage of passing the farm on to his children in an irrevocable trust as opposed to passing it on to them in an outright sale is that the father can handpick a trustee for it.

Now, what we have here is an *arm's-length sale* based on an objective appraisal. The father then takes back a long-term note and a small down payment, say $1,000. So what he's got is a note for $499,000 at a very reasonable interest rate. Under the Economic Recovery Tax Act of 1981, up to $500,000 in installment sales of land to relatives is eligible for an interest rate as low as 7 percent. If the buyer is a non-family member, the interest rate should not be below 9 percent because of the new imputed-interest law which allows the government to rewrite the transaction for tax reporting purposes using a higher interest rate.

The father reports the sale using the installment method. That means he doesn't have to pay tax on his gain until he receives a payment.

Let's assume that our farmer's cost basis for this land is $100,000. That's his historical cost, what he paid for it. If he had received cash for the property, he would have had a $400,000 taxable capital gain. But in this instance, since he's only getting $1,000 down, he only has to pay capital gains tax on about $800 of that $1,000 under current tax schedules. He doesn't have to pay any more capital gains until the note becomes due. The interest payments made each year, of course, would be taxed as ordinary income.

The next move is for our farmer, who still wants to farm the land, to enter into a lease with the owner of the property—namely, his children or the trustee. He leases it back, agreeing to pay a fair rental for the lease of the property. Now the annual lease payment he makes, to the trust or to the children, and the annual interest payment made to him may not be off-setting—that's an income-tax number crunch that has to be thought about, of course. But that's a separate and much lesser problem.

What has all this accomplished?

(1). The value of the estate has been frozen by means of a note. When the father dies, what will be in the estate is simply the balance due on the promissory note.

(2). The future appreciation of the property has been carried over to the next generation. If and when the land doubles or triples or even quadruples in value, it will belong to the children. So when the father dies, the children will not have to pay any transfer tax on that appreciated land. If the father's $500,000 estate were to double by 1987, at that point it would cost nearly 31 cents on the dollar to pay the tax on the extra $500,000. Now that happens to be $153,000 in taxes avoided by the estate-freezing technique used here. Even if the land is worth a million dollars by the time the father dies, his estate, remember, contains only the promissory note.

Now let's take this creative manipulation of value one step further. Suppose we have a taxpayer who has some improved real estate—that is, land with buildings on it—that he bought for $150,000 and depreciated to $100,000 for tax purposes, though it is now worth $500,000. He would like to sell or trade this property. But if he trades it for other "like kind"—that is, real estate for real estate, as opposed to real estate for, say, gold coins— he will not be stepping up the cost basis. He can't then redepreciate. So he will have the same cost basis–value dilemma with the traded property that he has with the property he now owns. He doesn't want to sell it, because he's worried that if he sells it he'll have a big capital-gains tax to pay.

Bear in mind that it's not prudent to sell property on an installment basis during inflationary times unless the sale is inflation-indexed. The one exception to this rule is selling property to your own children or to other members of your family.

How can our hypothetical taxpayer boost the cost basis of his improved real estate from $100,000 to $500,000 so it can be redepreciated for tax purposes and still be kept within the family? The answer is very simple. He can sell it to his children, taking back a long-term deferred-payment note. The children then have a new value for the property of $500,000 for tax purposes. Let's say the children allocate 80 percent of the value to the improvements. That gives them a $400,000 improved asset that can be subject to depreciation. And if they want the father to continue managing the property, they can enter into a management contract with him so that he has the control and the economic use of the property.

He has again accomplished two things:

Installment Sale Trust

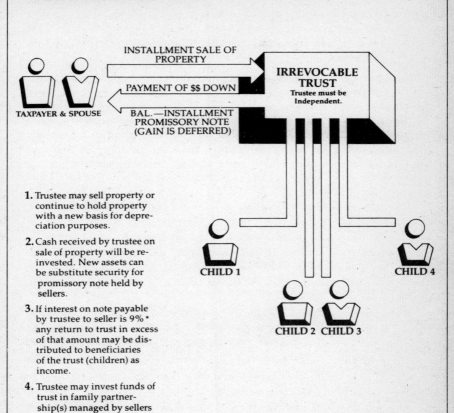

INSTALLMENT SALE OF PROPERTY

PAYMENT OF $$ DOWN

BAL.—INSTALLMENT PROMISSORY NOTE (GAIN IS DEFERRED)

TAXPAYER & SPOUSE

IRREVOCABLE TRUST
Trustee must be Independent.

CHILD 1

CHILD 2 **CHILD 3**

CHILD 4

1. Trustee may sell property or continue to hold property with a new basis for depreciation purposes.

2. Cash received by trustee on sale of property will be reinvested. New assets can be substitute security for promissory note held by sellers.

3. If interest on note payable by trustee to seller is 9%* any return to trust in excess of that amount may be distributed to beneficiaries of the trust (children) as income.

4. Trustee may invest funds of trust in family partnership(s) managed by sellers as general partners.

*Or 7% when the sale is to a family member and the land price is $500,000 or less.

1. He has kept the property in the family and increased his children's tax benefits from depreciation.
2. He has again frozen his estate for estate tax purposes at $500,000, where it will remain. And, in the process, he has shifted the future growth and appreciation of the improved property over to the children.

One drawback of installment sales, even those within the family, is that they force the parent to pay capital gains on the difference in price between what he paid for the asset and what he sells it to his children for. In the case of our hypothetical taxpayer whose real estate had appreciated in value from $100,000 to $500,000 before he sold it, there would be a $400,000 capital gains liability involved. However, the taxes due are spread out over the installment period, which eases the burden somewhat. After all, assuming inflation continues, the ongoing taxes will be paid with dollars of considerably less value.

One way to further minimize the effect of the capital-gains tax is to use a combination of a balloon payment and a very long term for the installment sale. Then the annual payments are low and the final installment represents a large part—the entire part liable for capital gains, in fact—of the sale price. With, say, a twenty-year payment plan, most of the sale price would probably be still unpaid when the parent dies. So it would be included as an asset in the estate.

Now that, in turn, means estate and capital gains taxes would have to be paid on the note balance. Or does it? In some instances, it used to be possible to include a provision in the original bill of sale specifying that all installment obligations are to terminate on the death of the seller. This seems too good to be true. But it's been done. The IRS challenged the plan once—and lost. No estate tax was imposed.

Another approach used was the idea that if the outstanding installment obligations are bequeathed to the child indebted for them, then the obligations merge right out of existence. To put it simply, the child got to keep the property without paying for it. And without having to pay taxes on the income of those annual payments that the child is not making to himself.

Neither of these techniques now work because of the new installment sales law.

NEW LIMITATIONS ON INSTALLMENT SALES

All good things should be brough to an end, according to the IRS. So, with the help of Congress, the agency pushed forth a piece of legislation, signed into law on October 19, 1980, to limit the effectiveness of installment sales in some situations.

The new bill calls for a number of new strategies in using this type of in-trust family sale.

First, the bad news—new limitations:

(1) If you make an installment sale to a "related person," a resale by that person within two years, in the case of property other than marketable securities, will cause a taxable gain to you. No longer can you use the old strategy of selling highly appreciated property to your son or daughter, who then turns around and resells it without tax liability. Meanwhile, you spread and defer your tax liability over twenty years or so.

(2) Once the sale is made, you cannot cancel the installment note or make a transfer of the note by will or trust to the related holder without income tax consequences. No longer can you escape tax on the installment note by canceling it when it comes due.

(3) You can no longer get a new basis on depreciable property by selling it to your spouse or to a partnership or corporation that is owned 80 percent or more by you and/or your spouse.

(4) When selling marketable securities to a related person on the in-stallment method, your note will be taxable whenever the securities are resold. In other words, the two-year rule is really an unlimited-year rule for marketable securities.

The good news is that there are still many other estate-freezing planning opportunities even under this new law. Here are a couple.

(1) A "related" person means your spouse, children, grandchildren, parents and partnerships, trusts and estates benefiting or owned by any of these same related persons. Brothers and sisters, sons-in-law, and daughters-in-law are not related persons. Property sold by you to a non-related person can be immediately resold without causing a tax on your installment note. The benefit of understanding this concept is that if there is an urgent need to resell shortly after the installment sale, for whatever reason, you should initially sell to your brother or some other trusted person who is considered a non-related person. Then the property can be resold, usually without tax.

The new law doesn't directly affect the case of our farmer who wants the property to remain in his family. However, it could have a very negative impact on a situation where it is desirable for the children to resell the assets of an installment sale in order to purchase a more profitable in-vestment vehicle.

On the whole, however, installment sales are still one of the most useful tools available for estate freezing. So let's look a little more closely at their mechanics and their implications.

Let's go back to a 2,000-acre farm again. You bought it, and now find out that a major highway is going to be built almost right through it. The property has already risen to $1,000 an acre in value and might well go to $2,000 or even $5,000 an acre in the next decade. You and your family are going to be rich. Correction. The IRS has struck a bonanza.

At $1,000 an acre, the death-tax cost of transferring this farmland to your four children would already be $718,000. If it went up to $5,000 an acre, this tax cost would escalate to $5,780,800. So much for the family farm. It would have to be sold to pay the taxes. So you decide to sell it yourself—to your children.

You enter into an arm's-length contract of sale, either with them or with a trust for their benefit. The down payment made the year the sale takes place is a minimal $10,000. That's $2,500 from each child. They get the money to make the down payment from you as a gift. Each gift is less than the $10,000 annual gift exclusion, so there are no taxes due. You have the buyer, who is either the children or a trustee, sign a long-term installment note for the payment of the balance of the purchase price. The terms of the note are as determined by you and the buyer, and they include interest at a rate no less than that offered at the time by T-bills. You structure the terms of the note to defer the principal payments until a time in the future which coincides with your income- or retirement-planning objectives, and you use the installment method of reporting under the Internal Revenue Code, Section 453.

The note is initially secured by a mortgage or a deed of trust on the real estate being sold. Once title has passed to the buyer, you lease back the property for a designated annual rental. The annual rental must be fair in light of existing and comparable farming projects, and it may be based on a per-acreage rental value or on a cropsharing arrangement.

Annually, you make your lease payments directly to your children or to the trustee, either of whom will make at least annual interest payments on the promissory note.

SELF-CANCELING INSTALLMENT NOTES

Because of a recent tax court decision, it may be possible for you not only to have the property you sell on the installment basis excluded from your taxable estate, but also to have the installment note excluded from your taxable estate! Here's how to do it. When you sell your property to your children, have the installment note contain a self-canceling clause. Basically it will say that when you die, your children's obligation to pay on the note will be canceled. This means that neither the property you sold nor the canceled note will be included in your taxable estate—your children own the property and the note is canceled. What you have done is completely escaped any estate taxes. This technique is new and still has some wrinkles to be worked out—however, it provides one of the best estate planning tools available today.

USING THE TRUST AS BUYER

The advantage of having a trust as buyer for the benefit of your children is that this arrangement gives more flexibility for the economic use and disposition of wealth to the next generation. For example, your children may be minors, or you may feel that a spendthrift provision, limiting the amount of money the beneficiaries receive as a distribution from the trust, is in order. Also, when you sell property to a trust with a single trustee, you need to deal with only one person, as opposed to the several persons you must deal with if you have more than one child.

Although the IRS has attempted to challenge similar transactions as a sham, their stance has been generally rebuffed in the courts. Now, however, there is the new installment sale law signed by President Carter on October 19, 1980, that will have some effect on the use of sales between family members as a technique for freezing an estate. Note also the retroactive effective date for "related party sales" in the new law—May 14, 1980.

To keep up with the fast shuffle of the IRS card game and get the most up-to-the-minute information on these and other changes you should consult a periodical specializing in estate and tax matters. There are several newsletters specializing in tax matters, including my own, *The Taxflation Fighter*. I'll be glad to send you a free sample copy. Simply write to P.O. Box 3000, 2411 Old Crow Canyon Road, San Ramon, California 94583.

SUMMING UP INSTALLMENT SALES

So much for the commercial break. Now back to your tax avoidance program. To sum up the current status of installment sales for estate purposes and tax planning, bear in mind the following points:

1. The parent seller must report a taxable gain for each installment payment received.

2. The buyer may deduct the interest paid from his or her income taxes and may also take a new depreciation for tax purposes, since the property will now be valued at its new, higher assessment.

3. At the death of the parent seller, the fair market value of the remaining installment payments becomes an asset of the estate. It is subject to estate

taxes. The actual value, however, may be open to adjustment. For instance, if there is $300,000 remaining to be paid on the installment note at an annual interest of 9 percent, and because of inflation the rate of interest paid on loans in the open market is 18 percent at the time, then a valid argument can be made that the note is actually only worth $200,000. That's because anybody with $200,000 at the time could get a yield in dollars equivalent to that from buying the $300,000 installment loan at a much lower rate.

4. Through the use of a self-canceling installment note, there is a chance that you may not only exclude the property from your estate but also from the installment note.

5. When the parent seller dies, the locked-in capital gains outstanding on the note will be taxed to the estate or heirs as payments are made. However, the estate or heirs are entitled to a deduction for the federal estate tax paid earlier on the same installment payments.

FAMILY ANNUITIES ANNUL THE ESTATE TAX

Private annuities are one form of estate freezing that can completely eliminate any future federal estate tax on the value of the underlying assets, such as a house, stocks, and so on. A private annuity must be based on an actuarially established program just like that of a commercial annuity with a life-insurance company or some other comparable institution.

The difference, as the name implies, is that the private annuity involves a private individual as payer. Typically, you transfer property to your children, or to a trust for their benefit. In exchange, you are given an *unsecured* promise of periodic payments of fixed income. The payments can be made monthly or annually, as you choose. But the amount of the payments must be based on actuarial tables for your age and life expectancy. They must also include a built-in interest assumption. That is, the lump sum placed in an annuity should be earning interest, and this interest must be included in the tables to determine the actual payout.

As you receive payments, they will be taxed as a complex combination of capital return, capital gains, and ordinary income. It is fortunate that no one has to figure out what the total tax would be, since its determination is just this side of using integral calculus. The various taxes involved are all combined in easy-to-read actuarial annuity tables that cover all the possible payments. Your financial planner will have the appropriate books with these tables for you to work from.

Payments must actually be made, of course. And unless they are made truly at arm's length, the transaction may be disputed by the IRS, which would prefer to call it a disguised gift and subject it to gift tax.

If you were to die, no part of the annuity would be included in your estate. No installment note, no portion of transferred property, nothing of assessable value—and there's nothing to tax.

Let's look at a typical example of the private annuity as used in a family. A father, seventy-four years old, has some low-yielding growth stock paying 2 percent annually. But it has risen in value from the $10,000 at which he bought it to over $40,000. Let's use the actual value of the stock, $42,749, for this example. Instead of selling the stock, which would incur a large capital-gains tax, in order to buy a high-income security he transfers the stock to his son in exchange for the son's promise to make annual annuity payments of $7,200 for the remainder of the father's life. (This $7,200 happens to be the appropriate figure specified by the annuity tables, which also predict that the father will live 10.1 more years.) The father's expected return under the annuity agreement is $72,720, the annual payment of $7,200 multiplied by the life expectancy, 10.1. Of each annual payment, $1,980 is tax free, $3,252.33 a year falls under the capital-gains tax, and the remaining $1,967.67 is taxed as ordinary annuity income. This proportion continues for the duration of the father's life, *except* that at the end of 10.1 years, which is his actuarial life expectancy at the beginning of the annuity, the $3,252.33 becomes taxed as ordinary income rather than as capital gains.

If you plan to use a private annuity, you will also, obviously, want to consult an accountant and an attorney. Most of these expenses will be tax deductible for you the year the annuity is formalized. What you want to look at now are the advantages and disadvantages of private annuities.

ADVANTAGES OF PRIVATE ANNUITIES

1. A portion of every annuity payment is tax free.
2. No portion of the asset will be considered part of the owner's estate, because the obligation to continue payments expires at the owner's death.
3. Once the asset is transferred, it receives a new stepped-up tax basis (in the example we've used, it goes from $10,000 to $42,749) to the fair market value—without any taxes becoming due. The annuity payer (the son, in our example) can therefore sell the property immediately and purchase a much higher-yielding equity to meet the annuity commitment without reducing the capital by taxation.

4. Property transferred through an annuity does not normally constitute a gift. Therefore no gift tax is involved.

DISADVANTAGES OF PRIVATE ANNUITIES

1. Annuity payments must be made regularly and on the basis specified in the agreement. *Any* variation may result in a tax liability disaster.

2. If the annuity owner survives well beyond the actuarial age, the annuity payer may be burdened with an ongoing-payments problem. Also, if the annuity owner (the father, in our example) does not consume all the annuity payments made after his actuarial death (after 10.1 years, in our example), the money left over will go back into the taxable part of his estate.

3. The annuity payer may not deduct for tax purposes any part of the payments made, even if they end up exceeding the fair market value of the property at the time it was received. This is because they are not considered a debt in the eyes of the IRS. Thus what might be considered interest, and consequently eligible for an interest deduction, is not really interest.

4. If the annuity owner dies earlier than scheduled to by the actuarial tables, the payer's tax basis for the assets given will be very low and considerable taxes will be due. Referring again to our example, if the father had died immediately after the transfer of assets to the annuity, the son's tax base for the assets would have been $10,000. Tax would have been due on the $32,749 difference between this base and the market value of the stock. The taxable basis would increase with each annual payment. After 10.1 years it would be $42,749, which would mean that the son would pay no taxes on that entire amount after this date. However, should the father outlive the annuity tables by some considerable time, the son would end up paying out more than $42,749 for the original $42,749 value. Whether he would stand to gain or lose economically throughout the life of the annuity, that stage would depend greatly on the interest values prevailing. In a period of continuing inflation such as we face today, the son would probably come out ahead.

5. The last problem is one of trust. The promise to pay must be unsecured in order for the annuity to be legal. The payer is bound to the annuity owner only by honor. The son could fail to make the

payments. Of course, he would be somewhat punished for this by having to pay taxes immediately on the entirety of the assets, which would negate the original tax-avoidance reason for setting up the annuity in the first place.

6. Then, too, there are the psychological implications of an annuity transfer. As one attorney couched it in a recent legal paper, "The transferee may develop an uncommon interest in the transferor's longevity, and this could disrupt an otherwise healthy family relationship."

CAPITALIZING ON RECAPITALIZING

There is a marvelous, much underutilized, and extremely complex way of freezing estates called *preferred stock recapitalization*. It essentially splits a company's shareholders into groups, the frozen group and the growth group. The founder of the company, who has already reached a comfortable living standard, is issued preferred stock. This preferred stock has a relatively low value and a fixed interest which takes precedence over the dividend of the common stock. That is, the preferred stock gets a preferential treatment, in that its dividends must be paid before those of the common stock. If the company does not earn enough to pay a dividend to both classes of stock, only the preferred gets it. The preferred stock has one other important feature—namely, that the owner of the preferred stock has complete control of the company.

The children receive the growth stock, the common stock. All the company's increase in value will be reflected in these shares. In essence, then, you, as founder, don't give up anything but the tax liability on the future growth of the company. And you can transfer this future growth to your children without paying a cent in taxes. Your children, in turn, need not pay taxes on the company's increase in value until and unless they sell the company sometime in the distant future.

The classic example of the use of preferred stock recapitalization involves one Dr. Joseph E. Salsbury, founder of Salsbury Laboratories, a pharmaceutical producer for the poultry industry. At the time of Dr. Salsbury's death, Salsbury Laboratories, which had really taken wing, boasted worldwide sales of almost $15 million. The company, which Dr. Salsbury controlled, was valued at $13 million by the IRS. However, due to a previous preferred stock recapitalization of the company, the actual value of the estate was deemed by the tax court to be only $514,000. Out of $13 million dollars, *12.5 million* went to the heirs without a cent of taxes being paid on it. The estate was well planned—but not unusual. The following generation of Salsburys is doing even better.

The concept of recapitalization can be used to great advantage with any number of rapidly appreciating assets such as the development of medical instruments and electronics and computer products. It is also applicable to licensable properties—literary, musical, and the like—if they are apt to produce ongoing revenue on an increasing basis. However, the device is a very specialized one, and it requires the framework of a corporation within which to operate. Specific details of its organization are covered in chapter 21, The Closely Held Business.

PARTNERSHIPS—THE TAX KEYSTONE IN BUILDING A FAMILY FORTUNE

Every family is essentially a partnership in responsibility. Some families, however, have more of the traditional values and cohesiveness in their partnership than others. For those families, the tax advantages of a family partnership in the business as well as in the social sense produce some startling economic gains.

Almost any family business can be adapted to the partnership strategy in one way or another. Farms, service companies with substantial assets, a mail-order operation in the basement—all would work well, as would real estate holdings and oil and gas properties, whose assets are best not put into a corporation.

In these cases the taxpayer's goal in using a family partnership is threefold: (1) to keep control, while at the same time (2) escaping any current gift tax, and (3) freezing the equity for estate purposes.

To accomplish these ends, the business assets are transferred to the family partnership in such a way that the parents' equity will be frozen for estate purposes. This is done by having at least two classes of partnership interest, just as in the preferred stock recapitalization. The enterprise is effectively divided into two separate ownership segments, that comprised by the parents, with the ownership of control and present value, and that of the children, with ownership of the potentially appreciating assets and rights to future income. The parents contribute the valuable assets that form the financial bedrock of the partnership: say, for example, an apartment building. The children contribute cash. It can be an insignificant amount in relation to the whole.

The partnership can provide that the father is the managing partner, retaining full control. He can also be entitled to the lion's share of the income as pay for his management services, as well as a preferred dividend, called a preferred distribution. The children as partners can receive some regular dividend income.

THE TAX ADVANTAGES OF A FROZEN FAMILY PARTNERSHIP

The most significant tax advantage of the frozen family partnership over the installment sale or private annuity is that the family partnership arrangement doesn't force the older generation family members to realize income—that is, be susceptible to future taxes—when freezing their estate.

Another important advantage of the frozen family partnership is that it's relatively easy to unravel from an income-tax standpoint, giving it a distinct advantage over the corporation. A frozen family partnership may also be useful if the assets in question, such as real estate, interests in oil and gas properties, and the like, are not normally put into a corporation. In addition, a family partnership with trade or business assets may qualify for installment payments of federal estate tax.

As a consequence of this ownership segmentation, any appreciation after the date the new partnership is created will bypass the frozen partner's estate. The obvious result is that such a freeze in value may reduce the estate taxes that would otherwise be assessed on such appreciation. In addition, the frozen interest provides a means for reducing the valuation controversy that often results whenever an estate is under review by the IRS.

A final advantage of the frozen family partnership is that it provides a way to avoid the 9 percent or higher interest payments required by the IRS for installment sales and the 6 percent minimum interest required by the IRS's annuity tables for a private annuity. A frozen family partnership permits the transfer of assets for future appreciation with a minimum preferred dividend computed on the value of the equity transferred.

Any property which has a potential for real and inflated appreciation is ideal for a contribution to a frozen partnership.

SHIFTING OPPORTUNITIES AND HELP TO YOUR FAMILY

All estate-freezing techniques need not be highly technical. Any approach whereby a wealthy individual can divert an income- or equity-generating opportunity to the next generation may have the same effect. Where a taxpayer is active in business or investing, opportunities for bringing the next-generation heirs into a profitable activity occur with regularity. The problem seems to be making the taxpayer conscious of the timing for the employment of such a technique and therefore not waiting until the asset is of such substantial value that any estate-freezing techniques will accomplish very little benefit.

Estate shifting could be accomplished by examining closely an existing business enterprise with the objective of finding one or more collateral activities which could be utilized more properly through a separate business entity, preferably a partnership, the owners of which would be the next-generation heirs of the taxpayer.

For example, assume you own a real-estate business which generates numerous clients requiring loans for primary and secondary real-estate financing. Collateral sources of income materialize in the form of brokerage fees. If you were to set up a partnership with your children in which they, by direct investment, became the major owners, the partnership enterprise could, by representing various institutions and noninstitutionalized lenders, derive fees and commissions and render a valuable service. The profits generated by the partnership after all overhead expense would be payable to the beneficiaries of the partnership—namely, your children. It would also possibly have the effect of providing a business vehicle to stimulate the children's interest in learning something about finance, real-estate appraising, and so on.

Here's another example. Let's say you acquired, historically, stock for the cost of $5,000. The stock now has a fair market value of $360,000 but is not considered as marketable securities. You have several children, one of whom has a dominant interest in photography and another who is aggressively interested in a career in computer programming. The stock pays no dividends and, in fact, generates no economic benefit to you at all but can be sold for $360,000. If you are in a substantially high earnings bracket, it would not be prudent for you to sell the stock directly for cash. What you decide to do is to establish an irrevocable trust with an independent trustee, in this case your certified public accountant, wherein the *income beneficiaries* are your six children and certain nieces and nephews to whom you have an interest in rendering financial assistance for education purposes. The *principal beneficiaries* might comprise an entirely different class, in this case your children only. Following the establishment of the trust and funding the same with a small amount of cash under the amount of the gift exclusions, you now enter into an installment sale of the stock for $360,000. The down payment is $1,000 and you receive back a $359,000 note. Terms of the note require no interest to be paid for the first three years and, thereafter, amortized annual installments including interest at 9 percent for a period of ten years.

Upon receipt of the stock, the trustee has an asset which was purchased for $360,000 and which now can be sold back to the issuing corporation for approximately the same price.* The sale is consummated for cash, and the trustee now has $360,000. Assuming the trust operates on a fiscal year ending June 30, on or before the ending of the next fiscal year the trustee can distribute any taxable income to one or more of the beneficiaries of the trust. The effect of the distribution is to shift the tax liability for payment from the trust, which is a single-person taxpayer, to one or more of your children or nieces and nephews, who themselves probably have no other income. The net result is that each beneficiary can receive $1,000 of passive income tax-free and pay only 14-percent federal tax on additional amounts received up to $3,400.

Now let's apply your special objectives as they relate to one or more of your children. The trustee is holding $360,000. This represents investment capital, and the trustee has total and absolute discretion as to how the funds are invested, as long as the investment meets a standard of prudence. You establish a family limited partnership, with yourself as general partner, and seek out two unrelated business opportunities, one in the field of photography or picture art, and the other in the field of computer software development or programming. Having found what looks like a fair investment opportunity, you then proceed to raise investment capital and enter into negotiations to acquire the businesses. The trustee can become a limited partner by making a substantial investment.

The son who has the interest in photography could be given $6,000 in cash, excluded from gift-tax reporting, by you and your wife. Your son could then make a direct cash investment in the family partnership. Other children might also become partners at your choice. The major amount of required cash, however, will be invested by the trustee of the irrevocable trust, who will become a significant limited partner. Thereafter, the partnership could operate with you as one of the general partners. The son whose dominant interest is in photography could also be a general partner.

When the profits are received, the lion's share will be distributed to the trust established for the benefit of all the children and the son who made a direct investment in the partnership, thus shifting the income-tax benefits to next-generation beneficiaries and, at the same time, using existing capital from an asset previously owned by you to assist with the vocational development of one of your children.

---

*Under the new installment sale law, the trustee would have to hold the shares for two years before reselling them to avoid paying an accelerated capital gains tax.

A similar family partnership would be created to engage in the business of computer software or programming, using the special talent of the son who is interested in that field. The possibilities for this kind of asset development become endless, limited only by your imagination. It is not only possible, but frequently the case, that parents can direct business to a new corporation owned by their children. They help it out with consigned inventory supported with experience in numerous ways and, in many instances, actually serve as officers and/or directors of the company, drawing only modest salaries.

The common factor in this technique is the transfer to your children of resources which are not subject to gift taxes. Because this strategy also has income-tax-avoidance implications, the income-tax law has some provisions which must be understood. If the salary you take from the business enterprise owned by the children is one which is considered grossly inadequate, the IRS may reallocate some of the profits to you. If the IRS does this, you, as the parent, will be taxed on the income only; you owe no additional gift or estate taxes.

Timing is the great equalizer. It is everything when it comes to making a transfer of a business interest or an idea for a business interest from one generation to the next. Having the sense to let go and make the transfer is a must. A taxpayer who simply wants to possess, in the conventional sense, the entire company and its future growth misses a great opportunity for estate freezing.

One such taxpayer has a large corporation which engages in the sale of industrial products with a pretax annual net of between $1 million and $2 million. Needless to say, his estate value comprising the majority of the stock would be between $6 million and $8 million, depending on the particular evaluation approach taken. It can easily be seen from the federal estate tax chart in chapter 6 that if such a single taxpayer dies after 1980, the amount of federal estate tax will be phenomenal, between $3,203,800 and $4,603,800.

The same taxpayer is a very intense and successful developer of new enterprises and has other ideas. It might appear that he has the Midas touch for creating successful businesses, since he regularly plunges into new company ideas. Business number two, after two to three years of operation, is now making a pretax net profit of $500,000. The value of this enterprise at the time of start-up, had it been transferred in whole or in part to the next generation, would have been less than $500,000. Its value today, for purposes of the same transfer, would be between $2 million and $3 million.

Future growth might be predicted at 30 percent per year based on experience. Yet the taxpayer refuses to relinquish the necessary controls or undergo the necessary planning—however simple or complex—in order to avoid a heavy tax burden at the time of death.

INTEREST-FREE LOANS

You may want to consider making interest-free loans to your children before completing any transfers. While there is continued uncertainty as to how long this estate-planning vehicle will be available, you can at this time pass benefits to your children without gift-tax consequences. A case recently tested in court involved trusts created for children and other relatives. The loans were made for the purpose of enabling the trusts to invest in limited partnerships. The loans were payable on demand and interest-free. In its decision, the court recognized that there were certain policy considerations for taxing interest-free loans as gifts but concluded that there had not been a transfer of property within the reach of the gift-tax provisions, as currently enacted, and left such enactment to Congress rather than the courts.

So long as the loan is enforceable and payable upon demand, it can be interest-free. The making of such a loan prior to sales of stock, etc., may avoid the argument of a *step transaction*—that is, the fusion of separate transactions into one, or vice versa, to determine the tax consequences of a transaction. The loans need not be secured, as we are assuming that the children are reliable and will not dissipate the money.

You may want to suggest to your children that the loan proceeds be kept in highly liquid investments. By keeping excess monies in relatively liquid investments, the children will have money available to repay their loans, in whole or in part, as you, the parent, derive a need for extra cash or as the personal representative of your estate requires for the payment of death taxes. In addition, a change in the law in this rapidly developing field may require repayment of the loans.

The major reasons for having this money in the children's names are:

1. Allowing the children, at low income-tax brackets, to realize the income from investments. Such investments in your hands would be taxed at the maximum rates and the net would be accumulated and added to their estates.
2. Even if invested in tax-free municipal bonds, the income is another additive to your estate. For example, if you keep $500,000 invested

in tax-exempt municipal bonds that have a 5-percent yield, it will add $25,000 per year to your estate.
3. The children will have assets on hand in the event they purchase stock from your or participate in a family partnership where capital is required.

The obvious disadvantages are:

1. The risk of possible gift-tax implications.
2. The relinquishment of the use of the funds and the potential income from those funds.
3. The risk the IRS will try to tax the income to you instead of to your children.
4. Certain unknown risks which may become significant in the event of new legislation or regulations.

Now let's go on to the idea of creating instant tax-exempt wealth for your family. There's a great deal of wealth to be made, wealth that can completely escape both your estate and any possible taxes.

12

How You Can Create Tax-Exempt Wealth

There is no wealth but life.

—John Ruskin

"Do you own any life insurance?"

If your answer is "Yes," you're in trouble. Why? Look at the question again. The key word is *own*. I'm not against life insurance. Far from it. Life insurance can be an essential ingredient in many estate plans. But you shouldn't own it.

There's a very simple rule involved here. When the owner of a life insurance policy dies, if he or she is listed on the policy contract as the owner and has paid the premiums—then even though the spouse and children are listed as the beneficiaries, the tax man shares in the policy proceeds.

If the estate is large enough to be subjected to, say, a 35-percent death tax and the policy is for $100,000, a good chunk of money, $35,000, without a marital deduction, is immediately handed over to the IRS rather than going to the intended beneficiaries. With a marital deduction, the taxable amount would be only $50,000 and the tax liability thus reduced to $17,500. Even that, however, is much more than you need to pay. So don't get caught in this trap.

Any incident of ownership will subject your life insurance to being included as part of your estate. You don't even have to be the registered owner. If you personally have the right to borrow against the life insurance, or the right to change beneficiaries, or even if the policy is held in a trust which you have the right to alter, or over which you have some other power, you have an incident of ownership.

So what can you do about it if you already own some life insurance? You can do something very simple. You can change the ownership and have someone else pay the premiums. Make your spouse the owner, for instance, and have him or her pay the premiums. You can do this even if your spouse doesn't have any income, by giving him or her the money each year.

To really keep the life-insurance ownership at arm's length, you must make sure that such gifts meet certain conditions. Let's say the premiums are $211.63 quarterly, for instance, and the next payment is due tomorrow. Don't sit down and write your spouse a check for $211.63 today. If you do, the IRS may conclude that he or she is merely your "agent" for the purpose of receiving the benefits and may decide to tax the insurance proceeds. Instead, annually or semiannually, give your spouse an amount larger by at least 10 percent than the premiums due for that period, and time your gifts so that they are completely out of sync with the insurance-premium bills. Your spouse should have a separate bank account in his or her name only, to receive these gifts. In addition, you should draw up a formal document to the effect that any money you deposit in that account is an outright no-strings-attached gift.

The same type of arrangement works with your children, In fact, under the annual gift-tax exclusion of $10,000 per individual, a considerable estate, instant and tax-free, can be built up for the whole family. That's the reason why life insurance may well be the most significant way—and it's certainly the most common way—to create tax-exempt wealth for a family's future. Check you policy. Don't let the technicality of ownership feed the IRS instead of your family.

If you do own life insurance, or have an incident of ownership in it, you should put this book down, call your agent, and consider getting rid of it at once.

LIFE INSURANCE CAN CREATE TAX-EXEMPT WEALTH

All right, now that you've disposed of one major estate problem, let's take a closer look at the role life insurance plays in creating tax-exempt wealth. There are many advantages to life insurance, and of course there are some significant disadvantages as well. However, there's a way around the disadvantages, and that's—you guessed it—a trust. But it's a rather different trust from the one we discussed before.

Life insurance serves two important purposes in the average estate plan. First, it assures your family that economically, at least, they could continue to live as they are doing now if you were to die. There's an infallible "law" to the effect that a family's life-style rises to meet its income. If your family was perfectly content and happy when your income was $20,000 a year, it's equally content and happy now if your income is $40,000 a year. Of course, this supposition sounds the optimistic note that your purchasing power, not inflation, has doubled.

But the chances are that your family could not sustain this level of life if your earnings were suddenly to cease. And if you're like most Americans, you probably haven't built up enough assets in your estate to generate a cash flow capable of supporting your family's dependency on the higher income. Hence the need for life insurance.

The primary focus of life insurance, then, is strictly as income replacement, not as an investment. There are no bargains in insurance. Insurance companies are in business to make a profit. When you go through the razzmatazz of a ten- or fifteen- or twenty-year projection showing what life insurance can do for you, and you decide you'd be making a great investment by buying it, you need to reevaluate your thinking.

Buy your life insurance as though you were going to die today. If you happen to be relatively young with more than two or three young children, income replacement should be a very major focus for you. What we're talking about is creating money that is going to support a life-style. So, for example, if you have a choice between buying a $25,000 whole-life policy that acts as a savings program as well as insurance and using the same premium dollars to buy $250,000 worth of term insurance, buy the term insurance. You'll get many more dollars' worth of coverage.

LIFE INSURANCE LIQUIDITY

The second purpose of life insurance is to provide estate liquidity. Real estate and other tangible property can make for a formidable estate. But if your earnings were to stop suddenly, what would your family use to sustain itself during the many months it might take to liquidate those assets at a reasonable price? Again, life insurance may be the answer for your family, although, as I will show you, there are other, less expensive ways to assure this liquidity.

THE WRONG LIFE INSURANCE

There is a third objective which people often use life insurance for—as a savings base for retirement. This is absolutely *wrong* thinking. In two words, forget it. Cash-value life insurance, which accumulates capital over the years, is not a good investment in inflationary times. You get fewer insurance dollars for your money. Trying to build up cash-value life insurance during double-digit inflation is like importing ice to the Sahara in order to build an igloo. The blueprints may look fine, but the end result vanishes even as you're trying to complete the project.

Remember, all insurance is pure protection—term insurance, in other words. Whole-life, or cash-value, insurance simply adds a savings account to the term. Would you try to build up your wealth by socking away a lot of money in a 5-percent savings account? Just think about that.

Life insurance is for dying. Investment is for living. Never combine the two.

INSURE YOURSELF

Use your accumulations to eventually become self-insured. Use term insurance when you need it. It's not for the rest of your life. It's only for the interim, until you are able to replace income by savings and investments.

If you are a candidate for a tax-deferred self-trustee pension plan, for instance, that is one means of creating tax-exempt wealth which usually is very, very liquid. Such a pension plan can be used in many ways to provide tax avoidance for your estate, as you will see in Chapter 17, The Ultimate Tax Shelter.

By now you should be sold on life insurance as at least a temporary part of your estate plan. And you should have eliminated any possibility of an incidental-ownership tax problem. Let's take our reasoning one step further. Let's look at a worst-case situation.

Both husband and wife in our hypothetical case are killed in a California freeway accident—unfortunately not an unusual occurrence, given the multiple collisons and freak accidents for which this fabled highway system is infamous. The wife, however, does not die instantly. She survives her husband by a couple of weeks—long enough to get that $100,000 life-insurance check. She doesn't even have to collect it physically. As long as the husband predeceases her, she is construed by law as having received the money. And if she is construed as having received the money, it naturally all passes through her estate. Never mind that she had no economic advantage from the money. The IRS may still tax it—and heavily—before it passes on to the children.

Is there any way such a situation can be avoided? After all, in many cases we're talking about $300,000 or $400,000 or more, because life insurance is the quickest way to build up a large estate. It is particularly so for the early-middle-aged executive, the self-employed individual, the professional person, and others in occupations where the middle years mark the beginning of a high earnings level and subsequent high living standards. This is a time when earnings may be high, but actual estate building has just begun.

THE ANCESTOR TRUST

The way to route insurance benefits around the inheritance roadblock of death taxes is an ancestor trust. The name *ancestor trust* is actually a descriptive generic name, originated in my offices, for an irrevocable life-insurance trust. One of the key advantages of this type of trust—especially in unstable economic times—is that it provides liquidity to your estate.

To refute the old maxim that the shoemaker's children always go barefoot, I'll use an example from my own life in explaining the concept. But before I start, please note that this simple trust arrangement could work in various situations—a single parent with several children, a husband and wife with minor children, or with adult children, or with no children but with a special bequest in mind, and so on. Various people could play the roles I have assigned to members of my family.

I have a son who is over the age of eighteen, so I designated him to create the life-insurance trust I had in mind. He became the grantor of an irrevocable trust. And he named himself as trustee. I have no connection with that trust. I am neither the grantor nor the trustee nor the beneficiary. I have nothing to do with it. From time to time, I transfer, no strings attached, some cash to my son as trustee. And, of course, if he doesn't do as I say, I'll disinherit him. But there are no strings attached to that trust.

My son established the trust, and then he made application on my life for a $500,000 life-insurance policy, which in due course he received. Note that I am neither the applicant nor the owner nor the beneficiary of the policy. My only function is that I am the warm body which is being insured.

My son is the owner of the policy. As trustee, he is also the beneficiary. When I die, he will receive a check for $500,000, and he will manage that money in accordance with his instructions in the trust, which are to support and give income and sustenance to his mother, the surviving beneficiary.

She would have the economic use of that $500,000. But at her subsequent death, whether it were a month or a decade later, the assets of the ancestor trust would be exempt from tax, because she has neither ownership nor control of them.

After her death, my son will distribute the balance held to the remainder beneficiaries, his brothers and sisters, according to the instructions in the trust.

One of my objectives in having this trust set up was to provide some equity—that is, cash—to pay death taxes on the other assets I haven't been able to dispose of. I have a revocable family living trust, and the assets I have are all in that trust. I am the manager, and if I die, my wife will be the next manager.

But there's not much cash in this trust. We keep fully invested so there's not much money available with which to pay taxes.

However, my wife, as successor trustee, can borrow money from her oldest son, who manages this other trust, the ancestor trust with the $500,000 in it. So there can be an arm's-length borrowing of money.

Better yet, if she is holding in the family trust some asset, such as an oil lease next to property where oil has just been discovered, which looks as though it's going to take off and become valuable, and we don't want it to be taxed when she dies, why not sell it to the ancestor trust? She would have the cash paid for it. As the beneficiary, she would have the use of it as well. And when she dies, this highly appreciated asset would pass tax-free to our children. They would get all the inflation-fattened dollars. The IRS would get nothing. She has really used inflation to beat the IRS.

That's the technique used to its fullest capacity.

Ancestor Trust

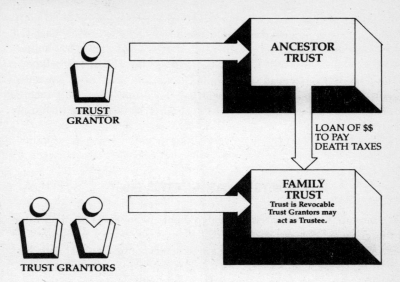

TRUST GRANTOR

ANCESTOR TRUST

LOAN OF $$ TO PAY DEATH TAXES

TRUST GRANTORS

FAMILY TRUST
Trust is Revocable
Trust Grantors may
act as Trustee.

1. Trust Grantor cannot be the insured
but may be an adult child of the insured.

2. The Trustee of the Trust can be a child
or children of the insured (Ancestor).

3. The Trustee is to be Owner and Beneficiary of
the Life Insurance on the life of the "Ancestor."

4. Upon the death of the insured (Ancestor)
the Trustee of the Ancestor's Trust will
receive the proceeds of the life insurance policy.
These funds may then be loaned to the Trustee of
the Family Trust for payment of various death taxes
and other costs or, in the alternative, these funds
may be used to purchase from the Family Trust
various assets with the money, when received by
the Family Trust, used for payment of death
taxes and other expenses.

5. Thereafter, the Trustee of the Ancestor's Trust can
be given the duty to support the surviving spouse
and, at the surviving spouse's death, to hold the
remainder of assets or to distribute such assets to
or for the benefit of the children or other beneficiaries
of the Ancestor.

YOU DON'T NEED MONEY TO SET UP AN ANCESTOR TRUST

One unique quality of an ancestor trust is that it's usually unfunded. Ordinarily, there is no actual money in the trust, nor are there any salable assets. Specific dispositive "what to do with the money" provisions cover the trust while you're still living. They concern the acquisition of life insurance and the payment of premiums thereon. Now there are other dispositive provisions to be made regarding the ultimate distribution of the trust's assets. These will need to be tailored to your specific family situation.

FIVE KEYS TO YOUR ANCESTOR TRUST

Let's sum up the basic provisions which should be included in an ancestor-trust agreement. These provisions will provide you with a framework for your planning. But remember, they are structural only. Don't let them hem you in, for the technique we are discussing is capable of wide variation.

(1) **The trustee should be authorized to purchase life insurance on the life of the ancestor.** It is imperative that only a new insurance policy, issued directly to the trust as original applicant, be acquired by the trustee. If an existing policy were to be transferred, the IRS would assert twin theories seeking to tax the proceeds. It would assert that the transfer was "in contemplation of death" and/or that the ancestor trust was the "agent" for the insured in providing for postdeath planning.

(2) **The trustee should be authorized to accept additions to the trust from any source acceptable to the trustee.** These additions are necessary to provide for premium payments.

(3) **The trust should contain a provision which will operate to qualify additions to the trust as gifts of present interests**, so they will qualify for the $10,000 annual exclusion from gift tax. Ordinarily, a gift in trust would not so qualify. However, where a beneficiary has the right to withdraw the addition, the gift of an addition to the trust will qualify for the gift-tax annual exclusion. So the trust should provide that whenever an addition is made to the trust, it is subject to withdrawal by a designated beneficiary or

beneficiaries. The right of withdrawal should be exercisable over some period of time, at the end of which it will lapse if not exercised. (For a sample clause that will accomplish this, see the Crummy clause in Appendix E.) Additions and premium payments should be staggered so that the trustee does indeed have property on hand during the period the withdrawal right may be exercised.

(4) **The trust should not terminate until a year or two after the ancestor's death** so that postdeath planning can be made with the trust fund intact.

(5) **Under express provisions in the trust agreement, following the ancestor's death, the trustee of the ancestor trust should be authorized to purchase assets at fair market value from the fiduciary of the ancestor's probate estate or from the trustee of the ancestor's revocable living trust, as well as to lend money to those fiduciaries, on agreed terms and conditions.** This fulfills the primary purpose of the trust, which is to provide liquidity to the ancestor's estate. The trustee of the ancestor trust should be authorized to enter into those transactions even though he or she may occupy dual fiduciary positions or a position as both fiduciary and beneficiary.

MAKING INSURANCE PREMIUMS TAX DEDUCTIBLE

If you own a family business, one way to fund your children's payment of the ancestor-trust insurance premiums is to put your children to work. In order to be on the payroll, however, they must perform legitimate services to the business, even if their task is only sweeping floors.

The business can deduct the cost of the children's wages. Thus, in a roundabout manner, the premiums are deductible. At the same time, the $10,000 annual gift-tax exclusion is left intact for other uses in case they arise. As a final psychological factor, there's something satisfying to both the "ancestor" and the children in some actual work being done for the benefits accrued.

A second way to fund the trust would be to transfer an income-producing asset to it. As a separate taxpayer, the trust will pay a much lower rate of income tax than you would, so there is a substantial tax saving in this maneuver.

TERMINATING AN IRREVOCABLE ANCESTOR TRUST

Although an ancestor trust is irrevocable, it can be readily terminated. Really it can. If conditions change and you no longer need an underlying term-insurance policy, all you have to do is to let the insurance policy lapse. Then, since the policy is the only asset of the trust, the trust ceases to exist.

On the other side of the coin, you, as the ancestor, cannot really disinherit an offspring trustee completely. Should there be a permanent separation between the two of you, as sometimes happens, there is nothing to keep the trustee from continuing to pay the insurance premiums if able to do so. As much as, wisely or foolishly, a parent may wish to cut a child off "without a penny," it can't be done.

SUMMING UP THE ANCESTOR TRUST

Properly structured, an ancestor trust coupled with the payment of premiums by annual gift-tax exclusion transfers from the ancestor can help you, as the ancestor, to do the following:

1. Reduce or stabilize the value of your gross estate, keeping death taxes and estate shrinkage to a minimum.
2. Provide your estate with adequate liquidity from the insurance proceeds to meet the death tax burden.
3. Have your prospective beneficiaries participate in the program, either as administrators and/or directly from their earnings.
4. Provide that the insurance proceeds, which are not includable in your gross estate, will, to the extent that they are not used to meet death-tax liabilities, be distributable to your beneficiaries as full or partial offset for the estate shrinkage caused by the death taxes.
5. Use inflation to beat the IRS.

CREATING TAX-EXEMPT WEALTH WITH A PRIVATE PENSION PLAN

Probably the best way to build tax-exempt wealth, for many people, is their own private pension plan. With such a plan, you are allowed to deposit before-tax dollars that can grow and grow for decades unimpeded by the tax man. Not only does the plan build up a tax-free capital base over the years but all its assets can be passed on to others without any estate taxes. In chapter 17 I'll show you all the little-known ins and outs of such a plan, that produces benefits often overlooked even by persons who have had these plans for years.

CATCH-79

Under Section 79 of the Internal Revenue Code, you may have your employer, in effect, pay your children. The catch is that the plan only works for corporate executives.

Usually, corporate executives are the beneficiaries of large amounts of employer-funded group term insurance as part of the fringe benefit package. With today's inflated dollar, it is not unusual for such insurance coverage to exceed half a million dollars for a well-paid executive. Even million-dollar policies are far from rare.

The ownership of this insurance is assignable. Children, other heirs, or trusts for their benefit can all be assigned the ownership. The proceeds are then excluded from the executive's estate.

In addition, no matter how high the premiums may become with the passing of time, no gift tax is involved. Since the executive is not paying the premiums on the insurance, these premiums aren't considered a gift from him, even though the continuation of premium payments is directly contingent upon his labors. On the higher scales of insurance coverage, some income-tax liabilities may be incurred by the executive. However, these possible liabilities are minor compared to the potential benefits of the nongift gift.

13

Lifetime Giving: A Family Solution to Your Tax Burden

Let him that desires to see others happy,
make haste to give while his gift can be enjoyed,
and remember that every moment of delay
takes away something from the value of his benefaction.
—SAMUEL JOHNSON

GIVING IT AWAY ISN'T WHAT IT USED TO BE

Since the Tax Reform Act of 1976, a number of very basic changes have occurred in gift planning. Since the Act equalized the estate and gift tax rates, and because the old $30,000 lifetime exemption was repealed and replaced by the unified gift tax credit (see chapter 6), the role of giving in tax avoidance has been radically altered. And the Economic Recovery Tax Act of 1981 has introduced even more changes.

But gifts to your family can still play a very important role in your overall financial planning. They are particularly valuable in keeping your estate from growing into the tax man's arms. So let's look at a gift the way the IRS does.

The IRS defines a gift as the "transfer by any person of property to the extent that the transferor does not receive in money or money's worth full and adequate consideration"—in other words, equal value. In addition, the law requires that the "intent" of the person making the gift, or donor, must be a specific and overt element of any transfer, since gifts can be reconstructed based on a variety of all the relevant facts and circumstances. The Internal Revenue Service can, after a review, conclude that a donor's intent in making a gift was really not to donate the gift at all but rather a motive of the donor as a taxpayer to avoid paying taxes.

That's how it all reads in legalese. In English, what it means is that the

IRS can call just about anything it wants to a gift unless there has been adequate payment, or "consideration," to you for whatever asset is involved.

Common examples of gifts are the transfer, without getting money or other valuables in return, of real estate, cash, stocks, and other personal property of significant value, such as jewelry, collectible items, paintings, gold, diamonds, silver, and so on.

Any of these assets may be transferred either directly to a recipient—a donee—or to an irrevocable trust in which the donor does not retain any "tainting" interest, but in both cases they will be considered gifts by the IRS. Even a transfer to a short-term trust constitutes a gift, in part, based on certain actuarial considerations. (Short-term trusts will be discussed in Chapter 18, Educating Your Children Tax Free.)

There are other gifts that are not so common, including forgiving debts, transferring property to joint-tenancy ownership or tenancy in common, and transferring property to a family partnership made up of other members of the family, or of assets to a corporation owned by others, or of ownership of stock in a closely held corporation. Assigning ownership in a life-insurance contract which has cash value to another, paying premiums under a life-insurance contract which is owned by someone other than the person paying the premiums, and making tax-free loans or otherwise permitting the use of property without adequate compensation or interest also constitute gifts, according to the IRS.

"Permitting the use of property without adequate compensation or interest" is a phrase covering a multitude of sins in the eyes of the IRS. High on the list of these transgressions are interest-free loans. Yet one very creative fellow who felt that an interest-free loan should be perfectly permissible went ahead and made one, ended up in tax court—which was to be expected under the circumstances—and won.

WHEN IS A GIFT NOT A GIFT?

Basically, what our enterprising taxpayer did was to transfer a lot of money—almost $2 million—to his children, taking back, in return, a non-interest-bearing demand note. The government attacked the transaction by saying, "Shoot, that's a gift. The kids don't have to pay back that money until you demand it, and you may never demand it. Your loan lacks substance. It really doesn't look like a debt or an arm's-length loan, especially since it doesn't bear interest." Nevertheless, the man won.

This particular case proves that it *is* possible to make an interest-free loan wihout paying a gift tax. More recently, however, the government has tried to attack the transaction by saying that any interest the $2 million earns for the children is a tax liability for the father. The whole plan, referred to as the Crown loan, is a bit of a gray area and is not likely to be cleared up for a few years yet.

Now a Crown loan to a responsible borrower for something like a college education is valid. However, it must involve a demand note and a reasonable expectation that you will indeed demand payment. Also, the loan must remain outstanding and subject to collection in order to avoid gift taxes. In addition, if the money earns interest for the loan recipient during the time it is out of your control, you may well be responsible for the income tax on that interest.

All in all, the Crown "interest-free" loan looks like an interesting proposition for future estate planning. Even though there is a question of who will be charged with tax on the income generated by the loaned assets, the chance of an audit appears to me to be slight. When the father loans money to his son interest-free with a demand note, there is no reason for him to report the transaction on his tax return. If the son deposits the money into an interest-bearing account, he will report the interest, and the IRS would, on the face of it, have no reason to ask where the income came from. On the other hand, if the matter is challenged by the IRS, you may have to stand up to a court challenge.

USING THE ANNUAL GIFT-TAX EXCLUSION

Since every taxpayer may transfer to any beneficiary $10,000 a year, to be excluded from reporting and, consequently, taxation under the gift-tax laws, a married taxpayer and his spouse may together transfer $20,000 to each beneficiary annually. So if a taxpayer's estate consists solely of assets that will not appreciate in value, embarking on an annualized gift-giving program can substantially reduce the estate over the ensuing years.*

Take, for example, the case of a husband and wife who have four children, eight grandchildren, and an accumulated estate of $2 million. Over a period of five years, the estate could be reduced to $800,000 simply by making the maximum annual gifts allowed to the twelve potential beneficiaries. Now if inflation happens to be running at 12 percent or less a year, the annual transfer of $240,000 would effectively keep the estate from

*Prior to 1982 the figures are $3,000 and $6,000 respectively.

growing. In other words, the goal of freezing the estate would be accomplished by this means alone.

The following table illustrates the effect of giving away $30,000 a year from a $500,000 estate for a period of ten years, with inflation at 10 percent a year.

DOUBLING UP THE EXCLUSION

A donor and his spouse can each claim half of a gift made to a third party. This device, known as *gift-tax splitting*, automatically doubles the annual gift allowance. The unusual feature of this gift-giving device is that the gift can be split regardless of who owns the property—this is automatically accomplished with a gift of community property.

For example, let's say a husband has $20,000 in cash in separate property which he gives to his son. His wife consents to join in the gift. He and his wife can split the gift so that each of them is able to take advantage of the $10,000 gift exclusion for the year, making the entire $20,000 gift tax-exempt.

CHANGES UNDER ERTA

In addition to increasing the annual exclusion from $3,000 to $10,000, the 1981 law made four important changes regarding gift taxes. First, there is no limit at all for gifts that are equal to the amount of tuition or medical expenses of the donee. The only requirement for this unlimited exclusion is that the money must be paid directly to a qualifying educational organization or health care provider.

Second, under the old law, all taxable gifts made within three years of a donor's death were included in the donor's gross estate. The new law repealed this three-year rule for outright transfers; it still applies, however, to transfers with retained life estates, revocable transfers, transfers taking effect at the death of the donor, powers of appointment, and gifts of life insurance.

Third, if a gift tax return is required (by reason of a gift in excess of $10,000), it is due, generally, on April 15 of the next calendar year.

Fourth, it is no longer possible to get a step-up in basis for property you give away, if you get it back upon the death of the donee and the gift was made less than a year before the donee died.

Fifth, and perhaps best of all, you can transfer an unlimited amount of property to your spouse without paying any gift taxes.

EFFECT OF ANNUAL $30,000 GIFT

Year One	Value	$500,000
	Gift	−30,000
	Remaining Value	470,000
	10% Appreciation	+47,000
Year Two		517,000
		−30,000
		487,000
		+48,700
Year Three		535,700
		−30,000
		505,700
		+50,570
Year Four		556,270
		−30,000
		526,270
		+52,627
Year Five		578,897
		−30,000
		548,897
		+54,890
Year Six		603,787
		−30,000
		573,787
		+57,379
Year Seven		631,166
		−30,000
		601,166
		+60,117
Year Eight		661,283
		−30,000
		631,283
		+63,128
Year Nine		694,441
		−30,000
		664,441
		+66,441
Year Ten		730,882
		−30,000
		700,882
		+70,088
Remaining Value of Estate		$770,970

GIFTS TO YOUR SPOUSE

That's right! Beginning in 1982, thanks to Auntie ERTA, you can transfer without any gift taxes an unlimited amount of your property to your spouse. The old law, however, created a quagmire of rules for gifts to your spouse. It sounds simple enough, but coordination with the estate tax rules is very tricky. And, unfortunately, the old law applies to any transfers made before 1982. Here's how the old rule works.

The first $100,000 of gifts made to a spouse is exempt from gift tax as a marital deduction. The second $100,000 of gifts receives no deduction. The third $100,000 is allowed the normal 50-percent marital deduction. Let's look at an example.

Assume a wife makes lifetime gifts to her husband of $175,000 after 1976 and before 1982. The first $100,000 of gifts qualifies for the marital deduction. Thereafter she dies, leaving an adjusted gross estate of $1 million, to which the maximum marital deduction of $500,000 is applied. This deduction will be reduced by the sum of $12,500 because of the lifetime gifts of $175,000 made by the decedent. The reduction amount ($12,500) is determined as the difference between the $100,000 of gift-tax marital deduction and one half of the total gifts made ($175,000), or $87,500.

Your strategy, then, if you calculate that your total transfers to your spouse will be less than $700,000, should be to coordinate the two deductions so that they total more than 50 percent of the transfers. The core of this tactic is to avoid any cut in the estate-tax deduction, so that the gift-tax deduction equals more than 50 percent of the gifts. The goal is lifetime gifts to the spouse of at least $200,000.

Suppose, as an example, you plan to give your wife $500,000. If you give her $200,000 during life and bequeath $300,000 in your will, the deductions will add up to $350,000, or 70 percent of the total transfers. If you give her only $100,000 during life, that amount will pass to her tax-free because of the gift-tax deduction, but only $200,000 of the remaining $400,000 bequest will be deductible. Thus the total marital deductions will add up to only $300,000, or 60 percent of the transfers to your wife. If you wait until death, the maximum estate-tax marital deduction will be $250,000, or 50 percent of the bequest.

GIVING STARTS WITH THE HOME

A common technique in tax planning, a way of reducing a husband's estate, especially in separate-property states, is to have him transfer his interest in the family residence, whether it's the total ownership, as in a separate-property state, or his half, in a community-property state, to his wife. The reasoning behind such a transfer is usually that if the wife is younger, or otherwise has a life expectancy longer than that of the husband, the husband will die first.

The Internal Revenue Code, Section 2036, has been interpreted as providing that when the property is transferred and the transferor—the husband, in this case—continues to retain the life use of the home, as established by the fact that he's still living there, the transfer will be considered ineffective for death-tax purposes and the value of the property at his death will continue to be part of his taxable estate.

The IRS has frequently litigated this question in an attempt to show that there was an agreement between the spouses that the transferor could continue to live in the home. But the IRS has lost most of the cases. So long as there is no written agreement allowing the donor spouse to live in the residence for the remainder of the marriage partners' joint life, this estate-planning tool remains a valuable one.

Where the family residence is transferred from parent to child with the parent or parents continuing to live in the house, it's much more likely that an implied agreement could be upheld by an IRS challenge. The result would be that the fair market value of the house at the transferor's death would be considered part of the gross estate for estate-tax purposes.

The way around this problem is for the parents to sell the house to a trust with the children as beneficiaries and then to lease it back.

ON THE CONTEMPLATION OF
INCOME TAX AND GIVING

One of the key considerations in planning a gift of property in order to reduce the taxable basis of an estate is a concept called the *stepped-up basis*. It's well worth illustrating, to see how it works.

Let's suppose that a man has a piece of property, perhaps a building lot, for which he paid $10,000. That amount becomes his *cost basis*, to borrow an income-tax term used in computing capital gains.

Now cost basis can be adjusted upward or downward. If the property is depreciated, the cost basis goes down as the asset is written off. If the lot is improved, by a septic system being put in, let's say, or some other work being done, then the cost basis is increased.

But suppose real-estate values in the area skyrocket and the owner decides to make no improvements on the property and sell it for the immediate profit. The lot brings in $100,000 cash. So he has an investment gain in the transaction of $90,000, the difference between his cost basis and the fair market value at which he's sold the lot. As a capital asset, if he kept that land for the required holding period—that is, twelve months—before he sold it, his profit would be taxed as capital gains.

Now let's assume something different. Let's assume he doesn't sell the lot, and he dies, leaving his wife a widow. From an estate-tax point of view, the property is subject to death tax at its fair market value, or $100,000. However, under Section 1014 of the Internal Revenue Code, the asset is also given a new stepped-up cost basis for income-tax purposes. The basis goes from $10,000 to $100,000, which is our value for death-tax purposes, and when the wife inherits the property, she has a new cost basis of $100,000. That means she could sell the lot for $100,000 cash and pay no income tax. Even if she sold it for $110,000, her taxable gain would be only $10,000, the difference between the stepped-up value and the price she received.

In community-property states, such as California, the stepped-up basis acquires even more importance. Suppose, for example, the $10,000 lot we're talking about is not the husband's separate property but rather community property. His half of the cost is $5,000, hers is $5,000. His half of the value is $50,000, hers $50,000. If they sold the property jointly for $100,000, each would have a $45,000 capital gain. However, what happens if just the husband dies before the property is sold? The basis of each share of the community property steps up from $5,000 to $50,000. His half has a stepped-up basis for tax purposes, which is to be expected, since it is transferred through his estate. But her half gets a stepped-up basis as well—a free ride, as it were.

If the same property were held in joint tenancy, the status of the tax law is such that the IRS would probably allow a new cost basis on his half of the property but not on hers. So, if a new basis is to be acquired on the entire estate, it has to be held as community property. A revocable trust can achieve this result simply by identifying the land as community property.

Now why should you be concerned about all this? Because when you have the choice of making a gift of property or letting property be inherited, the cost basis is going to be of considerable interest to you in terms of how and how much the property is taxed. Let's see why.

Suppose you have two pieces of land, parcel 1 and parcel 2. Since they are fairly equal in value and configuration, it really doesn't matter to you which one you give away to your family now and which one you hold onto until the time of your death. But you're going to give one to your children and let the other be inherited. Let's say the cost of parcel 1 was $10,000 and the cost of parcel 2, only recently acquired, was $90,000. The fair market value of each is $100,000. Here's the problem: Which parcel do you give as a gift and which one do you let be inherited?

Well, you want to give parcel 2 as a gift. And the reason is that when you give that one, your children will get a cost basis of $90,000. When they inherit the other one and get a new basis, their total basis will be $190,000. If you do it the other way around, the total basis will be only $110,000 and they end up with more income tax to pay on the ultimate sale of the property.

So the first rule in giving is to give away high-basis property or cash. It's the flip side of the trust coin. In establishing a trust, you usually want to use low-current-value, high-appreciation-potential assets for funding. To paraphrase an old Wall Street saying, Give high, trust low.

ERTA has a new provision which, before the new tax act was passed, could provide tax savings by gifting appreciated property to a terminally ill donee. Upon the donee's death the property was redistributed to the donor with a stepped-up basis equal to the property's fair market value. The original donor could then sell the property without any tax liability because the basis of the property was changed to its fair market value. ERTA simply provides that any property gifted by you which you reacquire within one full year from the date of your original gift will *not* receive a stepped-up basis.

GIVING THE FUTURE

A gift that can't be used right away, such as $10,000 given to a twelve-year-old daughter that she can't use until she is eighteen, may not really be a gift as far as the IRS is concerned, at least not when it comes to your availing yourself of the annual gift-tax exclusion. A *gift of future interest*, as such a bestowal is known, can pose a bit of a dilemma.

After all, giving a twelve-year-old that much money is an open invitation to the delivery to your home of truckloads of chewing gum or rock records. Your original intent, on the other hand, may have been to put the money aside for the child to use for a college education in the distant future.

One solution is the Uniform Gifts to Minors Act (UGMA). This act expressly allows you to make gifts which delay the full use and benefit of the property until a minor child comes of age. If the provisions of the act are actually complied with, transfers to a minor child will qualify for the annual gift exclusion.

The benefits of having a rich Uncle UGMA in the family will become apparent to you when you read chapter 18, Educating Your Children Tax-Free.

Another solution is to establish a trust where the beneficiary's use and enjoyment of the property may be deferred beyond age twenty-one and the trust includes provisions authorizing the beneficiary to withdraw up to $10,000 each year a gift is made to the trust (see Appendix E).

A QUESTION OF STATE

All the attractions and stumbling blocks of gift giving discussed here are on the federal tax level. However, many states have gift taxes of their own as well, and in some cases the state laws are at great variance with the parallel federal provisions. Before you make any gifts, check the state statutes to see what tax effect your gifts will have. It might prove worthwhile to change the type of property you use in your giving strategy.

14

Offshore Planning: Beware of the IRS Torpedo

Westerly weather to-night—
No need to explain that to an islander.

—ISLES OF ILLUSION

America has always been a nation of expanding frontiers. "Go west, young man" was an admonition followed by countless millions, even after the West had been won by freeways and fast-food franchisers, when the land, no longer cheap and readily available, had reached a stratospheric valuation no Easterner can comprehend.

Yet the yearning to go beyond is still there. The yearning to go beyond the IRS is also with most of us. So the tropical islands of the South Seas and the Caribbean call with a twin siren song of hidden beauty and sheltered wealth.

Breathes there a man or woman so meek as never to have dreamed of putting money offshore where the IRS couldn't touch it? Perhaps you've dreamed of following in person in later and wealthier years. Meanwhile, wouldn't an annual accounting be a tax-deductible vacation? Dream on. Those days are gone.

Currently the United States imposes income taxes on the worldwide income and estate and gift taxes on the worldwide assets of all persons who are either citizens or residents of the United States. To avoid U.S. taxes, you must not only move out of the United States permanently, you must give up your U.S. citizenship as well.

However, a trust is a separate entity altogether insofar as the IRS is concerned. What about establishing a trust abroad? If it's "born" there, certainly it can't be considered a citizen of the U.S.A. And if you move your assets to such a trust, with no intent of bringing the trust over to the United States, even for a visit, wouldn't the tax problem be solved?

THE GOOD OLD DAYS

A few years ago, before the passage of the Tax Reform Act of 1976 when the IRS torpedoed the whole concept of foreign trusts, the answer would have been yes. At that time, the establishment of a foreign trust offered substantial tax savings for Americans and their families. Now, this particular plan is almost worthless from a tax point of view, although there are still a few minor uses for an offshore trust.

Let's look at the offshore-trust concept for what it does *not* offer, simply because a lot of people are still touting this now-troublesome device. Under the law prior to the tax reform, a U.S. resident or citizen could create an irrevocable foreign trust with special provisions for the accumulation of income that would be viewed under U.S. law in the same manner as a nonresident foreigner. Since a nonresident alien generally pays no U.S. income or capital-gains tax on income from abroad, the theory was that if a new taxpayer, in the form of a trust, were created with its location outside of the United States—say, for instance, in the Grand Cayman Islands—this trust would be a nonresident alien. Its status would permit tax avoidance on any earnings the trust received and any capital gains, whether domestic to the Cayman Islands or foreign—for example, even income earned or generated in the United States. So by using a foreign-accumulation trust, American citizens could defer their U.S. taxes indefinitely until distribution was actually made to U.S. beneficiaries.

Although a gift tax might be due when the trust was established, as a rule, these foreign-accumulation trusts paid no income taxes anywhere in the world. Foreign or offshore trusts were widespread, and many United States taxpayers, with the proper technical planning and advice, built fortunes offshore. It was by far the best way to fly through the storm of inflation. After all, the trustee was permitted to invest and reinvest 100 percent of every dollar earned. The compounding return worked to its fullest, unhindered by any shrinkage from taxation.

Because the tax advantages were widely known, promoted, and, in many respects, flaunted by tax practitioners, in 1974 Congress began the study which culminated in the Tax Reform Act of 1976. This act slammed the door of opportunity on U.S. citizens and residents as far as foreign trusts went. The restrictive provisions now in effect can be summarized as follows:

1. An excise tax of 35 percent is levied on the transfer of appreciated property to a foreign trust.

2. Any accumulated capital gains in a foreign trust distributed to United States beneficiaries and not otherwise taxed to the United States grantor of the trust are treated as ordinary income. So you are actually taxed at a higher rate than if you left the money at home!

3. A nondeductible 6-percent interest charge on taxes due is imposed for every year money has been collecting in a foreign accumulation trust if the money has not been previously taxed to the grantor. This so-called throwback provision applies to the distribution of post-1976 accumulations from even a pre-1974 foreign trust.

4. Finally—and here's the real disaster—as a U.S. grantor of a foreign trust with one or more U.S. beneficiaries, you continue to be taxed on the foreign-trust income for the rest of your life, just as though you still owned the assets of the trust. This ruling applies not only to trusts where the document clearly identifies the grantor as a U.S. citizen but to trusts where you get an accommodation grantor, a foreign citizen whose only role is that of a nominal grantor. An additional trap is that the grantor is taxed on all the income of the trust if it's so much as conceivable that the trust could ever have a U.S. beneficiary.

In other words, foreign trusts have truly become untrustworthy for the American taxpayer.

THE LIMITED ADVANTAGES OF FOREIGN TRUSTS

"But you did say there were a few advantages to foreign trusts!" Well, there are, although these benefits are limited to very special situations. If your family circumstances happen to fall within the narrow range of still-useful tax-avoidance plans permitted under the new law, check the bibliography at the end of this book for titles you may find helpful.

For now, here is a list of the remaining legal uses of offshore trusts and some of their advantages:

1. A foreign grantor can still create a trust entirely for foreign beneficiaries. For example, a U.S. citizen married to someone who is a citizen of a foreign country may wish, for various reasons, to have the foreign spouse establish an ongoing benefit for other foreign citizens.

2. A U.S. grantor can still create a foreign trust for foreign beneficiaries none of whom are likely ever to become U.S. residents or citizens.

3. A truly bona-fide foreign grantor such as a grandmother, parent, or other relative—but not an accommodation grantor—can create a trust for U.S. beneficiaries. In this case, many authorities would choose a grantor trust which is currently taxable to the foreign grantor. Otherwise the accumulation trust would be subject to the throwback rules when it was distributed to the U.S. beneficiaries. U.S. taxes might consume most of the income compounded in the trust.

4. A nonresident alien who is planning to become a U.S. resident, not necessarily a U.S. citizen, can create a foreign-accumulation trust with the specific provision that the beneficiaries will not be U.S. citizens at the time they receive a distribution from the trust.

There are a few even more arcane uses for foreign-accumulation trusts that perhaps one person in a million might take advantage of, though even that person could probably find a better solution to his tax problems than offshore trusts. So when you hear about the various offshore tax schemes still being promoted, beware of the fact that they may involve not tax *avoidance* but tax *evasion*, which is against the law. Remember, tax avoidance saves you money. Tax evasion saves you money as well, but that's only because the room and board in jail are free.

SHOULD YOU BECOME AN EXPATRIATE?

What about moving out of the country altogether to escape the burden of onerous taxes? Now that's a distinct possibility. If you renounce your citizenship and never return to the United States as a resident, you will no longer be liable for U.S. taxes. Neither will you need this book any longer. You'll probably need a whole new library like it, though, to familiarize yourself with the tax laws of your new home. But don't count on the IRS's totally forgetting about you if you become a citizen of another country. The IRS can and does follow you to collect taxes on certain kinds of transactions connected with the United States. Let's take an example.

Suppose you have a small incorporated business which is now worth $1 million. Your cost for the stock, however, is only $75,000, and you are faced with a capital-gains tax on the equity when you sell it for cash. Thinking about the problem, you decide to become an expatriate. You relinquish your U.S. citizenship and move to Georgetown, Grand Cayman, in the Caribbean. Then you sell your business. Can the IRS tax you on the gain now that you are no longer a U.S. citizen or resident? The answer is probably yes. The only fail-safe solution to your dilemma is to choose a country that has a favorable tax treaty with the United States. In our example, the best choice, in order to avoid any tax on the sale of the business, would be Canada. Even though Canada is not a tax-haven country, under current Canadian law, a person becoming a new citizen there receives a stepped-up cost basis on all worldwide assets. Hence the basis of your stock would be adjusted under Canadian law from $100,000 to $1 million. When the business was sold, there would be no Canadian tax to pay. And because the United States and Canada have, in effect, an appropriate tax treaty, there would be no U.S. tax to pay.

CHECKING THE BOX ON YOUR 1040

A number of U.S. citizens with foreign bank accounts do not answer the question on their Form 1040 regarding such accounts. In a recent Congressional hearing, the director of the IRS was asked what the service does when a taxpayer fails to answer the question regarding a foreign bank account. His answer? "Nothing." In 1979, thirty-eight million taxpayers did not answer the question. Now what happens when a taxpayer in fact has a foreign bank account and answers the question with a no instead? He or she can be subject to fines and imprisonment.

You may be familiar with IRS efforts to look for U.S. citizens who have offshore bank accounts they're not paying taxes on. In the Caribbean, these IRS searches are known as "Operation Tradewind" and "Project Haven." The extent to which the IRS will go to obtain vital information on cheating taxpayers can be illustrated by an actual case.

A taxpayer residing in the Midwest maintained a bank account in a Caribbean bank. He did not report the existence of the account, and he checked the fatal box on his 1040 with a no.

A banker from the offshore bank where our taxpayer had his account frequently came to the United States to meet with bankers here on mutually beneficial banking business. Now the IRS had good reason to believe this offshore banker kept lists of United States taxpayers maintaining offshore accounts in his briefcase. So the IRS set the offshore banker up by arranging for him to date a certain young lady in Miami. During a dinner date, and with the permission of the young lady, an IRS agent went into her apartment, opened the briefcase, and, with a high-speed camera, photographed the contents. The contents included a list containing the name of our ill-fated taxpayer.

Three years later the taxpayer was indicted, tried, and convicted for criminal tax evasion. His appeal to the U.S. Supreme Court was heard during the spring of 1980 on the question of whether the information in the briefcase was unlawfully obtained and therefore inadmissible as evidence. For without such evidence, our taxpayer could not have been convicted. The result? The conviction was upheld. Taxpayers, beware.

TEMPORARY EXPATRIATES

A foreign assignment used to be the fast track to adventure and prosperity. Now it's more like a boring way station on the poverty route. With all the tax changes amplifying the dollar's declining international worth, a job abroad is more a hardship case than a means of accumulating capital.

If you are offered a chance to join some of the 1.5 million Americans working abroad, and the opportunity seems too good to resist, it probably isn't. Look closely at what you'll end up with. A $30,000-a-year construction engineer, for instance, needs roughly $100,000 a year in salary, housing, and education funds merely to stay even if he is assigned to the Middle East.

The United States is the only major industrial nation that taxes its citizens on salaries received abroad. There's the crux of the problem. With the higher salary needed to maintain your present standards abroad, you're automatically pushed into one of the highest tax brackets.

It's not only salary that the IRS nails you for when you're abroad. Unlike fringe benefits at home, which for the most part are not taxed, all those compensatory company payments for schooling, housing, and so on are chewed over by the IRS as ordinary income. International Telephone and Telegraph estimates that a foreign-based executive earning $40,000 annually may actually have to pay income taxes on $95,000 of gross income. That increases his tax liability by $33,000. Overall, almost his entire salary goes to Uncle Sam. He could probably save more by serving five to ten years in the penitentiary than he can being employed overseas.

Many companies pay the additional income-tax burden on top of the salary and perquisites. But that, according to the IRS, means more income, so these benefits are taxed yet again.

There is some hope for changes in these inequitable tax laws. But when those changes might occur and what they might actually be remain uncertain as of this writing. Right now, it looks as if there are precious few legal financial advantages in locating either your capital or yourself abroad. Better stay home and raise tax shelters.

15

Tax Shelters—Putting the Brakes on Inflationary Creep and Then Some

Beware of promoters bearing tax-shelter gifts in December.
—ANON.

If tax shelters were once only for the rich, inflation has now made them an economic necessity in the financial planning of millions of middle-income Americans. People who before were in tax brackets just high enough to be painful but not high enough to afford any remedy for the pain suddenly found that inflation was accelerating them into the stratosphere of the upper tax brackets. Their real earnings, in terms of buying power, had increased. But the take of the tax man had increased proportionately more. **Because of inflation, nearly one quarter of all the people in America are in a tax bracket high enough that they not only can but should use a tax shelter.**

The basic rule of thumb has always been that you should be in at least the 50-percent tax bracket before you even consider tax shelters. However, taxpayers in a lower bracket can take a smaller piece of the action and reap many benefits from a shelter. One of the reasons is that as bracket creep pushes you ever higher on the tax schedules, your marginal tax rate increases steeply. A married taxpayer earning $30,000 in 1982, for instance, pays $5,607, or 19 percent, in taxes. That's the average rate, 19 percent. On subsequent dollars, this taxpayer pays 33 percent. That's the marginal rate. The margin is where the income steps over from one tax bracket to the next one higher up. Of the $5,607 in taxes paid by our taxpayer, $33 is due from the last $100 earned. The answer is to shelter as much as possible of the marginal-tax-rate earnings. The last dollars earned will then be the first dollars sheltered.

Yet tax shelters have a tainted reputation in many people's minds. There's somehow something shady about them. The very term *tax avoidance* has a negative tone, even though in the form of tax shelters it's not only perfectly legal but actually encouraged by the Congress of the United States.

MAKING THE IRS YOUR PARTNER

Tax shelters are written into law as an incentive for you to invest in certain vital economic areas where there's a chance of personal loss due to the uncertainties of the investments. Government-assisted housing and oil and gas exploration are examples of such investments. To compensate for the above-average risk, you are given tax concessions. If the investment doesn't pan out, then, in theory, the IRS absorbs most or all of the loss for you. If you do strike it rich, you're allowed to keep more than you would be allowed to keep from other, less chancy investments. Heads you win, tails you win—if you are careful and know what you're doing.

A legitimate tax shelter—and there are plenty of schemes for illegitimate ones floating around—has as its main objective increasing your money. One whose only goal is the avoidance of taxes is not a tax shelter, and the IRS will make you aware of the fact in no uncertain terms. Upon reflection, that's a fair enough proposition.

As long as taxes remain below 100 percent, after all, there's no use throwing your money away simply to spite the IRS. Of course, if they ever go above 100 percent, then they become a different matter entirely. And don't think it can't happen. In Sweden, that model state of the future, Astrid Lindgren, the author of *Pippi Longstocking* and other classic children's books, ended up owing 103 percent of her total income in taxes one year. Isn't government logic wonderful?

WHAT IS A TAX SHELTER?

Tax shelters are investments which produce income-tax benefits above and beyond the normally taxed income from ordinary investments. In a tax-sheltered investment, you earn money and accrue income-tax fringe benefits at the same time. The fringe benefits can then be applied to your other income to decrease the amount of tax you would otherwise have to pay.

Tax-shelter benefits are a product of various accounting procedures ranging from a simple investment tax credit, which is subtracted right off the top of any taxes you might owe, to such complex procedures as accelerated depreciation, temporarily untaxed cash flow, and capital gains. A tax shelter maximizes these benefits through leverage, long-term tax deferral, or the conversion of an ordinary tax deduction into capital gains. It may sound confusing at first, but actually tax shelters are not difficult to understand.

A typical example involves real estate. When you take out a loan to buy a house, you are leveraging your investment in that property. For every $1,000 you put in, say you borrow another $5,000. So your first-year tax savings due to interest and other deductible payments may be well in excess of your actual $1,000 expenditure. Most of the initial payments of a mortgage loan are almost pure interest anyway, all of it tax deductible.

Now at some point in the real-estate investment, the appreciation of the building will have risen to a level where the taxes due on that profit will erode the value of the earlier years' tax savings. However, the appreciation increase will be taxed as capital gains, at a lower rate than that applied to your ordinary income. So you have shifted your profit from a highly taxed ordinary gain to a much lower-taxed capital gain.

Like most tax shelters, real-estate investment is a complex mixture of tax benefits and maximizing earnings. So you should get some outside legal help and do a lot of studying before tackling such an investment. Once you get started, you'll find the contest extremely interesting and fun, not to mention profitable.

CHECK IT OUT

Before you do anything about a shelter you're considering as an investment, investigate it thoroughly and ask four key questions.

1. Does the investment offer opportunities for "inflation-proof" investing? In other words, will the investment appreciate in value at least equal to the anticipated rate of inflation?
2. Is the whole structure of the investment economically sound with a reasonable prospect for an economic profit?
3. Does the investment offer "tax-advantaged" possibilities?
4. Can the proceeds of a later sale be taxed as capital gains and not ordinary income?

If you can answer yes to these four questions, you can and should feel good about the investment. Of course, there are other aspects to think about.

Sometimes you can't get a direct answer to all these questions. In that case, **make sure you know your promoter**, the person who is selling or structuring the tax shelter, very well. It's not very difficult to look over and evaluate the promoter's financial statements and past business history. Ask for references and recommendations, along with résumés of the promoter's previous dealings. See how those other deals are performing now.

Investigate the shelter itself, from all angles. Have your attorney look at the tax opinions or court decisions in similar cases. Examine any pertinent corporate or business-partnership documents and any permits required for the type of business involved. Visit the building or land or whatever—remembering that all the expenses, for such a trip, are probably tax deductible. Check that title to the investment is actually in the name of the entity in which you plan to invest.

Throughout your investigation, you may need the assistance of an attorney or an accountant, at least in planning your first shelter. As you become more knowledgeable in the field, you may find that you need to consult these specialists only on specific problems.

THE TAX SHELTER BENEFITS TRIPTYCH

Leverage, conversion, and *deferral* are the three major techniques for maximizing tax benefits in tax shelters. Let's look more closely at each of these tools in turn, to help you develop a sense of balance and a feel for which technique to use, and when, in your investment plans.

1. **Leverage is using borrowed money to increase a taxpayer's investment in a shelter,** thereby increasing the tax benefits. Suppose, for instance, that an investment of $10 in a given shelter will produce a 10-percent, or $1, deduction. If the investor borrows $190 and contributes that as well, he or she will receive the 10-percent deduction on $200, or $20. The deduction will thus exceed the investor's out-of-pocket contribution of $10. So using the bank's money allows the investor to increase the tax saving, at the same time freeing remaining cash for other ventures.

As a taxpayer, you should leverage a sheltered investment only if you are able to pay the costs of borrowing the money *and* if you can risk repaying the debt yourself if the investment goes under. The tax shelter should produce sufficient cash flow to cover the loan payments, or you must be willing to meet the payments from your other income. In addition, under the most recently passed laws, the tax benefits may be lost if you are not made personally liable for the loan.

The exceptions are real-estate shelters, which do not require personal liability, and recourse loans. With real-estate shelters, the taxpayer can walk away from the investment when the tax benefits are used up. All other tax shelters must have the taxpayer's money or liability actually at risk. The law will disallow deductions in excess of the amount at risk.

Leverage is commonly used to increase depreciation deductions. The cost of an asset that can be used in a business venture for more than a year must be deducted over the projected number of years of use. In other words, the cost of an asset, for example $10,000, divided by its projected useful life, let's say ten years, is the very least you'll be able to deduct each year. In this example it would be $1,000. Theoretically, this $1,000 is the amount by which the asset depreciates in value each year it's used. If you buy a more expensive asset, you can claim a larger depreciation deduction each year. Many tax shelters borrow funds to purchase expensive assets which will in turn produce large depreciation deductions.

Depreciation deductions are allowed only for property with at least a theoretically finite useful life. Land, then, is not depreciable, although buildings on it are. Inventories, stock in trade, and certain natural resources are by law not depreciable. Intangible assets such as patents, copyrights, licenses, franchises, and contracts having a limited useful life are depreciable. Goodwill in a business or profession, on the other hand, is not.

The interest paid on the loan used to leverage tax benefits is generally tax deductible in one of several ways. The deduction may be a business deduction or an itemized deduction. The type of deduction to be used depends on whether the money was borrowed to buy business property or income-producing property. The debt must arise from a real debtor-creditor relationship. As such, it must be based on an obligation to pay a fixed or determinable sum. If a promoter promises that the debt will be forgiven, you should probably ignore it, since in all probability the IRS wouldn't forgive you for taking the deduction. At the very least, discuss the matter thoroughly with your own attorney.

Leverage can put you into even lower tax brackets than you would have been in without inflation. If you're ready to invest $10,000 and borrow $90,000, you should have no difficulty finding a shelter that will produce tax savings of $10,000 to $40,000 immediately. You could easily find yourself paying less tax than you were paying years ago, even though inflation and hard work have raised your income. Leverage, then, can be a highly useful tool in offsetting the inflationary creep that is pushing you into ever higher tax brackets.

2. Conversion normally refers to changing ordinary deductions into capital gains. Suppose a tax shelter produces a $100 deduction for a taxpayer whom inflation has catapulted into the 50-percent bracket. This deduction will save the taxpayer $50 in taxes. But if the taxpayer then makes a $100 taxable profit from the tax shelter, he or she must normally pay $50 in taxes. However, if the profit is a capital gain, tax is due only on 40 percent of the $100 profit. Thus the taxpayer will pay only $20 in taxes.

Conversion sounds too good to be true. And to a large extent it is these days. It's now impossible in many tax shelters and only partially possible in others. Sections of the IRS code restrict conversion in equipment leasing, real estate, farming, and many other shelters. Generally, conversion is prevented by requiring that profits be taxed as ordinary income, not as capital gains, to the extent that they do not exceed deductions taken from the shelter. Any excess profits can usually be treated as capital gains.

Conversion should be used to your advantage wherever possible, because it directly offsets inflationary creep. By taking complete deductions measured in today's dollars and paying taxes on only 40 percent of tomorrow's dollars, you're using inflation very effectively to lower your taxes.

3. Deferral is reducing current taxes with the intent of paying them at a later time. By deferring taxes, you free current money to invest in other, more profitable enterprises than the government. Essentially this money is an interest-free loan from the government which can be repaid later with deflated dollars. Once again, time is on your side.

Deferral can also lower taxes. Let's say a doctor in the 70-percent bracket gets a $100 deduction from the ABC Flower and Melon shelter. He knows that five years later, when he sells the shelter, he's going to have to pay taxes on a $100 gain, but the $100 deduction saves $70 in current taxes. Five years later, the taxpayer, now retired, is in a 25-percent bracket. He has to repay only $25. Meanwhile he's had the interest-free use of the $70 for five years.

Deferral comes in very handy when you experience unusually large gains during a particular year. In such circumstances, you can lower your tax liability considerably by deferring taxation to future years when you will be in a lower bracket or until you die when an entirely different situation arises.

The concept of tax deferral can be continued until the property is transferred at death to your heirs. They will never have to pay tax on the deferred equity because of the stepped-up basis rules. For example, let's say you bought some real estate for $50,000. Through the process of depreciation, you write off $30,000 over the years. During the same period, the property rose in value to $200,000. If you sell the property, your combined equity for tax purposes is then $180,000 ($200,000 less the non-depreciated $20,000 of the original price). Retaining ownership of the property until you die causes the potential gain in value for income tax purposes to be eliminated. Because the equity passes through your estate and the basis steps up from $30,000 to $200,000, it then is subject to estate taxes.

TAX-SHELTER ORGANIZATIONS

Tax shelters come in any number of shapes and forms. The prime prerequisite in the formation of a tax shelter is simply that it be able to pass tax benefits on to the taxpayer. The most common types of organization used are limited partnerships, partnerships, joint ventures, and, occasionally, Subchapter S corporations. All these entities pass the tax benefits on to the investors directly, without affecting the entities' own taxes.

A limited partnership is the type of tax-shelter organization most commonly used. It is suited for both tax-shelter promoters and investors.

A limited partnership has two tiers of participants. General partners actively control and manage the partnership business, since they have the specialized knowledge to operate it profitably. Limited partners, the ones who actually invest in the business, do not have decision-making rights.

In theory, the limited partners share in the tax benefits and appreciation according to their percentage of the total investment. In practice, however, the general partners often will take a lion's share of the profits, leaving the limited partners to split the scraps. This is why it is so essential to go over every minor detail in a tax-shelter program before investing in it.

Of course, not everything is rosy for the general partners either. If the venture goes under, the limited partners are limited to losing their investment and any loan money for which they are personally liable. The general partners, on the other hand, are legally liable for all the other losses. Limited partners thus gain maximum tax benefits with a fixed downside risk in that they can't lose any more than they have invested or borrowed. General partners win a large profit potential if they succeed— and unlimited loss potential if they fail.

THE SELLING OF SHELTERS

A tax shelter is sold in one of two different ways, either as a public offering, in which case it must comply with the rules and regulations of the Securities and Exchange Commission and be presented to the public through a registered circular, or as a private offering, which is exempted from SEC rules.

A private offering needs to be very closely scrutinized. You must determine whether it really is exempt from the SEC rules and regulations. If, at some future date, it turns out not to be, SEC intervention could ruin the investment, even if its intervention was allegedly to protect the investors.

The investor in a private tax-shelter offering must also investigate and determine the risk of the investment. These risks are usually not as well disclosed in a private offering as they are in a public one. On the whole, I do not recommend an unregistered tax shelter for the first-time investor unless you know the managing partners.

THREE RULES OF THUMB FOR INVESTING IN TAX SHELTERS

Let's look at three rules of thumb for investing in tax shelters:

1. **Do your tax planning early.** That's the first rule. If it's already December, write off this calendar year's taxes to experience and begin planning right away for the year to come. The Christmas month brings all sorts of Santa Clauses out of the woodwork, including those bearing sackfuls of tax-shelter gifts. It's the end of the year, and suddenly millions of people realize that they're going to end up paying more in taxes than they thought they would. This makes them the natural prey of a myriad of deals, deals that will almost certainly be questioned by the IRS if you don't question them first.

The first and second quarters are prime tax-shelter planning time. The third quarter of the year barely gives you the opportunity to make a thorough analysis and get an accountant involved in the project before the tax year is over. The fourth quarter often leads to poor investments and tax mistakes.

2. **Avoid pyramiding more of a debt than you can handle if things go wrong.** Suppose you are approaching the end of the year when you suddenly realize that you have underestimated your income tax, and you're going to owe the government a considerable amount. Compounding your troubles is the fact that you've been living pretty well—well beyond your means. Unable to cover your tax bill out of cash flow, you may even have to borrow to pay the tax man.

Suddenly a white knight appears on the horizon in the form of Landlocked Seabed Mining and Milk, a limited-partnership tax shelter. "Sign this big note," says the salesman. "All you have to do is put up $5,000 in cash, and we'll give you an instant $50,000 write-off. Since you're in the 50-percent tax bracket, that will save you $25,000 in taxes."

"Salvation!" you exclaim. "Here's the solution to all my problems. Instead of paying the IRS twenty-five thousand dollars I don't have, I'll just invest five thousand instead."

That's fine, as far as it goes. But you are not considering the fact that potentially you're pyramiding the debt. When you lay out $5,000 cash, you're assuming an additional $45,000 obligation. If the deal goes belly up, you're on the hook for that $45,000. Better to pay the taxes due than to borrow almost double their amount to pay the tax shelter.

3. **Know what you are getting into, or it will probably be hot water.** There is no way I can stress this point too much. Study the subject. Adopt it as a hobby. Choose between oil and gas, or livestock, or leasing, or whatever else is available, almost as much for your own genuine interest in the field as for the potential tax advantages. Only by really becoming involved in the subject of your intended shelter will you ever be able to select the best one offered. Only by understanding the underlying economics of the field's particular goals will you be able to cull the lemons.

Look at the normal sequence of events that occurs when a tax-shelter investment, be it a ruby mine in the Mogok Valley of Burma or a drilling fund in Texas, is being promoted to you. First, you will receive the SEC-required prospectus. This prospectus will usually vary from fifty to a hundred pages and will be printed with type of the size used to list ingredients on cough-medicine bottles. These prospectuses are technically worded and hard to comprehend unless you're an expert.

You should hire an accountant to decode the prospectus for you, in the light of your particular financial situation. Let the accountant balance the economic benefits against the risks. Then see if it's for you. But don't make your final decision yet.

Check out the operation in person. If it's a reasonably small one, there's no reason why you can't talk to the management directly. After all, you are potentially their paymaster. Don't drop by to ask vague questions. Be prepared with specific, relevant queries.

Such a direct approach may not always be possible. Large independent oil developers and drillers, for instance, sell through brokerage firms. A one-to-one talk with management in such cases is very difficult to arrange, unless you're going to take a major financial position in what promises to be a very big deal. You're tangling with the remote-management concept here. You're relying on a presumably knowledgeable stockbroker, who's relying on a boss and a management-consultant firm and maybe half a dozen other levels of people, who presumably know what they're doing, until you finally get to someone who really knows what the operation offering the tax shelter is all about. In my opinion, there is no substitute for being able to look someone straight in the eye and determining for yourself whether or not you're dealing with an honest person.

The final decision is yours and yours alone. If you buy into the apartment house, invest in the horse, or help drill the hole, you end up owning all or part of the house, the horse, or the well. You can, and in most cases probably should, hire specialized advisers to help you with your decision. But in the end, there's really no one you can blame but yourself if the bottom line turns out to be a financial mistake.

Remember, lifetime savings and sizable fortunes have been and continue to be lost in tax-sheltered investments where people have been sold a bill of goods. They didn't have time to check it out. And the tax shelter became a remote investment rather than the direct investment it should be. **If you don't have time to make certain the tax-shelter investment you're interested in is sound—don't invest.**

Let me tell you a story that sums up all three of the rules for tax sheltering. I had two clients, men earning salaries of over $250,000 a year. They were well into the earnings bracket where they could comfortably afford the risk of a tax shelter when a promoter passed through the neighborhood in late November offering investment in what he called the "reworking of gas wells."

Now, basically that phrase meant revitalizing an old well. And whatever was necessary to get it flowing again, why, that was a tax-deductible cost. The gas was there, so it had to be a good deal. The gas merely had to be raised.

So each man put up $30,000 to $40,000 and signed a note with the bank for another $60,000 to $70,000. And they took a hefty write-off from their income taxes for that year.

The gas wells produced, and the investors' checks came rolling in for two years. Then they came a little bit less regularly, except in November and December, when the same salesman came into town again to sell more wells.

So these clients asked me to check out the situation. I know very little about gas wells. But I did go to southwest Texas to investigate. There I found a small pipe that had rusted to the ground a decade previously. It was my clients' well.

As it turned out, the salesman had continued to sell the same well over and over again to different people, using the proceeds from one sale to pay the earnings of the others. This scam is known as a simple Ponzi scheme. The U.S. Attorney finally stepped in, with the result that several of the participants were sentenced to jail.

THE BIG FOUR IN TAX SHELTERS

Every tax shelter has its own characteristics and drawbacks, which should be considered not only in terms of the tax-shelter benefits but in light of your particular financial situation as well. Choosing a tax shelter is like buying a suit. You're unlikely to settle for the first one you come across, even off the rack. So let's take a moment for a broad overview of the big four shelters—*real estate*, *equipment leasing*, *oil and gas wells*, and *livestock*—to see what might fit in with your investment plans. The final tailoring should be left to an accountant familiar with what part of your income can and should be sheltered.

THE REAL-ESTATE TAX SHELTER

Real estate is the most important and most frequently used tax shelter

available. It offers deferral, some conversion of ordinary deductions into capital gains, and leverage without personal liability. This limit on liability makes it ideal for the first-time shelter buyer and those with addquate but not immense resources at their disposal.

A real-estate tax shelter is usually formed when a limited partnership buys an existing office building or constructs a new building. As an investor, you should keep in mind what your financial objectives are and choose the type of real estate you invest in accordingly. For example, the financial advantage of investing in an older existing building is that it will already have tenants paying good rents. You need to balance this relatively secure income against the enticements of investing in a new building, which must attract tenants but which usually starts with a higher rent rate because of inflation. A new building can also be depreciated faster than an old building, so it may offer increased tax savings.

Leverage depreciation is the key to real-estate tax shelters. The income and expenses from a building usually come close to balancing out. That is to say, after the tenants pay you and you pay the bills—operating expenses, property taxes, and mortgage payments—the bottom line hovers monotonously around zero. In good times there's a little profit, in which case you have reportable income that is subject to tax. In bad times, there's usually a small loss, which may be tax deductible.

A building, however, is a wasting asset, with a limited useful life, and this is where you pick up the tax-sheltering profit. The building's total cost can be deducted over its theoretical life, and not just through straight-line depreciation, which is deducting the cost in equal portions for each year of the property's life. The cost can also be deducted with accelerated depreciation.

For the first year, accelerated depreciation can be twice the straight-line depreciation on new residential buildings and 1½ times the fixed-rate amount on new commercial buildings. Accelerated depreciation in the initial year you invest exceeds by a considerable amount the small taxable-gain income from rents, and so it can be deducted from your other taxable income.

For example, let's look at a limited partnership which purchases a building for $100,000 upon land for which it pays another $10,000. The investment in the land is neither tax deductible nor depreciable, so, for example, let's forget about it in our accounting. The $100,000 building cost has been financed by $10,000 in investors' funds and $90,000 in bank loans. The building rents for $5,000 a year, and all costs, including $1,000 in principal payments, come to $5,000 a year. The deductible costs, then, would be $4,000—the repayment of principal not being tax deductible. The rent less the deductible expenses is thus producing $1,000 in taxable income each year.

As a result of the Economic Recovery Tax Act of 1981, almost all real estate is deemed to have a productive life of fifteen years, after which time it will, in theory, be useless. If the partnership uses the straight-line method of figuring depreciation, the $100,000 cost of the building can be deducted at the rate of $6,667 per year. This $6,667 annual deduction would more than offset the $1,000 yearly taxable income, giving the investor $5,667 deduction against his or her other income. If accelerated depreciation were used, the deduction could be even greater.

The sale of this building could result in the conversion of these ordinary deductions into some capital gains. The sale's gain is measured by subtracting the remaining unrecovered cost of the building from the sale proceeds. For example, if the building was purchased for $100,000 and depreciated by $25,000, the remaining $75,000 is unrecovered cost. If it is sold for $100,000, the taxable gain on the sale is the $25,000 difference between the unrecovered cost and the sale price. If the taxpayer uses straight-line depreciation, the entire $25,000 is a capital gain, which means that only 40 percent of it will be taxed. If the taxpayer uses accelerated depreciation, some portion of the gain may be ordinary income and the remainder will be capital gain.

Even though ERTA applies to real estate acquired in 1981, there are a few unique rules of this new law worth noting. First, the old law (slower depreciation) will still apply to real estate owned by a relative in 1980 and purchased by you. Second, if you buy real estate and lease it back to any taxpayer who was the owner in 1980, the old law will apply. And finally, if you obtain property in a "like-kind" exchange, the old law will apply.

One important aspect of real estate investments is that they rely on appreciation as well as depreciation and possibly tax credits for their benefits. This makes real estate a superior investment during inflationary times. Real estate gives you tax benefits plus inflation indexing.

EQUIPMENT-LEASING SHELTERS

Equipment leasing offers large immediate deductions because it is highly leveraged. The tax savings result from both accelerated depreciation and investment tax credits.

An investor may purchase large commercial equipment which can then be leased to users, giving the investor a fairly quick-profit tax shelter. Typical examples of such equipment are airplanes, drilling rigs, trucks, railroad freight cars, computers, and heavy machinery for manufacturing. The investor provides the down payment on the equipment. The balance is financed by loans.

The lease payments are structured to cover the loan payment completely. Investors, however, must be personally liable for such loans, which often exceed a million dollars. The financial stability of the lessees, then, is a major investment consideration.

The Economic Recovery Tax Act of 1981 provides that equipment will have a five-year life for tax purposes. Since equipment has a shorter life than real estate, the cost recovery is much more rapid. Furthermore, such equipment may be depreciated at 175 percent of the straight-line rate.

The drawback of this shelter is that equipment leasing ordinarily offers no conversion of ordinary deductions into capital gains. On the other hand, there is a real advantage in that taxes may be deferred until the taxpayer is retired and in a lower tax bracket.

The investment tax credit is heavily used in equipment-leasing deals. Generally, the tax law gives an investor in new business equipment a tax credit of 10 percent of the investment. At first glance, 10 percent may not seem like a great deal, but remember that a tax credit is subtracted directly from the taxes you owe. It's not a simple deduction. If you are in the 50-percent tax bracket, for example, a deduction of $25,000 would save you $12,500 in taxes. A $25,000 tax credit, on the other hand, would save you a full $25,000—twice as much as the straight deduction.

Let me expand the example. A $250,000 equipment-leasing shelter would pass this 10-percent deduction, or $25,000, through to you, the investor. You, in turn, would have to put up only $25,000, since you could borrow the remaining $225,000 from the bank. Not only would the tax credit equal the actual down payment, but when the savings from accelerated depreciation were added in, you would actually be saving more in taxes than you were investing in the shelter!

There are two major risks in equipment leasing. The first has to do with **finding someone financially responsible** to lease the equipment. Usually, the promoters of an equipment-leasing plan secure reliable lessees before they begin selling the shelters.

However, you as an investor have a second risk to contemplate. You must carefully consider **whether or not the equipment is going to be technically obsolete before the lease expires.**

In the case of such items as rail cars and heavy equipment, this factor usually presents no problem. Computers, on the other hand, are quite a different story. Lloyd's of London used to write quite reasonable technological-obsolescence insurance on computer leases—until IBM came out with a whole new generation of computers that caused Lloyd's to incur the biggest claims loss in its history. Any high-technology leases must be approached with caution and a basic familiarity with the field.

A lesser risk of equipment leases used as tax shelters is that the IRS might decide your lease isn't really a lease. This could happen where the equipment has no real use after the lease expires, and where the lease payments are roughly equivalent to what installment payments would have been if the equipment had been sold in the first place. The IRS could then argue, rather logically, that the lease is actually a disguised indirect sale—that is, that essentially you bought the equipment and then resold it. That would mean the so-called lessee, not you, is entitled to the investment credit and the depreciation. For this reason it is crucial, when entering into an equipment-leasing deal, to look at any copies of the IRS rulings the promoter may have obtained. It's a good idea to get tax opinions from your own attorney as well, and be aware of the following points:

(1) An equipment leasing tax shelter is not for everyone. While most taxpayers will realize substantial tax savings in the early years of the lease, the long-range benefits may produce a negative result dependent upon the investor's personal financial position.

(2) An equipment leasing program has a high degree of risk and should only be entered into by those individuals who have a high tolerance for risk.

(3) An equipment leasing tax shelter is ideally designed for individuals whose income is high in the early years of the lease, but drops substantially after the crossover point.

(4) A prosperous equipment leasing tax shelter is highly dependent upon the equipment having a high residual value.

OIL AND GAS SHELTERS—THE GAMBLER'S CHOICE

Oil and gas shelters can provide large tax savings in their initial year of operation as well as income taxed on a reduced basis. They can also provide large losses, even with the best of tax benefits.

If the well is a dry hole, the leveraged investor will be called upon to pay back the pertinent loans entirely without any oil or gas income with which to make the payments. The deductions will not in themselves produce anywhere near enough tax savings to offset the cost. And considering that eight out of ten exploratory drilling ventures result in holes filled only with dust, you can readily appreciate the gambling factor involved. Of course, as any gambler will tell you, when you hit, you may really hit—which would mean huge ongoing tax-sheltered profits.

From an accounting point of view, the intangible drilling and development costs of investing in oil and gas shelters, such as ground preparation, surveying, and the construction of derricks, pipelines, and other structures, as well as the drilling and cleaning of the wells, are deducted as paid. These intangible drilling and development costs combined may run as high as 75 percent of the initial investment. The other initial costs are largely the expenses of acquiring mineral rights and heavy-duty equipment. These costs can only be recovered over a period of years.

Since even the best oil and gas wells rarely produce anything the first year, the immediately deductible costs will provide a large deduction to offset the investor's other income, thereby saving taxes. If the well is a dry hole, the remaining tangible costs can usually be deducted the year the well is capped. However, while these losses will offset some other income and produce tax savings, the outstanding loans will have to be paid. Overall, you'll end up with a large net loss.

If, as you hope, the venture is successful, its income will be offset by depletion deductions, saving you a considerable amount of taxes. Depletion is very similar to depreciation.

There are two types of depletion, the so-called cost depletion and percentage depletion. Since percentage depletion almost always gives the larger deduction, it is the one more frequently used. The highest depletion rate currently allowed for oil and gas shelters is 22 percent of gross income. This means that if your oil well produced $100,000 worth of oil a year, you get a $22,000 deduction on top of everything else.

FEEDING-AND-BREEDING SHELTERS

Along with recognizing the need to encourage housing and energy production via tax shelters, Congress has decided that feeding people is also a high-priority item worthy of encouragement. There are many tax advantages to be found in farming—or, for that matter, in growing just about anything, including tree crops and house plants.

The main tax-shelter benefits, however, are usually focused on the so-called feeding-and-breeding livestock operations. Ranging from cattle to chickens, these tax shelters produce two types of deductions. One is the highly leveraged fast-payout deduction for food. If you think feeding a family is costly, wait till you see the feed bill for a herd of cattle.

Typically, a feeding operation involves fattening already mature cattle for market. Stuffing them with tax dollars is an exercise which continues for a period of four to eight months during the first year. No cattle are sold during that year, however, since they're not ready for market. So the feed cost is completely deductible, with no offsetting earnings to lessen the reduction of your taxes.

The following year the fattened cattle are sold, one hopes for a profit. Part of the trick here is to be on the right side of the cattle curve. Herd building takes roughly five years. And there is a parallel rise and fall in prices as the supply swings through this long cycle. If there happens to be a long-term price decline in progress when you go to sell your cattle, your chances for a profit are greatly diminished.

At the same time, nature can increase your feeding-cost deduction dramatically. The unusual crop weather in 1980, for instance, increased feed prices by 20 to 30 percent in some areas. But while such an unexpected additional expense is tax deductible, its possibility must also be allowed for in advance, and its financial implications planned for, in your shelter program.

The tax advantage of a feeding operation, then, works on a one-year deferred basis. The large feed cost can be covered by loans repaid in turn from the proceeds of the following year's sale. The profit from this sale, it is hoped, will produce a gain equal to or greater than the initial deductions. This gain is fully taxable, unless you keep up your role as a cattle baron, buying another shelter the second year, and the third, and the fourth. . . . Theoretically, you can continue this indefinitely, along with the interest-free use of your tax savings each year. Just remember to look out for the declining part of the cattle cycle.

Breeding operations are primarily useful for their capital-gains advantages, but they do offer deferral of taxes as well. Breeding is a more intensive long-term operation than feeding. It starts with the purchase of cattle, sheep, or horses, and the initial group of animals is bred for years in a herd- or flock-building program.

The cost of raising the animals—feeding, breeding, and in some cases training them—is fully tax deductible. The later profits made as the animals are sold are actually only partially taxed as capital gains.

Most of the male animals, as well as the nonproducing females, are sold off, the proceeds going to loan payments or expenses. But such sales usually do not begin until the second or third year of the program's life. So the gains from them are taxed as capital gains. Meanwhile, the cost of raising the animals has been fully deducted.

At the final sale of an entire herd, only proceeds from the sale of the original breeders are subject to recapture. The proceeds from the sale of new animals are converted to capital gains.

Throughout the whole process, you can depreciate the breeding animals as well as receive an investment tax credit. The investment tax credit is available for cattle, hogs, sheep, goats, fur-bearing animals, and poultry but not for horses.

The IRS may argue that your breeding operation is a hobby. Since hobby expenses are deductible only to the extent of any profits derived from the hobby, they cannot be applied to the taxpayer's other income. As a hobby, breeding becomes at best a zero-sum game with no tax advantages.

Breeding activities must show a profit two out of every seven years in order to avoid the tax stigma of being classified as a hobby. So good planning and good records are absolute musts in such a venture, particularly where only a few animals are being raised, as on a family farm. On the other hand, you'll see in the next chapter that a family farm can be one of the best of all possible tax shelters. For it shelters not only your money but your way of life as well.

THE FOUR KEYS TO SPOTTING PROFITABLE TAX SHELTERS

1. The correct valuation of tax-shelter assets is of prime concern to the IRS. If real estate, coal mines, gifts to charity, development costs, or any other shelter items are inflated above their true value, you're in trouble right off the bat.

2. Prepayments resulting in deductions must make sense from a business viewpoint. There must be a really valid reason for paying costs up front. For instance, buying five years' worth of drilling pipe for oil exploration, all for one shipment and billing in December, might seem perfectly justifiable to you on the grounds that inflation will only keep driving prices up. But the IRS would probably not consider it good business planning. Five years' worth would simply be too big a supply. Then again, the IRS is not in the business of trying to stay ahead of inflation by any means except emptying your wallet.

3. Unless you are personally at risk for the investment, there's nothing the IRS is going to allow as a deduction except real estate. No matter what a shelter promoter says about leverage, and how you can deduct three times what you've invested, it just isn't so.

4. Every shelter must have economic substance. Its primary purpose should be to make a profit. If its structure is such that the primary purpose is to provide tax savings, rather than a profit, you're in trouble.

16

Special Tax Shelters That Outpace Inflation

> Look, we play "The Star-Spangled Banner" before every game.
> You want us to pay income taxes, too?
>
> —BILL VEECK

As inflation pushes more and more people into the higher tax brackets, a psychological mood of rebellion against the tax system is rising throughout the land. Witness California's Proposition 13 and Massachusetts' Proposition 2½, both attempts to put a brake on rapidly rising taxes. On the individual level, too, there's a spirit of catch-me-if-you-can, what with the underground economy passing funds back and forth behind the tax man's back in increasing amounts each succeeding year.

Changing the tax laws is difficult and time-consuming. Cheating, which is really what the underground economy is all about, is not only immoral, but can land you in grave financial difficulties as well. Not necessarily this year, or next, maybe not even in this decade, but if and when you're caught in the IRS net, you may find that, besides having to pay the piper, you'll be charged for all those no-show performances—with interest and penalties that will astound you if compounded over a number of years. Then, too, there's jail.

All of which may help to explain the boom in tax shelters. They are, after all, perfectly legal. And with careful planning, they can produce results equal to or better than those of most of their illicit counterparts.

THE TAX-SHELTER BOOM

Just to give you an idea of how explosive the growth of tax shelters has really been, in only three years the sale of shelter packages through Merrill Lynch went from $90 million in 1977 to well over $500 million in 1980.

As is true of anything hot in the money market, there are many operators out there, packaging the sizzle and not delivering the steak. Some of those shelters are outright frauds. But a large percentage of them have simply lost touch with basic market economics.

Consider the great boxcar shortage of the seventies. As late as 1978, Wall Street was offering boxcars for sheltered investments as if it were running a used-car lot, although in this case the cars were going for $40,000-plus apiece, a price level even inflation-bloated automobiles haven't reached yet.

Simple logic would have indicated that the railroads would run out of track on which to store all this equipment if the trend kept up. A lot of people didn't make that observation, however. At this writing, thousands of boxcars lie idle without accruing the per diem charges they collect when in use. They'll be leased again sometime in the future, so the investor's loss is not total. But for now, that meter just goes ticking right along.

THE ENERGY-SHELTER BOOM

Meanwhile, promoters are "into energy," as contemporary jargon puts it—not merely the old standbys of oil and gas but coal, the alternate-energy powerhouse which first entered the big-time shelter game in the mid-seventies and which now actually suffers from the same kind of glut as that afflicting freight cars. More novel and truly alternate energy forms such as gasohol plants, wind turbines, water power, and garbage-energy plants are on the way.

And the reason they are, besides energy's panache, is the Windfall Profits Act of 1979. In addition to the standard 10-percent investment credit available to regular tax shelters, many of these exotic tax-shelter offspring of the energy crisis—solar-power, wind-power, geothermal-power, and ocean-thermal-power projects—offer another 15-percent credit. Hydroelectric for some reason offers only 11 percent, and the garbage-to-fuel idea 10 percent. But add it all together, and it comes to about 20 to 25 percent in tax credits. You can even carry the credits back three years, which means the promoters can offer you the chance to make up for the past when you paid too much in taxes.

All these schemes I leave to the future. Look them over carefully if they interest you. But remember that when a concept gets hot on Wall Street, it often gets too hot for the investor.

THE THREE BEST TAX SHELTERS TODAY

The following three tax shelters are also very exotic in their own way. But the competition at the starting gate is a lot less for one of them and almost nonexistent for the other. The third . . . well, you'll see.

All three of these shelters offer you a direct hands-on position that eliminates the problems of the many-layered management promotion team. The first two involve livestock breeding, introduced in the previous chapter, and the family farm, respectively. When I talk about the family farm, I don't mean something that's going to tie you down to a six-in-the-morning-to-six-in-the-evening milking routine. Most investors would probably rather pay their taxes than transfer themselves to such an arduous life. No, what I have in mind is combining a summer or weekend home—though it certainly could just as well be your primary residence—with education for your children, wealth transfer, and tax shelter. That makes the country life sound pretty good, doesn't it?

HORSES THAT CAN SAVE YOU TAXES

Horse racing may well be one of those rare undertakings that are truly unaffected by business cycles. In times of financial prosperity people go to the races because they enjoy themselves there. When economic conditions take a nose dive, people still go—in order to forget their worries. In fact, historically, attendance and betting at the tracks *increase* during recessions.

Let's take a look at the tax-avoidance possibilities of quarter horse and thoroughbred horse breeding.

Sporting horses have a good record of appreciation. From 1970 to 1980, the average price of thoroughbred yearlings sold in North America rose from $7,670 to nearly $30,000, an annual increase of over 15 percent. Compare that with the Dow Jones on the chart, and you'll stop wondering why the farmer is still out in the country while the so-called "smart" money is on Wall Street.

The current investment potential of horses is perhaps best illustrated by the price yearlings have been bringing in auctions recently. In 1979 alone, the average price of American purebreds went up over 26 percent—an investment that does much more for your money than simply keep pace with inflation. And at the biggest auction of them all, the one held at Keene-

Average Thoroughbred Yearling Prices Compared to Dow-Jones Industrials Yearly Close, 1970–1980

Horse Prices

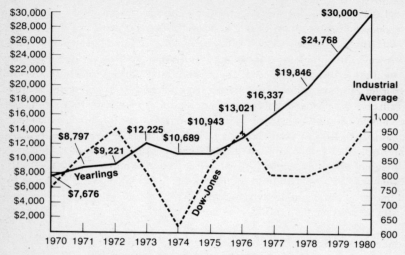

The Dow-Jones Industrial Average figure for 1980 is the closing average on November 1, 1980. The thoroughbred yearling price for 1980 is based on projections by the American Horse Council, Washington, D.C.

land, Kentucky, four horses were sold for more than $1 million apiece. These figures alone are impressive. Most investors find the tax savings even more so.

Let's say you have $50,000 to invest. Now you don't want to put all your money on one horse, even if it's insured—and, yes, you can insure horses, not for their future income, obviously, but for their current worth. However, the premiums are high. That's one of the reasons why you don't want to put all your money on one horse. There are training fees and feed to consider as well. Even though you'll be feeding the horse tax dollars, you're still going to need the cash flow. So if you have $50,000 to invest in a horse, allocate $30,000 of it to the animal itself and leave the other $20,000 in a money fund to earn interest and provide upkeep for the investment.

For $30,000 you can buy a thirteen-year-old brood mare in foal—that is, pregnant. Now, mares are considered to have a useful breeding life of sixteen years. So your mare can be fully depreciated in only four years. Your first two years' depreciation is $18,900, which gives you a tax saving of $9,450 if you're in the 50-percent bracket.

It will cost you roughly $3,600 a year to board, feed, and care for your mare, and about $3,000 a year to care for and train her offspring. Of course, you could decrease those expenses and actually increase your tax savings by keeping your breeding stock on the family farm.

Each year, when you breed your mare, you can expect to pay $1,000 or more in stud fees. The cost goes up both with inflation and with your attempt to improve the quality of your herd. For example, breeding your mare to Seattle Slew in 1979 would have cost you $100,000, although the charge would have included a guarantee of live birth.

Of course, all these expenses, and others associated with operating your horse-breeding business, are tax deductible against other ordinary income. In 1981, for instance, you might spend $10,000 to keep your two horses, the mare and her offspring, but you would immediately get another $5,000 back in tax savings along with your $10,000 in depreciation.

Yes, you can depreciate a horse; after all, it doesn't live forever. But that's not the crucial reason why livestock can be depreciated when you're breeding the animals under a genetic-improvement plan. Let me illustrate with an example. A bull raised for the purpose of producing better future bulls has no other economic use. He's literally used up—depleted—when his reproductive capabilities are gone. A bull raised for steak, on the other hand, ends up usefully on the barbecue spit. But the IRS says you can't eat your steak and deplete it too.

By definition, depletion occurs bit by bit in an irreplaceable asset over a long period of time—many years, in fact. Perhaps if that bull on the barbecue spit were really tough, and you chewed on it for four years, a depletion allowance might be permitted. However, the case would certainly end up in the tax courts.

When you buy breeding livestock, the purchase price is deductible over the useful life of the animal. Prior to the enactment of the Economic Recovery Tax Act of 1981, one of the most troublesome tax problems for those engaged in the breeding, racing, and showing of horses was the determination of the proper useful life. Old law placed the useful life of horses at anywhere from two to ten years depending on the age of the horse and the use to which the horse was put. The new law not only simplifies matters but generally reduces the useful life of the horse.

The new law simply provides that race horses over two years old when placed in service and other horses over twelve years old are given a three-year useful life. All other horses are given a five-year useful life.

The tax life and the biological life of an animal, of course, are two quite different matters. Consider the case of Naborr, the champion Arabian strutting around in the sixties. (Arabians, by the way, are show horses.) Tom Chauncey bought Naborr for $150,000 in 1969, when the horse was twenty years old. Biologically, that horse was eighty years old on our human scale. Eyebrows were raised in astonishment in horse circles. Yet, seven years later, Naborr was still bringing in $5,000 stud fees with regularity. Besides that, in 1973, the Arabian Horse Registry permitted artificial insemination for the first time, and though the offspring produced by this means are limited to fifty a year per stallion, Naborr's performance added another $250,000 to Chauncey's purse. The horses sired by Naborr and sold by Chauncey brought in $918,000 the same year. Not bad for a horse well over a hundred.

Of course, buying one good horse is no guarantee of anything. The same year that Chauncey bought Naborr, Mike Nichols, director and producer, acquired a $117,000 Arabian mare with excellent potential. She died of colic two days after he bought her. He more than recovered his loss with other horses in following years, but the case of colic points up one significant difference between horse breeding and other breeding operations.

Breeding once a year the way horses do is common to all livestock save sheep and pigs, in whose case extra cycles can be squeezed in because of the animals' short gestation periods. However, where, say, 100 percent of a herd of cattle or sheep usually becomes pregnant under intensive management, less than 85-percent pregnancy is the rule for horses. Pregnancy itself does not guarantee offspring, and here, too, horses are susceptible to problems besetting other livestock to a lesser degree. Only 60 to 70 percent of the mares carry to term and actually deliver. You're talking, then, about a yearly 50- or 60-percent foaling rate. In a well-managed sheep flock, by comparison, 150 to 200 percent lambing is the minimum acceptable range, depending on the breed, and 250 to 300 percent per year is not uncommon for good purebreds under intensive management.

NON-TAX PROBLEMS

Then there's that colic, or swamp fever, or screwworms, or flu, or any of a host of minor health problems. A sick mare can easily incur vet bills of $150 a day. And while they're a deductible expense, it's one deduction you'd rather not have.

Even considering all the tax benefits, horse breeding seems to involve a lot of problems and a high degree of risk. So why do people do it? Because the potential profits are commensurate with the risks—and, probably more than anything else, because investing in horses is more enjoyable than, say, investing in leased boxcars or oil wells.

THE IRS LETS YOU HAVE YOUR SHELTER AND ENJOY IT TOO

Enjoying an investment doesn't mean it's automatically not tax deductible. Even the IRS isn't enough of a Scrooge to say you can't whistle while you work. But business is business, and you're going to have to prove that you're in breeding for fun and profit, not just fun.

Besides the two profitable years out of seven required to qualify a breeding program for tax purposes, there are other factors that the IRS takes into account. In certain exceptional instances, it's possible to win your case for tax relief even if those two years are not profitable, provided all the following conditions, which apply to any kind of livestock shelter operation, are met.

1. Detailed financial records must be kept, including expected profit projections and a master business plan.
2. Flexibility should be evidenced and excercised. If profits look impossible to come by, your willingness to abandon or switch operations in an effort to secure a good return is an indication of the necessary profit motive.
3. There should be an ongoing acquisition of detailed knowledge in the field, including attending shows, auctions, and educational seminars for the purpose of improving your stock.
4. Shoveling manure—this is no joke—taking a hand in all aspects of the operation, including the menial tasks, is a solid argument for your trying to turn an operation into a profitable endeavor.

A final consideration, one that applies only to horses, concerns the breed you buy. Arabians are truly beautiful. But they are essentially show horses to put a $20,000 saddle on and ride in the Fourth of July parade. Their potential earning power is restricted to the value of their offspring in the show ring. Of course, this value may well skyrocket in the next decade or two, as the Middle East becomes increasingly sophisticated in its industrial technology and shifts its emphasis from such traditional businesses as horse breeding. When this happens, the oil wealth must seek all its horses abroad. In a similar vein, an acquaintance of mine is seriously considering raising camels, with the expectation that they will be in short supply in the not-too-distant future.

The point, however, is that a thoroughbred or a good quarter horse may have a higher earning potential than an Arabian. Above and beyond the stud fees and the sale of offspring, these horses have value because of their sporting potential. I'm not suggesting that you attempt to put together a string of racing horses. Your horses never have to set foot on the track, as long as they are bred for sporting purposes.

These points may be even more important to follow if you raise a horse or other livestock on your own farm. And that's a possibility which really allows you to double-scoop your tax savings.

DOWN ON THE FARM

America is a high-technology industrial state, but its moral base is still in the country. And while much of country living may be idealized, far more is underrated, particularly when it comes to raising a family. This is not meant to try to talk you into country living if you're adamantly against it. However, if you've simply never thought much about a family farm, or if you've dreamed about one but felt it just didn't make sense economically, read on.

A family farm can be operated to maximize tax deductions and fight inflation. Combining those two goals, you can even buy a $285,000 farm for less than $800 down, as I'll show you later in this chapter.

WHERE THE MILLIONAIRES ARE

Can you guess which state has the most millionaires as a percentage of its population? New York? California? Michigan? Florida? None of these. It's Idaho. That's right, Idaho. Twenty-six out of every 1,000 residents in Idaho are millionaires—many of them as a result of the large land holdings they have. Out of the top ten states with the highest percentages of millionaires per population, seven are farm states. This is no coincidence.

Of course, there are farms and then there are farms. Price levels for things that seem similar to the untrained eye may vary greatly. So I'm going to show you what I mean by a farm that provides both tax benefits and inflation-proofing—first by showing you what it's not. It's not a 150-head dairy operation calling for constant work seven days a week. Dairy farms are fine for building up a huge inflation-proofed net worth. But the life of dairy farming is not what the average individual has in mind. Neither is soybean farming on two thousand acres. Nor a million-layer egg factory.

These are all commodity farms, and they're like diamonds in the rough. Far more industrial-grade diamonds are sold than are those of fine jewel quality. And there's good profit to be made in industrial diamonds. But the real profit is in the flawless diamonds over a karat in weight.

The best is always worth a premium. And because it's the best, there's not too much of it around. And whether or not you believe that small is beautiful, there's no denying that scarce is profitable. Combine the small with the scarce—and you have the tax-advantaged small farm. That's beautiful *and* profitable.

For instance, instead of buying a horse and boarding it, with visitation rights three times a year, why not raise your Arabians or Thoroughbreds on your own farm? A farm offers you deductions on top of the tax shelter plus appreciation to combat inflation. It's plain horse sense to own the farm as well as the livestock. And by no means is your choice of livestock limited to the hoofed creatures just mentioned.

For instance, I have a friend who raises swans—for a $3,000-a-month profit. And did you know that there are super-rabbits bred specially for their fur that fetch $5,000 apiece? And prize-winning Suffolk rams that command prices topping $100,000? Just ten years ago, the top Suffolk ram went at auction for $1,000. That's 1,000 percent appreciation per year. The $5,000 rabbit started out at a value of zero and appreciated to $5,000 in one year! But the rabbit and the rams are not the kind that end up in the supermarket cooler. They're not commodity animals. They are purebreds, genetic wonders that should improve with each succeeding generation. In other words, they are the best of the crop in livestock.

This is the first aspect of the specialized family farm—what to do with it to make money. All the doing, of course, need not be done by you alone. You can use a farm or ranch on weekends for your own enjoyment and hire help to keep it running during the week or at other times when you're away.

LAND BANKING

Land banking is the second thrust in planning a family farm. As Will Rogers is often quoted as saying on the subject of buying land, "They ain't making any more of the stuff."

But buying raw land as an investment is a difficult gamble at best. Ongoing real-estate taxes, insurance, and carrying costs produce a negative cash flow. In such a speculative investment, your risk will be reduced if the acreage is in the path of an imminent development or if you can change its use to cause a dramatic appreciation. This tack, however, assumes that your knowledge and judgment are better than those of the seller, who has owned the property for a while and knows from personal experience what's happening in the area.

A much safer approach to land investment is what I call land banking. You approach your investment with an eye to the long-term appreciation of the land—which is inevitable if you hold onto it long enough. And you can if the land carries the payments on itself from the cash flow of your farming operation. You can then convert your ordinary income to potential capital gains as the land itself appreciates. Which brings us back full circle to our specialized breeding program.

What you are doing is buying a ranch or a farm the same way real-estate investors buy residential housing. The only real difference is that your tenants have four feet and can be depreciated. There are also other tax benefits of which investors in residential housing can't avail themselves.

TWELVE RULES FOR BUYING YOUR TAX-SHELTERED FARM

Let's take a look at the rules for acquiring your ranch or farm. Meeting the conditions of these rules is very important. Even if it takes months more than you'd planned on to acquire the property under the following conditions, wait and keep negotiating.

1. Pay no more than 10 percent down.
2. Arrange to buy the property with owner/seller financing.
3. The payback period in the acquisition contract should be twenty-five or more years, and interest should be included at no more than 10 percent.
4. Buy the property for 20 percent less than market value. Of course, this will mean developing negotiation skills and perhaps dealing with a distressed-seller situation.
5. The property to be acquired must be unique in character, considering topography, water rights, zoning, location, and so on. In simpler words, you don't want to buy the property in the valley that looks like everyone else's farm or ranch.
6. Make sure you negotiate for the release of some acreage from the mortgage with the down payment and each subsequent payment. For instance, a few acres of second-growth timber is useless from a farming point of view. This acreage, unencumbered by the mortgage, can then be sold for, say, recreational use, allowing you to meet future payments due on the farm out of the wooded land.
7. The contract must provide that you be able to prepay the principal and/or interest at any time, and that you have the right to apply those prepayments against the next fixed payment in the contract.
8. Make sure that the escrow is for as long a period as you can possibly negotiate with the seller to enhance property appreciation. Ideally, it should be at least six months.
9. Make allocations of the purchase price to, in order of priority,

expense items, then depreciable and investment-tax-credit items, and finally basic land cost.

10. When you sell the property, take 20 percent or more as a down payment.

11. The interest rate on the note to be carried by you when you sell should be at least 2 percent more than the interest rate you paid when buying the property.

12. Always sell with a short-term balloon payment from your buyer, ideally at five years.

BUYING A $285,000 FARM FOR LESS THAN $800 DOWN

So you've found the farm at last. It's in rural New England, where most people have discovered that commodity farming no longer pays. Or it's in Oregon or South Carolina, or one of the other states busily trying to entice industry while letting the farmer become obsolete. The property you've decided on is inexpensive by farm standards, precisely because commodity farming doesn't pay.

But stock breeding will. Seventy acres in New England isn't enough for a dairy farm to survive on. It's barely enough for a family farm to limp along on. But it's plenty for you to make a substantial income on. And it will give you a chance to refocus your life, to adjust its quality to a more meaningful relationship with Mother Earth. So buy it. The price is $285,000.

When you draw up the purchase contract, you want to allocate the various parts of the property to take advantage of tax deductions wherever possible. That means enumerating all those values you figured out in detail right on the contract, actually assigning prices to them in dollar amounts. These prices then become your basis for deductions. You can show in the contract how you established the base price for, say, your ram. After all, your farm is going to be a business. And a business is no business without accurate, detailed records from day one.

First, there are the items to be expensed—standing forage, supplies, tools, fuel, manure, and other items that are tax deductible on an annual basis. Let's give these a total value of $25,000—high, but possible. That thousand bales of hay in the barn, for instance, is second cutting and well worth $2 or $3 a bale. That's as much as $3,000 right there. So our $25,000 total is reasonable. It's also tax deductible the year you buy the farm.

Now those thousand bales of hay are to feed twenty-one sheep, including a $5,000 ram by the name of Larry Butts who is the super-stud of your new sheep generation. The twenty ewes are worth, say, $250 apiece. That's $10,000 altogether for the livestock. The new tax bill provides that sheep may be depreciated over a five-year life—giving us a $2,500 deduction the first year. Furthermore, we'll receive a $1,000 tax credit.

The land is worth $50,000, and there's nothing you can do with it but farm it. The IRS won't hear of any depletion allowance on hayfields, or any other deductions.

The same holds true for the house, to which we'll allocate another $50,000 of the purchase price. Assuming it's your residence, there's nothing you can do with it as far as tax savings are concerned.

The barn, on the other hand, and the fences, ditches, water lines, and stock tanks—even the shade trees in the pasture that provide the sheep with some shelter from the sun pelting down on their warm wool coats—these are all depreciable items. So we'll allocate $150,000 for these improvements.

If you think this is outrageous, incidentally, an acquaintance of mine just fenced in some sheep with a combination rail-and-livestock fence. The cost? A little over $1 per foot. Multiply that by ten or twenty thousand feet, add in $40,000 to $50,000 for a barn with a haymow, and you're up to $150,000 in no time.

Some of these improvements can be depreciated in as little as two years. Others, with a longer depreciation life, may also qualify for investment tax credit. Overall, let's say you have a $26,000 write-off the first year on this property.

Well, the $26,000 write-off plus the $25,000 in expenses plus the $2,500 by which you're depreciating the sheep's productive life all add up to $53,500. If you're in the 50-percent tax bracket, this sum represents a tax saving of $26,750. Add onto that the $1,000 investment tax credit, and you have a grand total of $27,750 in tax savings.

If you're paying 10 percent down for the farm, as you should be if you're playing by the rules, your down payment comes to $28,500. Subtract the $27,750 the IRS is giving you, and the out-of-pocket expense for your $285,000 farm comes to $750.

Now the land, you remember, was conservatively valued at $50,000. So what you have is a $50,000 deposit in the land bank and you're only spending $750 out of pocket for it. And this is an inflation-hedging deposit in land, not a deposit in paper currency.

The next step is taken once the farm begins to generate tax-sheltered

Family Farming and Land Banking

(Higher Risk)

LAND BANKING FARMS

(Conservative)

FAMILY FARM(S)

1. The goal with land banking is to financially support the family farm(s).
2. Land is held for long-term appreciation—but sold as market conditions allow for maximum return and safety.
3. Profits are recycled into the more conservative family farm operation(s).
4. With pyramiding of gains through notes receivable upon the sale of land banking farms, annual income will eventually become sufficient to support and subsidize the family farm(s) as required.

1. The goal is to acquire for long-term family operation a series of family farms, generally comprising best properties which are not for sale.
2. A portion of the profits from family farming should be channeled into land banking. Since land banking usually involves more risk, care should be taken not to overextend cash flow.
3. As profits become available from the sale of land banking properties, a second family farm should be purchased for family operation.

profits. These go into a second farm, and eventually maybe into a third or fourth. It can be done. A friend of mine has acquired a dozen farms this way, so I know it works. I know it well enough to be starting my own family farm.

But perhaps country life still appeals to you only in the abstract. Well, then, there's something almost as good—your own gold mine. If things get as bad as some people think they will, you and your family can survive on a family farm, which they can't in a gold mine. Outside of that limitation, precious metal mining may well be today's best inflation-sheltered investment.

KING SOLOMON'S MINES NEVER HAD IT SO GOOD

One of the most unique tax-advantaged investments for the eighties is direct participation in the mining and production of precious metals—gold, silver, platinum, and so on. A hard-money investor seeking a tax-advantaged investment can become part owner of an economic interest in the precious metal in the ground and, after taking full advantage of the exploration and development expenditures, can hold a share of the precious metals in inventory as a hedge against inflation. If it works, you are literally acquiring gold or silver with tax-deductible dollars and letting inflation build you a substantial future. There is no other single kind of investment that has as much opportunity for inflation tax planning.

Now I'm talking about an investment that has real economic substance, not the so-called precious-metal mining syndications, which seem to be no more than financing techniques, offering the potential for tax deferment but in all likelihood producing no precious metals.

A precious-metal mining operation begins to acquire real economic substance when a group of investors forms a partnership, perhaps a limited partnership, and hires a reputable, knowedgeable geologist to locate a desirable precious-metal property, perhaps gold. After going through the initial reconnaissance, along with actual assay reports on samples, the investors can decide whether the property looks favorable enough for further exploration. Core drilling would ascertain whether an ore deposit actually exists below the mineralized outcrops. On the basis of the core-drilling reports on assays, a program for development of the deposits and financial and economic projections could be made. Only then would mining actually proceed. Remember that you should be part of a syndicate which is truly interested in mining the precious metal, not one looking primarily for exploration expenditures as a tax write-off. A tax write-off for the sake of a tax write-off is a fraud, not only for the IRS but for yourself as well.

All exploration expenditures paid or incurred during a year are fully tax deductible the same year, provided they arise before the venture reaches the development stage. These expenditures include the expenses associated with the existence, location, extent, and quality of minerals. Geological surveys on core drilling are examples. For tax purposes, the development stage is considered reached when a sufficient quantity and quality of precious metals have been disclosed to justify commercial exploitation.

The significant tax consideration here is that when the venture achieves commercial production, the benefits and deductions taken for exploration will be subject to recapture. The venture may include all or a portion of the expenditures in its gross income for the year in which commercial production is achieved. As an alternative, it may forego depletion deductions in an amount equal to the benefits previously claimed.

Development expenditures arise after commercially exploitable quantities of a mineral have been confirmed but before the mine achieves commercial production. These expenditures include the costs of making the mine accessible, costs such as road building, tunneling, and driving shafts. **Developmental expenditures like these are deductible in the year paid or incurred.** They are not subject to recapture when the mine is in full production.

Once a venture reaches the production stage, operating expenditures, the ordinary and necessary expenses incurred in precious-metal mining, are tax deductible. These expenditures generally include payments for labor, equipment maintenance, transportation, milling, selling expenses, and commissions.

Depreciation and investment tax credit are both available to the mine if it purchases its own equipment rather than leasing it. The depreciation-deduction and investment-tax-credit rules then in effect will apply. New equipment may be depreciated using the 200-percent declining balance method. Used equipment may use the 150-percent balance rate.

The depletion deduction is to the mining of precious metals what depreciation deduction is to any business- or investment-related property. If you own mineral property which produces precious metals, **you will be entitled to a depletion allowance once the minerals are disposed of,** the act which generates taxable income. The percentage of your gross income allowable as a deduction is based on the type of deposit being mined. For gold, silver, and copper, the depletion percentage is 15 percent of the gross income from the minerals sold, subject, however, to the rule that the deduction cannot exceed 50 percent of the venture's taxable income.

What I have given you here is only the briefest possible sketch of the tax advantages involved in precious metal mining, because it is an area that is only now opening up to the private investor—or, I should say, reopening. A hundred years ago there were plenty of prospectors roaming the hills of America. There are still some around. But the vast majority have been replaced by $100-million conglomerates.

Now, however, with the explosion in precious metal prices and hard-money investors, more and more serious small mining ventures are being syndicated to investors. And no wonder. Gold in the ground is better than money in the bank these days, particularly when the IRS helps you find it. In some instances, investors are even going out on their own, hiring a specialized geologist, and proceeding with the exploration financing themselves. It's only when the actual development program indicating good profit has been completed that they look for outside financing for the high-cost development expenditures.

One of my clients discovered a valuable gold property in Mexico. I flew down in the midst of writing this book, to look around. It was absolutely amazing. Actually, I think I'll leave that story for my next book. The mine is still in the development stage.

Before we move on to the "ultimate tax shelter," let me give you one more gold nugget. Assuming you become an investor in a gold mine, you will most likely be taxed at ordinary income rates when the mine sells the gold (of course, the income will be set off to a great degree by development expenditures, ordinary and necessary expenditures, and depletion). However, there is a way you may realize capital gains on the sale of the gold—i.e., you will only be taxed on 40 percent of any gain realized on the sale of the gold. Here's how to do it. First, instead of receiving cash for your share of profits, have the mine distribute your share in gold. This will generally be a tax-free distribution. Next, you must hold the gold for a five-year period. If you are then holding the gold as an investment, you will be taxed at capital gains rates rather than ordinary income rates when you sell it. Remember, you will be taxed at capital gains rates on the value of the gold not only at the time of distribution but also on any appreciation after distribution.

The five-year period is essential. If the gold is distributed to you and you sell it before the expiration of the five-year period, you'll pay ordinary income on the sale gain even if you can prove you were holding the gold as an investment rather than as inventory. The five-year holding period (compared with the usual one-year period) is simply a threshold that Congress has established affecting distributed inventory from a partnership.

17

The Ultimate Tax Shelter

Never invest money in anything that eats or needs repairing.
                                                    —BILLY ROSE

"All these tax shelters are fine," you say, "but I don't like living in the country—even on weekends. I'm not interested in learning about oil wells, and frankly, I couldn't care less about horses. Besides, I can't take the risks involved." Fair enough. You should never take a financial risk unless you can handle the potential loss, both psychologically and economically. And there's no need to do so just for the sake of acquiring a tax shelter.

Probably the best tax shelter available, for many people, is their own private pension. The Keogh and IRA plans, by now probably familiar to you, and the lesser-known hybrid SEP, or Simplified Employee Pension plan, all offer significant sheltering of income for future years. However, it's the company-sponsored profit-sharing or pension plan, whether it be from a major corporation or a one-man concern, that maximizes the tax benefits for the high-income earner. And that's because corporate qualified pension plans allow much larger contributions.

The key element in a pension-plan shelter is that you are allowed to deposit before-tax dollars, and these deposits can continue to earn more money over the years, to the best of your, or some professional's, management ability—without paying a cent in taxes. You have to pay the piper eventually, but even that payment can be put off for years after your death, bypassing your estate entirely.

What makes this particular arrangement so valuable is that your money keeps earning money on itself year after year, without any cuts being taken by the IRS. It's a form of price compounding, and the increasing speed with which the funds grow can be compared to a free walk hand in hand with the IRS.

Go someplace where you can walk thirty feet in a straight line—someplace where no one will see you, if you're afraid of looking silly. Then take two steps forward and one step backward. Then three steps forward and one and a half steps back. Then four steps forward and two back. Keep up the progression, always half of the distance back after each move forward. That's the way your money walks with the IRS. Each year your funds grow, and a large part is taken away. They grow more the following year, and the IRS takes more away.

Now walk the same distance in your normal fashion. Faster, isn't it? It's the same with your money. Growing alone, it almost explodes in value after the first few years. No wonder Baron Rothschild is said to have called compound interest the eighth wonder of the world. He lived in an era before income tax, in an era before this wonder was hobbled. But now, thanks to private pension plans, once more you can enjoy watching your funds grow unimpeded, just as the Baron's did. Let's look over the four types of private pension plans.

THE FOUR MAJOR PRIVATE PENSION PLANS

1. **The Individual Retirement Account, or IRA**, program was signed into law by President Ford when he approved the Employee Retirement Income Security Act of 1974. Essentially it allows people not covered by an employer's retirement plan to start their own. An IRA is tax-sheltered, and it's deductible from the gross earnings when filing the federal income tax return. The Economic Recovery Tax Act of 1981 enables individuals to deduct 100 percent of such individual's compensation with a dollar limit of $2,000—except that there's a way around this limit if you are married. It's not much of one, but still, if an IRA is the only plan available to you, you may be able to expand your contributions by including your spouse in the plan. If your spouse does not work, you can match your IRA contribution with a contribution to another IRA for your spouse. If you contribute $500 to yours, for instance, you can contribute $500 to the other. Under the new tax law a married individual may deduct up to a total of $2,250 in IRA's for both the taxpayer and the taxpayer's spouse. Either way, that's a $250 improvement over what you could shelter alone.

In addition, lump sums received from a company retirement program may be reinvested in an IRA account with no limitation imposed on the amount. This feature was put in to accommodate job shifts. If you leave one employer for another, you can take your retirement plan with you and place it in an IRA account, provided you do so within sixty days, and you'll pay no taxes on it until it's withdrawn.

You can't take any money out of an IRA plan until you're fifty-nine and a half, and you must begin withdrawal by the age of seventy and a half. At that point, the distributions are taxed as ordinary income. Since, in theory, you are retired by then, your income-tax rate will be very low. IRA withdrawals, incidentally, being investment income, do not reduce Social Security payments the way salary income does.

Under the old law employees covered by a Keogh, a Simplified Employee Pension plan, or one of the corporate plans could not make contributions to a seperate IRA. The new act allows individuals to contribute to an IRA to the extent of $2,000 per year even though they are covered by an employer plan.

2. The Keogh pension program, intended for the self-employed, is older than the IRA. But it was radically changed by the same 1974 Employee Retirement Income Security Act. Allowable annual Keogh plan contributions were raised by ERTA to $15,000 or 15 percent of earned income, whichever was less. That represented a large step forward in the savings potential for the self-employed.

3. The Simplified Employee Pension plan, or SEP, for short, came into being with the Revenue Act of 1978. In the case of a SEP, the company you work for establishes IRAs for *all* its employees. You are allowed to contribute to the fund individually during any year in which the employer's contribution fails to reach the lesser of 15 percent of your salary or $2,000. The employer may contribute up to $15,000 per account or 15 percent of each employee's salary, again whichever is less, per year. What is contributed to one, however, must be contributed to all, on the basis of an allocation formula which gives everyone a fair share.

If you're beginning to wonder what the word *simplified* is doing in SEP, you're not alone. Most employers are wondering the same thing, and waiting for some of the paperwork dust to settle before they consider implementing an SEP plan.

4. Then there are the **Defined Benefit Pension Plan and the Defined Contribution Pension and Profit Sharing Plan,** both of which are structured for the corporation. Defined Benefit Pension Plans, or DBPs, are programs which provide employees with a fixed and determinable benefit after retirement or upon disability. In Defined Contribution Pension and Profit Sharing Plans, or DCPs, on the other hand, the specifics of accounting are placed at the input end rather than applied to the benefits. A specific percentage of the corporation's earnings is set aside for the pension each year. Seventy percent of all eligible employees must be included in the plan. The rules of eligibility automatically exclude part-time employees, those working less than 1,000 hours a year. You may also exclude any employee under twenty-five years-of-age from this pension plan.

DEFINED CONTRIBUTION PLANS

A Defined Contribution Plan (DCP) can be either a pension or a profit sharing plan or a combination of both. In a pension plan, the contribution percentage is fixed and, with some few exceptions, must be made by the employer corporation. A profit sharing plan, on the other hand, is discretionary. Each year the directors of the employer corporation can decide to make a contribution or not and the amount of the contribution can change from year to year. A combination Defined Contribution Pension and Profit Sharing plan will usually offer the most flexibility. Suppose, for example, you have a 10 percent pension and a 15 percent profit sharing plan. Since the profit sharing contribution can be less than the 15 percent, the employer corporation has the flexibility to contribute as little as 10 percent a year and as much as 25 percent a year of compensation for those employees who are eligible. If earnings decline suddenly in a given year, for any of various reasons—including simply taking a sabbatical—the contribution can decline proportionately. The corporation is not locked into a situation where an amount that would be a perfectly acceptable pension contribution one year is also required to be contributed in a year in which it might cause serious financial problems. That's one reason why the DCP is so popular.

CHOOSING A DEFINED CONTRIBUTION-TYPE RETIREMENT PLAN THAT'S RIGHT FOR YOU

Which private pension plan you choose will depend to a considerable degree on your own employment position. An IRA plan may be the only option open to you. On the other hand, if you can get an SEP, it will obviously be to your advantage to do so because (1) the potential contributions are larger and (2) your employer will help fund the kitty.

The self-employed professional and the small business owner have the best choice of all. They can elect either the Keogh plan or the Corporate Plan. Actually, their decision will probably be based on their level of earnings. Those with annual earnings in the $30,000 to $40,000 range will probably be better off with the Keogh plan, since their savings level is unlikely to exceed the plan's $15,000 annual limit. Once you reach the

$50,000 or better salary range, however, you should give serious consideration to incorporating and establishing a DCP.

Perhaps I should mention here that there is one cap on a corporate DCP. Contributions to the fund cannot exceed a total of $2,100,000 over the life of the trust. Now this is a minor problem for the vast majority of people. At $20,000 a year, for instance, it would take you 110 years to reach the limit. However, those few for whom it might pose a problem can put their excess funds into tax-free life insurance, which would then pass to their heirs without incurring estate or income taxes.

Let's compare the results of a Keogh plan and a DCP for a writer earning $60,000 a year. Mr. Writer can deduct $9,000 from his gross earnings and deposit it to his tax-sheltered Keogh plan. After also deducting business expenses of, say, $10,000, he has a taxable income of $41,000.

Writer, Inc., on the other hand, establishes a 25-percent Defined Contribution Plan, *defined* in this case referring to the fact that about 25 percent of each year's earnings has been earmarked as going into the combined profit-sharing and pension plan. Writer, Inc., pays expenses of $10,000, an annual salary of $40,000 to Mr. Writer, and deposits an amount equivalent to 25 percent of the $40,000 earnings, or $10,000, into the plan for the year. Mr. Writer then has taxable income of $40,000.

The net result of this simplified example is that with a DCP, the writer is able to put $1,000 more into his tax shelter for the year, In actual fact, the apparent lower income-tax level for the writer with the DCP may or may not turn out to be to his advantage, depending on state corporate taxes and other corporate variables. The point, however, is that a DCP should be given some serious thought at the $50,000–$60,000 earnings level. As the income of the self-employed professional increases further, DCPs look better and better.

TO INCORPORATE OR NOT—WHICH IS MORE PROFITABLE?

Let's take another example, a California doctor who is trying to decide whether he should incorporate his medical practice or not. He's thirty-five years old, and he estimates his average net income to be $80,000 after he's paid a salary of $6,000 to his part-time receptionist/aide. His income from investments averages $10,000 a year, and his living expenses are estimated at $42,700, leaving $8,652 a year for savings.

Now one fringe benefit of a DCP is that you can give your help a raise that doesn't incur any additional unemployment compensation tax or other costs for you, and doesn't increase income taxes for the help, either. This situation comes about because you must include all your help in the corporate pension plan as well as yourself, although not to the same financial degree. The contributions for the help are included as a specified percentage of the contribution to yourself.

Looking at the bottom line in the chart, you see that the cash the doctor can set aside for savings, including his contribution to the pension fund, is $18,942 under the corporate plan as opposed to the $8,652 he saves as an ordinary taxpayer. That's $10,290 more he gets to keep, instead of giving it to the IRS. As to the nurse, she gets a sheltered $1,500—a $1,500 raise she hadn't been expecting, at no "real" cost to the doctor.

The total $17,000 contribution, incidentally, is not an arbitrary figure. It represents 25 percent of the earnings of the doctor and the nurse. That's the 25 percent in the "25-percent Defined Contribution Plan," the maximum percentage of the corporation's earnings that may be set aside in the tax shelter. Less than 25 percent can be contributed, but not more.

	Before Incorporation	After Incorporation
Net professional income to corporation		$80,000
Less salary and bonus to doctor		(62,000)
Less contributions to pension plan		
For doctor		(15,500)
For nurse		(1,500)
Less franchise tax		(200)
Income to corporation		1,000
Add salary and bonus to doctor		62,000
Net professional income to doctor	$80,000	—0—
Add investment income	10,000	10,000
Less income tax		
Federal	(36,048)	(26,158)
State	(7,600)(Est.)	(5,500)(Est.)
Less living expenses	(42,700)	(42,700)
Add depreciation and amortization	5,000	5,000
BALANCE	$ 8,602	$ 3,442
Add contribution to pension	—0—	15,500
Cash set aside for savings or investment	$ 8,652	$18,942

Note the amount of cash available for investment or savings after incorporation is $18,942 compared to $8,652 without incorporation.

There are still other advantages to a Defined Contribution Plan, sometimes also referred to as Tax-Exempt Trust.

All the assets in a DCP are exempt from the restrictions generally applied to trust investments. There's no long-term or short-term capital gains tax, no minimum tax, no income tax, no excess-profits tax. Basically, what we're talking about here is the same kind of league IRA and Keogh play in, except that it's a bigger ball game.

Besides the disparity in size of permissible contributions, **one big profitable difference between DCPs and the Keogh and IRA plans is that you personally can borrow from the DCP.** This can be very valuable if you're in a profession characterized by large but irregular payments that prevent any semblance of an orderly cash flow.

DEFINED BENEFIT PLANS

A serious drawback to a DCP for high-level wage earners is that your permissible contributions are limited to 25 percent of your salary. With a DBP there's no such limit. In the DBP, age becomes a crucial factor in the permissible contribution formula. The plan allows a discriminatory feature in favor of older employees and against younger employees, which means you can put more away for yourself and less for your younger employees.

For example, at my age, which is forty-seven, if I had an opportunity, as the sole stockholder and sole principal employee of a small business, to earn $100,000 a year, I could establish a DCP and pay myself a salary of $80,000. I would then contribute to the plan for my own benefit an amount equivalent to the maximum 25 percent allowed, $20,000 a year.

Now on the other hand, if I were to establish a DBP, I could pay myself a $48,000 salary. I could then deposit $52,000 the first year as a tax-deductible contribution to my plan. The reason that I can make that large a contribution is the very nature of the DBP. Let's see how it works.

In the example just given, I would be earning $4,000 a month in salary for my $48,000 a year. The law permits me to establish a plan which, when growth is compounded and projected at a fixed rate of interest, will roughly, ten years from today when I retire, have a fund sufficient to pay me the same amount I'm making now, or $4,000 a month. Well, to get that contribution up to $52,000, I would amortize that payout in the most advantageous way—over the combined average age of myself, forty-seven, and my wife, forty-two. By using our combined average age instead of my age, which is higher, and our combined average life expectancy, which, again, is longer than mine alone because my wife statistically will outlive me, I can increase the number of years over which the funds are paid out. This allows me to make a much larger tax-deductible contribution than the DCP would allow.

I end up with a fund, ten years down the road from today, sufficiently large to make that $4,000 monthly payment. And, because I have only ten years to build the fund, my contribution can be very high.

Now let's see how the plan affects one of my employees, a receptionist who is twenty-five years old and earning $10,000 a year. If I set up a DCP, I have to put $2,500 away for her. And, remember, I am limited to putting away $20,000 for myself.

If I set up a DBP, on the other hand, I can put away $52,000 for myself and, assuming my employee's normal retirement age is fifty-seven, the same as mine, the first year's contribution for her will be less than $1,000. The reason—I have a total of thirty-two years to accumulate her funds, rather than ten years as in my case. Thus I can put away much more money for my own retirement and less for hers than I could do under a DCP.

BORROWING FROM YOUR RETIREMENT PLAN—TAX-FREE

Let's say Writer, Inc., sells a book that becomes a best-seller. His payments from the publisher arrive semiannually. Three months before a check is due, the writer comes across the perfect family farm. The only catch is he needs $50,000 up front to buy it.

His DCP is well funded. But the writer himself is strapped. What does he do? Instead of going to the bank to borrow money—you can't use the funds in a Keogh or an IRA as loan collateral under any circumstances—the writer borrows directly from his own DCP. He pays the going interest rate for personal loans (let's say it's 15 percent) upon retiring the loan.

The DCP then has its money back plus a 15-percent return, on which the pension plan pays no taxes. The writer, meanwhile, can deduct the 15-percent interest from his income taxes, just as if he'd borrowed from the bank. The DBP, like the DCP, allows you to borrow from yourself.

WHAT IF YOU GO BANKRUPT?

Not to pick on writers, but let's face it, someone who works on a free-lance basis, whose income may be highly irregular, is much more likely to go bankrupt than a professional, such as a doctor, or a person who works for a large company. So let's suppose the writer goes bankrupt. All the money in the pension plan is shielded. Trust assets are not subject to attachment, alienation, garnishment, judgment, or any other legal process save certain marital rights in certain states. Bankruptcy, personal or corporate, will not allow creditors to touch a single cent in trust.

UNLIMITED GROWTH

One of the biggest benefits of the DCP is that there's no restriction on the growth of the funds. A dramatic example of this involves a client of mine, a surgeon, who established a DCP in 1969. My client was the only person in his professional corporation eligible, and consequently the only participant in the plan. And each year as he made his (roughly) $100,000, he would contribute an amount equivalent to 25 percent of this income to the combination pension/profit-sharing plan, the DCP. Along the way, he made a fantastic investment in a small mining and energy company. It was risky, but he decided, as the pension trustee, to invest $100,000. The stock took off and split several times, and at this moment his pension investment is worth $8 million.

If this same client had a DBP he would have eliminated the possibility of any future years' contributions because the plan already had too large an asset pool once it hit about $2 million. However, he could have borrowed those funds from the pension plan, invested them personally in inflation-indexed assets, and kept the profits. As long as the plan document states that all participants on a nondiscriminatory basis can borrow, it's lawful. The IRS rule appears to me to indicate that if the plan is fully vested, or paid up, you can borrow without security up to your vested amount.

On the other hand, if it's a vesting that may go on over a long period of time, for example, ten years, and you're currently only 20-percent vested, then you can only borrow up to 20 percent of your fund without security.

COMPARISON OF DCP AND DBP

DEFINED CONTRIBUTION PLANS

Mr. A, an independent contractor, has two full-time staff employees, Miss Y and Miss Z. Mr. A is age 37 and his taxable income over the past two years has been approximately $50,000 per year. Miss Y receives a salary of $6,000 per year and Miss Z has an annual salary of $7,200. The following illustrates the contribution potential with a 10-percent pension and a profit-sharing plan permitting up to 15 percent contribution. One more ingredient—the pension is integrated with social security at $25,900 (applicable for 1980).

ASSUMED ANNUAL CONTRIBUTIONS

	Pension	Profit Sharing	Total	Percentage
Mr. "A" age 37 income $36,000*	$3,791	$5,400	$ 9,191**	75.0%
Employee #1 Miss "Y" salary $6,000	514	900	1,414	10.0%
Employee #2 Miss "Z" salary $7,200	615	1,080	1,695	14.0%
TOTALS	$4,920	$7,380	$12,300	100.0%

*Salary paid to Mr. "A" after incorporation.

**The actual maximum allowable is 25 percent of compensation (in this example $9,000). The solution would be to contribute less than 15 percent to the profit-sharing plan.

DEFINED BENEFIT PLANS

Defined Benefit Plans (DBPs) offer more dramatic tax-deductible contribution possibilities. Since *age is a factor to be plugged into the formula*, the amount of contribution will, of course, be much higher for an older employee than for a younger employee. And perhaps the best way to help you catch the vision is to give an example.

Doctor "Y," a physician 55 years of age, earned as a sole proprietor last year the sum of $175,000. He has incorporated and is now on a salary of $84,500, payable at $7,041 per month.

Doctor "Y" has one full-time employee, a nurse, age 43, who earns $7,416 annually, payable at $618 per month.

After establishing a Defined Benefit Plan, integrated with Social Security, and assuming nearly a 100-percent benefit level, the contributions for the participants are as follows:

	Monthly Salary	Annual Contribution
Doctor "Y" annual salary $84,500	$ 7,041	$83,348
Nurse annual salary $7,416	$ 618	$ 2,079
		$85,427

After incorporation, our doctor is able to take a tax deduction of $85,427 each year with 98% of that amount set aside and invested for his future retirement and use. He can, of course, be the trustee and manage the fund.

Thereafter you'd have to have a secured note. The note obviously would have to be fair in its terms and in the interest rate that you're going to charge.

One of the big disadvantages of the DBP, for some people, is that you have to make the contribution every year. Going back to our writer, he might find himself with some problems if his income suddenly declined.

THE BENEFITS OF TAX-FREE ACCUMULATIONS DRAMATIZED

Let's look at two professionals, a man and a woman both forty-five years old, who are saving $10,000 a year. And let's say those savings are bringing in what is probably an absurdly low interest, 5 percent. That's what the money would be earning in a bank, though by now most Americans are well aware of the fact that putting long-term money in the bank during inflation is a sure route to poverty. (As an aside, this aspect of savings may change with the phasing out of Regulation Q, which puts a ceiling on the interest that banking institutions are allowed to pay. By 1985 or 1986, it's not unlikely that banks will at last be able to offer rates in line with those of the money market overall.)

Now then, the professional without a qualified pension plan theoretically has $10,000 a year to put aside for his retirement. But before he can do that, he has to pay $4,000 in income taxes out of that amount, which leaves an actual $6,000 a year for the retirement fund. If his contributions earn 5 percent a year for twenty years, the total in his plan is roughly $208,000.

The second professional had a qualified pension plan. She has the same $10,000 a year for savings. However, since her plan is qualified, the entire $10,000 goes to the pension fund. Uncle Sam gets nothing. At the end of twenty years, the second professional had roughly $347,000. That's $139,000 more she's saved simply by spending half a day and maybe a few dollars setting up a qualified retirement fund. If we compare the results using 15-percent interest, which is probably a more reasonable estimate of return on money in the next twenty years, the regular saver had about $614,000 at the end of that time, the one with a qualified plan $1,024,000. The difference is $410,000. And whether you or the tax man gets the difference is up to you. The money is there for the taking.

DO YOU EVER PAY THE TAX MAN?

The contributions and the income, whether it's interest or a gain in capital—from any source, including such hard assets as gold—of any of the qualified private pension plans are tax free until the plan is paid out. If this payout is made over a period of time rather than in a lump sum, the payments are taxed in the years in which you withdraw them, just as annuity payments are.

Since the passage of the Tax Reform Act of 1976, it has also been possible to make a lump-sum withdrawal of all the plan's assets without being hit for the whole tax bill at the same time. You are allowed the option of having the distribution taxed under a ten-year averaging provision. **Spreading the money over ten years for tax purposes while actually taking possession of it in one year provides considerable tax savings.**

There is yet another tax advantage available to the professional corporation with a Pension Trust fund. Under the Internal Revenue Code, Section 2039, the value of an annuity is included in a professional's gross estate. But Section 2039(c) goes on to exclude the annuity from the gross estate if it goes to any beneficiary other than the executor, under the terms of a qualified amount. The portion excludable from the estate is limited to the payments attributable to *employer* contributions under the plan. Any *employee* contributions, on the other hand, must be included in the gross estate.

So if Writer, Inc., makes all the contributions to Mr. Writer's qualified pension trust fund, it's possible for the writer to name his wife as executor of the estate, and the children or favorite charity as the beneficiaries of the trust. If he does this, none of the pension trust fund money would ever be included in the estate for tax purposes.

The same Tax Reform Act of 1976 that made possible the spreading of the taxes due in a lump-sum pension-plan withdrawal for ten years into the future also limited the use of such lump-sum withdrawals in estate-bypass planning. Lump-sum withdrawals now end up being included in the estate for tax purposes.

There's an exception to the ruling, however. If the writer, in our case, decides to forego his ten-year tax liability-averaging privilege and takes his tax lump the same year he takes his lump-sum distribution, the lump-sum payment is again excluded from the estate. This holds true for all the qualified plans, including the IRA and Keogh.

A second change in the treatment of the lump-sum distribution allows the descendent's surviving spouse to roll the lump-sup distribution over into an IRA account in his or her own name. The rollover must occur within sixty days of receipt, however, if the current federal income tax is to be avoided. The provision permits the tax-free accumulation of the income from the assets until the surviving spouse actually withdraws the money.

Some state laws do not yet parallel these federal provisions—which once again highlights the crucial fact that you cannot plan your estate to avoid taxes without first carefully studying your state's statutes as well as those of the federal government.

IRA'S SPECIAL TAX-AVOIDANCE BENEFITS

The IRA rollover permits a very interesting tax-avoidance plan. Suppose, for instance, a woman receives a lump-sum distribution from a private pension trust forced by the death of her husband, the contributing spouse. The sum is excluded from her husband's taxable estate.

She then proceeds to roll the lump sum over into an IRA account of her own, well within the stipulated sixty days. By doing this, in effect she protects herself from having to pay income tax on the distribution and as the years go by, until she uses the fund.

This tax-avoidance technique can offer considerable tax savings for certain estates. If you think such a technique would be good for your estate, first ask yourself:

1. Will treating a death distribution as a part of the estate significantly increase the estate tax? If so, will the income-tax savings outweigh the estate-tax liability?

2. Will treating a death distribution as part of the estate really not affect the estate tax? If so, the favorable tax treatment available for lump-sum distribution should be put to good use.

If you haven't heard the news by now, Section 314(b) of the Economic Recovery Tax Act of 1981 contains a provision that has the net effect of prohibiting hard assets from pension plans.

Section 314(b) of ERTA, slipped in by Congressman James Shannon (D-MA) before the vote on the President's bill, provides that tax-advantaged money in self-directed pension plans, Keoghs, and IRA plans can no longer go into diamonds, gemstones, stamps, coins, gold, silver, art, antiques, or any hard asset defined by the Secretary of the Treasury as a "collectible," without being taxed in the calendar year it is purchased. The net effect is to prohibit collectibles from self-directed pension plans, including IRA's and Keoghs.

Most IRA's and Keoghs are guaranteed instruments of inflationary purchasing power erosion. Fixed-rate interest earned in pension plans has not even come close to keeping up with inflation.

Some studies have shown that from *December 1977 to December 1980* (for example), *those pension plans placed with banks, savings and loans, and insurance companies on a fixed rate of return suffered inflationary erosion resulting in a 35-percent loss of purchasing power* (as measured against the Consumer Price Index).

The rationale of those behind 314(b) is that a lot of money is no longer going into "traditional" investment vehicles but into "non-productive assets." Their change in the tax law was designed to divert money from flowing into hard assets and to send it back into savings institutions.

That's like saying that the coin or diamond dealer puts the money under his pillow and takes it "forever out of the market." But when someone buys or sells a stamp or any other collectible, he reinvests the money back into the economy.

A lot of pressure is now being put on Congress to repeal Section 314(b). And hopefully this prohibition will be repealed.

One note of caution, however, as you get worked up over this provision. *I think it entirely inappropriate to have your IRA, Keogh, or even your trustee under a self-directed account buy collectibles or other highly appreciating capital gains assets.* Remember, numismatic coins, rare stamps, and other collectibles rise in value tax-free outside of your pension plan until sold. Then the tax is at low capital-gains rates. (If the collector dies first, the gain will never be taxed.) On the other hand, when an IRA buys collectibles instead of, say, an interest-bearing investment, the favored tax treatment of a capital gain is lost.

Consider, for example, the case of a single taxpayer in a 40-percent tax bracket who puts $2,000 each year in a savings-type investment that earns 15 percent and $2,000 each year in an IRA which purchases collectibles that appreciate 20 percent annually. Retiring after 20 years, the taxpayer has $102,000 after tax in his savings-type investment. The IRA sells the coins and distributes $249,000 after ordinary tax based on 10-year forward averaging. The total value for this combination is **$351,000.** Now, if the taxpayer were to reverse the arrangement (the IRA into a savings-type investment and the taxpayer into collectibles) the net would be $298,000 after capital-gains tax on the collectibles and $153,000 after tax from the IRA. That totals **$451,000.** Which is better?

CHOOSING THE BEST INVESTMENT MANAGER FOR YOUR TRUST

Who is going to make the investment decisions for your qualified pension plan? That's a crucial question you must tackle before you set up the plan. The first rule of thumb is to forget about banks. Inflation will destroy a bank-sponsored IRA or Keogh account which must have institutional trustees. The trust department of a bank handling the larger Defined Benefits Pension Plans may well do the same. Their impressive credentials aside, bank trust departments have one of the worst investment-management track records around. In large part, this is due to their hewing to the prudent rule that trust money should be 40 percent invested in gilt-edged bonds. As true as this maxim has often been in the past, it's a fact that for the last decade and for many to come, inflation has rendered this once-prudent rule financially imprudent.

The best investment manager for your trust is you. It's your money and your future. This is not meant to preclude your seeking professional advice. Far from it. Use all the resources at hand before you make your decisions. But there are some responsibilities—raising children is one of them, and managing money is another—which simply cannot be foisted off on individuals who aren't aware of your values.

18

Educating Your Children Tax-Free

This is what is hardest:
to close the open hand because one loves,

—Nietzsche

Trusts can be structured in any number of imaginative ways to provide money for your family while keeping the tax man out of your wallet. One of the primary uses of trusts, for many people, is the education of their children.

AN INSTANT TRUST

There are trusts most people wouldn't even think of as trusts that can achieve the twin goals of providing funds for the children and at the same time minimizing taxes.

For example, under the Uniform Gifts to Minors Act, often called simply UGMA, you can give your child property such as stocks, bonds, or cash in a bank account—funds that you want to put aside for, say, the child's college education. And **the wonderful advantage of using the Uniform Gifts to Minors Act, as opposed to simply building up your own nest egg for your child's future, is that you don't have to pay any taxes on the money the investment earns.** Interest and dividends are essentially *tax-free*. This is because, by giving the money to your children, *they* become the ones responsible for paying the taxes. And even with today's exorbitant tax rates, most preteens and teenagers are in the zero income-tax bracket. What's more, they're likely to remain there even if they have thousands of dollars in the bank. With Uncle UGMA, uncle Sam doesn't get his cut. Your child gets it all.

YOUR CHILD GETS IT ALL

When I say your child gets it all, I mean that's exactly what happens. Once you have given the money to your son or daughter under the Uniform Gifts to Minors Act, it is no longer yours and never can be again. That's a vital factor to be considered before you give away money under this law, of course. Ten years from now, if you need $10,000 because of a temporary cash-flow problem, you'll have to borrow it from somewhere else, not from your child.

The other limitation to an UGMA account is your child's own spending habits and sense of responsibility. Most children have developed a certain degree of maturity by the time they are ready to embark on a college education. Then again, as a visit to almost any of the institutions of higher learning will demonstrate, a lot of them have not. Your child may well carry on the family values you have tried to teach and live by and apply all the funds in his or her UGMA account toward a college education. On the other hand, your child may not do either of these things. There is nothing to prevent him or her from saying, upon reaching the age of maturity, "Fork over, Dad," and taking the college fund to buy a sailboat for a round-the-world trip. Your child can do what he or she wants with the money. It belongs to your child, not to you. You have no control.

Maybe, in fact, a college education isn't the best thing for your son or daughter. That's something you will have to discuss with the child when the time comes. However, having $40,000 to $50,000 worth of unrestricted cash dropping into an eighteen-year-old's lap almost certainly isn't the wisest course to take. Few young people can handle that kind of responsibility. So, rather than investing in an UGMA account, maybe you'd rather have a trust that gives the trustee broad discretionary powers over the distribution of the funds. Let's take a look at what happens with such trusts.

THE LEGAL AND TAX IMPLICATIONS OF YOUR CHILDREN'S TRUST

Unless you include in your children's trust a provision similar to the Crummy clause (see Appendix E), a gift made in trust may not qualify for the annual gift-tax exclusion. This is because the person receiving the gift may not have the unrestricted right to the immediate use, possession, or enjoyment of the asset. The failure of a gift to qualify for the annual gift-tax exclusion works against you not only because it may increase the gift tax, but also because the IRS will lump the entire amount of the gift together with transfers made at the time of the donor's death when it computes the estate tax.

Since a major tax goal of an educational trust is to enable the income to be taxed at *lower* rates than would apply if the donor didn't make the gift, the trust must be structured quite carefully to ensure that the income falls into the right tax category. For example, trust income which conceivably could be used to satisfy parents' legal obligations toward their children, whether or not the money is actually used for such purposes, is taxable to the parents.

Similarly, in the case of a contractual obligation, such as the one where parents have contractually assumed the responsibility for payment of their children's college expenses, if trust income may be used for the purpose, the parents will be taxed on that income whether or not they actually use it this way. This rule applies even when the parents are not otherwise obligated under local law to provide a college education for their children. **As a parent, you should not contract with a college to pay for a child's tuition and other expenses if you plan to use a trust arrangement to make the payments.**

The rule is somewhat different in the case of support payments, as opposed to other legal obligations. Where the power to use trust income for the support of a beneficiary rests in a third person or in the donor, if he or she is a trustee or co-trustee, the donor will be taxed on the income only to the extent that it is actually used for support.

ARE YOUR CHILDREN LEGALLY ENTITLED TO A COLLEGE EDUCATION?

The question of whether the legal obligation of support which parents owe their children includes a duty to provide a college education must be considered. And the answer to the question is a matter of local law. Most attorneys conclude that where parents are still married, they rarely have a legal duty to provide a college education for a minor child. However, if the parents are divorced, the courts have often imposed a duty on a father to provide a college education for the minor children as part of his support responsibilities.

If there is a possibility that a parent may be held liable to provide a college education for a minor child, special consideration must be given to this point in the trust, because the trust income used for that purpose would then be taxable to the parent. To get around this problem before it arises, the trustee should be instructed to distribute the trust income directly to the minor during the time he or she is in college (and hope the minor will spend it on education).

Even when a parent is not the donor of the gift to the trust, he or she may be taxed on the trust income if it is used to support minor children. Where a grandfather, for instance, creates a trust to pay for his grandchildren's education, and the trust funds are distributed for that purpose while the grandchildren are minors, the income will be taxable to the parent if the local law states that furnishing a college education is a legal duty of parental support.

SHORT-TERM TRUSTS

Short-term trusts have a variety of applications. The most common one is probably to finance your children's education. However, such trusts can be used any time you want to shift income from assets from someone in a high tax bracket to someone in a lower tax bracket. The beneficiaries could be your children. They could also be your parents. Short-term trusts are frequently used to provide for aging parents without resources.

The beneficiary of a short-term trust, in fact, need not be related to the donor. As a donor, you can name anyone in a lower tax bracket than yours as a beneficiary for the purpose of avoiding taxes on the income from the assets. Note that I said the income, not the assets themselves. The basic short-term trust returns the assets to the donor after a specified period of time.

GOODBYE, MR. CHIPS; HELLO, MR. CLIFFORD

A Clifford trust is often referred to as a temporary trust, a family trust, or ten-year trust. Don't let the terminology confuse you. The principle is always the same. To be effective, the Clifford trust must, by its own specific terms, exist for not less than ten years. Assets used to fund the trust revert back to the trust's creator after a minimum of ten years and a day or at the death of the person for whom the trust was created, whichever is the shorter period. This time span is measured not from the inception of the trust but from the date on which the assets are actually transferred to the trust. The

Clifford Trust

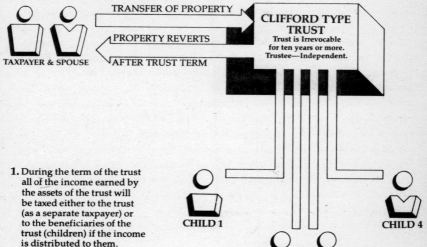

TRANSFER OF PROPERTY

CLIFFORD TYPE TRUST
Trust is Irrevocable for ten years or more. Trustee—Independent.

PROPERTY REVERTS

AFTER TRUST TERM

TAXPAYER & SPOUSE

CHILD 1

CHILD 2 CHILD 3

CHILD 4

1. During the term of the trust all of the income earned by the assets of the trust will be taxed either to the trust (as a separate taxpayer) or to the beneficiaries of the trust (children) if the income is distributed to them.

2. At the end of the term of the trust the property then reverts to the trust grantor (taxpayer) or other designated remainder reversionary beneficiaries.

ten-year limit is only a minimum. Should your plans benefit from a twelve-year or even a fifteen-year trust, a Clifford trust would be perfectly permissible.

A Clifford trust is, however, irrevocable. Once money has been placed in the trust, it must remain there until the date specified by the instrument. Income, on the other hand, may be distributed to the beneficiary either as it is earned or when the trust terminates.

Now, having said that only the earnings can be distributed before the trust is terminated, let me add that while this is the gist of the Internal Revenue Code's Section 673, it is open to a certain amount of interpretation. As long as the trust may reasonably be expected not to terminate within ten years, the reversionary rule of this section will be satisfied. Once more the matters of control and intent, those two very crucial factors in dealing with the IRS, enter the picture.

For example, if the family breadwinner should die unexpectedly and leave an estate insufficient to provide for the family's immediate needs, the trust could be terminated early. The argument would be that clearly the intent of the person who set up the trust was to provide for the children's education. Death unexpectedly intervened.

In order for this interpretation to be possible, two requirements must be met when the trust is first drawn up:

1. The breadwinner must be expected to live for at least ten more years at the time the trust is established.

2. The provision providing for early termination in case of unexpected death must be an integral part of the trust document.

DOUBLE YOUR PLEASURE, DOUBLE YOUR DEDUCTION

Clifford trusts allow a special tax advantage—doubling your personal exemption. The minor child benefiting from a Clifford trust can claim a $1,000 personal exemption. The parents, in filing their joint income tax return, can also claim a $1,000 deduction for the child. As long as they furnish 51 percent of the child's support, the child can be claimed as a dependent. Equipment trusts, which we'll discuss later in this chapter, also have this tax advantage.

GIFTS AND THE MAGIC NUMBER .441605

The biggest drawback to the Clifford trust is that, for tax purposes, the transfer of property to the trust results in a gift. But the value of the gift is measured by the so-called income stream flowing through the trust during its term. And, in computing this stream, there is a magic number, .441605, that can be used to your advantage in any ten-year trust.

Suppose, for instance, you deposit $30,000 in the trust to help pay for your child's education. Taking the $30,000 and multiplying it by .441605, or approximately 44 percent, you get $13,248.15. This is the actual amount considered a gift for tax purposes if the property reverts back to you when the trust terminates.

If none of the property reverts to you, then the entire fair market value of the contribution at the time it was made is the amount the IRS will consider as a gift. For instance, a thousand shares of Ford Motor Company stock worth $30 a share would then be worth $30,000 for gift-tax purposes—even if Ford came out with a 90-miles-to-the-gallon car the day after the stock was placed in trust, the share price rose to 65, and the cash-generating dividend for the trust subsequently tripled.

If the gift-tax consequences of a Clifford trust seem to you to be a major hurdle, remember the magic number—.441605. In an era of double-digit interest rates, being able to reduce the taxable gift to 44 percent of the value of the assets placed in trust still makes the Clifford trust a valuable tool for minimizing taxes.

Should the grantor or the trustee have any "tainting" power whatsoever in a Clifford trust—and the IRS interpretation of the word *power* is very broad—the trust will not succeed in shifting the income-tax burden as desired, and meanwhile you will still be liable for the gift tax as well. Before you set up any form of income-shifting trust, be sure to get the help of a skilled attorney.

WHAT IS SUITABLE FOR FUNDING A CLIFFORD TRUST?

Real property, owned free and clear of all mortgages and capable of generating a good cash flow, probably comes closest to being the ideal asset

for a Clifford trust. The best asset of all is unimproved land which can be leased to generate substantial annual income.

Properties encumbered by mortgages and loans for which the donor is liable, on the other hand, are not generally good assets for Clifford trusts, as they can produce unexpected income-tax problems as well as increasing the gift tax due. If the donor is not personally liable for the debt against the property, then at least there will be no income-tax problem.

Let's take an example of a real-property-based trust and see how it pans out. Suppose a gasoline marketer expands his business to a small chain of three gas stations surrounding a town in the Midwest. He operates the main one, which also deals in fuel oil for home heating, himself. The other two stations he leases to operators, one for $22,000 and one for $18,000.

Unfortunately, income taxes absorb $12,600 of the last $18,000, leaving only $5,400 in net income from that source. Meanwhile, it's costing our marketer $10,000 a year to send his three children to the local private school, an expense covered in part by the remaining income from the third gas station. The balance, $4,600, he must pay from other income, which has also already been heavily taxed.

So, with the help of an attorney, he places the last gas station in a Clifford trust. Now there are still real-estate taxes to pay, but they're only $1,000 a year, which leaves the trust a $17,000 net income annually. The full $10,000 cost for the private school is covered. Altogether, it will cost the three children about $1,000 in income taxes. The $6,000 yearly balance can be allowed to accumulate over the life of the trust with minimal shrinkage due to income taxes to help cover future college costs as well. During the ten-year life of the trust, the man's family gains over $100,000 in income for education, income which, without the trust, would have gone to the IRS.

Other assets that could be used to fuel this type of trust range from gold, silver, and money-market funds to leased equipment. However, the Internal Revenue Code specifically prohibits short-term trusts from including among their assets life insurance on either grantor or spouse, unless the income produced by the trust is taxed to the trust grantor—which, of course, negates the whole purpose of the trust in the first place.

A possible solution, if you are really determined to include life insurance, is to have the income of short-term trust A payable to short-term trust B. Trust B should be created by a different grantor, perhaps a child's nonrelated guardian, and it can own a policy on the life of the grantor for Trust A. The earnings of Trust B can then provide the income actually used for the benefit of your children.

As a rule, I do not recommend this cloning of trusts, particularly since it can lead to other tax problems. But I've included the example here to show how much more room there is for maneuvering within the framework of the Internal Revenue Code than people generally realize. All it takes is a little imagination—and a lot of technical work to make sure that absolutely nothing is overlooked.

SHORT-TERM TRUSTS AND CAPITAL GAINS

There's another curious twist that can be added to a short-term trust, and it concerns capital gains. The capital-gains tax due on the sale of property in a short-term trust is payable by the trust grantor. Even if the trust retains the capital gains, the grantor is liable for the tax. This is so because a short-term trust provides for the distribution of income only. The assets revert to the grantor. And since a capital gain is a gain in assets, the grantor is the person liable for the tax.

A way around this dilemma, however, is to include in the trust instrument a specific provision providing for the allocation of all capital gains to income. By this means, the value of the gift of income to the beneficiaries will be increased significantly. But, in using this tactic, the donor's taxable gift will be increased beyond the magic 44 percent.

The basic moves to keep in mind when you are funding a short-term trust are:

1. Transfer the assets you have that earn the greatest amount of taxable income.
2. Never transfer encumbered assets.
3. Transfer the assets that have a high income-tax basis.

What you want in a trust, in most cases, is property with a high rate of return but a low capital-gains potential.

LEASING AN EDUCATION

Equipment trusts offer an excellent way to pay for your children's education with tax dollars. The equipment involved in trusts is often the kind associated with technical professions, such as medicine, but could also include farm equipment, vehicles, furniture, leasehold improvements, other machinery, and so on. When picking an equipment trust, your imagination is the limit—as long as you stay within the IRS guidelines and previous court decisions as to what does and does not affect the legality of an equipment trust. For now, let's look at the common case of the local dentist. Dental equipment is very expensive, so it's an excellent source for fueling a trust.

Dr. No is a practicing orthodontist. He's married, and when he and his wife file their joint return, he's in the 50-percent tax bracket. With four children to educate, all of them between the ages of ten and fifteen, he is painfully aware of the fact that taxes are preventing him from putting enough money aside for their education. His lawyer suggests that he start an equipment trust.

The market value of his dental equipment, though it originally cost $40,000, is currently only $20,000. It's pretty well depreciated for tax purposes, and he owns it free and clear. So it can safely be placed in a trust without depriving him of any valuable depreciation on his own tax return. It can also be placed in an irrevocable trust without any residual interest due to the payment of loan installments.

So Dr. and Mrs. No, naming an independent party as trustee and their children as trust beneficiaries, set up an irrevocable equipment trust. The initial assets transferred to that trust are Dr. No's various pieces of dental equipment, worth $20,000. The equipment is to be held in trust and managed by the trustee according to the terms, provisions, and conditions of the trust agreement.

In order for the equipment to escape gift taxes, Dr. and Mrs. No include in the trust document a clause making gifts to the trust "gifts of a present interest," similar to the sample clause in Appendix E of this book.

After the trust has been established and funded, the trustee approaches Dr. No to negotiate a leaseback of the equipment. A real lease with realistic payments based on other commercial leases of the same nature is crucial here. Currently, a monthly lease rate of 2 to 3 percent of the equipment's value would be considered commercially acceptable. But this percentage is tied to the prevailing interest rates; 2.5 percent is conservative for a prime rate of 20 percent or lower. Adopting a rate of 2.5 percent, Dr. No would pay $500 per month to lease his equipment.

The trustee would collect $6,000 a year. This could be either retained temporarily by the trust or distributed to the beneficiaries immediately, depending on the age of the children and how the trust was set up. In either case, Dr. No would be able to pass $6,000 on to his children. He would still reserve the right to give each one $10,000 a year tax free. And he could deduct the $6,000 lease expense as a business deduction.

If you were to follow a course similar to Dr. No's, individual tailoring of the trust to your family's financial needs and goals would be essential. No fill-in-the-blanks approach to this kind of planning will work. To know whether or not such a course is possible for you, consult your attorney.

In order to satisfy the IRS, your equipment trust must meet the following conditions:

1. The taxpayer must give up control over the transferred property completely. This means that only an independent trustee can manage the irrevocable trust.
2. The lease arrangement must be in writing.
3. The lease arrangement must call for a reasonable rental in line with market conditions for similar equipment.

If the cost of leasing is to be made tax deductible for the lessee, the following conditions must also be met:

1. The leaseback must have a genuine business purpose. There should be some non-tax-related objective. In Dr. No's case, for example, the prevention of attachment by creditors in the event of a malpractice suit would meet this condition.

2. The trust grantor must not possess any retained interest in the property. That means more than giving up control. If the equipment were to automatically return to the taxpayer's ownership eventually, once the children completed college, for instance, the equipment trust would not pass IRS muster. But, of course, the taxpayer could repurchase the equipment.

Equipment Trust

OPERATING BUSINESS
Corporation, Partnership or Proprietorship.

LEASE OF EQUIPMENT

PAYMENT OF MONTHLY RENTAL

TRANSFER OF EQUIPMENT (GIFT)

IRREVOCABLE CHILDRENS' TRUST
Trustee must be Independent.

TAXPAYER & SPOUSE

CHILD 1

CHILD 2 **CHILD 3**

CHILD 4

1. Taxpayer(s) establish an irrevocable trust for children with an independent trustee.

2. Equipment is appraised and transferred to the trustee by gift.

3. Trustee leases the equipment to operating business. Monthly rental is 2 - 2.5% per month computed on the appraised fair market value.

4. Lease payments made by operating business constitute "ordinary and necessary" tax deductible business expenses.

5. Trustee may distribute the taxable income (lease payments) to the trust beneficiaries (one or more) prior to the end of the tax year of the trust.

Equipment Trust (Continued)

Problem:

Assume that taxpayer is a dentist paying 50% tax on all earnings. Assume further the taxpayer has as a personal objective to transfer $6,000 per year to four children for their education. He wants to know the least costly way from a tax perspective. Under the doctor's present program he must earn $12,000 to save $6,000 for his children's education. A good solution is to establish an irrevocable equipment trust.

Solution:

Doctor has equipment appraised by an equipment supplier for the amount of $26,136.50.

He makes a gift of the equipment to the trustee of the irrevocable trust.

The equipment is then leased back by the doctor for the monthly rental of $522.73 which is 2.0% per month on the appraised value of the equipment.

Result:

The trustee will, prior to the end of the trust fiscal year distribute the amount of $1,568.18 to each child for deposit into a special account for education purposes. Each child must report income of $1,568.18. After a $1,000 personal exemption the balance of $568.18 will generate a federal income tax of $68.18 leaving the amount of $1,500 each year to accumulate for education purposes.

In this example the gross earnings of the doctor required to save $6,000 for the children is $6,272.73. Compare this with the $12,000 required with the doctor's present program.

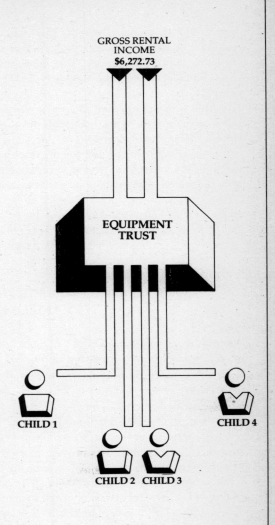

GROSS RENTAL INCOME
$6,272.73

EQUIPMENT TRUST

CHILD 1

CHILD 4

CHILD 2   CHILD 3

IT PAYS TO PAY YOUR CHILDREN

Many people still feel that their children should earn their own way through college. Maybe they shouldn't have to pay for all of it, but their education might be enhanced by an early contact with the real world and the responsibilities it imposes. Also, the very fact that students pay at least part of the cost of their education may make the education something more valued.

I'm not advocating child labor. But **employing your children is an excellent way for them to acquire a sense of values as well as earnings—and for you to acquire a tax deduction.**

Even if you intend to pay for all their college costs, employing your children can give them a chance to feel more independent and responsible, attitudes which often actually strengthen family ties.

If you have a business such as the family farm discussed in the chapter 16 on special tax shelters, or if you're in a business in which the children might legitimately be able to help, hiring them can be a tax-shelter plus.

HOW YOU AND YOUR CHILDREN CAN USE INFLATION
TO BEAT THE IRS

When a taxpayer, even a child, earns passive income—that is, dividends, interest, money from a trust, and so on—the *first $1,000* of this income is tax-free because of the personal exemption. Income over $1,000 is taxed at the standard progressive rate of 14 percent and up. In the case of earned income, on the other hand, the *first $3,300* is tax-free. That's because of the addition of the $2,300 zero bracket amount. The passive income a child receives from a trust cannot be used for clothing and other items normally considered part of the parents' responsibility without tax complications. But money the child earns can be spent on anything.

For example, I have a daughter who cleans my law office. In compensation for her work, she earns $200 a month—$2,400 a year— and pays no income tax on those earnings. All that is necessary for her to receive this money tax-free is that she perform some task that I can justify as being worth retaining her services. So she cleans the office, and I pay her $200 a month. That comes to $2,400 a year in tax-free income for her, which I deduct as a business expense. She can buy her own clothes, records, or whatever else she wants with that money. I also have two teenage sons who have, in the past, worked as process servers and messengers for my firm. If, for example, I paid each of my sons $200 a month for their services, that would be $2,400 tax-free earned income for each of them and an additional $4,800 business deduction for me.

If you have a big family, think of the possibilities. I have seven children. If I can figure out some way to get them all involved in my business, I can pay them each up to $3,300 a year tax-free income. And that's a yearly tax deduction of as much as $23,100 for me.

If there's any way that you can legitimately put your children to work in your trade or business, it makes sense to do so. You'll get the deduction. They'll get a real-world education and money besides. And with inflation making it increasingly difficult for most families to afford even the essentials, you and your children will have extra money for whatever you choose. Just make sure you pay them a fair wage.

TOO LATE TO TRUST?

"But," you interject, "I just now picked up this book, and my son is going to college this fall. An equipment lease wouldn't generate enough cash flow to pay the college bills. And though I'd be happy to have him work for me, as a college student working summers, he won't have time to earn enough to make it worthwhile. And as far as a trust goes, it's too late to start one."

Well, it's not really too late.

You can start a short-term trust—I like to call it the instant-scholarship trust—and fund it with as little as $100. Of course, $100 won't generate enough interest to pay for a textbook, much less an education. But there's a twist to this idea.

Once the trust is established, you can lend it $10,000 or $20,000 or whatever is necessary to cover your child's college expenses. You must lend the money on a demand basis. The loan cannot call for payments to be made at fixed periods, annually, semiannually, or quarterly. As soon as your child's education is completed, you can call the loan, or take your money back, letting your initial $100 deposit ride in the trust for the remainder of the trust's ten-year life.

INTEREST-FREE LOANS

A plan similar to the instant-scholarship trust involves giving your child an interest-free loan. The trust approach guarantees you'll get the principal back, of course. But more than that, part of an interest-free loan will be considered a gift.

The interest the money would have earned if you hadn't lent it out interest free is the amount considered to be a gift. If the loan is for a specific period of time, the assumed interest for the entire term of the loan constitutes the gift, on the date the loan is made. On the other hand, if the loan is a demand loan, only the assumed interest for each calendar quarter during which the loan remains unpaid is considered a gift.

If it's starting to seem as if you really can profit from giving, read the next chapter. You may view the IRS even more charitably.

19

Charitable Giving: Good Deeds that Save You Taxes

Avarice hoards itself poor,
charity gives itself rich,

—OLD GERMAN PROVERB

Charitable giving is not just for the wealthy. It's true that many foundations and charitable trusts that benefit the nation as a whole were set up by millionaires. But in today's tax environment, the middle class can profit financially as well as morally from transfers to charity.

Next to caring for one's family, charitable giving may be the best way to express one's beliefs and hopes for the future direction of the world. You may not be able to change the world single-handedly, any more than you can alter the tax laws by yourself. But you can use the tax laws to promote your own vision of a better tomorrow for all mankind.

To this end, the IRS has charitably conceded some special privileges for those who give money to worthy causes. If you've never thought of this broader approach to savings and taxation, try it. It will make both you and your checkbook feel good.

CHARITY CHICANERY

First, however, a warning. There's something about charity that attracts hustlers. I'm not sure exactly what it is that does so. Maybe, in our somewhat spiritless world, charity has become associated with a soft touch in many people's minds. Or maybe it's because cynicism has become so ingrained in our daily life, where the news always seems focused on the seamy side. Whatever the cause, you should both be aware of and beware of charitable tax shelters.

These questionable objects of charity come in all forms, from the donation of inflated gems to a museum to giving dry-rot-infested schooners to the Sea Scouts. One of the latest scams involves Bibles. A promoter was selling cases of Bibles at a time, for prices that were way below wholesale. Buyers were told that if they held onto the Bibles for a year, they could then contribute them to charitable organizations and deduct the full, much higher retail cost as a charitable donation.

The IRS agreed with everything but the price. "The charitable deduction is based on the fair market value of the Bibles at the time of the contribution, and the best evidence of the fair market value at that time is the price at which similar lots of Bibles are being sold to others."

Of course, the promoter could have sold each lot of Bibles and increased the price each month. There's no end to the possibilities, in fact. But let's face it, that's not what the charitable deduction is all about. **A charitable deduction should be a meaningful gift first and a deduction second.**

A GIFT WITH NO GIFT TAX

The IRS recognizes the special character of charitable giving and does not subject such gifts to gift or estate tax. Whether you transfer your assets to a charity during your lifetime or after you die makes no difference to the IRS. What counts is that the IRS recognizes your charity as bona fide. State, federal, and municipal agencies all qualify for charitable tax deductions. Religious, social service, scientific, literary, and educational organizations also qualify for tax deductions.

There is a certain quality control in charitable giving that restricts your generosity to prevent private organizations from hiding in charitable clothing. If you're like most people, you probably already have your own specific charitable goals in mind. Before you actually give, however, it's a good idea to check the official status of the charity. Every year, the United States government publishes a list of charities that qualify for a tax deduction. When in doubt, you or your attorney should check this register.

THE TAX IMPLICATIONS OF CHARITABLE GIVING

First of all, there's the matter of when to give. Tax considerations favor your giving the money during your lifetime, while you're in your peak earning years, if that is feasible. If you do not need the income from the assets you're thinking of giving away, then you could probably use the income-tax deduction.

Under federal income tax and the estate and gift-tax laws, there are no limits on how much you can *give* to charity. There are, however, limits on how much you can *deduct* from your income tax.

Each taxpayer is allowed an annual deduction of up to 50 percent of adjusted gross income for charitable gifts made to public or government-supported agencies or to certain approved private foundations. Such institutions are called *50-percent, or public, charities.* Public charities are those defined as having broad public support. They include legitimate churches, educational institutions, and other broadly based organizations, such as the American Red Cross, American Cancer Society, and the like.

All other charitable gifts come under the category of *20-percent charities*, with the deduction limited to 20 percent of your gross income. This allowable deduction is double the traditional 10-percent tithe, so it should leave plenty of leeway for most people.

Any donor who contributes more than 50 percent of adjusted gross income in one year to a 50-percent charity may carry over the excess deduction to any one or more of the following five years. Which of those years you choose is up to you. There is no carry-over allowed for the 20-percent charities, however.

These limitations on charitable giving apply only to individuals and certain partnerships. Corporations are limited to a deduction of 5 percent of their taxable income.

WHAT TO GIVE

Giving a gift of appreciated property has a multiplier effect that has important tax consequences. Appreciated property, simply speaking, is property that has gone up in value since it came into your possession. But *how* it appreciated has significant tax implications.

First there's *ordinary-income property* to be considered. This is property which would not be eligible for capital gains were you to sell it rather than give it away. As a deduction, therefore, its fair market value is reduced by its appreciation. Let's say, for instance, you have a painting that costs $3,000. Nine months after buying it, you decide to give it to a museum, which appraises it at $4,000. You cannot deduct $4,000. You can deduct only the fair market value, $4,000, less the appreciation, $1,000, or $3,000.

This rule includes diaries, letters, and other comparable documents accumulated during a life of public service. Henry Kissinger's letters, for instance, are worth the value of the paper they're written on as far as charitable deductions go.

Second, there are gifts of *appreciated property*. And the rules for such gifts fall into two categories.

Category 1. If you donate that painting we were talking about to a charity whose charitable function is not directly related to art—the Red Cross, for example—the IRS limits the amount of your deduction to the cost of the painting plus 50 percent of the appreciation, or $3,500.

The same holds true for transfers to private foundations. If a private foundation does not make a qualifying distribution equal to the amount of your contribution within two and a half months of the end of the year in which you make your contribution, you will be limited to the 50-percent appreciation deduction. A qualifying distribution in this case means the foundation must spend an amount equal to the value of your contribution for the purpose for which the foundation was established.

Category 2. This category relates to gifts of appreciated capital-gains property not covered by the first category. It includes diamonds, rare coins, stocks, and other such nonpersonal property as defined by the Internal Revenue Code which is held for over twelve months. When you contribute appreciated capital-gains property to a charity, your deduction ceiling is reduced from 50 percent to 30 percent of your adjusted gross income. However, you may elect to take a 50-percent reduction in appreciation, in which case the ceiling is raised to 50 percent.

Let's see how the two approaches work out on a dollar basis. Suppose a taxpayer with a $20,000 adjusted gross income makes a charitable contribution of part of a painting collection to a museum for display purposes. The contributed portion of the collection has a cost basis of $50,000, but it is valued at $100,000 on the date contributed, which is during 1980. Under the general rule, the taxpayer has made a contribution of $100,000. During

1980, the taxpayer may deduct $6,000 (30 percent of $20,000) and have a five-year contribution carry-over of $192,000, subject to the annual 30-percent adjusted-gross-income limitation.

Now suppose, alternatively, that the taxpayer decides to value the contribution at $75,000 (the $50,000 cost basis plus 50 percent of the $50,000 appreciation). In this case, the taxpayer could deduct $10,000 during 1980 (50 percent of $20,000), with a contribution carry-over of $65,000, subject to the 50-percent carry-over rule. A taxpayer making a contribution of highly appreciated property probably would not wish to elect the 50-percent rule.

If you regularly contribute 10 percent of your gross income to an established church which clearly qualifies as a 50-percent charity, you should seriously consider satisfying this commitment by transferring appreciated property instead of cash.

CHARITABLE TRUSTS

Trusts have a valid tax-sheltering function in charitable giving. By using a charitable trust, it's possible to give away a substantial amount of money, receive a tax deduction, and still be able to use most of that money. Some of it eventually goes to the chosen charity, of course, although this has not always been the case.

There have been some severe cutbacks of charitable trust benefits since 1969, when Congress drastically altered the laws governing gifts of future interest to charity. It used to be possible to take a large deduction by setting up a remainder trust, under which the named beneficiary, or beneficiaries, had life use of the entire trust, including the capital, and the charity received the remainder, what was left of the trust, only upon the beneficiary's death. This law has now been changed. The beneficiary must now receive a sum certain equal to either an annuity equal to not less than 5 percent of the gift originally placed in trust or a specific percentage equal to not less than 5 percent of the fair market value of the assets valued annually.

It might seem logical for the charity to be the one to receive a specified percentage. But the purpose of the percentage breakdown is to permit a more specific computation of the remainder interest to establush the worth of the deduction, rather than to control what the charity actually receives.

THE CHARITABLE-REMAINDER ANNUITY TRUST

You can transfer property to a charitable-remainder annuity trust and deduct the value of the remainder, meanwhile assuring a life income for yourself and your spouse. The remainder deduction under the new rule, however, is greatly reduced, and the trust must meet the following criteria to qualify:

1. The trust must pay a fixed sum to at least one noncharitable beneficiary, who must be living at the time the trust is created.
2. The amount paid cannot be less than 5 percent of the initial net fair market value of the contributed property.
3. The fixed sum must be payable at least annually, either for a term of years, but not more than twenty years, or for the life or lives of the noncharitable beneficiary or beneficiaries.
4. The trust may pay no other amounts to or for the use of any person other than a qualified charitable organization.
5. The remainder interest must be transferred to or for the use of a qualified charitable organization or be retained by the trust for such use.

The initial contribution to a charitable-remainder annuity trust is the only one permitted by law. No additional contributions are allowed. However, there's nothing that says you can't start another trust.

When a charitable-remainder annuity trust is formed, the grantor must select an independent trustee. The grantor may be the trustee. And the grantor may retain the right to remove the trustee and appoint a successor. The grantor may also, at any time, substitute a different charity for the original one to which the remainder is to be bequeathed. The grantor can even set up a public foundation, in order to have more say in the design of the charitable program. However, such a foundation must precede the trust itself.

The benefits to the grantor of this charitable act are many:

1. There is no tax on the proceeds of any sale of property by the charitable trustee.
2. The trustee selected will have whole dollars for investment and can be encouraged to choose inflation-proof investments.
3. The grantor is assured of an annual annuity.
4. The grantor receives an immediate tax saving from the deduction allowed in transferring the property to the trust.

5. The grantor may design a foundation program with the purpose of, say, educating Americans on the merits of the free-market system, or any other similar cause he or she wishes to support.

YOU PROFIT FROM INFLATION WITH A CHARITABLE-REMAINDER UNITRUST

The charitable-remainder trust can be improved even more by taking inflation into account. Using a so-called *unitrust*, the annuity payments to the grantor can be made variable, tied to a percentage of the trust's increasing assets. Besides the tax benefits it offers, such a trust, in inflationary times, provides a valuable hedge against the erosion of purchasing power.

A unitrust must meet the following conditions, similar to those of the remainder annuity trust, but with significant differences:

1. The trust must pay a fixed percentage, not less than 5 percent, of the net fair market value of its assets to at least one noncharitable beneficiary, who must be living at the time the trust is created.
2. To determine the amount of the payment to the noncharitable beneficiary or beneficiaries, the trust assets must be valued annually.
3. The payments to the noncharitable beneficiary or beneficiaries must be payable at least annually, either for a term of years, but not more than twenty years, or for the life or lives of the noncharitable beneficiary or beneficiaries.
4. The trust may pay no other amount to or for the use of any person other than a qualified charitable organization.
5. The remainder of the trust must be transferred to or for the use of a qualified charitable organization or retained by the trust for such use.

The crucial difference between a charitable-remainder annuity trust and a charitable-remainder unitrust, then, is that in the unitrust the grantor and the charitable beneficiary are united in their battle against inflation. The assets are revalued each year, and the annuity adjusted accordingly.

Let's see how that difference pays out. Taxpayers John and Mary Jones, fifty-eight and fifty-five years old respectively, have, among their other assets, a parcel of unimproved real estate which they purchased over ten years ago for $50,000. With a proposed highway about to be constructed near the property, an offer of purchase from a shopping-center developer is in the making.

The price to be paid for the property is $240,000, and a down payment of 29 percent is to be made in the year of the purchase. The balance, including interest at 9 percent, will be paid over the next five years.

John is still practicing medicine, and he earns over $100,000 a year. Considering his taxable income and the long-range objective of both himself and his wife to have a certain charitable institution receive a percentage of their estates after their death, a charitable-remainder unitrust would offer excellent planning potential.

After consulting with their tax adviser, the Joneses agree to establish such a unitrust. They transfer the real property to the trust.

In turn, the Joneses will receive, beginning in five years when John retires from his medical practice, an annual annuity equivalent to 7 percent of the value of the trust assets as appraised each year. So, assuming the trust's assets are inflation-indexed, the annuity will be too.

Since the trust is a charitable entity, the large gain of $190,000 ($240,000 less the $50,000 cost basis) is not subject to any capital-gains tax. In addition, the IRS will allow the Jonese a current income-tax deduction of approximately 18 percent of the value of the property, or $43,200. This amount is the value irrevocably earmarked for charity when the trust is established. Of course, there's the 30-percent-of-the-gross-income limit to the amount of the deduction the Joneses can use in any one year. But the balance of the deduction can be carried ahead to the following years.

GIVE NOW, REAP FROM INFLATION LATER

A charitable-front trust can lead to even larger tax savings for very sizable estates. Here, we're usually talking in the $1-million-plus range. The problems of such a lofty estate bother only a few of us, so let me merely state that this device is structured in such a way as to allow the trust assets to pay a fixed sum annually to a charity for a specified number of years. After that period, the full ownership of the trust property and its income revert to noncharitable beneficiaries.

If the trust is going to be in effect for over twenty-four years, it is possible to get a current estate or income-tax deduction for more than three quarters of the assets put in trust. The reason the deduction is so high in this instance is that it is based on the actuarial value of the gift spread over its life.

At the end of twenty-four years, however, the trust assets, given inflation, will be considerably higher in value than the original amount of the donation. They will be so even after a generous and continuous stream of income for the charity.

PRIVATE FOUNDATIONS AREN'T VERY TAX ADVANTAGEOUS ANYMORE

Private foundations are sometimes touted as the way to keep all your money and give it to charity as well. There are certain cases where a specific charitable goal becomes the central focus of someone's life, and a private foundation may then play a significant role. But, on the whole, **private foundations are not really viable tax-avoidance alternatives.** The idea of a private foundation may be intriguing to, say, a small business wishing to set up a mini Ford Foundation. But any prudent persons contemplating a private foundation for the purpose of tax avoidance had better consult the Tax Reform Act of 1969. They'll soon discover that there are better ways to control and pass on the assets of a closely held business.

20

Tax-Deferral Techniques, or, How to Put Off Paying Taxes Indefinitely

A fair exchange was no robbery.

—SMOLLETT

In 1979, close to $100 billion worth of nonmonetary transactions took place in both international and domestic trade. The IRS complains that most of it went untaxed, as well. Depending on who you listen to, barter is either the greatest tax avoidance program yet devised or is just another, more creative, way of doing business.

The truth is that barter does offer several unique tax savings opportunities, but tax evasion is *not* one of them.

BARTER, THE ALTERNATE ECONOMY?

The fact is that barter—the exchange of one asset for another—is not by definition a way to avoid taxes, even though many people promote it as such. There's a right and a wrong way to approach barter if you intend to stay within the law.

It would be a big mistake to assume that all barter transactions are taxable. The tax advisers who suggest this are as wrong as the hustlers who claim that all barter is tax-free because no actual money is involved. As in all potential tax situations, much depends on the circumstances involved. The services and products involved also are crucial to the final tax outcome.

As Jesse Cornish, a well-known expert on inflation-proof investments, once put it, "Tax advantages in barter resemble beauty, because they are in the eye of the beholder." In other words, when one embarks on the barter trail, either by way of the rapidly expanding barter exchanges or just between friends and neighbors, one enters that vast gray land in the tax code that is open to interpretation.

THE TAX ADVANTAGES OF BARTER

The tax law permits you to barter, or exchange, certain property tax-free. You aren't really absolved from paying the taxes due. They don't just vanish. But they are deferred, either indefinitely, for all practical purposes, or until a time in your life when you're in a potentially lower tax bracket, such as during your retirement. This gives you two distinct financial advantages.

First, if you can defer paying taxes for several years, it means that when you do eventually pay the tax, you will actually be paying less. This is because inflation erodes the dollar's value with each successive year, and so **you will be paying the tax you owe with dollars that have less value.** Meanwhile, you can profitably invest the amount you defer until repayment is actually required.

A second advantage to tax-deferred barter is that you save the money you would have had to pay for taxes if you sold the same asset you are exchanging, paid tax on the profit of the sale, and then purchased another asset with cash. In other words, **tax-deferred barter allows you to keep your money without tax costs,** whereas an ordinary sale and purchase requires you to tie up your money and pay taxes besides.

WHAT MAKES A BARTER TAX-DEFERRED?

The fundamental requirement for a tax-deferred barter, or exchange, under the Internal Revenue Code, Section 1031, is that **the properties to be traded must be of "like kind." They must also be held for productive use in a trade or business or for investment.**

"Like kind" refers to the nature, character, or class of the property, not to its grade or quality. Real estate, for instance, whether improved or unimproved, is property of like kind. The existence or lack of improvements merely affects its grade or quality. The location of the property to be exchanged is likewise of no importance. A ranch in the United States and a ranch in a foreign country are like-kind properties.

Other examples of like-kind exchanges are a used automobile or truck exchanged for a new one to be used for the same purpose; trades of uniform player contracts owned or controlled by major league baseball or football clubs; bullion-type gold coins minted by one country for bullion-type coins minted by another country, where the coins are no longer a circulating medium of exchange within their respective countries, and hence not money.

The Internal Revenue Service recently ruled that an exchange of non-circulating, or numismatic, gold coins, for instance U.S. $20 gold pieces for circulating gold coins—say, South African Krugerrands—would not be tax free, as the coins are not considered to be of like kind. The reason given was that the U.S. coins are collector-type coins, whose value is determined by factors such as rarity and aesthetics. The Krugerrands' value is established solely by their metal content. In short, an investment in numismatic coins and an investment in bullion-type coins represent investments which are not of the same nature or character.

To further illustrate the intent of Congress on the crucial question of what properties are of like kind, Section 1031(e) of the Internal Revenue Code gives the specific example that the exchange of livestock of one sex for livestock of the other sex is not an exchange of property of like kind. Why? Different sexes of livestock represent investments of different types: in one case, an investment for breeding purposes; in the other, an investment in livestock raised for eventual slaughter.

INVENTORY AND SECURITIES ARE NOT INCLUDED

The tax-free exchange rules do not cover bartering for inventory, stock in trade, or other property held primarily for sale; stocks, bonds, notes, choses-in-action (the right to bring an action to collect a debt for money), certificates of trust or beneficial interest, or other securities or evidences of indebtedness or interest. Thus, you cannot legally barter many investment and business assets without paying taxes.

These exceptions can produce unexpected results. For example, though tax-free real-estate barters are generally permitted, if a real-estate dealer, as opposed to a real-estate investor, trades real estate for real estate, the dealer must pay taxes on the transaction. According to the IRS, the dealer is keeping such real-estate property primarily as inventory, not as an investment, and so must pay taxes on it.

UNDERSTANDING THE TAX IMPLICATIONS OF BARTER

The key to understanding the potential tax liability in barter lies in determining the fair market value of the bartered goods. How do you define the fair market value? Take the case of a camera. Is the fair market value the retail price? The wholesale price? Or what you would be willing to pay for the camera, for example, if you already owned a camera and didn't really need another one but were offered a deal you couldn't refuse?

In an attempt to resolve this problem, the IRS regulations state, "Fair market value is defined as the price at which the property would change hands between a willing buyer and a willing seller; neither being under any compulsion to buy or sell, and both having reasonable knowledge of the relevant facts"—a definition which still leaves a lot to the subjective judgment of both parties.

It's not at all unreasonable to assume that the same product or service may vary considerably in price. For example, a discount store might sell a camera for $400. Exactly the same camera might sell for $600 at a local full-price store. But is either of these the real price? A bank offering you the same camera as a gift for opening a $10,000 account would, in effect, be giving you the camera for free. Is the price of the camera then zero?

The same ambiguity holds true in the case of professional services. For example, a dentist may have some charity cases. Even for regular clients, prices may not be the same. Our family dentist, for instance, charges $15 for a semiannual checkup. But last time he didn't charge at all for one of my children. It had just become obvious that the child would need considerable orthodontal work at a later date. In the joyful contemplation of future income from the expenses of braces, the dentist didn't bother to charge for the present visit.

When you think about it, faith in the capitalistic system under which we operate, if to a lesser degree than before, requires one to believe that prices will reflect "whatever the market will bear." Taxpayers are under no more compulsion to set the "fair market value" at the highest possible level than they are to pay the highest possible income tax. Rather, both logic and the desire to minimize taxes would dictate that the lowest possible values be assigned by all parties in most transactions. However, the final valuation must take into account what would be considered reasonable and defensible in the tax court.

BARTERING TAX-FREE WITH ADDITIONAL PROPERTY

If you barter property for property of like kind but, because the properties are not of equal value, money also changes hands in the transaction, any profit you receive from the money portion of the transaction could be liable for tax. In addition, under no circumstances can you deduct a tax loss for such a trade.

UNUSUAL TECHNIQUES FOR TAX-FREE BARTER

Many times you may want to barter property tax-free but either cannot find a buyer who owns property to barter in exchange or cannot find suitable property to barter for. There are two solutions to such problems, the *multiparty exchange* and the *nonsimultaneous exchange*.

THE MULTIPARTY EXCHANGE

The multiparty exchange is used to barter tax-free when you cannot find a trade partner who is willing to barter with you. For example, A owns property and wants to exchange it tax-free. B will buy A's property but does not have property of equivalent value or property for which A wants to exchange. C is selling property which A would be willing to exchange property for, but C is unwilling to exchange. A, B, and C can all get what they want if they take the following steps:

1. B buys C's property from C. This achieves C's objective of selling.
2. B then exchanges properties with A. This achieves B's objective of acquiring A's property. It also achieves A's objective of a tax-free exchange for C's property.

This kind of transaction is usually considerably more complex because the value of the properties being exchanged is rarely equal. Often, money, mortgages, and so on must also be exchanged to balance the equity position of all parties. You must be careful to follow each step of the barter in the proper order, as specified by your attorney. It may also be necessary to have trusts or escrow arrangements, extensive negotiations, and purchase agreements. Before you agree to any such transaction, seek the advice of an independent tax attorney.

NONSIMULTANEOUS EXCHANGES

Another way to barter when normal barter is not possible is to *barter for property in the future.* Often, a person who owns property wants to exchange the property tax-free and has found a buyer but has not found suitable like-kind property to receive in exchange. The person wishing the exchange wants neither to pass up the willing buyer nor to pay the tax that would be incurred with an outright sale of the property. Remember, a multiparty exchange, as described above, will not work unless suitable like-kind property is found.

Let's say that A wants to exchange property for other like-kind property. B wants to buy A's property but does not own suitable like-kind property to exchange. The solution is as follows:

1. A agrees to transfer the property to B. B agrees to find and purchase suitable like-kind property and transfer it to A.

2. Sometime later, B acquires suitable property and transfers it to A.

Up until recently, the IRS claimed this was not a solution because A's exchange was delayed in time, or nonsimultaneous. The law had been unclear whether such an exchange qualified for tax deferral or not. Taxpayers said it did; the IRS said it didn't. The case of *T. J. Starker* v. *U.S.* decided the matter in 1979. *The taxpayers won.*

THE *STARKER* CASE: A VICTORY FOR TAXPAYERS

The most significant ruling of the Starker case is that a nonsimultaneous exchange can qualify for tax deferral under Section 1031. In the *Starker* case, the taxpayer transferred real estate to Crown Zellerbach, a large paper and lumber concern, in exchange for Crown Zellerbach's agreement to provide the taxpayer with suitable like-kind real estate or cash within five years. The taxpayer wanted real estate. The deal was closed two years later when Crown Zellerbach provided the taxpayer with the real estate. The Ninth Circuit reversed the District Court and held that the exchange qualified for tax deferral under Section 1031. The court held that it is not important that the exchange transfers of title were separated by a "substantial" period of time, as long as all the other requirements of Section 1031 were met.

The court also held that the possibility of the taxpayer's receiving cash instead of like-kind property did not make Section 1031 inapplicable. The "mere possibility at the time of agreement that a cash sale might occur does not prevent the application of Section 1031." Even where taxpayers have the option to receive payment in cash rather than in property, the possibility that the taxpayers might have received cash does not make the transaction taxable.

THE TAX IMPLICATIONS OF NONSIMULTANEOUS EXCHANGES

The *Starker* case also decided that where a gain is recognized, the gain is taxed in the year the taxpayer transfers the property, not in the year he or she receives property in exchange. The transfer is thus not completed for tax purposes until it is determined whether or not the taxpayer will receive cash or like-kind property in payment. If the taxpayer ultimately receives cash, however, the tax he or she owes will be assessed in the year he or she actually transferred the property.

STARKER AND NON-REAL-ESTATE EXCHANGES

The *Starker* ruling is very broad and is not limited to real-estate transactions. **Because of this ruling, taxpayers should be able to get a tax deferral for nonsimultaneous exchanges of all types of like-kind properties.** The case does not specifically state this. But there is no logical reason why real estate could be exchanged non-simultaneously and other assets could not.

PLANNING OPPORTUNITIES

Starker has made it possible for taxpayers to transfer property before receiving suitable like-kind property in exchange and qualify for tax deferral. As a taxpayer, it will now be easier for you to exchange property when you have difficulty finding suitable like-kind property to exchange for, when it is difficult to get all the parties involved in the exchange together to achieve a simultaneous exchange of deeds, and when the terms and conditions of the trade require time to be worked out.

You also have the option of receiving cash or like-kind property and getting a tax deferral as long as you establish that you *prefer* to receive suitable like-kind property if it can be found. You should enter into an exchange agreement stating this specifically *before* the title to the initial property is transferred. As long as you do not receive any cash payment, you can wait until you find suitable property and still qualify for tax deferral under Section 1031.

The *Starker* ruling does not set a time limit for this type of transaction. However, to be on the safe side, you should set a two-year time period for completing the exchange. In this way, you will not exceed the time limit established in this precedent.

THE PROBLEM OF TRADE PARTNERS' CREDIT

A *Starker* trade assumes that the partner with whom you're trading will be financially able to acquire suitable like-kind property. In *Starker*, the trade partner was Crown Zellerbach, which could easily afford to purchase suitable properties. But the taxpayer who trades first risks a loss if the trade partner is later unable to deliver.

IRS Letter Ruling 7938087 discusses a method of solving this credit risk. For example, suppose X planned on trading existing property to Y for suitable like-kind property which Y was to find in the future. To consummate the trade, X transferred property to a trust with an independent trustee. The trust sold the property to Y and held the proceeds to purchase suitable like-kind property. This gave X absolute security. If Y could not find suitable property by a specified date, X would receive the cash being held in the trust.

The IRS initially ruled that this transaction would qualify as a tax-free exchange at the time the like-kind property was acquired and transferred. The IRS cited the *Baird* case as an example that using a trust with an independent trustee was a valid means of achieving a tax-free exchange.

However, in a later IRS Letter Ruling, 8005049, the IRS informed the taxpayer that it was reconsidering its position and that the taxpayer could no longer rely on the previous letter ruling. The IRS gave no reason for this turnabout.

In my opinion, the initial ruling would probably be upheld if it was challenged in tax court. There is ample authority that a trust can participate in a Section 1031 exchange, particularly where there is an independent trustee. The *Baird* case is one example. If a trust can participate, there is no reason why the *Starker* rule should not apply to the trust in the same way it applies to an individual taxpayer.

PERSONAL PROPERTY BARTER

Most used-personal-property trades should prove to be tax exempt. Why? Because, in most cases, personal property is used property, and so it has depreciated in value.

If you were to hold a garage sale at your home, you would not have to declare any income gained from the sale because, in all likelihood, the earnings you receive from the sale wouldn't come anywhere near the original cost of the items you sold. The same would apply to the sale of your automobile, except in the case of certain antique cars that are increasing in value.

As a result, if you swap personal property for other personal property, the trade should be tax-free, no questions asked. Besides, it would be extremely difficult to decide what is fair market value here. Normally, the trade would be a loss transaction. But, alas, the IRS won't let you take a loss on personal property except in the case of a casualty loss.

Typically, then, no taxable event takes place at flea markets, garage sales, or other such open transactions involving personal goods.

How about home exchanges for a two-week vacation? You offer your home for two weeks in exchange for someone else's home located in a vacation spot. Are you liable to pay tax on the income you could have gotten if you had rented out your home? The law is unclear. The IRS will undoubtedly argue that there is income. They have ruled that the use of a home or apartment in exchange for a work of art is taxable income. But in this situation aren't you simply reducing the cost of vacationing? Or, if there is income, can you now depreciate your home as you can other income-producing property?

Or suppose a lawyer wants a house painted, and a house painter needs legal advice? They get together, either through a formal exchange club or as friends, and barter their services. Are they liable for tax, and if so, how much? According to a recent IRS ruling (Revenue Ruling 79-24), the lawyer is supposed to count as income the fair market value of the paint job, and the painter the value of the legal advice.

Yet there are still some questions left unanswered. What if the lawyer and painter were friends? How could the IRS prove that their services were not mutual gifts, which are exempt from tax? Moreover, who is to decide the fair market value of the services rendered?

The only time that barter of a service or item is not considered as taxable income is when it is given as a gift, or "gratuitous transfer with no intention of repayment," according to Wilson Fadely of the IRS Public Affairs Office in Washington, D.C. This means that if I take you out to lunch, we fight over the bill, and I win, you don't have to declare the "free lunch" as taxable income. That is, you don't unless I happen to say, "You can pick it up next time," in which case you'll face the wrath of the IRS for failing to report your share of the lunch as income.

Obviously, under our "voluntary" tax system, the lawyer and the painter are expected to estimate by themselves how much the income from an exchange should be. Normally, let's say, the lawyer charges $50 an hour. Is that fair market value? Not necessarily. Certain clients may be charged more, depending on the technical nature of the case; widows and friends less. Perhaps the lawyer offers discounts from time to time and on other occasions donates both time and services to charity.

In other words, it is up to the lawyer and the painter to make the decision as to the value of the exchange. From a practical point of view, the IRS isn't going to involve itself in such a confusing situation if it's an isolated occurrence. In the words of Vernon K. Jacobs, senior editor of the newsletter *Tax Angles*, "In our opinion, a good tax lawyer could have a field day with an attempt by the IRS to place a value on a pure exchange of services."

THE PROBLEM WITH BARTER CLUBS

However, there would be a more serious problem if the swapping of services were done on a large, organized scale, as in the case of an exchange club. Some barter organizations have developed a "check" or "credit" program in which nominal values are assigned to the various barter transactions. Whenever these credits are used by a club member, the amount is recorded on the club's central-computer bank. The credits are usually at near-retail levels, which may not be a fair representative of value for value.

Obviously, there are expenses related to finding barter partners, and those fees and expenses can legitimately be deducted from the income accrued. However, a recent IRS ruling (Revenue Ruling 80-52), states that, for tax purposes, one trade credit equals one dollar, and that income should be reported when the trade credits are received, not when they are spent. Now, in reality, trade credits are not anywhere near equal to a dollar in value. Also, the IRS is aggressively seeking to obtain the transaction and membership records of such clubs with the intent of auditing the members. Therefore, trade clubs may offer more tax disadvantages than advantages.

NO GAIN, NO TAX

If you don't show a gain or a profit as a result of a transaction, whether it's cash or barter, obviously there is no tax event. So if you were to make a habit of trading at cost, taxes would be the least of your worries. Not even the IRS can compel you to make money just so it can take it away.

In the cash economy, unless you at some time show a profit in your business career, that career is likely to be short. In barter, showing a profit is not only unnecessary but often irrelevant as well.

Utility, not monetary value, is the key concept in barter. The utility of a given item or service does not change when various prices are assigned to that item or service.

For example, if I am trading some gems that I acquired at a very good price for a series of metal etchings that you acquired years ago while in Europe, at an equally good price, we could approach the transaction in one of two ways. First, we could blow smoke at each other. I could produce an appraisal indicating a highly inflated fair market value of the gems, a value at least four times my actual cost. And you could play the same game by giving me a real song and dance about this great unknown artist whose work is so rare that it can't be accurately appraised—bringing to mind the word *priceless*. We could each assign unrealistically high values and go on to make the trade only because we both know that what each of us is giving up isn't worth what we say it is. In this trade, only the IRS would benefit, as we would both show substantial profits.

Or, we could both acknowledge that we want what the other has—I want prints, you want gems—that the values of what we're trading are roughly comparable, and that the prices we assign are totally irrelevant. As long as we get what we're bargaining for, showing a profit not only doesn't matter but is actually counterproductive as well. If we arrange our documentation to honestly indicate that the exchange was a wash, tax problems can be minimized.

ONE WARNING ABOUT THE IRS AND BARTER

In its never-ending battle to get every last nickel, the IRS has recently cracked down on the abuse of barter deals. The new *Audit Technique Handbook for Internal Revenue Agents* instructs agents to pay special attention to barter, particularly the swapping techniques used by reciprocal trade agencies, or trade clubs. Agents are to ask taxpayers if they have engaged in any barter, or if they have traded services for inventory or for "personal goods and services, such as vacations, houseboats, luxury cars, use of vacation home or condominium, or payment of personal or stockholder debts."

As you can see, the IRS seems to feel it has the right to know about everything in your personal and financial affairs—an invasion of privacy that comes, apparently inevitably, with the federal income tax.

SUMMING UP BARTER

The basic conclusions we can draw about barter, then, are as follows:

1. The Internal Revenue Code specifically exempts certain like-kind exchanges.
2. The exchange of most personal property is exempt from taxation.
3. The exchange of services for other services or products is taxable at the fair market value of the service or product rendered. For tax purposes the lowest reasonable value should be assigned to a transaction. Remember, however, if you are audited, IRS could reject your estimate and it would be up to you to prove you are right.
4. The IRS generally ignores isolated barter transactions that don't involve substantial income. But IRS auditors have been alerted to large-scale organized barter exchanges. Members should check

with their tax advisers on the value they should place on such barter arrangements.

5. The mutual exchange of gifts is income-tax-free as long as neither party expects compensation. Clearly, the motivation for an exchange of services or products is in the eyes of the beholder, and it would be difficult for the IRS to disprove your charitable motives.

6. Where there is no gain, there is no tax.

USING SILVER COINS TO DEFER TAXES

Requesting that you be paid in silver coins when selling a house or boat or some other asset could result in all your taxes being deferred to a much later date. It costs the buyer no more than paper money or a check. And not only do you defer taxes, you manage to switch into hard, inflation-proof assets at the same time.

If pre-1965 United States silver coins are exchanged for any other property, the provisions of Section 1031 I've mentioned before would seem to indicate a tax-deferrable exchange only if the exchange items are "like" the pre-1965 silver coins. So what makes these coins, minted prior to 1965 and containing 90-percent silver, unique barter items offering a possible tax deferment in transactions involving "unlike kinds" of property?

Pre-1965 silver coins are distinguished from most other coins which have a metal value far in excess of face value by the fact that they are still considered legal tender by the U.S. government.

Let's take as an example a seller of real property who chooses to defer taxes by accepting pre-1965 silver coins in payment for the property. The taxpayer owns a parcel of real property which has a market value of $200,000. The present basis of the property—that is, its original cost, less depreciation, plus capital improvements—is $10,000. If the property were sold for cash and the taxpayer received $200,000 in Federal Reserve notes, he would have a taxable gain of $170,000. However, the seller could ask the buyer to pay not in Federal Reserve notes with a face value of $200,000 but in pre-1965 silver coins with a face value of, say, $16,000 but a silver metal value of $200,000. He would then report a sale of real property for $16,000. After subtracting the cost basis, $10,000, the recognized taxable gain would be $6,000. The balance of the gain, or $164,000, would be tax deferred. The basis of the coins received would be $16,000. If and when the coins were later converted to other property, including Federal Reserve notes, the taxpayer would have a taxable gain of the difference between $16,000 and the face value of the other currency received.

Right now it's not known how the courts would perceive such a transaction, because a transaction involving the specific issue of pre-1965 silver coins being legal tender and giving rise to tax deferment has not as yet been challenged by the IRS.

However, the bellwether of the IRS position on pre-1965 silver coins is contained in a ruling issued in 1976. This ruling (Revenue Ruling 76-249) holds that a taxpayer exchanging real property for silver coins realizes a taxable gain, a gain based on the excess of the fair market value of the coins over the adjusted basis of the real property. In arriving at this conclusion the IRS gave no discussion of the issue of the coins as being legal tender. It stated only that the coins were to be considered property within the broad definition of certain IRC sections.

SILVER COIN PAYMENTS—THE CONGRESSIONAL VIEW

The most direct authority for deferment lies with the United States Constitution and various laws passed by Congress. Under its constitutional powers, Congress passed the Coinage Act of 1965 under Title 31 United States Code (U.S.C.), Section 392. That section states, "All coins and currencies of the United States (including Federal Reserve Notes and circulating notes of Federal Reserve banks and national banking associations), regardless of when coined or issued, shall be legal tender for all debts, public and private, public charges, public taxes, duties and dues." That section clearly indicates that legal tender of the United States still includes pre-1965 silver coins. Even the legislative history to this law states

> It is of critical importance to the public and to the economy that there be a smooth transition from our present coinage system to a new system. . . .
> To this end, it is important that there be no incentive for the withdrawal from circulation of the existing subsidiary silver coins or of the new ones.
> The official agencies of the Treasury Department will continue to exchange lawfully held coins and currencies of the United States, dollar for dollar, for other coins and currencies which may be

lawfully acquired and are legal tender for public and private debts.

The argument can then be made that the value of a certain coin is fixed on its face as well as by statute and regulation. The fact that a coin is a circulating silver coin should not be reason for making that coin worth more than its face value in transactions with the United States government. The IRS briefly touched on the subject in a 1974 ruling (Revenue Ruling 74-218) referring to foreign currencies. The ruling discussed the meaning of United States currency. It stated, "Currency in its usual and ordinary acceptation means gold, silver, other metals, or paper used as a circulating medium of exchange."

Today, under the new laws cited in chapter 4, Inflation Indexing, it is perfectly legal to specify gold or silver coins in payment of obligations. The courts have consistently held that the Constitution leaves the power to declare what shall be legal tender for payment of all debts to Congress. The pronouncement of Congress in the Coinage Act of 1965, then, should be the final say on the matter. Accordingly, the person who sells property, receives payment with pre-1965 silver coins, and reports the sale price at the face and not the silver value of coins, is only acting in accordance with the Constitution, federal law, and public policy.

As a further example, consider what would happen if a taxpayer took coins to the U.S. Treasury and requested Federal Reserve notes computed on the silver value: The Treasury would decline payment. Likewise, a taxpayer tendering payment of a federal income-tax liability with pre-1965 coins would be given credit only for the coins' face value. Under the Federal Reserve Act, the U.S. Treasury is only required to give Federal Reserve notes at the face value of those coins, not at an increased value.

WHAT IS LAWFUL MONEY?

A letter from the Board of Governors of the Federal Reserve system, responding to an inquiry regarding redemption of Federal Reserve notes, noted that the term *lawful money* generally means any medium of exchange which freely circulates from hand to hand as money under sanction of law. Although there was a certain time when it was necessary to make a distinction between *lawful money* and *legal tender*, this is no longer the case.

Prior to 1933, only certain types of currency were declared by statute to be legal tender, in which a creditor was legally obligated to accept payment. However, after 1933, it was specifically provided that all coins and currencies of the United States heretofore or hereafter coined or issued shall be legal tender for all debts public and private. So when a person with a Federal Reserve note tenders it at the U.S. Treasury and demands payment in gold or silver or specie, the U.S. Treasury has the right to tender payment in *either* paper reserve notes or other standard coins or coinage. This coinage could be pre-1965 silver coins. But the U.S. Treasury has the option of paying whatever currency it desires. One brave soul recently tested this and demanded that his $50 Federal Reserve banknote be redeemed in lawful money of the United States, which, he said, *must* be gold or silver. The Ninth Circuit Court of Appeals found he had no such right and poetically observed:

> While we agree that golden eagles, double eagles, and silver dollars were lovely to look at and delightful to hold, we must at the same time recognize that time marches on, and that even the time-honored silver dollar is no longer available in its last bastion of defense, the brilliant casinos of the houses of change in the State of Nevada. Appellant is entitled to redeem his precious note, but not in precious metal.
>
> *Milan* v. *U.S.*, 524 F.2D, 629, 9th Cir., 1974, memo dec.

The government is in the unique position of being able to have its cake and eat it too. It will accept payments in any lawful money, including pre-1965 silver coins, at face value—and return payments in Federal Reserve notes at face value.

The central question remains: Are pre-1965 U.S. silver coins legal tender? The IRS, in its efforts to prevent tax rebels from refusing to pay taxes on the constitutional grounds that Federal Reserve notes are not legal tender, or lawful money, has gone to great pains in describing and defining such notes as being equal in acceptability to gold or silver coins. Yet, when circumstances seem to reveal a possible tax advantage in using silver coins as legal tender, the IRS doesn't hesitate to reverse its previous position. It then concludes that such coins are property for income-reporting purposes and legal tender for purposes of tax payment. The rationale for this inconsistency is clear only to the IRS. The rest of us, including the courts and Congress, assume that any United States coin or paper currency that is still in circulation, regardless of any intrinsic or metal value, is legal tender. The fact that these coins remain in circulation and are accepted at banks, pay telephones, candy machines, and government offices as legal tender is significant.

At present, silver coins are the only form of legal tender that has a melt value in excess of the face value. But this may soon change. When copper prices climb above $1.46 per pound, the level at which the metal and the face value of a penny are equal, it may be possible to demand payment of obligations in pennies—at least if you're the owner of a trucking firm.

THE BOTTOM LINE

The use of silver coins should not be taken too far. Paying wages in silver coins and declaring them at face value, for instance, has greater risks than using silver coins in a sale or exchange. The IRS has already won a major court battle in 1980 involving gold numismatic coins. The taxpayer was a stockholder who received gold coins as dividends on his shares of stock and reported the face value of the coins as dividend income. The IRS successfully contended the income-tax value was the fair market value.

Wages are not measured under IRC Section 1001, but rather Sections 61 and 83, among others. These sections do not distinguish between money and other property. Generally, wages paid are measured in terms of compensation, regardless of the form. The language of Sections 61 and 83 is broad enough to allow the IRS to argue that the fair market value of coins is the amount of compensation, and the face amount is irrelevant. The taxpayer could argue that the standard of measurement here is the statutory standard of value, which is a gold dollar, not a Federal Reserve note. This area of the law is undecided. But it's likely to be resolved in favor of the IRS.

A recent District Court opinion (*Joslin*, D.C., Utah, February 27, 1981) was faced with this dilemma. Mr. Joslin, an attorney, billed his clients at the rate of $100 per hour, payable in silver coins minted prior to 1965. He reported his income at the $10 hourly rate, but the IRS said his actual income was equal to the fair market value of the coins, which amounted to more than $100 an hour. While the court agreed with the IRS, it completely ignored the legal tender issue. The *Joslin* case is currently on appeal to the 10th Circuit Court of Appeals.

The possible advantage in using silver coins is limited only to tax deferral and should not be viewed as a scheme to evade taxes. One IRS agent with whom this idea was discussed cautioned that, to enjoy any tax benefits of this deferral, the coins must be legal tender. And as soon as they are sold or further exchanged for any consideration whose value exceeds the tax basis of the coins, a gain must be reported. As with any deferral, your real profits from inflation accrue because the payment of taxes is postponed to a later, more convenient date.

LIKE-KIND EXCHANGES OF MINERALS

Does the exchange of one precious mineral held for investment for another precious mineral held for investment qualify as a tax-deferred exchange under Section 1031? This is a question of increasing importance as we enter an era of resource scarcity, where investments in such minerals as chromium, rhodium, and vanadium may well outpace inflation better than any other assets. The answer is simple, but the reasoning is complex. Let's start with the revenue rulings on a mineral in the form of coins.

In Revenue Ruling 76-214, Mexican bullion-type gold coins were deemed to be of a like kind with Austrian bullion-type gold coins. The crucial test for this decision was based on Regulation 1.1031(a)-1(b), which, as I have noted, states that like kind refers to the nature or character of the property, not to its grade or quality, and, additionally, that one kind or class of property may not be exchanged for a different kind or class of property.

The ruling states that the differences between the Mexican and the Austrian coins are primarily in size, shape, and gold purity. These are matters of grade, or quality. But the nature or character of the two coins is the same. Both derive value solely from their gold content. They represent investments in gold.

Now contrast this with another ruling, Revenue Ruling 79-143, which held that gold bullion-type coins are not of a like kind with numismatic-type coins, because numismatic coins have value attributable to their age, the number minted, history, art, and aesthetics, as well as metal content. "The bullion-type coins, unlike numismatic-type coins, represent an investment in gold on world markets rather than in the coins themselves." The ruling pointed out that "investments in gold on world markets" are a distinct kind or class of property in comparison to collecting coins.

Investors, however, generally buy minerals, whether gold, silver, diamonds, titanium, or coal, for the same reason—namely, to hold the assets until the price goes up. That all these minerals can be deemed like-kind property is indicated by IRS Letter Ruling 8020107, dated February 15, 1980, which acknowledges that investments in gold and silver are of a like kind. In that letter ruling, a quantity of silver bullion held for investment is exchanged for a quantity of gold bullion held for investment. The letter ruling states, "In the intent case, there is an exchange of *bullion for bullion* and under the rationale of Revenue Ruling 76-214, such a transaction would qualify as an exchange for property of a like kind" (italics mine). The equation of bullion with bullion seems to indicate that other minerals could be of a like kind as well if they are held for investment in bullion form. Significantly, the letter ruling does not even mention the differences in the two metals; their chemical composition, usage, lore, and so on are not factors.

FUTURES ARE DIFFERENT

A direct investment in minerals, however, cannot be exchanged, under Section 1031, for indirect investments, such as futures or other commodity rights. Section 1031(a) specifically excludes securities. In addition, many cases require identical title for like-kind properties. For example, future oil and gas royalties are not of a like kind with business real estate, while unlimited mineral rights are. In addition, an investor with future rights to minerals should wait for delivery of the minerals before entering a Section-1031 exchange.

An investment in raw, uncut, or unprocessed minerals should be of a like kind with an investment in pure or cut minerals. Both are investments in the metal market. The differences are merely matters of grade or quality. Revenue Ruling 76-214 found differences in size, shape, and gold content to be irrelevant in bullion coin exchanges. Other property exchanges show similar flexibility. *Wylie* v. *U.S.* (281 F. Supp 180 [N.D. Tex, 1968]) found a trade of common cattle for registered Aberdeen Angus to be like-kind. A new truck was like-kind with a used truck in *National Outdoor Advertising Bureau, Inc.* v. *Helvering* (89 F.2d 878 [2nd Cir., 1939]). Since differences in grade or quality are easily shown with minerals, they should not be confused with differences in kind or class.

There are insufficient authorities to exactly delineate the breadth of the class of like-kind mineral investments. Clearly, silver and gold are in the same class. But are gems, cut or uncut, in the same class? The investment purposes are the same, so they should be included. How about investments in tungsten, coal, or other less popular investment minerals? Certainly the investment purpose—to hold the asset until the price rises and then sell—is the same. Logic would dictate that the class should include all minerals held for investment, but that manufactured minerals, such as numismatic coins or silverware, should be excluded.

The legislative history of Section 1031 supports this approach. The major factor cited there is whether the investor has cashed out of the investment or left the money tied up in the same kind of property. The report accompanying the 1934 Revenue Act stated that

> profit or loss is recognized in the case of exchanges of notes or securities, which are essentially like money; or in the case of stock in trade; or in case the taxpayer exchanges the property comprising his original investment for a different kind of property; but *if the taxpayer's money is still tied up in the same kind of property as that in which it was originally invested, he is not allowed to compute and deduct his theoretical loss on the exchange, nor is he charged with a tax upon his theoretical profit.* The calculation of the profit or loss is deferred until it is realized in cash, marketable securities, or other property not of the same kind having a fair market value. [H.R. Rept. No. 704, Revenue Act of 1934, 73rd Congress, 2nd Session; italics mine.]

An exchange of mineral investments for manufactured or useful goods is a form of cashing out. But switching from one mineral to another leaves the investor's money in the market.

THE IRS DIDN'T WANT YOU TO TAKE LOSSES—BUT NOW YOU GET THE GAINS

The IRS can be expected to take a narrow view on like-kind mineral interests. Minerals are highly appreciating properties in today's market, and there is considerable revenue at stake. Section 1031 was originally enacted in 1924 to prevent losses as much as gains. The 1934 Revenue Act renewed it because, during the Depression, "claims for theoretical losses would probably exceed any profit" (H.R. Rept. No. 704). Inflation has changed all that and turned Section 1031 into a pro-taxpayer provision. The IRS cannot be expected to like it.

21

The Closely Held Business— The All-American Way to Beat the IRS

> Government in the U.S. today is a senior partner in every business in the country.
>
> —NORMAN COUSINS

Any business with a limited number of owners, whether it's a supermarket owned by a single individual or a light manufacturing company owned by half a dozen people, is known as a *closely held business*—as opposed to a publicly held business, where the ownership is held by a larger number of people. A closely held business faces particularly difficult tax planning problems. As a business, it usually has a long-range plan to foster its growth and economic development. Sales projections, capital projections, and cost projections are all made regularly. The more structured of these projections may well carry five, ten, or even twenty years into the future. Yet somehow, when it comes to estate planning, the business is all too often simply left as an asset that will somehow continue to churn along its profitable route by itself. And so it does, right up to the day its founder dies. Then chaos ensues.

PLANNING AHEAD TO MINIMIZE TAXES

Some of the most important estate decisions a business owner may ever have to make may actually be made shortly after a new business is established, and some of those decisions can be costly if all their future ramifications aren't carefully considered. Let me show you what I mean. I have a client with a large estate that includes two very successful manufacturing corporations. One grosses about $20 million in annual sales, the other about $4 million. The first company may be worth $5 or $6 million, the second $3 million. So this man has a pretty good-sized estate, and he's facing some pretty stiff death taxes.

Just after my client had achieved success with his first business, when it was worth about $3 million, and before he'd started his second, I said to him, "Look, when you form this new business, why don't you create two classes of stock in the corporation. You can put up the operating capital, let's say $150,000, and keep the preferred stock with all the voting control in your name, so you run the business. But give your three children the common stock. Let each of them put up $500. That way, if this business ever becomes worth a lot of money, your equity for tax purposes will be frozen at $150,000."

He couldn't see the long-range tax advantage of this suggestion. He was stuck on the idea of retaining total control of the business, and he didn't want his children owning anything in his estate at that point. So he didn't do it. He owns 100 percent of the stock of that corporation. But not too long ago, he came to my office and announced, "Now I'm ready to give away half of my estate to my kids. How can I do it tax-free?"

He'd given me an impossible task. The only thing I could advise him to do lawfully was to give $10,000 a year to each of his three children and have his wife do the same. That would be a total of $60,000 a year.

Do you know how long it takes to give away $4 million at the rate of $60,000 a year when your asset is appreciating at 10 percent a year? You can't do it. The time when he should have given his kids stock in the business was when he first started it, or when it was worth only a small amount of money and he could have had it appraised at a reasonably low value. But because he waited until his business was a success, with buyers queueing up and offering to pay him more for it than he ever dreamed it would be worth, his options for protecting his profits from the IRS have been severely limited.

People in a situation like this are often attracted to the offshore trusts and certain onshore programs that I describe in chapter 23, Trusts *Not* to Trust. Such desperation measures don't work. All they achieve is litigation and penalties.

There are people who have what I call the Midas touch of business accruement—the ability to start new enterprises, to buy right, to do things that make money. Why not do it in such a way that the future growth of those new enterprises is diverted to the next generation *now*, before the ventures are worth anything? It can be done in such a way that you do *not* relinquish control. It takes some creative thinking, and it takes some expert advice, but it can be done.

So let's look at the various forms of closely held businesses to see how they would affect your taxes, particularly estate taxes, in the long run.

SOLE PROPRIETORSHIPS

A sole proprietorship, as the name implies, is a business that has a single owner. The proprietorship theoretically ceases to exist on the owner's death. It may also cease, or go into suspended animation, if that owner becomes seriously ill or disabled.

All of a business operating as a sole proprietorship becomes an asset of the estate once the owner dies. These assets may be distributed through a will or through a living trust. But the point is, there is no real allowance made for the business to continue once the owner dies. It's like building a major highway mile by mile across the plains. When you run out of funds, the highway stops abruptly. Someone may come along to complete the road. But as often as not it remains a highway to nowhere—or the IRS.

Because of this lack of continuity and planning for the future, sole proprietorships on the whole are not really a satisfactory method of conveying assets to the next generation. They're an all-or-nothing proposition restricting the owner as well, since temporary incapacitation here can disrupt the business enough to render it worthless. Even when the owner recuperates and is ready to dig in once more, the business may be back on base one.

PARTNERSHIPS

A partnership offers the small business many distinct advantages over one-person ownership. Not the least of these advantages is that the founder can bring family members into the business either as full or silent partners—either as working partners, that is, or as partners merely sharing in the profits. The form the partnership takes, however, must be considered in light of how it will affect your future.

For instance, oral partnerships—where the business is founded on a verbal agreement between partners—present a serious disadvantage in that they make it much more difficult at the time of death to dispose of the dead partner's interest. This is particularly serious because it counteracts the tax-saving advantages otherwise possible through careful planning.

Partnership agreements should always be written, with specific attention to what will happen to the business should one of the partners die. The buy-out provision in a partnership can be crucial.

Let's take the case of two partners, I'll call them Mr. Aaron and Mr. Bell, who are both married and have been working together for some twenty-odd years under the most auspicious circumstances. They genuinely enjoy their work and their partnership. And with everything coming up roses, neither of them has given any thought to the possibility that one or the other might die an untimely death, much less providing for it in their partnership agreement.

They have at least each drawn up a last will and testament. Each has stated that, in case of death, his widow is to receive all his distributable assets. Unexpectedly, Aaron has a heart attack and dies. Under the terms of his will, his wife, Adrienne, could become Bell's partner. But Bell, as much as he liked Aaron, doesn't want to continue the partnership with Adrienne. She'd really much rather have cash anyhow. Unfortunately, Bell doesn't have enough money to buy out her share. There are only two things he can do. He can personally borrow money to buy out her shares or he can tie up the partnership assets by borrowing against them to buy out her shares.

If Aaron and Bell had planned more carefully, such a transition would have been a lot smoother. For instance, Aaron could have taken out a life-insurance policy on Bell's life, and vice versa. Then, at Aaron's death, Bell would have had the income-tax-free funds with which to buy out Adrienne. She would have had the money. He would have become sole proprietor and thus been able to choose his own new partner.

Personal liability is the most often cited disadvantage of a partnership. For instance, if any partner causes loss or injury to anyone during business activities, the partnership as a whole is liable for any damage claims that ensue. A partnership agreement might include special clauses to try to eliminate this problem—but they wouldn't. The provisions would not be binding on anyone who was not a partner. So the injured party, not being a partner, could sue any and all partners, no matter what the partnership agreement says. Partners, then, are exposed to unlimited business risks. The solution in the case of a partnership in which you plan to become a passive investor, as opposed to being engaged in active management, is to be sure that yours is a limited partnership. The solution for a family business may also be a Subchapter S corporation.

THE SUBCHAPTER S CORPORATION

A Subchapter S corporation is a hybrid between a regular corporation and just plain ownership, as in the case of a proprietorship or a partnership. Subchapter S tries to give the best of both worlds to the owners of small companies by providing the limited liability of a corporation and the tax structure of individual ownership. In this type of company, any liabilities incurred are restricted to the corporation. If it goes bankrupt, for instance, there is little chance the creditors could attach your personal property.

At the same time, the Subchapter S corporation is *not* a separate entity for tax purposes. Any losses incurred by the company can be deducted from your personal income when it comes to paying your individual income tax each year. This makes the Subchapter S corporation a tempting form for new companies that can be expected to incur losses during the first few years of operation. In the long run, however, the Subchapter S corporation has its limitations.

The most severe drawback to its use for a family business, particularly in inflationary times, is that it does not provide the same means of tax-free wealth transfer that the regular corporate structure does. So let's look more closely at partnerships and the standard corporate form of family business ownership, your two most useful organizational alternatives to paying high death taxes.

LIMITED PARTNERSHIPS

Many states have adopted a Uniform Limited Partnership Act authorizing a special class of partners. Under this law, limited partners contribute cash or property to the business, but the management services are contributed by the general partners. It is precisely this limitation which, if the partnership has been established in strict compliance with the law, assures you that you will not be held personally liable for any debts of the partnership. In return, you forfeit any control over the business, and your name cannot appear in the partnership name, unless, of course, it's identical to that of one of the general partners, as often happens in family businesses.

A limited partnership complying with your state's version of such an act is the type you will, or should, choose when you plan to use a tax shelter like cattle feeding, oil drilling, and large-scale agricultural ventures—ventures, in other words, where your role is basically that of an outside investor, even if you are contributing all the money for the company's operation.

Before the 1976 Tax Reform Act, this dual arrangement within a partnership offered limited partners a leveraged tax deduction. That advantage has now been all but eliminated, since deductions larger than the investment "at risk" can no longer be deducted. In other words, you cannot deduct an amount greater than that of your investment or a loan to the partnership for which you take personal responsibility. If, say, you invest $25,000 in a partnership, and the partnership then borrows an additional $30,000 from a bank, you must be personally liable for that bank loan in order to take a full $55,000 deduction. Before the 1976 Tax Reform Act, you could have deducted that additional $30,000 loan without being personally liable, or "at risk," for it. You could have taken a $55,000 deduction while sustaining at most a $25,000 potential loss. In effect, this meant that if you were in the 50-percent tax bracket, it was cheaper to throw your money away on a tax shelter with no real chance of economic reward than to pay your taxes. Now, while your risks are still limited, so are your tax deductions.

Any tax-shelter plan that requires you to become a general partner rather than a limited partner should be scrutinized with extreme care.

USING A FAMILY CORPORATION TO TRANSFER MONEY TAX-FREE

A family corporation is exactly what the name suggests—one in which all the stock is owned by members of the same family. A discussion of the benefits, hazards, and planning requirements of a family corporation, be it a Subchapter S corporation or other variety, would require a book all to itself. There are many factors besides limited liability to be considered in the forming of a family corporation. Not the least of these factors are the way profits will be taxed and the availability of tax-free benefits for the employee's family. To decide whether your family enterprise should be a partnership or a corporation, you need the assistance not only of a knowledgeable attorney but of a certified public accountant as well.

A corporation is a separate taxpayer and is taxed on its earnings by the federal government as follows: 17 percent on the first $25,000 of income; 20 percent on the next $25,000*; 30 percent on the next $25,000; 40 percent on the next $25,000; and 46 percent for all income thereafter.

If the corporation, after receiving income and paying the appropriate

*By 1983 the percentage of tax on the first two brackets will be lowered to 15 and 18 percent respectively.

tax, decides to declare a "dividend" to the stockholders of the corporation, then such distributions constitute a nondeductible payment by the corporation and are taxable as income to the stockholders. This procedure is sometimes referred to as "double taxation." Of course, not all small corporations pay dividends and indeed it would be imprudent for most to do so.

The most crucial aspect of corporate planning for the family may well be using the business entity, the corporation, to pass on appreciating assets *without incurring a transfer tax*. However, families often neglect this very important tax-avoidance technique at the time they set up their corporation. Let's discuss it here.

HOW A FAMILY CORPORATION CAN FREEZE ITS ASSETS

Corporations, except Subchapter S corporations, have the option of classifying their stock as either common or preferred stock or both. Preferred stock has a fixed value. The value of common stock, on the other hand, is limited to the asset value of the corporation. It will fluctuate, increasing or decreasing in value with the company's worth. Preferred stock has a fixed dividend, established at the time of incorporation. Common stock, on the other hand, has no dividend requirement. It can pay as much or as little as management deems prudent. Either class of stock may comprise voting or nonvoting shares. And therein lies the key to a very successful estate-management plan.

To see how it works, let's follow the progress of a hypothetical Mr. Grace and his new Sunshine Solar Cell Company, a high-technology business which, with a little luck and a lot of effort, may be worth a considerable fortune a decade from now. Mr. Grace is primarily interested in developing Sunshine Solar Cell into a substantial income source for himself and his wife, should she outlive him. Retirement is not really on his mind. He's one of those individuals who would much prefer to keep on working.

Mr. Grace has two sons and a daughter. The boys are twenty-two and eighteen years old, the girl thirteen. The children may or may not want to enter the business, but Mr. Grace would at least like to give them the opportunity to do so when they are older. On the other hand, the oldest son is already twenty-two years old, and, frankly, Mr. Grace doesn't want to take a chance on losing control of the company to anyone, even his children. He's not paranoid, but there are simply too many cases where this has happened. Mr. Grace could give his family 49 percent of the company, retaining 51 percent and control. However, if that 51 percent of Sunshine Solar Cell were to do as well as he expects it to, it could add an immense tax burden to his estate. And, because they would not be able to afford the taxes, the family might lose control of the business to the IRS. If, for example, the family needed to sell stock in order to pay the death taxes, it could be put in a position where it retained enough stock to control the company, but not the 51 percent it would need for absolute control.

This is where the two-class stock system comes in. Mr. Grace can take 100 percent of the preferred stock and place it in a revocable trust with himself and his wife as beneficiaries. The children could be given 100 percent of the common stock. The preferred stock, although it pays a dividend, has limited claim on the assets and therefore has a very low but fixed evaluation for tax purposes. The preferred stock is also the only class with voting rights.

So, by using the two classes of stock, Mr. Grace can retain 100-percent control, including the right to give himself raises, perquisites, and anything else he might legitimately desire. He can also provide retirement income that will pass on to his wife through the trust. The children, in the meantime, have inherited the corporation for tax purposes *before* it becomes a big success.

Let's say the worth of Sunshine Solar Cell is $100,000 at its founding. At the death of Mr. and Mrs. Grace, the children inherit the whole company, which by then has a worth of $3 million, partly because of the success of its products, but just as much because of inflation. There is no death tax on that $2.9 million. And the tax on the $100,000 preferred stock is minimal at most.

Of course, the tax man has to be paid sometime. Or does he? Not really. Although a zero tax may be impossible to achieve, taxes on the estate—the estate of Mr. Grace's children, that is—can in turn be reduced to a negligible amount if the children act early in the game.

The preferred stock held by Mr. Grace can be retired by the company. That is to say, it can be bought back and eliminated. Then there is only a single class of stock, the common stock, outstanding.

Mr. Grace's children can then proceed to undertake a tax-free stock recapitalization. To do this, they once again split the company's shares into two classes. This time they receive only the dividend-paying, voting shares of preferred stock, divided among themselves in proportion to their prior holdings of common stock, originally given to them when they were young.

The new common stock is issued to Mr. Grace's grandchildren.

The company's $3 million worth is pegged almost completely to the preferred stock, leaving the grandchildren's common stock very little of value. What the common stock does have, however, is all the future growth potential of the company. So yet another generation will receive, tax-free, all the benefits of the company's growth and increase in value due to inflation. There will be no death taxes, because the common stock has next to no value when it's given to the grandchildren. There will be no gift taxes for the same reason. The grandchildren will be responsible for the income tax on any dividends—if and when the common stock pays them.

When Mr. Grace's three children pass on, each with $1 million worth of preferred stock in the estate plus a lifetime of other accrued assets, there will be death taxes due on the value of the preferred stock. But will it really be worth $1 million? Certainly not. Assuming Mr. Grace's children lived another twenty inflationary years after his death, by the time their estate comes due for taxes the actual purchasing power of the $1 million will be somewhere in the vicinity of $10,000. Maybe $2,000 worth of this purchasing power will then go to the IRS. Meanwhile the company will probably be worth $30 million. If there are six grandchildren, each of them will have stock worth $5 million.

So Mr. Grace, in other words, can pass on to a second and third generation some $40 million—for a total estate tax perhaps as low as $5,000 in terms of purchasing power. Now that's really using inflation to beat the IRS.

22

Special Estate Problems for Singles and Retirees

Woe to him that is alone when he falleth;
for he hath not another to help him up.

—ECCLESIASTES 4:10

As a rule, single people, young and old alike, are less likely to think in terms of estate problems and trusts than couples are, especially those with children. Now it may well be true that you can't take it with you. But there are two good reasons why single people, even if they have no living relatives, should have an estate plan.

First of all, you **you should provide for your old age** in an era in which inflation can wipe out a lifetime's earnings within only a few years, and the tax man takes it if inflation doesn't. To give you an idea of how beneficial a trust can be under such circumstances, even for a single person with no heirs, I'm going to discuss the hypothetical case of a widow, sixty-five years old, with a problem asset—namely, a small commerical building worth $100,000 which her husband gave her years ago. The building is not appreciating much because the neighborhood is past its prime and decaying.

What the woman would really like to do is sell the building and reinvest the assets in something that would keep up with inflation. Unfortunately, her husband originally purchased the building for $10,000. Selling it now would mean a paying an ordinary tax on $36,000. So, instead of selling it, she gives the building to a charitable-remainder unitrust set up for her by her attorney. The gift is irrevocable, and in exchange she is to receive a 15-percent-a-year annuity.

The trustee appointed by the widow sells the building and invests the proceeds in inflation-indexed bonds, gold, and other assets that can be expected to rise in value. There is no capital-gains tax due on that $90,000 profit from the building. Remember, the trust is a charitable entity.

On top of eliminating the capital gains tax, the IRS also allows her a $40,000 charitable deduction. The $100,000 the building is worth at the time she contributes it to the trust is, after all, a gift, which entitles her to a charitable deduction. And as a final bonus, her future income is now indexed to inflation. Although she receives only 15 percent of the trust's worth a year, this holding can be expected to increase dramatically as time goes on. The building, on the other hand, because of its location, can be expected to remain worth $100,000 at best, with inflation and maintenance actually decreasing the purchasing power of those dollars substantially.

When the widow dies, the remaining proceeds of the trust will be distributed to the charity she chose when setting it up. So everybody comes out ahead, the widow, the charity—well, actually, not everybody. The IRS comes out far behind, but I doubt if any of you are shedding crocodile tears about that.

THE PSYCHOLOGICAL BENEFITS OF A TRUST

Like the widow in the example I've used, any single elderly person can profit greatly from a trust in yet another way. The profit I refer to here is not measured in dollars and cents but in peace of mind. Think, for just a moment, of what would happen should you suffer a crippling heart attack. Or be stricken by a debilitating disease or have an accident that made you unconscious for a period of a month. What would happen to your affairs during that time? If you were alone, your world might come to a grinding halt during your incapacitation. And when you recovered, you'd return to financial chaos, chaos that could be as debilitating as the illness itself.

You need to prepare for growing older. **You need some instrument lawful in your state to deal with things if you become disabled** and cannot look after your own affairs. There are unethical people who prey on the elderly. But it needn't happen. And if you set up a trust, it shouldn't happen.

POWER OF ATTORNEY

A power of attorney gives another person the right to make financial and other decisions for you in your stead. And a power of attorney given to a trustworthy person could keep the machinery of your life running smoothly in your absence. There is no need to fear that a power of attorney would cost you control of anything or be abused. Obviously, choosing a responsible attorney or banker as the recipient of that power may be the wisest course in some circumstances. However, you may also retain the right to let the power of attorney be delivered only when your appointee needs to act in your behalf. In other words, **the power of attorney gives no one any power until such time as you are actually incapacitated.**

Some states have a durable power of attorney, a very simple one-page document, that does not terminate on disability. Others do not. In such states powers of attorney become void when the person giving the power becomes disabled. If this is the case in your state, a living trust with a child or other person named as trustee or co-trustee is a much better solution. If you are single, I urge you to consider this.

THE LIVING WILL

At the same time, you might consider drawing up a living will. As of this writing, only a few states accept the powers granted in a living will. However, the eighties will probably be the turning point for this document. Without going into the ethical arguments concerning a living will and its potential results, I'd like simply to mention its provisions, in case you aren't aware of them. Again, this instrument is one offering no real monetary return, but for some it could offer real peace of mind.

Today's world of medical science has produced previously inconceivable methods of saving people's lives, in certain cases prolonging them by artificial means far beyond all expectation, even when there is no chance whatsoever of a return to consciousness. Some people, if they were to be reduced to a vegetablelike existence completely dependent on an artificial support system, would not wish to have their unconscious life extended at such cost. If you feel this way, **you may execute a living will stating that you do not wish to be kept alive by artificial means.** The central clause of such a living will is usually something like the following:

> If the situation should arise in which there is no reasonable expectation of my recovery from physical or mental disability, I request that I be allowed to die and not be kept alive by artificial means or heroic measures. I do not fear death itself so much as the indignities of deterioration, dependence, and hopeless pain.

A living will should be supplemented by other documents that permit the transplant of organs, should you desire to do this. These documents may be executed with any of a number of organizations. But remember that it is not sufficient merely to notify the institution concerned or to have a provision in your will or some other document about organ transplants. All close members of your family should be fully aware of your intention to donate, because time is very much of the essence following death. You should also have a card in your wallet or among your other identification papers giving instructions to immediately contact a certain physician or institution upon your death in order for the organ transplant to be accomplished. In Appendix G you will find two sample living wills and in Appendix F a sample power of attorney.

The decision about whether or not to make a living will is a moral and ethical one and, as such, can only be made on an individual basis. You should, however, be aware that there is increasing interest in this aspect of estate planning.

DIVORCE, MARRIAGE, AND THE TAX MAN

A few years ago, there was a television show about a man who had a large capital gain toward the end of the year and couldn't decide what to do. His tax adviser suggested various options, including tax shelters, oil drilling, and horses, and finally concluded that the best thing for him to do was to find a woman with a large capital loss and get married. This he did, and the IRS tried to attack the marriage as a sham, calling it a tax-conceived marriage. But that's not a real-life situation. So let's talk about preventive tax planning for single persons.

It is important to know that in either a community-property state or a separate-property state, what you have as a single person belongs to you and is called your separate property. If you marry, that property can remain your property provided it does not change hands during the marriage. For instance, suppose a single man living in California had property worth $100,000. Then suppose the man married. The money he earned as salary after he was married would automatically be owned half by him and half by his new wife, as would be half of any salary she earned. But the $100,000 that he had before marriage would remain his separate property, and his wife would have no rights over it, provided he didn't commingle it—that is, join it with her money in the same bank account or in the same investment. He could keep it in a separate bank account or investment vehicle, subject to use or withdrawal by his name alone.

On the other hand, an unmarried woman with money in her maiden name who later marries should consider leaving the money in her name. That would suggest her intent to keep it separate. The money might be put into a revocable living trust under the separate management of the spouse to whom it belonged, and the trust could specify that everything in it was separate property. This provision would be important in case of divorce or death.

Let's suppose our hypothetical taxpayer with the $100,000 worth of separate property marries, and there is some question about how that property will be distributed when he dies. Let's assume our taxpayer has written a will which says, "I leave all my community property to my surviving spouse, and I leave all my separate property to my children by my previous marriage." If he does not specifically state who owns the $100,000, controversy may arise over whether it is separate property, and goes to the children, or community property, and goes to the wife. It used to be that in California, where our hypothetical taxpayer lived, you could change the character of property by an oral agreement. It didn't have to be in writing. In the instance I've cited, the wife could have gotten on the witness stand, been sworn, and said, "I realize it was in his name, but there was a time when he told me that that property belonged to both of us."

If you intend property to be separate, keep it separate, and make it clear that it is your separate property.

Premarital agreements are recognized in most states as valid antenuptial contracts. Such agreements must be signed before the date of the marriage. In a premarital contract, the parties can agree that the property listed is and will always be the husband's, and the wife waives all rights to its future inheritance, and vice versa. Such an agreement usually provides that the only way this can be changed is by written instrument. You can change your mind, but you must document it.

An antenuptial contract can be handled sensitively, without disturbing the relationship between the partners, and often it is what both parties really would want done if one or both of them have been married before and there are children from the previous marriages.

An agreement made after marriage, on the other hand, is subject to many complications. And some states don't consider a postnuptial contract enforceable, whereas an agreement reached before marriage is part of the marriage consideration.

SECOND-MARRIAGE ESTATE PROBLEMS

Conflicting interests may pose a degree of dilemma in financial tax planning where a second marriage is contemplated, particularly if there is property jointly owned with a right of survivorship involved and if there are children from a previous marriage. For example, I have a widower client who is worth $300,000 and has two children. At the age of sixty-five, he decided to remarry. But the children had conflicts with the stepmother-to-be. They didn't want the marriage, and they tried to have him put his property into an irrevocable trust for them.

Their rationale was that their mother and father had earned this money, and they, rather than his second wife, should receive it upon his passing away. On the other hand, the man was very lonely, and if he remarried and his wife gave him a number of years of companionship, why shouldn't he give her his property? The choice was really his.

Compare this with another case, that of a newspaper editor eighty years old whose wife of fifty years died. He went to Alaska to take his mind off things, and the first woman he met, thirty years younger than himself, he begged her to marry him. He kept writing passionate letters to her, and in his last letter he said that if she married him and if he died, she could spend $50,000 a year for ten years, assuring her that he would put that provision in his will. So she married him. She got an attorney to put in the husband's will an agreement that its provisions could never be altered unless the marriage terminated in divorce or annulment.

The marriage didn't last long. After about three months of it, the eighty-year-old man asked me to represent him and filed for a divorce. Well, in those days it took an entire year to get a divorce, and my client was beside himself because he couldn't change the will until the final decree. He was worrying himself to death. So we petitioned for an annulment and paid her for that.

A second marriage, then, presents certain problems beyond those of the first. When each of the spouses decides to leave his or her property to the other outright, the following problems might occur:

1. The estate of the survivor may be unnecessarily taxed. If both husband and wife have inheritances from their previous marriages, these will pass through the tax man's hands once again.
2. The surviving spouse could cut the deceased spouse's children out

of their inheritance. If the assets were held in joint tenancy, everything would go to the surviving spouse, who, perhaps feeling neglected, could easily change his or her will to exclude them.

3. The surviving spouse could, for what might seem perfectly good reasons at the time, transfer some assets into joint tenancy with a child. Such an arrangement could then override the gifting intent of the first-deceased spouse.

4. The delays caused by probate, which might take up to a year or more, could deny the surviving spouse of some economic benefits for a time. And when you are elderly, a year is a lot of time to take out of what remains of your life.

DIVIDING ASSETS SAVES TAXES

The solution might be to divide assets and establish two trusts. In the case of a widow or widower remarrying at an older age, the two marriage partners' assets are often of the same magnitude. A widow, having inherited the estate of her deceased husband, usually enters matrimony anew with as much, if not more, money than the second husband has.

The first practical step for a couple in these circumstances would be to split their combined assets as closely down the middle as possible. Any special assets, such as family heirlooms, designated to be passed on to the children or grandchildren should probably be given at this time unless the donor feels a need to hold onto them personally.

After the couple's assets have been divided, there should be no joint property left except for a small bank account for day-to-day living expenses and emergencies. The divided assets should then be placed into two separate trusts. The husband's trust would leave the income from the assets to his wife, with the principal going to his children upon her death. If for any reason the wife needed extra funds, the trustee could be empowered to invade the principal to cover the emergency. In the same way, the wife's trust would be set up for her husband's benefit, with the eventual disposition of the assets to her children. Furthermore, under the new provisions relating to terminable interests, it is possible to have one of the trusts qualify for a marital deduction.

RETIREMENT—THE TAX DIFFERENCE

The south calls retirees like geese in fall, and they flock to a new home in the sun, but taking flight does not necessarily leave the tax man behind. Those states imposing income taxes and death taxes may hold an individual liable for these taxes even if he or she has moved out of state permanently. This requirement can lead to double taxation—even triple taxation if you count the federal government's cut.

This problem most commonly occurs when someone moves from a super-taxing state such as New York or Illinois to one like Arizona, which has a much lower tax rate, or Florida, which uses not only sun but the complete absence of a state income tax to lure retirees to its shores. Theoretically, an individual can have only one domicile, or permanent home, at a time for tax purposes. Yet **having a winter home in Florida and business ties or property in a high-tax state may lead not only to income-tax liabilities in the high-tax state but to estate taxes on the property in both states as well.**

Consider the case of seventy-nine-year-old Wilfred Owen, retired chairman of the Extra-Strength Pool Pulsator Company. After retiring, he moved to Miami and bought a co-op. However, he retained a pied-à-terre in New York, close to his old offices, and the family farm in New Jersey, the scene of many happy childhood days. When he died, all three states tried to tax his estate. Needless to say, the litigation involved was time-consuming and most costly.

While there may sometimes be compelling personal reasons for not complying with all of the following suggestions, the more you can do to regroup your life legally in the new state, and the sooner you can do it, the more successful you are likely to be in establishing your domicile in that state for tax purposes.

1. Change your automobile registration and your driver's license. Then notify each department in your old state of the change in residence. Don't simply mail back the registration and the license plates. Write a covering letter specifically stating that you are now residing in the new state.

2. File for a homestead exemption to establish a partial immunity from the taxes on real property if the new state allows one. Also apply for a certificate of domicile. And register to vote.

3. Obviously you will be opening local bank accounts in the new state. What may be less obvious is that you should also close out all your accounts in the old state, including that ancient one with

$16.32 in it that you've just never gotten around to doing anything about.

4. Sell the old homestead. This may be the most difficult part of the program. If it's personally impossible for you to sell it, you could give it to your children. Of course, this might lead in turn to gift-tax problems, as well as intrafamily disputes. Only you can judge the merits for your specific situation. If it's a workable alternative, you could arrange to visit as a guest in the house. But you should not retain any interest in it.

5. When you file your last tax form in the old state, send with it a letter indicating your change of residence. Also notify the Social Security Administration that you want all checks sent to your new address or bank. The federal income-tax return and the state return, if any, must be filed from the new state.

6. Have a new will prepared by a local lawyer giving the new domicile as your residence. All the witnesses to this will should be local. Out-of-state witnesses can add to the legal expenses of probate.

If you are thinking of moving after your retirement, and you're moving for the climate rather than because you've always wanted to live in, say, New Orleans, you might want to consider which states would impose the least tax burden on your estate. In Appendix H you will find a complete state-by-state breakdown of the death-tax burden the various states impose. Do not move to a state simply because of its tax-advantaged locale. But if you really want to move to make yourself and your life more comfortable or for health reasons, be sure to consider the tax advantages of the move as well.

23

Trusts *Not* to Trust and Tax-Avoidance Programs that Will Get You into Trouble with the IRS

The safest way to double your money is to fold it over once and
put it in your pocket. —KIN HUBBARD

The difference between legal tax avoidance and tax evasion may be difficult
for many taxpayers to understand. So you must stay up-to-date on the
changing moods of the IRS and the tax courts. About the only certainty is
that if a purportedly legal tax-avoidance plan seems too good to be true—
well, it probably is.

Everybody wants to pay lower taxes. Some people are willing to go to
extreme lengths to accomplish this, including the use of shelters they
suspect may be illegal or quasi-legal. But instead of checking on the legality
of these schemes, they duck their heads in the sand, hoping no one will
actually find out about it. This is no way to minimize taxes. It's a way to
maximize your trouble.

At the same time, **tax-shelter swindlers have declared open season on the
ever-increasing number of people who find themselves in the position of
needing a tax shelter for the first time.** Suddenly, inflation and inflationary
incomes have pushed these people into a higher tax bracket than they had
ever expected to be in. And so, in their eagerness to protect their money,
they are particularly open to anyone who comes along peddling a tax
shelter. Unfortunately, many people who find themselves in this situation
are unable to distinguish the good shelters from the bad. This leaves them
vulnerable to the tremendous number of pure promoters who are great
salesmen, but whose products are the financial version of selling the
Brooklyn Bridge. Let's look at some of these nonshelter shelters, beginning
with trusts.

TRUSTS *NOT* TO BE TRUSTED

Just because the word *trust* appears in the sales literature doesn't mean you have to trust it. Currently, a large number of trusts are being marketed, bearing such names as double trusts, pure equity trusts, Patrick Henry trusts, educational trusts, and constitutional trusts. They come in both onshore and offshore varieties to suit the gullibility of the buyer.

THE OFFSHORE PURE TRUST

The offshore version is being peddled by numerous solid-sounding organizations which set you up with a trust program in the Turks and Caicos Islands, in the Bahamas or some other location under common-law jurisdiction. And the claim made is that you, as a United States citizen and taxpayer, can filter your income through the island trust to avoid paying taxes on it. Now if you've read this far in the book, you know it can't be done. But if there's still a question in your mind about it, let me tell you, this plan is pure bologna, and the IRS will slice you up mighty thin if you try it.

Here's the typical scenario—right from the IRS:

> The taxpayer attends a two-day seminar where he is provided with lectures and instructional materials relating to the use of foreign "pure trust organizations" to avoid taxes. After this session, the taxpayer authorizes a representative of the promoters to travel to Central America and to pay a small fee to a Central American citizen to sign formal documents purporting to establish a series of foreign trusts.
>
> The Central American citizen, who is described by the promoters as an individual having no information whatsoever about the documents which he is asked to sign, is designated as the "creator" in documents labeled "contract and Declaration of Trust." These documents allegedly create three foreign trust entities, which purport to be governed by the laws of a Central American country.
>
> The taxpayer then signs additional documents stating that nominal sums of money have been transferred to two of the trusts in exchange for "Trust Certificates" or "Certificates of Beneficial Interest" issued to the taxpayer. The taxpayer also signs documents stating that the taxpayer's real and personal properties including his business equipment have been transferred to one of the foreign

trusts in exchange for Trust Certificates. The taxpayer is named the trustee of one of the foreign trusts, and that foreign trust (for convenience, called trust #1) is in turn named as the trustee of each of the other foreign trusts.

After all these documents are signed, the taxpayer attempts to eliminate all or a substantial portion of his own taxable income. He does so by purporting to enter into transactions with one of the three trusts.

For example, during the first year of the plan, the taxpayer signs documents stating that the taxpayer has assigned his rights to the instructional materials he received from the promoters of the plan to one of the foreign trusts in exchange for the certificates. At the same time, the taxpayer purports to "negotiate" with that trust (for convenience, this trust is numbered trust #2) to "purchase" the materials back from trust #2 for a stated sum of $50,000. The taxpayer then claims a $50,000 deduction with respect to this transaction on his own individual income tax return.

Trust #2, to which the $50,000 is paid, files a non-resident alien tax return reporting the $50,000 from the taxpayer as income. However, the taxpayer also causes trust #2 either to make a "distribution" to, or enter into another transaction with, one of his other foreign trusts (trust#3). This "distribution" or transaction allegedly gives rise to a $50,000 deduction for the non-resident alien trust #2 which it claims on its tax return. Thus, trust #2 reports no taxable income.

Trust #3 which received the $50,000 allegedly paid or distributed (and deducted) by trust #2 does not file a Federal income tax return. Trust #3 claims that it conducts no business in the United States and thus is not required to file a return.

Finally, as part of this overall plan, the taxpayer arranges to have the $50,000 which is now in foreign trust #3 either "loaned" or "gifted" back to himself.

A modification of this offshore plan is the foreign double trust. The *double* in its name refers to the fact that there are two trusts involved. But what it should probably refer to instead is that a double trust gets you in double trouble—back taxes plus penalties. And, like all tax evasion, it may land you in jail as well.

In the double trust, a foreign agent is named as the creator of a trust, while you are named trustee. The creator doesn't have to know what he's doing. In fact, according to some promoters, it's best if he simply puts his X on the dotted line. Once the trust is set up, you transfer your assets to it— a move like that alone takes nerves of steel. Then this creative creator creates another trust in the same country, and with the same provisions, but naming the first trust as trustee. The income from the first trust goes to the second trust and then to whomever you, as trustee of the first trust, direct. And if all this sounds like a ring-around-a-rosy sham, that's exactly what it is. From the IRS's point of view, these trusts are only spinning their wheels while you sink deeper and deeper into debt.

Oh, I know, this isn't the kind of upbeat how-you-can-save-taxes information you wanted to hear about these trusts. But if you're going to look out for number one, you really have to look out for the IRS too. Before you read on, you might want to reread chapter 14 to review the new rules and limited application of foreign trusts.

Believe me, I can cite chapter and verse from IRS case rulings on why such offshore programs won't work. If you're curious, go ahead and investigate them. But there's no magic there. You don't even get to deduct the sizable promoters' fees and other costs of these nontrustable trusts.

Nor is there any magic in the onshore type of family estate type trust, whatever name it may go by. Knowing what won't work, however, is as important to your planning as knowing what will, so let's look at a typical example of such a trust you shouldn't trust.

THE TYPICAL FAMILY ESTATE-TYPE TRUST

The usual onshore family estate-type trust created by a taxpayer is based on an educational home-study course using copyrighted materials. Using the knowledge gained from these materials, the taxpayer drafts a personal family estate trust agreement.

Though it's quite possible for you, with the help of an attorney, to draft a workable family trust that will meet with IRS approval, the family trust we're about to detail is not one of them.

The content of the typical family estate-type trust being peddled today is as follows:

1. A trust based on educational course materials is created.

2. The grantor (creator) transfers all of his or her assets, both income- and non-income-producing, including residence, automobiles, real estate, securities, and the family farm or business, if any, to the trustee(s) of the trust. The lifetime services of the grantor are also assigned to the trust,

including all future income the grantor earns, regardless of the source. The trust will later contract with third parties for the grantor's employment and will receive income for these services. In exchange for the transfer of assets and assignment of lifetime services, the grantor receives 100 percent of the trust's "units of beneficial interest"—something similar to receiving stock in a corporation.

Where the grantor's spouse owns property, the non-grantor spouse first turns over his or her ownership interest in such property to the grantor spouse. In exchange for this, he or she receives a trust receipt entitling the non-grantor spouse to a percentage of the units of beneficial interest equaling the portion his or her pro-rata property interests transferred bear to the total of all property transferred. The grantor spouse will then act alone as grantor of the trust by conveying the total interest (that of the grantor and that first conveyed by the non-grantor spouse) to the trustees in exchange for 100 percent of the trust's units of beneficial interest.

3. In order to take advantage of the purported tax savings that result from such income splitting, the units of beneficial interest are divided and redistributed among the family members. The object of such a redistribution is to create multiple tax entities for income splitting.

First, the grantor distributes the pro-rata portion of units allocated to the non-grantor spouse in accordance with the trust receipt previously given. If no units are distributed to a non-grantor spouse because the non-grantor spouse did not own or turn over any property, the non-grantor spouse presumably nevertheless receives, by gift, a distribution of units of beneficial interest originating from the property transferred by the grantor spouse. In any event, the non-grantor spouse is directed to receive or retain a fairly large percentage of units of beneficial interest in an effort to ensure status as an "adverse party." Other units are distributed to the remaining family members. The grantor is directed to retain few, if any, units of beneficial interest.

4. The certificates establishing units of beneficial interest entitle the person who receives them to only two rights—namely, the right to a proportionate share of income in the event the income is distributed and the right to a proportionate share of any distribution of assets when the trust terminates. Both events are under the sole control of the trustees. The certificates are also considered transferable.

5. The trust is operated by a board of trustees, usually composed of three individuals, of whom the grantor may be one. While the grantor is sometimes cautioned not to be an original trustee, provision is usually made

for the grantor to assume office at a later date. (I have never seen any literature on the family estate trust where the grantor is prevented from serving or succeeding as a trustee.) The trustees are given broad powers to do anything which individuals may legally do with their own property.

The trust is irrevocable, and it is established for a specific number of years, the minimum being ten years. The term of the trust may be shortened or extended by unanimous action of the trustees. Except where termination of the trust is involved, the trustees are to act by majority vote.

When and if the trustees exercise their absolute discretion to distribute income, distribution must be on a pro-rata basis among the holders of certificates of beneficial interest.

6. The grantor and possibly other family members purportedly become employees of the trust. Employees receive consultant fees for their managerial services as well as other compensation in the form of the right to live in the residence and to use the automobile (both formerly owned by the grantor for services rendered to or on behalf of the trust).

PURPORTED TAX BENEFITS OF THE FAMILY ESTATE-TYPE TRUST

The promoters of onshore pure trusts assert that these trusts:

1. Reduce income-tax liability by means of income splitting following a division of the units of beneficial interest among the grantor, his or her spouse, and other family members.

2. Generate substantial tax deductions through the trust business and administration expenses, under sections 162 and 212 of the Internal Revenue Code.

3. Exclude from taxable income the items furnished by the trust to the grantor in kind, items which under section 119 are considered to be "furnished for the convenience of the employer."

According to the promoters, once the creator's income is shifted to the trust, the trust is supposedly taxed only on undistributed net income. Generally, almost all the living expenses of grantor and family are deducted on the trust's fiduciary income-tax return as alleged business expenses of the trust. The balance is often distributed to the creator's family or to a separate nonprofit educational trust, so-called, leaving little or no taxable income to be reported.

As the section title indicates, the above are *purported* tax benefits, purported by promoters whose ultimate concern is getting your money, not helping you protect it.

WHY YOU SHOULD BEWARE OF THESE TRUSTS

The IRS position on these trusts is that they are an illusion for tax purposes. And it has published numerous rulings completely discrediting such schemes for tax purposes. The IRS position has been upheld by the United States Tax Court, which has repeatedly rejected the taxpayer's argument that assigning all earnings to a family estate-type trust effectively eliminates any need to list those earnings on an individual income-tax return. The Tax Court has also repeatedly asserted that any income from sources other than the taxpayer's earnings—income such as interest, for example, paid to the trust—is taxable to the taxpayer.

What the IRS and the Tax Court are trying to tell you is, no matter how you work it all out, these alleged shelters simply will not be recognized. And the promoters' answer to that, in many cases, is simply to make the trust setup even more complex. After all, their reasoning goes, the more legal-sounding something is, the more legal it must be.

There isn't much that can be added to this barrage of rejection except the warning that you are responsible for the accuracy of your tax return even if you engage professional help in preparing it. A penalty of 5 percent of the additional tax due can be assessed against a taxpayer for negligent or intentional disregard of the tax rules and regulations. If the IRS establishes that you have willfully understated your taxes due, the penalty goes up to 50 percent of the additional tax due.

AN OUNCE OF PREVENTION . . . CAN SAVE YOU AND YOUR FAMILY MONEY

Don't be embarrassed to seek professional advice! Skilled professionals— doctors, dentists, engineers, you name it— people making a very good living applying their skills and talents, feel they should somehow be able to handle everything else. They feel inadequate to the task of making in-

vestment decisions. Yet they go ahead and do so merely because they feel
even more inadequate asking for outside advice. To such people, I would
like to say that, as an attorney, I don't fill my own tooth when I have a
cavity or set my own broken leg. I have no qualms about consulting the
appropriate professional when a part of my body hurts or is in pain.
Similarly, as a taxpayer, if you find it hurts in your pocketbook and the IRS
is causing you pain, see a professional.

THE IRS IS WATCHING YOU

What follows is a list of fake "answers" to your tax problems—that is,
common tax-avoidance schemes the IRS will *not* accept as legitimate.
Without going into all the excruciating details of why they'll get you into
more trouble than they're worth, suffice it to say that all the little reasons
add up to one big one in each case—using any of the so-called tax-avoidance
programs I'm going to mention will immediately raise a large red flag for
the IRS. The IRS will come after you. And it will get you. It's as simple as
that.

TAX STRADDLES WILL GIVE YOU SADDLE SORES
NO MATTER HOW YOU RIDE THEM

A tax straddle is a scheme that attempts to convert ordinary gain into
capital gain, or tries to shift taxable income from one year to the next, or
both. A scheme like that can become very involved. The basic principle,
however, can be best and most simply demonstrated in the once-popular
silver straddle. Let's follow its course.

You buy and sell equal amounts of silver futures contracts. The risk is
supposedly nil because, even though the price of silver may fluctuate
wildly, you are both long and short. So the loss in one contract presumably
will be offset by the profit in the other. Now, as any commodity trader will
tell you, this is simply not the case. It's quite possible, and it often happens,
that a contract for a near-term delivery goes up while one for a distant
delivery goes down, or vice versa. About the only infallible rule is that, no
matter which way the spread widens, somehow you always end up on the

losing side. Of course, that will give you a small tax loss. If actually losing your money is what you are after, there's no problem. The real benefits, however, come from a series of new purchases and sales as the years go on, each series designed to move the "profits" from one year into the next while at the same time balancing out losses. You sell the losing half of the straddle, which gives you, naturally enough, a loss. But then you buy it right back again, balancing your position. And you haven't really lost anything, except for tax purposes, because the other half of the straddle has theoretically gained as much as your loss.

Unfortunately, **the IRS does not recognize a risk in this kind of transaction.** The trade, as far as it's concerned, is a sham. This ruling may well be overridden by the tax courts in the future, since there truly is a risk involved. While it is a smaller risk than that involved in ordinary commodity trading, straddles do play a serious role in an overall commodity strategy. For now, however, a silver straddle or any other commodity straddle used in an attempt to defer taxes will cause you a lot of grief. Commodity straddles have become a prime target for the IRS.

To restrict the tax avoidance opportunities in commodity futures straddles and to curb abusive tax shelters, the Economic Recovery Tax Act of 1981 provides a number of specialized rules that virtually eliminate the use of straddles for most taxpayers as a tax savings tool. These specialized rules apply to straddles entered into after June 23, 1981. Three basic rules were created by the Act:

(1) *Regulated futures contracts market to market.* The United States commodity futures exchanges employ a unique system of accounting for every contract's gain or loss in cash on a daily basis. Basically, a taxpayer in commodity futures maintains an account with his broker, and each day his account is credited with the net paper gain or debited with the net paper loss on all his futures contracts. Any net paper gain credited to his account may be withdrawn by the taxpayer at any time, but any net paper loss must be covered by the taxpayer before the next business day. The Tax Code now refers to a contract under this type of system as a regulated futures contract.

Under the Act, gains and losses from regulated futures contracts that have not been closed by year's end must be treated as if sold on the last day of the year, and the amount of any gain or loss is to be determined by the contract's fair market value on the last day. Any capital gain or loss is treated as if: (a) 40 percent of the gain or loss were short-term capital gain or loss, and (b) 60 percent of the gain or loss were long-term gain or loss.

(2) *Non-regulated futures contract straddles losses postponed.* Tax straddles that are not on the market-to-market system and that are not entirely

composed of futures contracts must postpone paper losses to later years in certain circumstances. Such straddles are referred to as "non-regulated futures contract straddles." Basically, the rule mandates that recognized "losses on non-regulated futures contract straddles" are deductible only to the extent that they exceed unrealized gains from the same straddle. Taxpayers who have "mixed straddles" (i.e., regulated futures contracts and personal property positions) may elect to be taxed under this rule or as if they were a "regulated futures contract."

(3) *Identified straddles, losses deferred only when entire straddle is sold.* An identified straddle is one where all original positions (i.e., future or forward contracts, options, and personal property other than actively traded stock) are acquired and disposed of on the same day. No losses on identified straddles are recognized before the day on which the straddles are sold.

Furthermore, special tax rules from which commodity straddles were previously exempt—the wash sale and short sale rules—now apply to tax straddles. The Act prohibits the current deduction of interest and carrying charges related to a position except to the extent that such interest and carrying charges are offset by current income generated by the position.

THE CRACKDOWN ON BARTER

Direct mail merchants aren't the only buyers of mailing lists these days. The IRS has got its list as well. And it's from the barter companies. Now, as I pointed out in chapter 20, barter can be a perfectly legitimate way of reducing taxes through the use of the fair market valuation of goods and tax-deferred exchange. However, barter clubs, where members accumulate credits by providing goods or services and then use these credits in exchange for other goods or services, are another matter entirely. Yet the barter clubs are spreading with a speed almost as amazing as that with which the dollar is losing its value.

To take just one small example, in Arizona there are already ten established barter clubs, as of this writing. And the IRS is watching all of them. Raymond Lipton, a local IRS agent, says that of all the returns examined by the IRS there, those involving barter failed to report bartering income in over 60 percent of the cases. "We're going to look at all the barter companies this year," Lipton promised. "With the big ones, we'll be getting a list of their members, the activities of their members, and the returns of the members themselves—maybe on a sample basis." The courts may eventually take a dim view of such fishing expeditions. But the IRS is moving in on barter clubs nationwide. Forewarned is forearmed.

Even the IRS will admit that there is nothing intrinsically wrong with barter clubs. What is wrong, in its eyes, is companies or individuals failing to report the net profit from bartering on their returns. This is fraud. In other words, you can keep right on bartering. Just draw the line where the IRS would.

DON'T BE FOOLED BY THE "RELIGIOUS" APPROACH

Many do-it-yourself churches are now spreading a money-saving message. And it may be a reasonable enough message, considering that In God We Trust is the motto found on United States currency. Some people have begun to take this creed very seriously—when it comes to paying taxes. The IRS is not amused.

For example, the Bubbling Well Church of Universal Love has as its only voting members and directors John Calvin Herberts, his wife, Catherine, and their son, Dan. But Bubbling Well's limited congregation were all denied their tax deductions. On a larger scale, do-it-yourself churches like this are sold by mail. They require no experience, no education—in fact, no particular qualifications other than the ability to make a $50 donation to "purchase" the church's charter.

One leading promoter of such mail-order ministries, Reverend Kirby J. Hensley, founder of the Universal Life Church, indicates that he doesn't really care what you believe, or even if you believe at all. His only concern seems to be spreading the word about the tax advantages made possible by forming your own church. And that, he claims, is as easy as falling off a log.

For a $50 donation, the Reverend Hensley will ordain you and send you your credentials of ministry. He will charter your church as a branch of the mother church, put you on the mailing list for the *Universal Life Church News*, and regularly inform you of the niceties of the tax laws as he and his advisers interpret them. For additional donations, Reverend Hensley will add to your credentials by making you a doctor of divinity, a bishop, a cardinal, or even a saint.

According to Reverend Hensley, you need to find two members for your church—your spouse or your children will serve. And you must hold regular meetings. You must also profess a sincere belief in your religious calling. This, Reverend Hensley claims, puts you in the religion business and offers the promise of paradise today, which is to say, freedom from nearly all forms of local, state, and federal taxation.

Reverend Hensley had his day in court in 1974 and won federal recognition of the Universal Life Church, so he argues that anyone receiving a charter from him is safe.

With charter in hand, he suggests, you can own property in your church's name, receive income or donations, and operate a church-related business. To be exempt from taxes, any income from the business you donate to the church must really be church-related. A publishing business would qualify, of course, if it printed religious tracts, sermons, and so on which were for sale. A radio or television station used to propagate the faith would also qualify.

As the ordained minister of a legally recognized church, you are not subject to Social Security taxes, because you earn no income as such. All of your living expenses come out of what is called a parsonage allowance. The Internal Revenue Code, Section 107, provides that a minister or religious worker in the employ of a church can get a tax-free cash allowance for the fair rental value of a furnished home, including utilities, and living expenses. The only kicker in keeping the allowance tax-free is that the amount must be designated by the church's board of directors in advance of receipt and entered into the official minutes, or it will be disallowed by the tax man.

If this seems like another one of those propositions that sound too good to be true, think it over. It is. There is no question that our tax codes were constructed to favor and, in a way, foster the growth of organized religion in the United States. Some will even argue that this represents a breach of the separation of church and state. But most of those attracted to the "mail-order ministry" are unconcerned with either religious or constitutional issues. They see it as a way to eliminate virtually all of their taxes—a way to render unto God (or themselves) instead of Caesar.

What they fail to see is that in obeying, or at least appearing to obey, the letter of the law, they may lose track of its intent. And when the IRS and the courts get around to examining their personal intentions, these "ministers" could find themselves in a lot of trouble.

Section 501 of the Internal Revenue Code lists tax-exempt organizations. The language is unusually clear for the Internal Revenue Code. Exemptions are given to "corporations organized and operated exclusively for religious purposes no part of the net earning of which inures to the benefit of any private shareholder or individual."

In other words, **the IRS will examine and interpret your motives in organizing your own church.** If it is seen primarily as a tax sham, something constructed solely for the purpose of avoiding taxes, you can forget it. Appearances won't mean a thing.

The Internal Revenue Service attacks these sham churches on several grounds. Revenue Ruling 78-232 describes a "funneling" scheme involving "donations" and "exempt allowances." In this case a church was set up with a taxpayer as minister and his spouse, two minor children, and a few friends as members. The church retained some of his earnings, but the bulk came back to the taxpayer.

The ruling began by disallowing the taxpayer's donations to the church. The IRS reasoned that the taxpayer gave the money expecting a return— namely, the payment of his living expenses. A gift, so the reasoning went, should not have such strings attached to it.

The ruling went on to suggest that tax exemptions can be taken only if the church is operated exclusively for religious purposes. What those religious purposes might be is not important when other nonreligious purposes (like the benefit of the taxpayer) clearly exist.

Fortunately, not even the IRS attempts to define religion. But it has outlined, as follows, several characteristics common to legitimate religions:

1. A distinct legal existence.
2. A recognized creed and form of worship.
3. A definite and distinct ecclesiastical government.
4. A formal code of doctrine and discipline.
5. A distinct religious history.
6. A membership not associated with any other church or denomination.
7. A complete organization of ordained ministers ministering to their congregations.
8. Ordained ministers selected after completing prescribed courses of study.
9. A literature of its own.
10. An established place of worship.
11. Regular congregations.
12. Regular religious services.
13. Sunday schools for the religious instruction of the young.
14. Schools for the preparation of its ministers.

Of course, all these characteristics need not be present to satisfy the IRS. In fact, a great deal of interpretation on the part of both the IRS and the courts goes into determining the legitimacy of each individual case. And that is the biggest trap the unwary fall into—believing that if their elaborate tax dodge is carefully constructed to obey the letter of the law, their motives don't matter. Such naiveté virtually guarantees an audit with all kinds of disallowances. The do-it-yourselfer who chooses to fight can expect to spend a minimum of $10,000 in legal or accounting fees, win or lose. And the loser at best pays some stiff penalties, at worst ends up in jail.

It's just not worth the risks.

On the other side of the coin, while the IRS is examining the motives of those starting their own churches, you should be examining the motives of those selling the do-it-yourself kits. It may be more than just their scheme to get rich quick. The Reverend Kirby J. Hensley makes his motives clear: "I do not believe anybody in America should have tax-exempt status except the Federal Government. I'd like to see all religious tax exemptions set aside. I want to see the church system, as we know it today, die."

Hensley's church has been found tax-exempt. But the law states that each chartered church must stand on its own, and many who bought his scheme have lost thousands in his crusade to tear down the system. Whether or not they share Hensley's beliefs is unknown, but as crusaders they are "slaughtered before they even see the lights of the city."

CAN YOU ELIMINATE SOCIAL SECURITY TAXES LEGALLY?

The onerous burden of Social Security taxes is increasing as rapidly as the income tax itself. And in the case of the Social Security tax, there's not even a chance to reduce the amount through legitimate deductions. No wonder people would like to get out from under this unfunded program, which in all probability will be unable even to sustain its payout for more than a few years. However, contrary to many ideas promulgated by some so-called tax advisers, **there is simply no legal way to avoid paying Social Security taxes.**

Becoming a minister of a mail-order church to avoid Social Security taxes is a recommendation I've disposed of earlier. Using a Subchapter S scheme to pay yourself strictly with dividends, as has also been recommended by some, doesn't work either, since the IRS takes the position that these "dividends" are subject to Social Security taxes.

OTHER SCHEMES TO AVOID

To handle the growing number of tax protesters, the IRS has issued a set of guidelines for its agents. These cover not only the aforementioned plans and schemes but also such obviously questionable tactics as filing a return giving only the taxpayer's name and address, the rest being left blank by taking the Fifth Amendment against self-incrimination. The Supreme Court threw this argument out in 1927. In a recent case, the IRS won tax and penalties from the recalcitrant tax protester.

The fair-market ploy fails in the same unworkable category. In this case, the taxpayer makes a large adjustment in his gross income because the purchasing power of the dollar has been so badly eroded. The adjusted gross income then becomes small enough so that all taxable income is eliminated.

Let's face it: These schemes, along with refusing to pay part of your taxes due because you don't like the way the government is spending the money, are nothing but open invitations to trouble. And with the Illegal Tax Protesters Project in effect since January 1, 1978, on all returns identified as being from tax protesters, you're liable for criminal sanctions as well as pecuniary punishment.

Besides avoiding obvious problems, the best way of staying out of trouble with the IRS is to heed the advice of competent professionals. Sure, you'll have to pay for it. But the advice is usually tax deductible. And gambling with the tax man is gambling with loaded dice—loaded in his favor.

ADDITIONAL COSTS OF TRUSTS NOT TO TRUST

The new tax bill should provide the impetus for most taxpayers to avoid these ill-conceived schemes. Starting February 1, 1982, an interest rate of almost 25 percent will be charged for the underpayment of taxes. Furthermore, a negligence penalty of 50 percent of the interest due from underpayment of taxes may be assessed. Thus you may be paying 35 percent in interest for underpayments deficiencies in the amount of taxes you owe. Even in today's market 30-percent interest is a pretty high cost for borrowing money. And remember you (hopefully not you) could be liable for additional negligence penalties and subject to possible criminal charges. It simply isn't worth it.

24

Finding the Right Professional Advice

> In the multitude of counsellors there is safety.
>
> —PROVERBS 11:14

For better or for worse, in sickness or in health, the IRS is your partner for life. When it comes to other partners, however, your options are open. Choosing these partners, whether they be trustees, CPAs, or members of your tax-sheltering partnership, involves a number of crucial decisions.

Let's start by choosing a *comprehensive* financial planner or an attorney. He or she will probably be the linchpin of your tax-avoidance and estate plans.

THE ROLE OF A COMPREHENSIVE FINANCIAL PLANNER

As a practicing tax attorney for nearly two decades, I have found that over half of the clients seeking my services were really looking for someone who could offer more broad financial ideas and assistance than a lawyer traditionally gives. What many of these clients wanted was a financial adviser who could act as a kind of financial quarterback in the development of their overall personal financial plan. True, they wanted estate-planning advice and usually some help on basic tax-avoidance strategies, but they were also looking for investment advice. And they had questions about specific investment products—diamonds, gold shares, how much and what kind of life insurance, tax shelters, and the like.

Now, it so happens that as a lawyer, I was expanding my advising spheres to include this kind of planning, but you must understand this is not typical. Lawyers are specialists. And most lawyers can be viewed as financial planners in handling the specialist role—advising and approving wills and trusts, preparing other legal documents needed in your financial plan, and sometimes offering counsel on ideas.

Just as many lawyers, accountants, and other specialists are quite specific and sometimes limited in their role as financial advisers, many traditional financial planners also have a limited perspective in their approach to solving your problems.

If a financial planner is a single-product salesperson, there is the tendency to solve your investment needs with the product he or she happens to be selling. An insurance salesperson always includes insurance or annuities. Stockbrokers usually suggest stocks. Real estate people push real estate, and so forth. I'm not saying that this is always bad. My point is that it may not always be the *best* answer to your financial needs. Your individual needs require a totally balanced and thoroughly coordinated approach.

The planning you want is what I call "comprehensive" financial planning—and you need someone who is broadly skilled to help in the full development of your total financial program. The kind of planning questions that should be answered by your plan would include the following:

1. How much Federal Estate (death tax) can you and your spouse expect to pay on your current estate values, assuming a projected inflationary rate?

2. What strategies could best reduce your income tax over the next several years?

3. Considering the double whammy of income taxes and inflation, will your current investment program provide you with sufficient retirement income to live the way you choose?

4. Considering the future cost of education, what options are available to you to educate your children with either tax-free or low-tax dollars?

5. Should you establish a revocable "living" trust as your principal estate-planning document?

6. How could you best redeploy your assets to stay ahead financially during the decade of the 1980s?

Two more suggestions before we talk further about attorneys. The kind of financial planner you should seek will be one who is not using up his one-investment product, but who has available a cafeteria of investments. This way, your personal needs are more likely to be satisfied. Also, the good financial planner advises when specialists are needed and how to work with them. To do a solid job of estate planning, you will need a lawyer. Likewise, an accountant will be needed for various aspects of your planning. The financial planner can be the quarterback and may call the signals, but the specialist plays a big role in your financial success.

WHERE *NOT* TO LOOK FOR AN ATTORNEY

The worst thing you can do is to call the local or county bar association. In one California community, the local bar association runs a large advertisement which says, "If you need a lawyer and you do not know one, call this number. This is our public service to the community."

Now, down at the office, they have clerks with little file boxes of three-by-five cards, one for each attorney who wants referrals. Typically, the only ones in the box are those who have just hung up their shingle. That's your first problem.

Your second problem is that they pull the names on a rotation basis. Which is like pulling them out of a hat.

You call them up with your tax problem or estate problem or trust problem, and they say "We've got just the right lawyer for you" and pull out the next card. Not only is the lawyer new to practice but he or she may be focusing on criminal law, which you don't really need for tax problems—unless of course your problem is evasion.

The next worst place to look for a lawyer is your bank. It might seem logical for you to ask one of your bank's trust officers to recommend an attorney, particularly if you're contemplating setting up a trust. Nothing could be further from the truth. The trust department often has sweetheart arrangements with different lawyers. You fill my wallet and I'll fill yours. So the lawyer the trust officer sends you to may well name the bank as the executor of your estate and the trustee of your trust, whether you need it or not—whether you want it or not.

Moreover, the bank is one of the worst places to deposit that kind of responsibility and power in inflationary times. Banks simply don't believe in hard-money investments. They're still living in the bond days of the 1940s. I have a client who is the beneficiary of a $1 million estate under a bank's management in the Midwest. It's a very prudent bank, so prudent that it finds the concept of buying gold or any other hard assets irresponsible. The bank has agreed, however, to resign the trust management and allow its transfer to another bank. With a lot of searching, we at last managed to find a bank willing to invest 25 or 30 percent of my client's inheritance in hard money.

THE BEST PLACES TO LOOK FOR AN ATTORNEY

What you do want to do, if possible, is to locate an attorney with a reputation in the field of trusts or taxes or estate planning. This might be an author in the field or one of those attorneys asked by the state to help educate other lawyers in a particular specialty. He or she might also be a part-time member of a law school faculty.

One way to locate an attorney in a particular field is through the *Martindale-Hubbell Law Directory*. It offers every lawyer in the country a chance to place a biographical summary indicating a legal specialty after his or her name. But remember, that blurb is an indication only of specialty, not of competency. You will have to be the judge of that—or let your friends be. Referrals from friends and business acquaintances whose opinions in financial matters you respect, as well as accountants and others who normally have contact with lawyers, are your best single source for finding a competent attorney.

Besides the five checkpoints that follow for assessing professional help, one telltale sign of an attorney's suitability for your needs is the office library. It should be filled with tax service bulletins from the Commerce Clearing House, Prentice-Hall, Tax Management, Mertens on Taxation, Cavitch on Business Organizations, and the like. If it's not, this is not the right attorney for your tax-avoidance planning.

One secret in finding a good estate attorney is knowing where and when he or she takes a vactation. If it's Miami in January, it's probably for more than a tan. The best professional seminar on estate planning for lawyers and accountants is sponsored that month by the University of Miami. Lawyers who keep up with what's happening in the field usually attend or send an associate.

Choosing an accountant follows more or less the same search pattern as that for choosing an attorney. Be sure your accountant is not only a specialist in taxation but a CPA as well. The April specialists that bloom in storefronts come spring every year are obviously not good choices.

Here are five clues to determining the quality of any professional in taxation, finance, and estate planning:

1. Is this person well organized? How orderly is the office? A chaotic room with piles of folders and open books everywhere may indicate an intense involvement with a project. On the other hand, it's just as likely to indicate a chaotic mind. And speaking of files, how long does it take to locate information in your file, if one has been started, or to answer your questions if you request specific examples? "It's here somewhere" should send you somewhere else.

2. Is this adviser a good problem solver? Are the questions you are asked pertinent? Concise? At the same time, are your replies considered carefully? Are interruptions such as telephone calls kept to a minimum during your conferences? In other words, does this person focus on your specific problems? Defining the problem, after all, is half the battle.

3. Does the professional know his or her limits? An adviser who has a pet answer for every question may be superbly informed and on top of the situation. More likely, this is someone who is unable to say, "I don't know." Admitting one doesn't have all the answers indicates a basically honest character and an adviser unlikely to shoot from the hip. Of course, there must also be the follow-through to get you the answers you seek when they're not immediately forthcoming.

4. How good at dealing with other advisers is this candidate? Is he

confident and unafraid to take advice from others in related fields? Can you get advice put in writing quickly, both for you and for any other consultants you might wish to ask for an opinion? Incompetent advisers have a difficult time letting themselves be pinned down in black and white.

5. You should look not only at the adviser but at the quality of the support staff as well. Do they appear satisfied and loyal? Is a lot of the work delegated to them? If not, perhaps your adviser is incapable of delegating. That's a bad sign. By delegating routine work, a good manager is able to deal with more crucial questions for more clients, which provides more experience—exactly what you're looking for.

Once you've gotten over the hurdle of selecting your adviser, the question you should ask is, "How much do you charge?" Remember, this is business.

In my opinion, it pays to have a written fee agreement between you, as a client, and the attorney, as the person whose services you are retaining. This agreement should spell out how much the attorney will charge you and what exactly he or she is expected to do. You can't have one without the other. **A detailed written agreement is the best insurance against any misunderstandings** or feelings of resentment by either party later on.

The second matter to be considered besides price is deadline. When is the attorney going to have what you need done? Lots of lawyers, like lots of other people, are dilatory. Make sure you have an agreement as to when you can expect a finished program or plan. Make the lawyer accountable, and then don't be afraid to follow up if matters become delayed.

After all, if in reading this book you have been motivated to take decisive steps against inflation and the IRS, the worst thing you can do is to get an adviser who doesn't produce any documents for a year. Be assertive: It's your money and your future.

CHOOSING A FIDUCIARY

A *fiduciary* is most simply defined as a person who holds something in trust for someone else. When dealing in wills and trusts, administrators, executors, and trustees all act as fiduciaries. Their powers, however, vary.

Both administrators and executors are short-term appointees whose office rarely exceeds two years. They simply wind up the estate and distribute the assets according to the law and/or your will.

The trustee's work, on the other hand, extends over decades, perhaps even over a whole lifetime. This is an ongoing management position. Choosing such a long-term fiduciary, then, is not only exceedingly important but exceedingly difficult as well.

The qualities you need to look for in a trustee are integrity, genuine compassion, and an understanding of your family or the other particular beneficiaries of your trust or estate. These qualities are ones institutions rarely offer.

If you choose a bank as trustee, for instance, you should give your spouse a certain limited power to change the trustee. Then, if your spouse finds it difficult to deal with the particular person chosen to represent the bank, he or she has the power to threaten to terminate the bank's trusteeship services unless someone more amenable is put in charge of the account.

The powers of the trustee should be broad where they concern the ability to make investment decisions. Anything less could be disastrous. For example, John Jones and his wife, Mary Jones, both lived through the stock-market crash of 1929 and as a result lost a considerable amount of their estate. John was so embittered by the experience that he took what remaining cash he had and bought approximately $400,000 worth of paid-up life insurance. He named an institutional banking trust company as trustee, and he specifically stated that the trustee, upon his death and after collecting the insurance proceeds, could invest the proceeds only into a certain class of government obligations which paid approximately 2½ percent per annum. He died in 1930. His widow lived until 1972.

Following his death, the banking trust department collected the insurance proceeds and promptly invested the funds as designated, paying 2½ percent per annum, which generated approximately $10,000 in income a year for the widow. Needless to say, during the Depression years she was in excellent financial shape, with plenty of money on which to live and raise her children. But as time went on and inflation began taking its toll, the amount of income Mary Jones received became very inadequate. She requested the bank to change its investment designation. They refused because of the direction established by her late husband. As a result, the purchasing power of the trust's assets began eroding.

In 1970, when her plight was discovered by a new attorney, she was desperate. The attorney, employing some statutory provisions of law, was able to remove most of the assets from the bank's management and to reinvest them in property less susceptible to being eroded by inflation. But by then most of the damage had been done.

Hindsight would show that, had the $400,000 of insurance proceeds been invested in almost anything else during the thirties and forties, by the time of Mrs. Jones's death, in 1972, she could have been worth several million dollars. As it was, however, her estate was worth $350,000—because the powers of the trustee had been too limited.

The instrument giving power to the trustee should outline not only the investment goals for the assets, in broad terms, but the survivor's needs as well. Don't make the instrument a straitjacket for your trustee. Make it a charter of freedom to further your desires for the survivor's benefit.

25

What We Can Expect from Congress and the IRS

Future, n. That period of time in which our affairs prosper, our
friends are true, and our happiness assured.
—AMBROSE BIERCE. *THE DEVIL'S DICTIONARY*

The Economic Recovery Tax Act of 1981 goes a long way in an effort to
save family businesses, farms, and estate property from the onerous transfer
taxes of the government. The Act does not go as far as many claim it has.
True, the new maximum $600,000 exemption from gift and estate taxes
will have a major impact, but this full exemption does not go into effect until 1987. Meanwhile, if your estate is worth $225,000 in 1982 (which is the
exemption equivalent for 1982), with just normal inflation (12 percent) you
could well have an estate of over $700,000 in ten years. In other words,
even a middle-sized estate is not totally excluded from estate tax planning
by the new Act.

ERTA also provides us with more creative taxation changes. At long last,
we see a sound approach to business expansion through tax
incentives—instead of transfer payments—as the way to reduce unemployment, spark the economy and, hopefully, control inflation. But will it work?
Sadly, unless Congress is now willing to go much further in the way of taxation changes, I think not.

During the time President Reagan was campaigning for the presidency,
Nobel-laureate Milton Friedman, one of President Reagan's economic advisers, qualified his optimism for the eventual turning back of inflation,
even with the passage of ERTA (or the Kemp-Roth bill, as it was then
known). Mr. Friedman outlined a series of steps which, he stated, must be
realized if the economy was to turn around. According to Friedman, to rid
ourselves of inflation we must cut taxes, pare government spending, reduce
regulation of private enterprise, and stabilize the money supply. Even
though I believe President Reagan is a remarkable and courageous man,
and his first major step toward these objectives has been taken through the
recent tax act, the political realities are such that it may be difficult indeed
for the kind of changes advocated by Milton Friedman to be made and fully
implemented.

And while we hope it may happen, it would be economic suicide to simply sit back and wait for Congress to solve our tax and inflation problems.

We need to start implementing the techniques discussed in this book now.

We know what Congress *should* do to continue the direction of our "Ship of State." But what *will* Congress do? Remember, Congress still has a major conflict of interest in the area of inflation. Inflation increases its real spendable income through bracket creep, which has not been totally eliminated, while at the same time reducing its debts. And reducing the budget by cutting out various social programs also places members of Congress on the horns of a dilemma. Knowing what must be done for the good of the country does not ease the pressure brought by the various voting constituents who will be affected. In short, Congress benefits politically from proposing additional tax cuts, but economically from inflation-increased taxation, and when reelection is at stake the "immediate interests" of the voters usually come first.

In the meantime, what can we expect from Congress now that the initial reaction to Reaganomics has been recorded? My first answer is—I simply don't know. Why? At the time these book revisions were being made (October 1981), the staff at the Treasury Department, the Senate Finance Committee, and the House Ways and Means Committee were all extremely closed-mouthed. This hush-hush attitude in Congressional circles was because of the condition of Wall Street. It was literally on its tail. And rumors were being circulated that Congress would retreat on many of the provisions of ERTA because of increased tax needs to meet budget demands.

Now, for my best guess about some of the significant tax changes we might expect:

Capital Gains. Elimination of capital gains and/or a redefining of the holding period for qualifying property to six months from the current one year.

Energy Credit Repeal. The residential energy tax credits of up to $4,300 and the business energy tax credits of up to $4,300 and the business energy tax credits of somewhere between 10 and 15 percent of expenditures could be repealed.

Employee Benefits. Possible elimination of business deductions for some employee benefits such as medical insurance, at least on the higher income levels where these perks include company cars and other tangible benefits.

Unemployment Benefits. Possible increase of taxes on compensation received by unemployed workers.

Tax Exempt Bonds. A scale-back on tax-exempt industrial development bonds.

One last hopeful note is a bill introduced by Representative Mike Lowry (D., Wash). This bill proposes that individuals who "substantially prevail" in fighting the IRS will be reimbursed for their legal fees and expenses. Under the terms of this proposed bill, if the IRS position is deemed reasonable, the individual taxpayer will be reimbursed by the government's general fund. Better yet, if the IRS position is deemed not reasonable—if, that is, they're just harassing you as they often do—then the legal fees you, as a taxpayer, incur will be paid to you directly by the IRS.

The IRS has to pay at last.

APPENDIXES

A. QUESTIONNAIRE

Date Prepared: _____ By: _____

FAMILY INFORMATION

	Husband	**Wife**
Name:	_____	_____
Usual Signature:	_____	_____
Home Address:	_____
	_____ Zip _____

Telephone: ( ) _____

Present or Past Occupation: _____

Employer:	_____	_____
Business Address:	_____	_____
	_____ Zip____	_____ Zip__
Business Phone:	_____	_____
Birthdate [present age]:	_____ [ ]	_____ [ ]
Birthplace:	_____	_____
Social Security Number:	_____	_____

Date and Place of Marriage: Date: _____ Place: _____

State of Residence at Marriage: _____

Value of Property Owned at Marriage: _____

What states have you resided in since the date of your marriage, including dates of residency?

_____[19   -19   ]   _____[19   -19   ]   _____[19   -19   ]

Any marriage agreements settling property rights:

Prior to Marriage? _____ After Marriage? _____
                        Yes/No   Yes/No

If Yes send copies.

CHILDREN:

Indicate relationship as follows:
Child of client husband and wife (HW)
Child of client Husband (H)
Child of client Wife (W)
Adopted child or grandchild (A)

Living Children:

Name	Relationship	Birthdate	Age

Deceased Children:

Name	Relationship	Birthdate	Age

Children of Deceased Child:

Name	Deceased Parent	Relationship	Birthdate	Age

EXISTING ESTATE-PLANNING DOCUMENTS

Will: Dated _____

    Does Will create a trust for spouse? _____

Trusts:

    Created by Husband: _____

    Created by Wife: _____

    Created by Third Parties: _____

WILLS AND TRUSTS

Are you or your spouse a beneficiary of one or more trusts? _____

Do you or your spouse have any powers (rights) over the assets of any trust in which you or your spouse are not trust grantor(s) or beneficiary(s)? _____

If the answer to either of the two questions immediately above is yes, complete the description of the trust(s) below.

	Date Trust Established	Name of Trust Guarantor(s)	Relationship to Trust Guarantor(s) to You or Your Spouse	Name of Trustee(s)
TRUST #1	_____	_____	_____	_____
TRUST #2	_____	_____	_____	_____
TRUST #3	_____	_____	_____	_____

Relationship of Trust Beneficiary(s) To You or Your Spouse	Name of Trust Beneficiary(s)	Relationship of Trust Beneficiary(s) To You or Your Spouse	Is the Trust Revocable or Irrevocable	Purpose for Which the Trust Established
_____	_____	_____	_____	_____
_____	_____	_____	_____	_____
_____	_____	_____	_____	_____

Additional information: _____

_____

_____

_____

_____

_____

_____

_____

_____

_____

_____

_____

ESTATE-PLANNING OBJECTIVES

Are you more interested in meeting the current needs of the surviving spouse or in conserving the value of your estate to pass it to your children? Please elaborate _____

_____

_____

Would you want all your children treated on an equal basis or should special consideration be given to one or more? _____

_____

Do you also want to plan for your grandchildren? If yes, to what extent or for what specific purposes (i.e., education)? _____

_____

_____

Do you want to establish a program for educating your children with tax deductible or low tax funds? _____

_____

Is avoiding probate one of your objectives? _____

Do you intend some portion of your estate to be used for charitable purposes? Describe _____

_____

_____

Are you willing to plan now for reducing either income tax or estate tax liabilities by the shifting of income or changing the ownership of existing assets? _____

If our analysis indicated it would be feasible, would you be interested in "freezing" the value of existing estate assets to reduce the impact of inflation on estate settlement costs?

_____

If an estate-freezing device, such as an installment sale of a major asset to a trust or partnership, would be advantageous, would you want us to consider this alternative?

_____

_____

If creation of an irrevocable life insurance trust would reduce estate taxes for you, would you be willing to create such trust (sometimes called an ancestors' trust)? This would require you to relinquish all rights and incidents of ownership including the power to change beneficiaries. Comment. _____

_____

_____

Do you have a family business which you are interested in transferring intact to later generations? _____

What average rate of inflation do you expect in the next 5 years? _____

CURRENT AND PROJECTED INCOME

	1981		1982		1983		Year Proceeds Terminate?	
	C	S	C	S	C	S	C	S
Base Salary	$_____	_____	$_____	_____	$_____	_____	$_____	_____
Commissions/Bonus	$_____	_____	$_____	_____	$_____	_____	$_____	_____
Professional Fees	$_____	_____	$_____	_____	$_____	_____	$_____	_____
Director's Fees	$_____	_____	$_____	_____	$_____	_____	$_____	_____
Net Self-Employed Income (Schedule C)	$_____	_____	$_____	_____	$_____	_____	$_____	_____
Partnership Distributions	$_____	_____	$_____	_____	$_____	_____	$_____	_____
Sub-Chapter S Corp. Distributions	$_____	_____	$_____	_____	$_____	_____	$_____	_____
Trust Distributions	$_____	_____	$_____	_____	$_____	_____	$_____	_____
Deferred Compensation	$_____	_____	$_____	_____	$_____	_____	$_____	_____
Pension and Annuity Income	$_____	_____	$_____	_____	$_____	_____	$_____	_____

Please estimate totals for each calendar year.

1. This information should be made available from your 1981 Federal Tax Return, W-2's, 1099's etc. If it was aggregated on your tax return, please allocate as shown here.

2. For 1982 and subsequent years, base your forcast on the information presently available (promotions, retirement, etc.) plus what you may reasonably expect. Your estimates need only be approximations for planning purposes.

CURRENT AND PROJECTED INCOME (CONTINUED)

	1981		1982		1983		Year Proceeds Terminate?	
	C	S	C	S	C	S	C	S
Dividends	$_____	_____	$_____	_____	$_____	_____	$_____	_____
Taxable Interest Income	$_____	_____	$_____	_____	$_____	_____	$_____	_____
Tax Exempt Interest Income	$_____	_____	$_____	_____	$_____	_____	$_____	_____
Net Rental Income (Sched. E, Part II)	$_____	_____	$_____	_____	$_____	_____	$_____	_____
Short Term Capital Gains (Losses)	$_____	_____	$_____	_____	$_____	_____	$_____	_____
Long Term Capital Gains (Losses)	$_____	_____	$_____	_____	$_____	_____	$_____	_____
Other Income (Royalties, Judgments)	$_____	_____	$_____	_____	$_____	_____	$_____	_____
Anticipated Inheritances	$_____	_____	$_____	_____	$_____	_____	$_____	_____
Alimony Received	$_____	_____	$_____	_____	$_____	_____	$_____	_____
Farm Income (Sched. F)	$_____	_____	$_____	_____	$_____	_____	$_____	_____

CURRENT AND PROJECTED EXPENSES

Tax Related Expenditures:	1981	19__ (1)	19__ (2)
IRA and Keogh Contributions			
Alimony Paid			
Medical Expense (net of ins.)			
Nursing Care			
Medical Insurance Premiums			
State (& City) Income Tax			
Real Estate Taxes			
Personal Prop. Taxes			
Investment Int. Expense			
Contributions—Cash			
Contributions—In Kind			
FICA, Social Security, SDI			
Casualty and Theft Losses			
Discretionary Expenditures:			
Recreation & Entertainment			
Vacation			
Domestic Help			
Major Purchases—Describe			

Living Expenses	1981	19__ (1)	19__ (2)
Food			
Clothing			
Mortgage or Rent			
Life Insurance Premiums			
Property Ins. Premiums			
Liability Ins. Premiums			
Telephone and Utilities			
Commute Expenses			
Other Car Expenses			
Car Payments			
Education			
Home Furnishings			
Home Upkeep & Maintenance			
Debt Repayments			
Other—Describe			

Notes:

1. Use this column to indicate what you expect these expenses to be after some major anticipated change in your lifestyle, such as a job-related transfer, a move to the country, back to school, children out of college, etc.

2. The second column is intended for a post-retirement or similar period when job-related income would be sharply reduced.

FINANCIAL INFORMATION

ASSETS

Residence

Location and Description: _____

Estimated Value: _____

Indebtedness Outstanding: _____

Date of Maturity of Debt Obligation: _____

Title: Jt. Ten._____ Ten. Com._____ Comm. Prop._____ Other—specify_____

Bank and Savings & Loan Accounts

Checking

Name/Address of Institution:	In Name(s) of:	Balance:
_____	_____	_____
_____	_____	_____

Savings

Name/Address of Institution:	In Name(s) of:	Balance:
_____	_____	_____
_____	_____	_____
_____	_____	_____
_____	_____	_____

Stocks, Bonds, and Money Market Funds:

No. of Shares	Company	In Name(s) of:	Estimated Value:
_____	_____	_____	_____
_____	_____	_____	_____
_____	_____	_____	_____
_____	_____	_____	_____
_____	_____	_____	_____
_____	_____	_____	_____
_____	_____	_____	_____

Notes, Mortgages, and Accounts Receivable

Debtor	Creditor (H and/or W)	Face Amount	Present Value	Maturity Date	Security
_____	_____	_____	_____	_____	_____
_____	_____	_____	_____	_____	_____

Employee Benefits (e.g., pension and profit-sharing plans)

Briefly describe source, amount, and present beneficiary designation.

_____

_____

Miscellaneous Assets (at current value) (Please note title as Joint Tenants, Community, Tenant in Common or other)

1) Jewelry/Gems: _____

2) Precious Metals: _____

3) Works of Art:_____

4) Antiques: _____

5) Collections (e.g., coin, clock, stamp): _____

_____

6) Oil/Gas: _____

7) Farm Machinery: _____

8) Harvested but Unsold Grain: _____

9) Livestock: _____

10) Other: (specify) _____

_____

Life Insurance

Policies Owned by Husband on His Life

Face Value	Company	Type	Beneficiary	Source of Premiums
_____	_____	_____	_____	_____
_____	_____	_____	_____	_____
_____	_____	_____	_____	_____

Policies Owned by Wife on Her Life

Face Value	Company	Type	Beneficiary	Source of Premiums
_____	_____	_____	_____	_____
_____	_____	_____	_____	_____
_____	_____	_____	_____	_____

Policies Owned by Wife on Life of Husband

Face Value	Company	Type	Beneficiary	Source of Premiums
_____	_____	_____	_____	_____
_____	_____	_____	_____	_____
_____	_____	_____	_____	_____

Policies Owned by Husband on Life of Wife

Face Value	Company	Type	Beneficiary	Source of Premiums
_____	_____	_____	_____	_____
_____	_____	_____	_____	_____
_____	_____	_____	_____	_____

Policies Owned by H/W on Life of Others

Face Value	Company	Type	Beneficiary	Source of Premiums
_____	_____	_____	_____	_____
_____	_____	_____	_____	_____
_____	_____	_____	_____	_____

REAL ESTATE, BUSINESS INTERESTS, TAX SHELTERS AND OTHER INVESTMENT ASSETS[1]

Property #1

Name and Description _____	Lender _____
	Original Balance $ _____
Location _____	Date Obtained ___/___/___
Original Cost $ _____	Term (Maturity) _____
Plus Improvements $ _____	Current Balance $ _____
Less Accum. Deprec. $ _____	Interest Rate _____%
Net Tax Basis $ _____	Monthly/Quarterly Payment: $ _____
Purchase Date ___/___/___	Special Principal Payments $ ___;___/___/___
Source of Funds _____	(List Amounts and Due Dates) $ ___;___/___/___
Form of Title (e.g. Joint Tenancy etc.) _____	
Estimated Market Value $ _____	

Receipts:	1981	1982	1983
Gross Cash Receipts			
Net Taxable Income—Ordinary			
Depreciation/Amortization/Depletion			
Sales Proceeds Less Selling Experience[3]			
Allocated Basis[3]			
Accelerated Depreciation Recapture[3]			
Payments:			
Additional Cash Investment			
Debt Service—Principal			
Debt Service—Interest			

1. Use this form for notes receivable, contracts receivable, investments in first and second mortgages and deeds of trusts, installment sales, interests in partnerships and joint ventures, and tax shelter deals. Some or even major portions may be inapplicable to a particular investment. If so, indicate "N/A."

2. Provide last year for comparison purposes and to facilitate our analysis.

3. These apply if a business interest or other investment asset has been or will be sold, for example on an installment basis where you have provided or will provide financing.

REAL ESTATE, BUSINESS INTERESTS, TAX SHELTERS AND OTHER INVESTMENT ASSETS[1]

Property #2

Name and Description _____

Location _____

Original Cost	$ _____
Plus Improvements	$ _____
Less Accum. Deprec.	$ _____
Net Tax Basis	$ _____
Purchase Date	___/___/___
Source of Funds	_____

Form of Title (e.g. Joint Tenancy etc.) _____

Estimated Market Value $ _____

Lender	_____
Original Balance	$ _____
Date Obtained	___/___/___
Term (Maturity)	_____
Current Balance	$ _____
Interest Rate	_____ %
Monthly/Quarterly Payment:	$ _____
Special Principal Payments	$ ___;___/___
(List Amounts and Due Dates)	$ ___;___/___

Receipts:	1981	1982	1983
Gross Cash Receipts			
Net Taxable Income—Ordinary			
Depreciation/Amortization/Depletion			
Sales Proceeds Less Selling Experience[3]			
Allocated Basis[3]			
Accelerated Depreciation Recapture[3]			
Payments:			
Additional Cash Investment			
Debt Service—Principal			
Debt Service—Interest			

1. Use this form for notes receivable, contracts receivable, investments in first and second mortgages and deeds of trusts, installment sales, interests in partnerships and joint ventures, and tax shelter deals. Some or even major portions may be inapplicable to a particular investment. If so, indicate "N/A."

2. Provide last year for comparison purposes and to facilitate our analysis.

3. These apply if a business interest or other investment asset has been or will be sold, for example on an installment basis where you have provided or will provide financing.

LIABILITIES

Notes Secured by Mortgages or Deeds of Trust:

Outstanding Balance   Owed on What Property

_____   _____
_____   _____
_____   _____

Notes Owed on Autos:

Outstanding Balance   Owed on What Property

_____   _____
_____   _____

Unsecured Notes:

Outstanding Balance   Owed on What Property

_____   _____
_____   _____

Taxes Accrued:

Outstanding Balance   Owed on What Property

_____   _____
_____   _____

Other Liabilities:
(Credit Cards, Charge Accounts, Etc.)

Outstanding Balance   Owed on What Property

_____   _____
_____   _____

ESTATE SUMMARY

I. ASSETS

	Husband	Wife	Jointly Owned % Paid for by Husband	% Paid for by Wife
A. Real Estate, Business Interests, Tax Shelters				
B. Cash and Bank Accounts				
C. Stocks, Bonds, and Money Funds				
D. Notes, Mortgages and Accounts Receivable				
E. Residence				
F. Life Insurance (face amount)				
G. Employee Benefits				
H. Miscellaneous				
TOTAL				

II. LIABILITIES

	Husband	Wife	Jointly Owned % Paid for by Husband	% Paid for by Wife
A. Note Secured by Mortgages or Deeds of Trust				
B. Notes on Autos				
C. Unsecured Notes, Taxes and Other Liabilities				
TOTAL				

DOCUMENT INVENTORY

	Client				Spouse				Present Advisor/Contact (Lawyer, Accountant, Trust Officer)	May We Contact (Indicate)	
	Does It Exist		Copy Attached		Does It Exist		Copy Attached		NAME, ADDRESS, TELEPHONE	YES	NO
	YES	NO	YES	NO	YES	NO	YES	NO			
WILLS (Please attach copy):											
Present will	☐	☐	☐	☐	☐	☐	☐	☐	_____	☐	☐
TAX RETURNS (LAST 3 YEARS) (Please attach copies):											
Federal income tax (joint or individual)	☐		☐		☐		☐		_____	☐	☐
State income tax (joint or individual)	☐		☐		☐		☐			☐	☐
Federal gift tax	☐	☐	☐	☐	☐	☐	☐	☐	_____	☐	☐
State gift tax	☐	☐	☐	☐	☐	☐	☐	☐		☐	☐
Federal corporate/ partnership(s)	☐		☐		☐		☐			☐	☐
State corporate/ partnership(s)	☐		☐		☐		☐			☐	☐
TRUST AGREEMENTS (Please attach copy):											
Created by client	☐		☐		☐		☐		_____	☐	☐
Created by third party for benefit of client, spouse or family	☐		☐		☐		☐		_____	☐	☐
EMPLOYEE BENEFIT SUMMARY											
Client	☐	☐	☐	☐	☐	☐	☐	☐	_____	☐	☐
Spouse	☐	☐	☐	☐	☐	☐	☐	☐	_____	☐	☐
FAMILY AGREEMENTS (Please attach copy):											
Separation or divorce	☐	☐	☐	☐	☐	☐	☐	☐	_____	☐	☐
Property Settlement	☐	☐	☐	☐	☐	☐	☐	☐	_____	☐	☐
OTHER AGREEMENTS (Please attach copy):											
Installment sale	☐	☐	☐	☐	☐	☐	☐	☐	_____	☐	☐
Other (indicate)	☐	☐	☐	☐	☐	☐	☐	☐	_____	☐	☐

B. SAMPLE GOLD CLAUSES

Attached are several sample forms and clauses utilizing the concept of payment of obligations in gold or gold-value dollars. The specific language and options to be placed in such a contract in actual use can be most varied and also can include references to payment in foreign money currency. A brief reference follows as to each sample form, setting forth some of the significant differences and considerations. *Care, however, must be exercised by the user to seek advice from competent legal counsel on the specific merits of use for the particular transaction being considered.*

Form No. 1: LEASE RENTAL CLAUSE. To be utilized in a lease of real or personal property. Calls for adjustment to rent each year during the lease term. Adjustment is based on a gold-value index. Payment in gold or U.S. currency based on gold value.

Form No. 2: NEGOTIABLE CORPORATION PROMISSORY NOTE. This note calls for payment of specific monthly installments of principal *plus* interest. Principal payment is to be adjusted in gold-value dollars annually during the forty-eight-month term of the note. Interest is payable in non-gold-value dollars on original principal sum only. Note is secured by security agreement covering assets of maker. *Caveat:* With negotiable promissory note must consider Uniform Commercial Code.

Form No. 3: NEGOTIABLE INDIVIDUAL PROMISSORY NOTE. This note is similar to Form No. 2 and is secured by deed of trust on real property. Same *Caveat* regarding UCC is applicable. Interest, however, is payable on the annually adjusted principal-sum payments, and user must consider the matter of usury.

Form No. 4: NON-NEGOTIABLE INDIVIDUAL PROMISSORY NOTE. Payment of principal to be in U.S. Federal Reserve notes. Cash equivalent of specified number or ounces of gold, or gold bullion or bullion coins. Interest payable only in lawful currency of the U.S.

Form No. 5: NON-NEGOTIABLE LOAN AGREEMENT WITH SINKING FUND. Funds are borrowed by corporation and guaranteed by individual. Trustee designated for sinking fund funded by a percentage of corporation receipts and as beneficiary of life insurance policy on life of individual guarantor. Terms of payment similar to Form No. 4.

FORM NUMBER 1
LEASE RENTAL CLAUSE

MINIMUM RENTAL CLAUSE

Tenant shall pay to landlord as minimum rent, without deduction, setoff, prior notice, or demand, the sum of _____ Dollars ($_____) per year for a term of ten (10) years, which sum is subject to possible adjustment as provided in Paragraph ____. The equivalent number of ounces of gold determined by the London Gold Spot quotation set by the London Metal Exchange, England, on the date of this lease is ____. Such sum shall be payable in advance of the first five (5) business days of each year, beginning on the date the term commences, and continuing during the term. All rent shall be payable to landlord at the address to which notices to landlord are given. Payment shall be made in the form of standard U.S. currency or gold bullion of standard weight and fineness, whichever the landlord elects.

PERIODIC GOLD VALUATION ADJUSTMENT

The minimum yearly rent provided for in Paragraph ____ shall be subject to adjustment at the commencement of the second year of the term and every year thereafter. The adjustment shall be as follows: The basis for computing the adjustment is the London Gold Spot quotation of Troy ounces in U.S. dollars, as set by the London Metal Exchange (index) on the close and fix of the first day commencing the new term, or the setting nearest the date of commencement of the term (beginning index). If the gold quotation fixed nearest the adjustment date (extension index) has increased over the beginning index, the minimum yearly rental for the following year shall be set by multiplying the price per ounce of gold of present standard weight and fineness as traded on the London Metal Exchange by the number of ounces set

in the beginning index. In no case shall the minimum yearly rent be less than the minimum yearly rent set forth in Paragraph ____ above. On the adjustment of the minimum yearly rent as provided in this lease, the landlord and the tenant shall immediately execute an amendment to the lease stating the new minimum yearly rent. If for any reason there is a change in the methods of fixing the price of gold on the London Metal Exchange, then at the landlord's election, the landlord and tenant shall mutually select such other gold-fixing index which is satisfactory to both. If the parties cannot agree, then such index shall be selected by three arbitrators in accordance with the rules of the American Arbitration Association, and such determination shall be final and binding on the parties.

EXAMPLE FOR GOLD-VALUE ADJUSTMENT

Assuming the January 1981, fixing of London gold is Seven Hundred Dollars ($700.00) an ounce on a Seventy Thousand Dollars ($70,000.00) per year lease, the rental sum would be equivalent to 100 pure Troy ounces of gold. If, at the beginning of January 1982, the London Spot is at One Thousand Dollars ($1,000.00) an ounce, this sum shall be multiplied times 100 (the number of Troy ounces of gold at beginning index). The landlord can either receive 100 ounces of gold or the U.S. currency equivalent to the gold value ($100,000.00).

FORM NUMBER 2
NEGOTIABLE CORPORATION PROMISSORY NOTE

PROMISSORY NOTE

$18,000.00   Walnut Creek, California
                                                            May 1, 1980

For value received, the undersigned promises to pay to JOHN E. DOE, Payee, or order, at Walnut Creek, California, the sum of Eighteen Thousand Dollars ($18,000) in gold or in gold value over forty-eight (48) monthly principal installments of Three Hundred Seventy-five Dollars ($375.00) each (as adjusted each new twelve-month period) beginning on the first day of June, 1980, and continuing on the first day of each and every calendar month thereafter until paid.

Payment of Interest

In addition to the principal payment as set forth, the undersigned shall also pay to JOHN E. DOE interest on the unpaid portion of the original principal (without adjustment) at the rate of nine percent (9%) per annum. Interest shall be payable monthly in lawful currency of the United States only.

Adjusting of Principal Payment

The minimum monthly installment due, provided for in the first above Paragraph, shall be subject to adjustment at the commencement of each new twelve-(12)-month period thereafter as follows: The base for computing the adjustment is the London Gold Spot quotation of Troy ounces in U.S. dollars, as set by the London Metal Exchange, England (index), on the close and fix of the first day commencing each new twelve-(12)-month term, or the setting nearest the date of the commencement of the term (beginning index), equivalent to one month's payment of Three Hundred Seventy-five Dollars ($375.00). If the gold quotation fixed nearest the adjustment date at the beginning of the next twelve-(12)-month term (extension index) has increased over the beginning index, the minimum monthly installment for the following twelve-(12)-month period shall be set by multiplying the latter price per ounce of gold as traded on the London Metal Exchange by the number of ounces equivalent to a monthly payment as set in the beginning index.

In no case shall the minimum monthly installment be less than the minimum monthly installment as set forth in the first Paragraph hereof. On adjustment of the minimum monthly installment payment as provided in this Promissory Note, Maker and Payee shall immediately execute an amendment to this Promissory Note, stating the new minimum monthly installment.

This promissory note principal sum shall be payable in U.S. dollar currency, or equivalent quantity in gold bullion of standard weight and fineness, whichever the payee elects.

If for any reason there is a change in the method of fixing the price of gold on the

London Metal Exchange, then at Payee's election, the Payee and Maker shall mutually select such other gold-fixing index which is of satisfaction to both. If the parties cannot agree, then such index shall be selected by three arbitrators in accordance with the rules of the American Arbitration Association, and such determination shall be final and binding on the parties.

If any installment is not paid when due, it shall bear interest from the due date, until paid, at the rate of nine percent (9%) per annum.

This Note is secured by a security agreement covering all securable assets of that certain business known as ABC, Incorporated, located at 1234 Law Street, Suite B. Walnut Creek, California 94595.

This Note and any pledge or security agreements securing same are hereby declared by the undersigned, and by acceptance hereof, Payee agrees that this Note and pledge securing it are subordinate to any indebtedness of Maker, ABC, Incorporated, to DEF Bank now or hereafter existing, including any extension or modification thereof. Payee, by acceptance hereof, agrees to and shall, when requested, execute whatever documents or instruments are required by such lender as further evidence of such subordination.

Should default be made in the payment of any installment when due as provided herein, then, at any time during such default, the entire amount of principal and accrued interest, if any, at the election of the holder, become immediately due and payable without notice. In the event of any such default, the undersigned agrees to pay all costs of collection, including a reasonable sum of attorney's fees and costs of suit.

IN WITNESS WHEREOF, ABC, Incorporated, has caused this note to be signed by its president and secretary, and its Corporate Seal to be affixed.

Executed and delivered in Walnut Creek, California, on the date first above written.

ABC, INCORPORATED

BY: _____

    MARK ROE, President

BY: _____

    LINDA ROE, Secretary

FORM NUMBER 3
NEGOTIABLE INDIVIDUAL PROMISSORY NOTE

PROMISSORY NOTE

$18,000.00   Walnut Creek, California
                                                      May, 1, 1980

For value received, the undersigned promises to pay to JOHN E. DOE, Payee, or order, at Walnut Creek California, the sum of Eighteen Thousand Dollars ($18,000.00) in gold or in gold value over forty-eight (48) monthly principal installments of Three Hundred Seventy-five Dollars ($375.00) each (as adjusted each new twelve-month period) beginning on the first day of June, 1980, and continuing on the first day of each and every calendar month thereafter until paid.

Payment of Interest

In addition to the principal payment as set forth, the undersigned shall also pay to JOHN E. DOE interest on the unpaid portion of the remaining principal (after adjustment) at the rate of nine percent (9%) per annum. Interest shall be payable monthly in lawful currency of the United States only.

Adjusting of Principal Payment

The minimum monthly installment due, provided for in the first above Paragraph, shall be subject to adjustment at the commencement of each new twelve-(12)-month period thereafter as follows: The base for computing the adjustment is the London Gold Spot quotation of Troy ounces in U.S. dollars, as set by the London Metal Exchange, England (index), on the close and fix of the first day commencing each new twelve-(12)-month term, or the setting nearest the date of the commencement of the term (beginning index), equivalent to one month's payment of Three Hundred Seventy-five Dollars ($375.00). If the gold quotation fixed nearest the adjustment date at the beginning of the next twelve-(12)-month term (extension index) has increased over the beginning index, the minimum monthly installment for the following twelve-(12)-month period shall be set by multiplying the latter price per ounce of gold as traded on the London Metal Exchange by the number of ounces equivalent to a monthly payment as set in the beginning index.

In no case shall the minimum monthly installment be less than the minimum monthly installment as set forth in the first Paragraph hereof. On adjustment of the minimum monthly installment payment as provided in this Promissory Note, Maker and Payee shall immediately execute an amendment to this Promissory Note, stating the new minimum monthly installment.

This promissory note principal sum shall be payable in U.S. dollar currency, or equivalent quantity in gold bullion of standard weight and fineness, whichever the payee elects.

If for any reason there is a change in the method of fixing the price of gold on the

London Metal Exchange, then at Payee's election, the Payee and Maker shall mutually select such other gold-fixing index which is of satisfaction to both. If the parties cannot agree, then such index shall be selected by three arbitrators in accordance with the rules of the American Arbitration Association, and such determination shall be final and binding on the parties.

If any installment is not paid when due, it shall bear interest from the due date, until paid, at the rate of nine percent (9%) per annum.

Should default be made in the payment of any installment when due as provided herein, then, at any time during such default, the entire amount of principal and accrued interest, if any, shall, at the election of the holder, become immediately due and payable without notice. In the event of any such default, the undersigned agrees to pay all costs of collection, including a reasonable sum of attorney's fees and costs of suit.

This Note is secured by a deed of trust dated even date herewith.

Executed and delivered in Walnut Creek, California, on the date first above written.

_____

MARK ROE

_____

LINDA ROE

FORM NUMBER 4
NON-NEGOTIABLE INDIVIDUAL PROMISSORY NOTE

PROMISSORY NOTE

$18,000.00
Walnut Creek, California
May 1, 1980

For value received, MARK ROE promises to pay to JOHN E. DOE, Payee, on January 1, 1982, without grace, at Walnut Creek, California, the principal sum of Eighteen Thousand Dollars ($18,000.00) in gold or gold value (as adjusted by the gold value index as set forth).

In addition to the principal payment as set forth, the undersigned shall also pay to JOHN E. DOE on June 1, 1980, and on the first day of each month thereafter, interest at the rate of nine percent (9%) per annum. Interest shall be payable only in lawful currency of the United States.

Principal shall, at the option of JOHN E. DOE, be payable as follows:

(a) either by check, cashier's check, or money order, denominated in United States Federal Reserve notes,

(b) in the cash equivalent of the fair market value of _____ ounces of gold bullion, or

(c) in gold bullion or bullion coins equal to Paragraph (b) above.

The number of Troy ounces of bullion in Paragraph (b) is to be determined by taking the average price of the Second London daily dollar denominated gold fixing for the last five (5) trading days prior to the receipt of funds, and dividing it into the principal amount of this loan.

The fair market value of the bullion in Paragraph (b), for purposes of repayment, will be determined by the average closing price of the Second London daily dollar denominated gold fixing over the last five (5) business days prior to the payment date of this contract, multiplied by the number of Troy ounces of gold in Paragraph (b).

If Payee chooses to take delivery in gold or bullion coins, Payee agrees to be responsible for shipping charges, insurance, and sales taxes, if applicable, and if coins are chosen, Payee will absorb any market premium incurred by Maker in the course of making purchase.

Payee must notify Maker in writing by certified mail, prepaid, and addressed to Maker at _____, thirty (30) days prior to the payment date as to which method of payment he chooses. If such notice is not received by Maker three (3) days prior to the payment date, Maker may, at his option, select any of the repayment methods permitted under this agreement, but in no case will repayment be less than the dollar face amount of balance due on the amount borrowed.

If Payee chooses to receive the gold cash equivalent described in Paragraph (b), payment will be mailed no later than one week after the payment date, to allow time for the necessary computations.

If Payee chooses to take repayment in gold or in bullion coins, said gold will be delivered to payee no later than thirty (30) days after the payment date, to allow time for purchase, packing, and shipping. Said gold will be shipped C.O.D. to the address and by the carrier method specified by Payee, consistent with standard market procedures, and will be in bullion or coins, at the option of Maker.

If for any reason there is a change in the method of fixing the price of gold on the London Metal Exchange, then at Payee's election, the Payee and Maker shall mutually select such other gold-fixing index which is of satisfaction to both. If the parties cannot agree, then such index shall be selected by three arbitrators in accordance with the rules of the American Arbitration Association, and such determination shall be final and binding on the parties.

Should default be made in the payment of any installment when due as provided herein, then, at any time during such default, the entire amount of principal and accrued interest, if any, shall, at the election of the holder, become immediately due and payable without notice. In the event of any such default, the undersigned agrees to pay all costs of collection, including a reasonable sum of attorney's fees and costs of suit.

This Note is secured by a deed of trust dated even date herewith.

Executed and delivered in Walnut Creek, California, on the date first above written.

_____

MARK ROE

FORM NUMBER 5
NON-NEGOTIABLE LOAN AGREEMENT WITH SINKING FUND

LOAN AGREEMENT

_____, A Corporation organized and existing under the laws of the State of California (hereinafter referred to as Borrower), acknowledges receipt of a loan in the amount of _____ from _____(hereinafter referred to as Lender).

Both parties agree to the following terms and conditions:

1. Borrower agrees to repay the principal balance _____ (_____) months from date of this agreement. Repayment will be made, at the option of Lender,
   - (a) either by check, cashier's check, or money order, denominated in United States Federal Reserve notes,
   - (b) in the cash equivalent of the fair market value of ____ ounces of gold bullion, or
   - (c) in gold bullion or bullion coins equal to Paragraph (b) above.

2. The number of Troy ounces of bullion in Paragraph 1(b) is to be determined by taking the average price of the Second London daily dollar denominated gold fixing for the last five (5) trading days prior to the receipt of funds, and dividing it into the principal amount of this loan.

3. The fair market value of the bullion in Paragraph 1(b), for purposes of repayment, will be determined by the average closing price of the Second London daily dollar denominated gold fixing over the last five (5) business days prior to the payment date of this contract, multiplied by the number of Troy ounces of gold in Paragraph 1(b).

4. If Lender chooses to take delivery in gold or bullion coins, Lender agrees to be responsible for shipping charges, insurance, and sales taxes, if applicable, and if coins are chosen, Lender will absorb any market premium incurred by Borrower in the course of making purchase.

5. Lender must notify Borrower in writing by certified mail, prepaid, and addressed to Borrower at_____, thirty (30) days prior to the payment date, as to which method of payment he chooses. If such notice is not received by Borrower three (3) days prior to the payment date, Borrower may, at his option, select any of the repayment methods permitted under this agreement, but in no case will repayment be less than the dollar face amount of balance due on the amount borrowed.

6. If Lender chooses to receive the gold cash equivalent described in Paragraph 1(b), payment will be mailed no later than one week after the payment date, to allow time for the necessary computations.

If Lender chooses to take repayment in gold, as described in Paragraph 4, said gold will be delivered to Lender no later than thirty (30) days after the payment date, to allow time for purchase, packing, and shipping. Said gold will be shipped C.O.D. to the address and by the carrier method specified by Lender, consistent with standard market procedures, and will be in bullion or coins, at the option of

Borrower.

7. Borrower agrees to make quarterly interest payments denominated in United States Federal Reserve notes at the rate of ten percent (10%) per annum.

8. Borrower anticipates sufficient income from product sales over the term of this agreement to meet the terms of this agreement and all similar agreements contemplated.

9. Borrower agrees to protect Lender's interests by the following methods:

(a) Beginning six (6) months from the date of this agreement, Borrower will appoint _____ as Trustee, who will be under the following instructions:

(1) Trustee will establish a separate trust account into which each month all income will be deposited, until [i.e., *one-twelfth (1/12)*] of the principal amount of this agreement, plus accrued interest, has been collected. Thereafter Borrower will be free to use remaining monthly revenues for any other purposes.

(2) This procedure will be repeated each month, commencing on the first business day of each month, until the due date of this obligation, at which time the pertinent funds in trust will be distributed to Lender by the Trustee.

(3) Borrower and Trustee will certify to Lender once each quarter that the necessary funds have been properly placed in the trust account.

(4) These funds will be invested in Treasury Bills, gold, silver, or a Money Market Fund. There can be no other use of these segregated funds without the consent of Lender. Such investment decisions will be made by Borrower, and the Trustee will assure that the funds are invested in no other way.

(5) _____, President of _____, is personally guaranteeing the indebtedness of this agreement.

(b) Borrower will protect its ability to meet the gold option provisions of this agreement, in the event of a substantial rise or fall in the price of gold, by "hedging" through the purchase of future contracts for the total number of ounces specified in this and all similar agreements.

10. Borrower will obtain and maintain an insurance policy on the life of guarantor payable to the Trustee in the event of guarantor's untimely death, which will be used to repay all indebtedness incurred under this contract, including accrued interest. If such liquidation becomes necessary, Lender will be given thirty (30) days to determine the preferred method of payment, and payment will be made no less than sixty (60) days later.

11. Borrower may, at any time, with thirty (30) days' notice, repay all or part of the principal and interest due under this contract without prepayment penalty, provided that Lender is given an additional ten (10) days' notice in which to specify the form of repayment.

12. The proceeds from this loan will be used by _____ for the following purposes:

(a) To repay current short-term obligations of _____;

   (b) For general overhead of_____,
including salaries and all normal operating expenses;

   (c) To hedge with future contracts as described in Paragraph 9(b);

   (d) For advertising, promotion, and sales efforts in connection with the sale
of _____ products;

   (e) The purchase of additional inventories and manufacturing equipment;

   (f) Any other normal business purposes associated with _____
methods of operation.

DATED: _____

                         LENDER:

                         _____

                         BORROWER:

                         BY: _____

                                            President

   The undersigned does hereby guarantee the obligation of Borrower to repay under the terms and conditions of this loan agreement the principal and interest as set forth and does hereby waive demand or notice being first made or given to Borrower.

                                 _____

                                       Individual

C. FOREIGN FIDUCIARY STATUTES

FIDUCIARY, EXECUTOR, ADMINISTRATOR, AND TRUSTEE PROVISIONS OF THE CODES IN FIFTY STATES, ACCORDING TO THE MOST RECENT STATE CODE BOOKS AND SUPPLEMENTS AVAILABLE

A review of Amjur, Corpus Juris, ALR 1, 2, 3, and treatises and law reviews available determined that this information is not located in one place; therefore, the code books of each state were consulted. A comprehensive study of this subject was made in 1951 but has not been updated since (see 37 Va. L. Rev. 1119 [1951]).

The issues were: if there is a death in State A, and a California resident or some other State B resident is appointed executor, administrator, guardian, or trustee of an inter vivos or testamentary trust, which states authorize the State B resident to serve in that fiduciary capacity in State A?

All states did not make a distinction between a living trust and a testamentary trust for the purposes of this study. Some states did not address the issue by statute, and therefore the words "no prohibition" were used. Case law was not checked. Some answers were not directly yes or no, but had qualifications, and these are noted. Statute supplements were checked to the most recent pamphlet.

State	Foreign Executor Allowed	Foreign Trustee Allowed
Alabama	Yes, §43-2-191.	Yes by inference from §19-3-212. *Ingalls v. Ingalls*, 263 Ala. 106, 81 So. 2d 610.
Alaska	Yes, §13.21.000–13.21.075	Yes, §13.36.010.025. Registration required.
Arizona	Yes, §14-3203.	Yes, §14.7203–14.7305, "at a place appropriate to the purposes of the trust and to its sound, efficient management."
Arkansas	Yes, 62-3101. Must appoint local agent, 62-3103.	Yes, 58-405 (no prohibition in code).
California	Yes, 405.1	Yes, no prohibition.
Colorado	Yes, 15-12-301(2)(d); 15-12-402(1)(b); 15-12-203(1)(a).	Yes, 15-16-105. Registration, qualification of foreign trustee.
Connecticut	Yes, 52-60. Certificate of Appointment must be filed.	Yes, 52-60; 45-191. Must appoint local agent.
Delaware	Yes, 12 §1565.	Yes, Code Ann., tit. 12, §1506. Must appoint local agent. Nonresident subject to court confirmation, Code Ann., tit. 12 §3501.

State	Foreign Executor Allowed	Foreign Trustee Allowed
District of Columbia	Yes, §20-1505, 4.	Yes, Code 1967, §20-365. Must appoint local agent.
Florida	Yes, 21 §733.304, but only if: (1) legally adopted child or parent of decedent; (2) related by lineal consanguinity to decedent; (3) spouse or brother, sister, uncle, aunt, nephew, niece, niece of decedent; or (4) spouse of a person otherwise qualified under this section.	21 §737.105. Registration not required to receive distribution; otherwise may register, §737.101 et. seq.
Georgia	Yes, 113§2401-406.	Yes, 108 §701-707.
Hawaii	Yes, §560: 3-203; 560: 3-601; tit. 30A.	No prohibition. Tit. 30, §554-2.
Idaho	Yes, 15.3-203	Yes, 15.7-105.
Illinois	Yes, 3 §262.	Yes, by implication. Tit. 148, 102(2)-103.
Indiana	Yes, 29-2-1-3(7-751).	OK, Same as executor.
Iowa	Yes, 32 §633, 503.	Yes, same as executor. Must appoint local agent and subject to court approval. Code Ann. §633.64 and 633.71.
Kansas	59-1706 (yes) must register "Any fiduciary."	Yes, same as executor.
Kentucky	tit. 34, §395.005; Letters needed §395.105 No, except if: (1) Spouse of decedent, (2) related to decedent by consanguinity, (3) Spouse of a person related by consanguinity, (4) Father, mother, brother, or sister of the Spouse of the decedent, or (5) The legally adopted child or adoptive parent of decedent.	Same, as 34, §395.005. "Any fiduciary."
Louisiana	Yes, but must first qualify in a Louisiana court, 4 §3401 et seq.	Yes, 9 §1783. "Any citizen of the U.S. who has capacity to contract can be a trustee."
Maine	18 §1410, must file letters; §1601 (appointment); §2152 (proof of appointment).	Same, 18 §4004. Service of process on nonresident trustee. Must appoint local agent.
Maryland	Yes, §5-501-5-503. "Any foreign personal representative may exercise in Maryland all powers of his office."	Same as executor.

State	Foreign Executor Allowed	Foreign Trustee Allowed
Massachusetts	Yes, ch. 204, §3. Must file appointment.	Ch. 203, §10 Required to take out letters of trust from the court. Must appoint local agent, ch. 203, §15.
Michigan	Yes, §27.5532 (sec. 531). Resident of state is given *preference*. Nonresident OK if (1) bank or trust co-authorized to do business in the State; (2) last will and testament nominates two or more persons as personal representatives or trustees, and any, but less than all, are nonresidents; and (3) foreign fiduciary for purposes of ancillary administration (as enacted July 1, 1979).	Same.
Minnesota	No, §524.4-706. Except if there is no administration or application therefore pending in this State. Any application or petition for local administration terminates the power of foreign personal representative to act (discretionary with court).	§303.25 OK *Doerr v. Warner*, 247 Minn. 98, 76 N.W. 2d505 (quasi-in-rem over trust res). See also Stat. Ann. §501.33 as amended.
Mississippi	Unclear. Yes, by implication from Miss. Code Ann. §538 and §91-7-251.	Same.
Missouri	Unclear. Probably no by implication from §507.020 and Mo. Rev. Stat. Ann. §10, 390 and 459.	Unclear. Yes, if resident appointed co-trustee, Stat. Ann. §443.350. §456.120 no, foreign corporation may act. See also Stat. Ann. §456.210 giving courts jurisdiction over nonresident.
Montana	No prohibition. §91-3202.	No prohibition, 86-507(7914); 86-205(7882); 86-208 (7885). Seems to be implied residency requirement, since must be registration and accounting in county of trust situs, 86-513.
Nebraska	Yes, 30-2501, et seq.	Unclear. No prohibition.
Nevada	Yes, 12 §138.020	Yes, 13 §164.010. But district court of county wherein trustee resides or has his place of business shall consider the application to confirm appointment of trustee.
New Hampshire	Yes, ch. 553:2. Right to administer discretionary to court under 535.5; looks at character integrity, soundness, capacity In re Quirin Estate, 116 NH 845, 367 A.2d 594 (1976).	Yes, 564:12; 554:27. Appointment and accounting required. Must appoint local agent. Court has discretion to deny local agent. R.S.A. §553:5.

State	Foreign Executor Allowed	Foreign Trustee Allowed
New Jersey	Yes, 3A §6-11. Must file foreign appointment; 3A: 12-7 actions by or against.	Yes, 3A: 12-6, -7; 3A: 6-13; 3A:12-14. Must appoint local agent.
New Mexico	Yes, ch. 45-4-207.	Yes, ch. 47-7-105. Corporation must be qualified. Individual must register.
New York	Yes, CPLR §302	Yes. Surrogate's Court Act, §167. Must appoint local agent.
North Carolina	Yes, 28A-26-1. Heavily prejudiced toward home-state admininstration. Any administration outside state can be ancillary only.	Yes, §28A-22-4. Must appoint agent for service.
North Dakota	Yes, 30.1-24-02 (4-201), if there is a nonresident decedent. Any local administration terminates power of foreign state representative to act 30.1-24-07 (4-206).	59-04-01, situs of trust in state gives county power; 59-04-12, -14, must register, post bond, agent, etc.
Ohio	Yes if nonresident is spouse or next of kin. No all others. See §2109.21 and 2113.05.	Unclear. No authority.
Oklahoma	58 §262 Upon proof and motion foreign executor or administration has same power as home state.	Unclear§175.3(c); 175.6. No prohibition.
Oregon	No, 43.180, 116.263, .163	No, 713.012, business trusts. Yes, 128.560, other.
Pennsylvania	No, 20 §4101. Yes, if no administration in state; must register and record; affidavit required.	Yes, but must appoint local agent and court may require appointment of local co-trustee. See 20 Pa. C.S. §7102 and 7103.
Rhode Island	Yes, 9-5-33; 33-18-9.	No prohibition, 18-2-1.
South Carolina	Yes, §21-13-310, if bond and consent to service. No foreign corporations, 21-13-320.	Yes, if 21-13-310, other. No, corporations 21-29-40(6)(a).
South Dakota	Yes, if agent in state and appointed in South Dakota 30-13-2; oath needed, 30-13-1.	Yes, must have certificate, 55-5A-1.

State	Foreign Executor Allowed	Foreign Trustee Allowed
Tennessee	Yes, if either a resident is appointed co-trustee or a local agent is appointed, bond is posted, etc. See §35-618.	Same.
Texas	Probate Code §78(d); nonresident if agent for service of process.	7425b-7,7425b-4, No prohibition found.
Utah	Yes, Prohibition Code 75-4-204, 4-206, but only if local application for administration is pending.	No prohibition in Code General fiduciary, §22-1-1.
Vermont	No, 14§904, unless requested by: (1) surviving spouse, (2) surviving children, (3) surviving parent or guardian	Yes, if local agent appointed. See Stat. Ann., tit. 14 §904 and 368.
Virginia	No, unless a resident of state or company in state is appointed as co-trustee, 26-59.	Same, except testamentary trustee allowed if local agent appointed. See Code 1950, §26-7.1 to 27-7.3.
Washington	No, unless appoints agent, files papers, 11.36.010.	Same. Stat. Ann. §2-52.
West Virginia	No, 44-5-3. Testator who is nonresident at time of death may name nonresident executor. Decedent who was resident at time of death must give bond, consent to service, and must be husband, wife, father, mother, brother, sister, child, grandchild, or sole beneficiary of such resident decedent.	Same.
Wisconsin	Unclear. OK when decedent is a nonresident, §777.16. No authority when decedent is a resident.	271.28
Wyoming	No, unless a resident is appointed co-administrator, §2-4-203.	Unclear. No prohibition under §4-1-102 definition.

D. SAMPLE TITLE TRANSFER DOCUMENTS FOR REVOCABLE LIVING TRUSTS

DEED

Documentary Transfer Tax $ _____

_____ Computed on Full Value of Property Conveyed

_____ Or computed on Full Value Less Liens and Encumbrances
      Remaining at Time of Sale

_____

Signature of Declarant or Agent Determining Tax

FOR VALUABLE CONSIDERATION, the receipt of which is hereby acknowledged, JOHN Q. TAXPAYER AND MARY TAXPAYER [do not include as *joint
tenants*, etc.], hereby grant to JOHN AND MARY TAXPAYER, CO-TRUSTEES,
THE TAXPAYER FAMILY TRUST, DATED JULY 1, 1980, all that real property
in the County of Contra Costa, State of California, more particularly described in
these instruments recorded in the Official Records of the County of Contra Costa,
State of California, as follows:

[Example] Document No. _____ Book _____ at Page _____ recorded
_____, 19____, Accessors Parcel No. _____.

DATED: _____19____   _____

                                     John Q. Taxpayer

                                _____

                                   Mary Taxpayer

State of _____)
)SS
County of _____)

On the _____ day of _____, 19____, before me, the undersigned, a Notary
Public in and for said County and State, personally appeared JOHN Q. TAXPAYER
AND MARY TAXPAYER, known to me to be the same persons whose names are
subscribed to the within instrument and acknowledged that they executed the same.

WITNESS my hand and official seal.

                                _____

                                  Notary Public

(SEAL)

ENDORSEMENT OF NOTE

The within Promissory Note, dated _____, made by _____
_____and payable to JOHN Q. TAXPAYER AND MARY TAXPAYER, in the
amount of _____[written amount]_____ ($_____),
is hereby endorsed to the order of JOHN Q. TAXPAYER AND MARY TAXPAYER,
CO-TRUSTEES, THE TAXPAYER FAMILY TRUST, DATED JULY 1, 1980.

Dated this _____ day of _____, 19____.

_____
John Q. Taxpayer

_____
Mary Taxpayer

STOCK POWER
ASSIGNMENT SEPARATE FROM CERTIFICATE

FOR VALUE RECEIVED, _____JOHN Q. TAXPAYER_____
hereby sells, assigns and transfers to _____JOHN Q. TAXPAYER AND MARY_____
_____TAXPAYER, CO-TRUSTEES, THE TAXPAYER FAMILY TRUST,_____
_____DATED JULY 1, 1980_____
Capital Stock of the _____
standing in _____ names on the books of said _____
_____ represented by Certificate No. _____ herewith
and do hereby irrevocably constitute and appoint _____
_____ attorney to transfer the said
stock on the books of the within named Company with full power of substitution in
the premises.

Dated _____

[the only signature
required is that of the
holders of the certificate] _____

Signature Guaranteed _____

Social Security or Tax Reporting Number

_____

ASSIGNMENT OF DEED OF TRUST

FOR VALUE RECEIVED, the undersigned hereby grants, assigns, and transfers to JOHN Q. TAXPAYER AND MARY TAXPAYER, CO-TRUSTEES, THE TAXPAYER FAMILY TRUST, DATED JULY 1, 1980, all of their right, title, and interest in and to that certain Deed of Trust dated _____, 19____, executed by _____, named as Trustor, and wherein _____, a corporation, is named as Trustee, and JOHN Q. TAXPAYER AND MARY TAXPAYER, husband and wife, as joint tenants, are named as Beneficiary, and which Deed of Trust was recorded on _____, 19____, in Volume _____, at Page _____, Official Records of _____ County, State of _____.

_____
John Q. Taxpayer

_____
Mary Taxpayer

State of _____)
) SS
County of _____)

On the _____ day of _____, 19____, before me, the undersigned, a Notary Public in and for said County and State, personally appeared JOHN Q. TAXPAYER AND MARY TAXPAYER, known to me to be the same persons whose names are subscribed to the within instrument and acknowledged that they executed the same.

WITNESS my hand and official seal.

_____
Notary Public

(SEAL)

E. THE CRUMMY CLAUSE

Withdrawal by Beneficiary of Additional Transfer.

Each designated beneficiary or, during any period that a designated beneficiary lacks legal capacity, the legal guardian (or, if there is none, the natural or general guardian) of the designated beneficiary may demand in writing payment over to such beneficiary of his or her share of qualifying property transferred to the beneficiary's trust.

The term "qualifying property" refers to a transfer to a beneficiary's trust with respect to which the Trustee has received written notice from the transferor that the property transferred (or some specified portion of it) shall be subject to withdrawal under the provisions of this paragraph.

The term "designated beneficiary" refers to a beneficiary with respect to whom the Trustee has received written notice from the transferor of additional property that such transferred property (or some specified portion of it) shall be subject to withdrawal by such beneficiary under the provisions of this paragraph.

Within thirty (30) days of receipt by the Trustee of such qualifying property, the Trustee shall give notice to the designated beneficiary or beneficiaries (or to the legal or natural or general guardian of the designated beneficiary) in writing and mailed by certified mail, return receipt requested, of the transfer of qualifying property and of the designated beneficiary's right to make withdrawal from such qualifying property.

Commencing from the date of receipt of notice given by the Trustee, a designated beneficiary (or the legal or natural or general guardian of the designated beneficiary) shall have ninety (90) days within which to notify the Trustee in writing of the beneficiary's exercise of the withdrawal right granted a designated beneficiary under the provisions of this paragraph. This right shall be exercisable notwithstanding any other provision of this agreement.

The right of withdrawal of a designated beneficiary (or the legal or natural or general guardian of the designated beneficiary) shall be noncumulative and to the extent that the right of withdrawal has not been exercised by the end of such ninety (90) day period, it shall lapse.

The Trustee shall, at all times while any such withdrawal right is outstanding, retain from the qualifying property sufficient assets to satisfy all such withdrawal rights then outstanding.

The Trustee shall deliver assets withdrawn to the designated beneficiary within fifteen (15) days of receipt of notice of exercise of the withdrawal right.

If there is any disability on the part of a designated beneficiary on whose behalf such right of withdrawal has been exercised, which would make the beneficiary unable to hold the assets withdrawn, the Trustee may make distribution to his or her legal guardian, or if no guardian has been appointed, to his or her natural or general guardian. Alternatively, the Trustee may, in his discretion, turn the assets over to a custodian under an applicable Uniform Gifts to Minors Act. Assets received by any such guardian or custodian pursuant to the exercise of this withdrawal right shall be held by such guardian or custodian for the designated beneficiary's use and benefit. The receipt of such guardian or custodian shall be a complete discharge of the Trustee.

Any provision of this paragraph to the contrary notwithstanding, no such right of withdrawal shall be effective to require the delivery over to a designated beneficiary of property of a value in excess of the maximum gift tax exclusion allowable under the Internal Revenue Code.

F. POWER OF ATTORNEY

I, _____of _____, appoint _____ (referred to below as "my attorney"), a sample of whose signature appears below, my true and lawful agent and attorney, for me and in my name with reference to any interest from time to time owned by me in property, real or personal, wherever located ("property"), or other matters in which I from time to time may have a personal or financial interest:

1. To deposit in or withdraw from any bank, trust company, savings association, safe deposit company, broker or other depositary or agent any moneys or other property and to examine or receive related records, including canceled checks.

2. To open and enter on my behalf any safe deposit box rented or held by me alone or jointly with others, at any time to deposit in such box and to remove from such box any part or all of the contents thereof, including any security or tangible personal property, as often and as freely as I could do if personally present, and to cancel or modify the lease under which such box is rented and to surrender or exchange the same.

3. To pay my ordinary household expenses, to arrange for and pay the costs of services of a companion for me, medical, nursing, hospital, convalescent and other health care and treatment, including admission to hospitals and consent to treatment, and to make application for insurance, pension or employee benefits related to such health care and treatment.

4. To retain, invest in, acquire by purchase, subscription, lease or otherwise, manage, sell, contract to purchase or sell, grant, obtain or exercise options to purchase, options to sell or conversion rights, assign, transfer, convey, deliver, endorse, exchange, pledge, mortgage, abandon, improve, repair, maintain, insure, lease for any term and otherwise deal with all property, and to release and waive any right of homestead therein, if any.

5. To enter upon and demand possession of, maintain, manage, improve, subdivide,

resubdivide, raze, alter, dedicate, vacate, partition, release, lease or renew, amend, or extend leases for any term, contract to make leases, grant options to lease or to purchase the whole or any part of the reversion contract regarding the manner of fixing present or future rentals, grant easements or charges of any kind on or with respect to, and cultivate, irrigate and operate, all interests in real estate and how or hereafter owned by me, including beneficial interests in any trust and leasehold interest, and related improvements, equipment and supplies, alone or with others, by general or limited partnerships, trust agreements, joint ventures, corporations, associations, sharecrop agreements, leases, management or agency agreements, participation in government programs or otherwise.

6. To borrow from any source for any purpose and mortgage or pledge any property to any lender, including my attorney individually.

7. To demand, sue for, receive and otherwise take steps to collect or recover all debts, rents, proceeds, interest, dividends, annuities, securities for money, goods, chattels, bequests, income from property, damages and all other property to which I may be entitled or which are or may become due me from any person or organization; to commence, prosecute or enforce, or to defend, answer or oppose, contest and abandon all legal proceedings in which I am or may hereafter be interested; and to settle, compromise,or submit to arbitration any accounts, debts, claims, disputes, and matters now existing or which may hereafter arise between me and any other person or organization to grant an extension of time for the payment or satisfaction thereof on any terms, with or without security.

8. To continue to carry, purchase, cancel or dispose of fire, casualty, property, or income protection, medical, hospital, life, liability or other insurance and to pay any premiums thereon.

9. To vote and give proxies to vote securities and approve or oppose mergers, consolidations, foreclosures, liquidations, reorganizations or changes in the financial structure of any organization, and all other matters which may come before the shareholders; and to enter into voting trusts and other agreements restricting the voting, transfer or other use or disposition of interest in any organization.

10. To retain, continue, operate, manage, organize, or acquire, invest in, terminate and dispose of, alone or with others, proprietorships, corporations, limited or general partnerships, joint ventures, land trusts or other business or property holding organizations under the laws of any jurisdiction, to lease, sell, purchase or otherwise transfer any property to or from, make further investments in or advance or loan funds to, with or without security, and incur obligations on account of or for the benefit of, any such organization; and to employ any persons for such purposes and delegate to them such powers and discretions as my attorney considers advisable.

11. To undertake performance of any and all acts, whether or not otherwise specifically enumerated herein, including the sale of any property or the borrowing of any funds, which my attorney considers necessary or appropriate in order to purchase United States treasury bonds redeemable at par in payment of federal estate taxes; provided, however, that nothing herein shall be construed as requiring my attorney to acquire any such bonds.

12. To appear and represent me in regard to and to take all actions convenient or appropriate in connection with taxes imposed by any municipal, state, U.S. or foreign authority or government relating to any tax liability or refund, abatement or credit (including interest or penalties) due or alleged to be due from or to me or any other person or organization, association or trust for which I am responsible for the preparation, signing, executing, verifying, acknowledging or paying of any tax due or filing of a return or report, including without limitation federal or state income or gift tax, for any and all taxable years or periods; and for such purposes to inspect or receive copies of any tax returns filed by or for me, reports or other papers or documents, compromises or adjustments of any and all claims.

13. To prepare, draw, make, sign, execute, seal, acknowledge, verify, discount, accept, endorse, with or without recourse on me, waive demand, notice and notice of protest, file and delivery on my behalf any and all checks, options, orders, notes, drafts, overdrafts, certificates of deposit, bills of exchange, deeds, directions to land trustees, mortgages, leases, powers of sale, drafts, bonds (of indemnity or otherwise) and contracts, transfers, assignments, proxies, agreements, receipts, releases, release deeds, composition agreements, discharges, income or personal position agreements, income or personal or intangible property or gift or other tax returns, estimates, declarations, certificates, schedules, statements, claims of abatement, refund or credit, protests, requests (including requests for rulings from proper authorities), applications, waivers (including waiver of restrictions on the assessment or collection of any deficiency or additional tax), acceptances (including acceptance of any determination or proposed determination of additional tax or overassessment or overpayment of taxes, including interest and penalties), consents or waivers or agreements for a later determination and assessment and collection of taxes than is provided by applicable statutes of limitations, closing agreement (whether in respect of a tax liability or a specific matter or otherwise), and any other papers, documents or writings or things, with or without guarantees, surety obligations, covenants, warranties, indemnifications, representations, powers of substitution, affirmations or otherwise.

14. To appoint and employ, with or without compensation, any accountants, attorneys at law, investment counsel, agents, servants or other persons, including their agents and associates, and to dismiss or discharge the same and appoint or employ any others in their stead as my true and lawful attorneys, to appear and represent me as to all matters covered by this power of attorney, or for any other purpose, including, but not limited to, appearance before the Treasury Department, the Tax

Court, The U.S. Court of Claims, or any other court in the U.S., in any state, municipal or foreign court, and any department or official of the U.S. government or any state, municipal or foreign government, with full power and authority to such agents and attorneys to do any and all acts convenient or appropriate in connection with such matters, including the specific acts described above, to substitute attorneys and agents subsequent to the date of such appointment and prior to any revocation thereof, and to delegate or revoke the authority so granted to them.

15. To pay, as my attorney shall think fit, any debts, or interest, payable by me, or taxes, assessments, and expenses due and payable or to become due and payable for my use and benefit, or for the use and benefit of any person to whom I have a legal obligation of support.

16. To the extent my attorney thinks I might have done, to make, unconditionally or upon such terms and conditions as my attorney shall think fit, such donations or contributions to publicly supported charities, private operating foundations and private foundations, all as defined in present IRS Code § 170 or equivalent statute. My attorney shall have sole discretion in making such donations or contributions, or my attorney may also make subscriptions, for any reason that my attorney determines such donations, contributions or subscriptions shall be made.

17. To the extend my attorney thinks I might have done, to make, unconditionally or upon such terms and conditions as my attorney shall think fit, such gifts to any one or more of those persons consisting of my spouse, my descendants and the spouses of my descendants in my attorney's sole discretion and for any reason my attorney determines.

18. To substitute and appoint in my attorney's place and stead (on such terms and at such salary or compensation as my attorney shall think fit) one or more attorney or attorneys to exercise for me as my attorney or attorneys any or all of the powers and authorities hereby conferred, and to revoke any such appointment from time to time, and to substitute or appoint any other or others in the place of such attorney or attorneys, as my attorney shall, from time to time think fit.

19. Finally (without prejudice to and in enlargement of the authority above conferred) to execute each and every instrument, to undertake each and every obligation, and to take from time to time any and all action of whatsoever nature and with relation to any matters whatsoever, whether or not specifically mentioned herein, and to exercise in respect thereto as full and complete power and discretion as I myself might or could do.

My attorney shall exercise or omit to exercise the powers and authorities granted herein in each case as my attorney in my attorney's own absolute discretion deems desirable or appropriate under existing circumstances. I hereby ratify and confirm as good and effectual, at law or in equity, all that my attorney, and any agents and attorneys appointed by my attorney, and their agents, associates and substitutes, may do by virtue hereof. However, despite the above provisions nothing herein shall be construed as imposing a duty on my attorney to act or assume responsibility for any matters referred to above or other matters even though my attorney may have power or authority hereunder to do so.

If any power or authority hereby sought to be conferred upon my attorney should be invalid or unexercisable for any cause or not recognized by any person or organization dealing with my attorney, the remaining powers and authorities given to my attorney hereunder shall nevertheless continue in full force and effect.

Each person, partnership, corporation or other legal entity relying or acting upon this power of attorney shall be entitled to presume conclusively that this power of attorney is in full force and effect unless written notice shall have been given by me to such person, partnership, corporation or other legal entity that his power has been revoked. In addition revocation of the appointment of my attorney shall not be effective until my attorney has received actual notice of its revocation in writing from me and delivered to my attorney; until receipt of such actual notice, my attorney shall not be liable to me for any action taken by my attorney.

No person, partnership, corporation or legal entity relying upon this power of attorney shall be required to see to the application and disposition of any moneys, stocks, bonds, securities or other property paid to or delivered to my attorney, or my attorney's substitute, pursuant to the provisions hereof.

It is my intent that this power of attorney shall remain in full force and effect and that the power granted herein shall continue without interruption until my death unless previously revoked by me, or in the event that I become incapacitated or incompetent or a disabled person as established by any court.

If I am adjudged to be a disabled person, I name _____, as guardian of my person and estate. If he or she fails or ceases to act as such guardian, I name _____,

_____

as such guardian in order of their respective ages.

Reproduction of this executed original (with reproduced signatures and the certificate of acknowledgement) shall be deemed to be original counterparts of this Power of Attorney.

Specimen signature of my attorney:

_____

_____

_____

I certify to the correctness of the signatures of my attorneys and I execute this Power of Attorney on

_____   _____
                    Date   Witness#1

_____   _____
              Signature   Witness #2

                              Notary:_____

G. SAMPLE LIVING WILLS

DIRECTIVE TO PHYSICIANS

Directive made this _____ day of _____, 19____.

I, _____, residing in the County of _____, State of California, being of sound mind, willfully and voluntarily make known my desire that my life shall not be artificially prolonged under the circumstances set forth below, do hereby declare:

1. If at any time I should have an incurable injury, disease, or illness certified to be a terminal condition by two physicians, and where the application of life-sustaining procedures would serve only to artificially prolong the moment of my death, and where my physician determines that my death is imminent whether or not life-sustaining procedures are utilized, I direct that such procedures be withheld or withdrawn and that I be permitted to die naturally.

2. In the absence of my ability to give directions regarding the use of such life-sustaining procedures, it is my intention that this directive shall be honored by my family and physician(s) as the final expression of my legal right to refuse medical or surgical treatment and accept the consequences from such refusal.

3. If I have been diagnosed as pregnant and that diagnosis is known to my physician, this directive shall have no force or effect during the course of my pregnancy.

4. I have been diagnosed and notified at least 14 days ago as having a terminal condition by _____, M.D., whose address is _____, and whose telephone number is _____. I understand that if I have not filled in the physician's name and address, it shall be presumed that I did not have a terminal condition when I made out this directive.

5. This directive shall have no force or effect five years from the date filled in above.

6. I understand the full import of this directive, and I am emotionally and mentally competent to make this directive.

_____

The declarant has been personally known to me and I believe him or her to be of sound mind.

Witnesses:

_____   Residing at _____

                                                      _____

_____   Residing at _____

                                                      _____

GENERAL DECLARATION

To my family, my physician, my lawyer, my clergyman:

To any medical facility in whose care I happen to be:

To any individual who may become responsible for my health, welfare, or affairs:

Death is as much a reality as birth, growth, maturity, and old age. It is the one certainty of life. If the time comes when I can no longer take part in decisions for my own future, let this statement stand as an expression of my wishes while I am still of sound mind.

If the situation should arise in which there is no reasonable expectation of my recovery from physical or mental disability, I request that I be allowed to die and not be kept alive by artificial means or "heroic measures." I do not fear death itself as much as the indignities of deterioration, dependence, and hopeless pain. I therefore ask that medication be mercifully administered to me to alleviate suffering even though this may hasten the moment of death.

If I have executed a valid form of bequeathal of any of my organs for transplant or other purposes, I do, however, authorize and request that I be kept alive by artificial means for a time sufficient to enable a physician or physicians to harvest after my death the organ or organs to be transplanted.

This request is made after careful consideration. I hope you who care for me will feel morally bound to follow its mandate. I recognize that this appears to place a heavy responsibility upon you, but it is with the intention of relieving you of such responsibility and of placing it upon myself in accordance with my strong convictions that this statement is made.

_____

_____
Date

_____
Witness

_____
Witness

H. STATE INCOME AND DEATH TAXES COMPARED*

The residents of different states do not pay equal taxes. Many states impose large income and death taxes on their residents. These taxes must be paid in addition to the federal income and estate taxes. Other states have minimal or no income and death taxes. This appendix will briefly compare the fifty states and the District of Columbia's (hereinafter "the states") income-tax and death-tax systems.

State income- or death-tax planning can be accomplished by moving to a state with low or nonexistent income or death taxes. Such a move is impractical in most situations. But a retiring couple, a mobile executive, and many others often have a wide choice of where they will move. Florida's lack of income and death taxes partially explains the great number of people who have retired there.

It is also important for state residents to understand how their state's taxes compare to those of other states. This may lead to reducing the burden on taxpayers in many of the states with high taxes. California, for example, has very high income and death taxes; there is a movement under way to repeal the death taxes and to cut the income taxes. Oregon, which formerly had very high death taxes, has passed legislation which will eliminate these taxes by 1986.

INCOME TAXES

There are four types of state income-tax systems. First, there are *states with no income taxes*. Alaska is the most recent state to join this group, having repealed its income tax law on September 24, 1980.

Second, there are *states which tax only a few forms of passive income at relatively low rates*. For example, New Hampshire does not tax wages, salary, or self-employment income. It only taxes interest and dividends, and then at 5 percent. These systems only burden a small number of taxpayers.

Third, there are *states with low flat tax rates or very low progressive rates*. For example, Indiana taxes all income at 1.9 percent. Ohio has a graduated or progressive system, but its highest rate is 3.5 percent for income above $40,000. These systems have been ranked in the following table, from the state with the lowest final rate to the state with the highest final rate.

Final, there are *the vast majority of states with graduated tax rates reaching high final rates*. These states include those which impose a tax based on a percentage of the federal tax liability. (Since the federal tax is progressive, any fixed percentage of that tax is also progressive.) The states in this category range from Virginia, with a high final tax rate of 5.75 percent, to Vermont, with a highest final tax rate of 16.1 percent. (The Vermont highest rate is 23 percent of the highest federal rate of 70 percent; 23 percent of 70 equals 16.1 percent.)

The following table ranks the states from least burdensome to most burdensome in terms of income taxes. However, these rankings may not take into account your

*This appendix reflects current law up to the summer of 1980.

individual situation. The states are graduated at different degrees. Thus a taxpayer may have a smaller tax burden in a state nearer the end of the list in some situations. The rankings are based on the typical application of each state's taxes to a taxpayer.

When examining these charts, keep in mind that the tax imposed is *in addition to* the federal income tax but deductible when making the federal determination. The federal income tax reaches 70 percent for a married taxpayer with income over $215,400. In Vermont, for example, this taxpayer would pay a total of 86.1 percent on any income above $215,400. This table reflects rates for married taxpayers where rates differ depending on marital status.

INCOME TAX RANKINGS

I. States with no income taxes (listed alphabetically):

1. **Alaska**
2. **Florida**
3. **Nevada**
4. **South Dakota**
5. **Texas**
6. **Washington**
7. **Wyoming**

II. States with taxes only on specified types of passive income. Ranked from least to most burdensome.

8. **New Hampshire** Tax on interest and dividend income at 5%.

9. **Tennessee** Tax on interest and dividend income at 6% with lower 4% dividend tax if corporation is 75% taxable in Tennessee.

10. **Connecticut** Tax on dividends and capital gains if taxpayer's adjusted gross income (AGI) equals or exceeds $20,000. Dividends tax begins at 1% and rises to 9% if taxpayer has AGI of $100,000 or over. Capital gains tax is 7%.

III. States with flat tax rates or very low graduated rates. Ranked from lowest final tax rate to highest final tax rate.

11. **Indiana** Flat rate of 1.9% of AGI.

12. **Pennsylvania** Flat rate of 2.2% on classes of taxable income.

13. **New Jersey** 2% up to $20,000; 2.5% above $20,000.

14. **Illinois** Flat rate of 2.5% of taxable net income.

15. **Ohio** Graduated rate from 0.5% to 3.5% above $40,000.

16. **Mississippi** 3% up to $5,000; 4% above $5,000.

17. **Michigan** Flat rate of 4.6% of AGI.

18. **Maryland** Graduated rate from 2% to 5% above $3,000.

19. **Alabama** Graduated rate from 1.5% to 5% above $5,000.

20. **Massachusetts** Flat rates of 5% on earned income and annuities and 10% on interest, dividends, and capital gains.

IV. States with graduated tax rates or rates based on percentage of federal tax liability. Ranked from lowest final tax rate to highest final tax rate. Rates based on a fixed percentage of federal tax liability are converted to highest final rate by taking the fixed percentage of the highest federal final rate, which is 70%.

21. **Virginia** Graduated rate from 2% to 5.75% above $12,000.
22. **Louisiana** Graduated rate from 2% to 6% above $50,000.
23. **Oklahoma** Graduated rate from 0.5% to 6% above $15,000.
24. **Georgia** Graduated rate from 1% to 6% above $10,000.
25. **Missouri** Graduated rate from 1.5% to 6% over $9,000.
26. **Kentucky** Graduated from 2% to 6% over $8,000.
27. **Arkansas** Graduated rate from 1% to 7% over $25,000.
28. **South Carolina** Graduated rate from 2% to 7% above $10,000.
29. **North Carolina** Graduated rate from 3% to 7% above $10,000.
30. **North Dakota** Graduated rate from 1% to 7.5% above $30,000.
31. **Idaho** Graduated rate from 2% to 7.5% above $5,000.
32. **Utah** Graduated rate from 2.25% to 7.75% above $4,500.
33. **Colorado** Graduated rate from 3% to 8% above $10,000.
34. **Arizona** Graduated rate from 2% to 8% above $6,000.
35. **New Mexico** Graduated rate from 0.8% to 9% above $6,000.
36. **Kansas** Graduated rate from 2% to 9% above $14,500.
37. **California** Graduated rate from 1% to 9% over $14,500.
38. **West Virginia** Graduated rate from 2.1% to 9.6% over $400,000.
39. **Wisconsin** Graduated rate from 3.4% to 10% above $40,000.
40. **Maine** Graduated rate from 1% to 10% over $25,000.
41. **Oregon** Graduated rate from 4% to 10% over $5,000.
42. **Montana** Graduated rate from 2% to 11% above $35,000.
43. **Hawaii** Graduated rate from 2.25% to 11% above $30,000.
44. **District of Columbia** Graduated rate from 2% to 11% over $25,000.
45. **Nebraska** 17% of federal tax liability. Equivalent of 11.9% highest rate.
46. **Iowa** Graduated rate from 0.5% to 13% above $75,000.
47. **Rhode Island** 19% of federal tax liability. Equivalent of 13.3% highest rate.
48. **Delaware** Graduated rate from 1.4% to 13.5% above $50,000.
49. **New York** Graduated rate from 2% to 14% above $23,000.
50. **Minnesota** Graduated rate from 1.6% to 16% above $27,500.
51. **Vermont** 23% of federal tax liability. Equivalent of 16.1% highest rate.

DEATH TAXES

The states have no uniform system of death taxation. Nevada is the only state which has no death taxes at all. The remaining forty-nine states and the District of Columbia collect death revenues at least equal to the federal pickup tax. Many states also have either an inheritance tax, an estate tax, or both.

The pickup tax is a form of revenue sharing. The federal estate tax gives a credit for death taxes paid to the states. The amount of this credit is limited. If a state imposes a tax equal to the credit, the estate will pay the amount of the credit to the state rather than to the federal government. But the estate's total tax burden will not be increased. For example, assume someone dies in 1981 with a taxable estate of $500,000. The tax due the federal government would be $108,800 minus any credit for taxes paid to the state. The maximum credit allowed for a $500,000 estate is $10,000. If the person died in Florida, which has a pickup tax only, the estate would pay $10,000 to Florida and $98,800 ($108,800 minus $10,000) to the United States. Nevada's state constitution bars death taxes. If the person died in Nevada, the estate would pay the full $108,800 to the federal government. There would be no tax credit to subtract from this amount, and nothing would be paid to Nevada.

Most states have taxes which exceed the pickup tax on large estates. Only the states ranked 2 through 13 in the following State Death Tax Rankings have pickup taxes only. The remaining states use the pickup tax to back up their other death taxes. Only where their other death taxes are less than the maximum federal credit do they pick up the difference. For example, in the situation used in the rankings, Texas imposes a normal inheritance tax of $31,500. The maximum credit at this level is $32,200. So Texas imposes an additional pickup tax of $700 to take full advantage of the revenue-sharing opportunity. Otherwise, this $700 would be paid to the federal government. The estate in this situation pays the same amount whether the money goes to the federal government or to Texas.

Where the state tax exceeds the pickup tax, the estate or the heirs pay more than the total federal tax without the death-tax credit. Again, take an example from the rankings. In this situation, New York imposes a tax of $49,900. The federal tax is $303,300 minus the state death-tax credit of 32,200. The full credit is available because the state tax is equal to or, as here, exceeds it. The taxpayer thus pays $271,000 ($303,300 minus $32,200) to the federal government and $49,900 to the state government, for a total of $321,000. If the person died in a state with a pickup tax only, or a normal tax which did not exceed the pickup tax, the total tax obligations would not have exceeded $303,000.

It is only in situations where the state death tax exceeds the pickup tax that the state taxes will increase the estate's or the heirs' tax burden. The states that impose tax which can exceed this level are listed as 14 through 51 in the rankings. Many times their tax levels will not exceed the pickup tax. But they all are capable of imposing taxes in excess of this level. If possible, these states should be avoided for tax planning purposes. If you cannot avoid them, you must carefully plan around their tax systems.

These excess-tax states generally use either an inheritance tax or an estate tax. An inheritance tax imposes a tax on the separate shares of the estate which pass to different heirs. The tax rate is determined by relationship of the heir to the decedent. Generally, the closer relationships will have lower taxes. For example, surviving spouses generally have the lowest rates imposed on their shares. Surviving children have moderate rates. Unrelated persons who inherit have the highest rates imposed on their shares.

An estate tax is imposed on the total amount of property the dead person owned at death without regard to whom it passes. The tax is technically on the decedent's *right to pass* the property rather than on the property itself. The rate is generally the same regardless of who inherits, although some states exempt certain amounts, depending on the relationship of the survivors. The federal tax system is an estate tax.

It is very difficult to rank state death-tax systems, simply because comparing inheritance-tax and estate-tax systems is like comparing red and yellow apples. The bottom line, of course, is the amount of money an heir will owe the state government. The ranking system used here is very simple. It has been assumed that a surviving spouse dies, leaving an estate of $1 million to a sole adult child. The states are ranked by the amount of tax due in this case.

This situation was chosen as a measure of the relative death taxes because it represents the classic estate-planning problem. Estate planning becomes most difficult when the estate is to be passed on to younger generations. Most states impose very little death tax on property that passes between spouses. Death taxes are also relatively low on property below the $1 million level. The following table illustrates the problems presented by the various state tax systems in passing on a substantial estate of more than $1 million to someone in a younger generation. The table shows the federal tax as well as the state tax so that you can see the total tax burden.

There are many ways to compare state death taxes. For a more complete picture, also compare the death taxes as described in the next section under State-by-State Death and Inheritance Tax Summary.

STATE DEATH-TAX RANKINGS (1980)

State	State Initial Tax	State Pickup Tax	Federal Tax	Total
1. Nevada	None	None	$303,300	$303,300
2. Alabama	None	$32,200	$271,100	$303,300
3. Alaska	None	$32,200	$271,100	$303,300
4. Arizona	None	$32,200	$271,100	$303,300
5. Arkansas	None	$32,200	$271,100	$303,300
6. Colorado	None	$32,200	$271,100	$303,300
7. Florida	None	$32,200	$271,100	$303,300
8. Georgia	None	$32,200	$271,100	$303,300
9. New Mexico	None	$32,200	$271,100	$303,300
10. North Dakota	None	$32,200	$271,100	$303,300
11. Utah	None	$32,200	$271,100	$303,300
12. Vermont	None	$32,200	$271,100	$303,300
13. Virginia	None	$32,200	$271,100	$303,300
14. New Hampshire	$ 0	$32,200	$271,100	$303,300
15. Nebraska	$ 9,900	$22,300	$271,100	$303,300
16. Maryland	$ 10,000	$22,200	$271,100	$303,300
17. Wyoming	$ 19,334	$12,966	$271,100	$303,300
18. Louisiana	$ 29,650	$ 2,550	$271,100	$303,300
19. Mississippi	$ 30,589	$ 1,611	$271,100	$303,300
20. Texas	$ 31,500	$ 700	$271,100	$303,300
21. Kansas	$ 41,750	$ 0	$271,100	$312,850
22. New York	$ 49,900	$ 0	$271,100	$321,000
23. Indiana	$ 51,950	$ 0	$271,100	$323,050
24. District of Columbia	$ 52,000	$ 0	$271,100	$323,100
25. Missouri	$ 52,300	$ 0	$271,100	$323,400
26. Connecticut	$ 53,900	$ 0	$271,100	$325,300
27. Delaware	$ 55,470	$ 0	$271,100	$326,570
28. South Dakota	$ 56,850	$ 0	$271,100	$327,950
29. North Carolina	$ 58,000	$ 0	$271,100	$329,100
30. Ohio	$ 58,040	$ 0	$271,100	$329,140
31. Pennsylvania	$ 59,880	$ 0	$271,100	$330,980
32. South Carolina	$ 60,200	$ 0	$271,100	$331,300
33. Oklahoma	$ 50,700	$ 0	$271,100	$331,800
34. New Jersey	$ 70,700	$ 0	$271,100	$341,800
35. Michigan	$ 71,300	$ 0	$271,100	$342,400
36. Tennessee	$ 72,000	$ 0	$271,100	$343,100
37. Hawaii	$ 72,500	$ 0	$271,100	$343,600
38. Iowa	$ 73,425	$ 0	$271,100	$344,525
39. Montana	$ 75,940	$ 0	$271,100	$347,040
40. Minnesota	$ 77,000	$ 0	$271,100	$348,100
41. Kentucky	$ 85,350	$ 0	$271,100	$356,450
42. Washington	$ 85,500	$ 0	$271,100	$356,600
43. West Virginia	$ 89,700	$ 0	$271,100	$360,800
44. Maine	$ 90,000	$ 0	$271,100	$361,100
45. Illinois	$ 91,600	$ 0	$271,100	$362,700
46. Rhode Island	$ 96,250	$ 0	$271,100	$367,350
47. Massachusetts	$103,100	$ 0	$271,100	$374,200
48. Wisconsin	$107,875	$ 0	$271,100	$378,975
49. Oregon*	$111,600	$ 0	$271,100	$382,700
50. Idaho	$113,000	$ 0	$271,100	$384,100
51. California	$113,000	$ 0	$271,100	$384,100

*No tax after 1986 except pickup tax.

STATE-BY-STATE DEATH AND INHERITANCE TAX SUMMARY

The individual death-tax systems should be closely examined in any estate-planning situation. Most state death taxes can be avoided through estate freezing, insurance trusts, and so on. The following list describes each death-tax system in the various states, including the type of tax or taxes, the range of rates, and most available exemptions.

Alabama. Pickup tax.

Arizona. Pickup tax.

Arkansas. Pickup tax.

California. Pickup tax and inheritance tax. Transfers to surviving spouses are fully exempt. To minor child, $40,000 exempt; rates from 3% to 14%. Lineal ancestors and descendants $20,000 exempt; rates from 3% to 14%. Brothers, sisters, nieces, nephews, $10,000 exempt; rates from 6% to 20%. Others, $3,000 exempt; rates from 10% to 24%.

Colorado. Pickup tax.

Connecticut. Pickup tax and inheritance tax. Surviving spouse, $100,000 exempt; rates from 3% to 8%. Parent, child, grandchild, $20,000 exempt; rates from 2% to 8%. In-laws, stepchildren, half-bloods, $6,000 exempt; rates from 4% to 10%.

Delaware. Pickup tax and inheritance tax. Surviving spouse, $70,000 exempt; rates from 2% to 4%. Lineal ancestors and descendants, $3,000 exempt; rates from 1% to 6%. Brothers, sisters, nieces, nephews, $1,000 exempt; rates from 5% to 10%. Others, no exemption; rates from 10% to 16%.

District of Columbia. Pickup tax and inheritance tax. Surviving spouse, lineal ancestors and descendants exempt; rates from 1% to 8%. Others, $1000 exempt; rates from 5% to 23%.

Florida. Pickup tax.

Georgia. Pickup tax.

Hawaii. Pickup tax and inheritance tax. Surviving spouse, $100,000 exempt; rates from 2% to 7%. Parents, children, grandchildren, $50,000 exempt; rates from 3% to 8%. Others, $5,000 exempt; rates from 3% to 10%.

Idaho. Pickup tax and inheritance tax. Surviving spouse, minor children, $50,000 exempt; rates from 2% to 15%. Lineal ancestors and descendants, $30,000 exempt; rates from 2% to 15%. Brothers, sisters, in-laws, nieces, nephews, $10,000 exempt; rates from 4% to 20%. Aunts, uncles, $10,000 exempt; rates from 6% to 25%. Others, $10,000 exempt; rates from 8% to 30%.

Illinois. Pickup tax and inheritance tax. Surviving spouse, children, $40,000 exempt; rates from 2% to 14%. Parents, lineal ancestors, $20,000 exempt; rates from 2% to 14%. Brothers, sisters, $10,000 exempt; rates from 2% to 14%. Uncles, aunts, nieces, nephews, $500 exempt; rates from 6% to 16%. Others, $100 exempt; rates from 10% to 30%.

Indiana. Pickup tax and inheritance tax. Surviving spouses, all exempt. Orphans, $5,000 exempt for each year under 21; rates from 1% to 10%. Children, $5,000 exempt; rates from 1% to 10%. Lineal ancestors and descendants, $2,000 exempt; rates from 1% to 10%. Brothers, sisters, nieces, nephews, $500 exempt; rates from 7% to 15%. Others, $100 exempt; rates from 10% to 20%.

Indiana. Pickup tax and inheritance tax. Surviving spouse, all exempt. Orphans, $5,000 for each year under 21; rates from 1% to 10%. Children, $5,000 exempt; rates from 1% to 10%. Lineal ancestors and descendants, $2,000 exempt; rates from 1% to 10%. Brothers, sisters, nieces, nephews, $500 exempt; rates from 7% to 15%. Others, $100 exempt; rates from 10% to 20%.

Iowa. Pickup tax and inheritance tax. Surviving spouse, $80,000 exempt; rates from 1% to 8%. Children, $30,000 exempt; rates from 1% to 8%. Parents, lineal descendants, $10,000 exempt; rates from 1% to 8%. Brothers, sisters, in-laws, stepchildren, no exemption; rates from 5% to 10%. Others, no exemption; rates from 10% to 15%.

Kansas. Pickup tax and inheritance tax. Surviving spouse, $250,000 deduction; rates from 0.5% to 2.5%. Lineal ancestors and descendants, in-laws, $30,000 deduction; rates from 1% to 5%. Brothers, sisters, $5,000 deduction; rates from 3% to 12%.

Kentucky. Pickup tax and inheritance tax. Surviving spouse, infant children, $20,000 exemption; rates from 2% to 10%. Parents, children, grandchildren, $5,000 exemption; rates from 2% to 10%. Brothers, sisters, aunts, uncles, nieces, nephews, $1,000 exemption; rates from 4% to 16%. Others, $500 exemption; rates from 6% to 16%.

Louisiana. Pickup tax and inheritance tax. Surviving spouse, lineal ancestors and descendants, $5,000 exemption; rates from 2% to 3%. Collateral relations, $1,000 exemption; rates from 5% to 7%. Others, $500 exemption; rates from 5% to 10%.

Maine. Pickup tax and inheritance tax. Surviving spouse, $50,000 exemption; rates from 5% to 10%. Parents, children, $25,000 exemption; rates from 5% to 10%. Lineal ancestors and descendants, in-laws, $2,000 exemption; rates from 5% to 10%. Collateral relations, $1,000 exemption; rates from 8% to 14%. Others, $1,000 exemption; rates from 14% to 18%.

Maryland. Pickup tax and inheritance tax. Parents, surviving spouse, lineal descendants, no exemption; 1% tax. Others, no exemption; 10% tax.

Massachusetts. Pickup tax and inheritance tax. General exemption of $30,000; rates from 5% to 16%.

Michigan. Pickup tax and inheritance tax. Surviving spouse, $75,000 exemption; rates from 2% to 10%. Parents, grandparents, lineal descendants, $10,000 exemption; rates from 2% to 10%. Others, no exemption; rates from 12% to 17%.

Minnesota. Pickup tax and inheritance tax. Exemption of $175,625 in 1981 and after; rates from 1% to 16%.

Missouri. Pickup tax and inheritance tax. Surviving spouse, $20,000 and up to half of the estate; rates from 1% to 6%. Insane, blind, incapacitated lineal descendants, $15,000 exemption; rates from 1% to 6%. Lineal ancestors and descendants, $5,000 exemption; rates from 1% to 6%. Brothers, sisters, nieces, nephews, in-laws, $500 exempt; rates from 3% to 18%. Aunts, uncles, their descendants, $250 exemption; rates from 3% to 18%. Brothers or sisters of grandparents, $100 exemption; rates from 4% to 24%. Others, no exemption; rates from 5% to 30%.

Montana. Pickup tax and inheritance tax. Surviving spouse, all exempt. Minor children, grandchildren, $15,000 exemption; rates from 2% to 8%. Lineal ancestors or descendants, $7,000 exempt; rates from 2% to 8%. Brothers, sisters, in-laws, $1,000 exempt; rates from 4% to 16%. Uncles, aunts, first cousins, no exemption; rates from 6% to 24%. Others, no exemption; rates from 8% to 32%.

Nebraska. Pickup tax and inheritance tax. Surviving spouse, $10,000 and homestead exempt; rates from 0 to 1%. Parents, lineal descendants, $10,000 exempt; rates from 0 to 1%. Uncles, aunts, nieces, nephews, $2,000 exempt; rates from 6% to 9%. Others, $500 exempt; rates from 6% to 18%.

Nevada. No death taxes.

New Hampshire. Pickup tax and inheritance tax. Surviving spouse, lineal ancestors and descendants, all exempt. Others, no exemption; rate of 15%.

New Jersey. Pickup tax and inheritance tax. Grandparents, parents, spouse, and lineal descendants, $15,000 exempt; rates from 2% to 16%. Brothers, sisters, $500 exempt; rates from 11% to 16%. Others, no exemption; rates from 15% to 16%.

New Mexico. Pickup tax.

New York. Pickup tax and inheritance tax. Surviving spouse, marital deduction up to the greater of $250,000 or half the adjusted gross estate, $20,000 exempt. $500 credit. Lineal ancestors and descendants, $500 exempt, $500 credit. Others, $500 credit; rates from 2% to 21%.

North Carolina. Pickup tax and inheritance tax. Surviving spouse, $3,150 credit; rates from 1% to 12%. Lineal ancestors and descendants, remaining $3,150 credit; rates from 1% to 12%. Brothers, sisters, aunts, uncles, nieces, nephews, no exemption; rates from 4% to 16%. Others, no exemption; rates from 8% to 17%.

North Dakota. Pickup tax.

Ohio. Pickup tax and inheritance tax. General exemption of $5,000. Surviving spouse, $30,000. Minor children, $7,000. Adult children, $3,000. Rates from 2% to 7%.

Oklahoma. Pickup tax and inheritance tax with two classes. Parents, lineal descendants, $60,000 exemption; rates from 1% to 10%. Others, no exemptions; rates from 2% to 15%.

Oregon. Pickup tax and inheritance tax. General exemption of $70,000 in 1980. By 1987 inheritance tax will be eliminated. Surviving spouse, minor or incompetent children, credit of $51,600 in 1980; 12% tax rate. Others, 12% tax.

Pennsylvania. Pickup tax and inheritance tax. Grandparents, parents, lineal descendants: $2,000 deduction; 6% tax. Others, no exemption; 15% tax.

Rhode Island. Pickup tax, estate tax and inheritance tax. Estate tax is 1% in excess of $50,000 to surviving spouse and $10,000 to others. Inheritance tax; Surviving spouse, $50,000 exempt; rates from 2% to 9%. Grandparents, parents, lineal descendants, $10,000 exempt; rates from 2% to 9%. Brothers, sisters, stepchildren, and parents, $5,000 exempt; rates from 3% to 10%. Nieces, nephews, children of adopted children, $3,000 exempt; rates from 4% to 11%. Others, $1,000 exemption; rates from 8% to 15%.

South Carolina. Pickup tax and inheritance tax. Exemption of $120,000. Marital deduction of the greater of $250,000 or half the adjusted gross estate; rates from 5% to 7%.

South Dakota. Pickup tax and inheritance tax. Surviving spouse, $100,000 exempt; rates from 4.5% to 6%. Descendants, $30,000 exempt; rates from 3% to 6%. Lineal ancestors, $3,000 exempt; rates from 3% to 12%. Brothers, sisters, nieces, nephews, in-laws, $500 exempt; rates from 4% to 16%. Aunts, uncles, $200 exempt; rates from 5% to 20%. Others, $100 exemption; rates from 6% to 24%.

Tennessee. Pickup tax and inheritance tax. Marital deduction of the greater of $250,000 or half the adjusted gross estate. Surviving spouse, lineal ancestors and descendants, brothers, sisters, $120,000 exempt; rates from 5.5% to 9.5%. Others, $10,000 exempt; rates from 6.5% to 16%.

Texas. Pickup tax and inheritance tax. Surviving spouse, lineal descendants or ancestors: $200,000 exempt in 1980; rates from 1% to 6%. U.S. if used in Texas: $25,000 exempt; rates from 1% to 6%. Brothers, sisters, their descendants, $10,000 exempt; rates from 3% to 10%. Uncles, aunts, $1,000 exempt; rates from 4% to 15%. Others, $5,000 exempt; rates from 5% to 20%.

Utah. Pickup tax.

Vermont. Pickup tax.

Virginia. Pickup tax.

Washington. Pickup tax and inheritance tax. Surviving spouse and minor children, $100,000 exempt; rates from 1% to 10%. Adult children, $10,000 exempt; rates from 1% to 10%. Brothers, sisters, nieces, nephews, $10,000 exempt if no other heirs; rates from 3% to 20%. Others, no exemption; rates from 10% to 25%.

West Virginia. Pickup tax and inheritance tax. Surviving spouses, $30,000 exemption; rates from 3% to 12%. Parents, brothers, sisters, children, $10,000 exemption; rates from 3% to 13%. Grandchildren, $5,000 exemption; rates from 3% to 13%. Brothers, sisters, no exemption; rates from 4% to 18%. Other relatives, no exemption; rates from 7% to 25%. Others, no exemption; rates from 10% to 30%.

Wisconsin. Pickup tax and inheritance tax. Surviving spouse, $250,000 exemption; rates from 1.25% to 6.25%. Lineal issues or ancestors, $10,000 exemption; rates from 2.5% to 12.5%. Brothers, sisters, nieces, nephews, $1,000 exemption; rates from 7.5% to 30%. Others, $500 exemption; rates from 10% to 30%.

Wyoming. Pickup tax and inheritance tax. Surviving spouse, $200,000 exempt; 2% tax. Children, parents, brothers, sisters, $33,300 exempt; 2% tax. Grandparents, grandchildren, half-brothers or sisters, $15,500 exempt; 4% tax. Others, no exemption; 6% tax.

COMBINED RANKINGS

The last table shows the rankings of the states when their income and death tax rankings are combined. Nevada leads the list, as it is the only state without either type of taxes. Alaska and Florida are, for most purposes, equal as neither has income tax and both have a pickup estate tax. Near the bottom of the list are the country's two most populous states, New York at 28 and California at 33. Rhode Island takes the bottom spot.

COMBINED INCOME AND DEATH TAX RANKINGS

Overall Rank	State
1	Nevada
(tied) { 2	Alaska
2	Florida
3	Wyoming
(tied) { 4	Texas
4	Alabama
5	New Hampshire
6	Virginia
7	Georgia
(tied) { 8	Arkansas
8	South Dakota
9	North Dakota
10	Indiana
(tied) { 10	Maryland
10	Utah
(tied) { 11	Colorado
11	Mississippi
(tied) { 12	Connecticut
12	Arizona
13	New Mexico
14	Louisiana
(tied) { 15	Pennsylvania
15	Washington
(tied) { 16	Tennessee
16	Ohio
17	New Jersey
18	Missouri
19	Michigan
20	Vermont
21	Oklahoma
22	Kansas
23	North Carolina
24	Illinois
(tied) { 25	Nebraska
25	South Carolina
(tied) { 26	Kentucky
26	Massachusetts
27	District of Columbia
28	New York
29	Delaware
30	Hawaii
31	Montana
(tied) { 31	West Virginia
31	Idaho
(tied) { 32	Maine
32	Iowa
(tied) { 33	Wisconsin
33	California
(tied) { 34	Oregon
34	Minnesota
35	Rhode Island

Further Help and Reading

SERVICES

Updating: To be of most use to you, the information in this book needs to be as up-to-date as possible. For that purpose, my associates and I have established a newsletter, published monthly, dealing with the overall topics of inflation/tax planning. Also covered will be strategies dealing with related financial, investment, and estate matters. The name of the newsletter: *The Taxflation Fighter*. Subscription information can be obtained by writing to:

P. O. Box 3000
2411 Old Crow Canyon Road
San Ramon, California 94583

or by calling:

(415) 837-4504

Overall Financial and Tax Shelter Planning: Financial and tax planning services, commencing with a computer-based study and leading to a complete investment and tax review with specific recommendations:

Financial Planners International
1835 South State Street, Suite 299
Orem, Utah 84057
(801) 226-0845

Financial Planning Help and Service: This Utah-based company below conducts personal financial planning *seminars* throughout the United States and also markets a *home-study financial planning course*. These programs are designed to help most people. The same company is in the business of creating a variety of investment products that are sold through professional financial planners. To receive a recommendation to a comprehensive financial planner, call:

Financial Planning Services
1835 South State Street, Suite 450
Orem, Utah 84057
(801) 224-9800

Investment Products with Proper "Due Diligence": If you're not interested in the services of a financial planner but you need some timely investments, and tax shelters have been carefully reviewed and approved, call:

B.H. Newcastle Financial Group
(800) 453-1466

TAX-SHELTER STRATEGIES

The Ultimate Tax Shelter: Planning questions or a request for a preliminary corporate pension and/or profit-sharing plan design can be directed to:

> Harold Smith
> 1835 South State Street, Suite 450
> Orem, Utah 84057
> (801) 224-9800

Livestock Breeding: The Family Farm: Land Banking: Frequent seminars are conducted at various locations throughout the U.S. on this tax shelter strategy for inflation-proof investing. For information contact:

> George R. "Ron" Wright
> 3886 Winona Road
> Grants Pass, Oregon 97526
> (503) 479-8328

Precious Metal Mining:

> Financial Planners International
> 1835 South State Street, Suite 299
> Orem, Utah 84057
> (801) 226-0845

> Leon Hansen & Associates
> Consulting Geology & Geosciences
> 3333 South 900 East, Suite 230
> Salt Lake City, Utah 84106
> (801) 487-7439

Oil, Gas, & Real Estate Programs:

> Financial Planners International
> 1835 South State Street, Suite 299
> Orem, Utah 84057
> (801) 226-0845

> B.H. Newcastle Financial Group
> (800) 453-1466

BOOKS

Tax Shelters Generally:
TAX SHELTERS, A COMPLETE GUIDE
Robert and Carol Tannenhauser
1095 Harmony House
New York, New York

TAX SHELTERS AND TAX FREE INCOME
William C. Drollinger
Epic Publications, Inc.
Orchard Lake, Michigan

TAX SHELTERED INVESTMENTS HANDBOOK
Robert J. Haft and Peter M. Fass
Clark Boardman Company, Ltd.
New York, New York

TAX PLANNING FOR INVESTORS
by Jack Crestol and Herman Schneider
Dow Jones-Irwin
Homewood, Illinois

International Offshore Tax Planning:
PRACTICAL INTERNATIONAL TAX PLANNING
Marshall J. Langer, Esq.
Practicing Law Institute
New York, New York

MONEY DYNAMICS FOR THE 1980's
Venita Van Caspel
Reston Publishing Company, Inc.
Reston, Virginia

Financial Planning:
SURVIVE AND WIN IN THE INFLATIONARY 80'S
Howard J. Ruff
New York Times Books
New York, New York

Estate Planning:
THE DOW JONES-IRWIN GUIDE TO ESTATE PLANNING, Most Recent
Edition
William C. Clay, Jr.
Dow Jones-Irwin
Homewood, Illinois

Index

About the Author

B. RAY ANDERSON is an Attorney-at-Law and Member of the California and Wyoming State Bar Associations. An expert in inflation/tax planning, he is Certified as a Tax Specialist by the State Bar of California and is authorized to practice before the U.S. Tax Court. A member of the California Society of Public Accountants, Mr. Anderson has also been an attorney with the Internal Revenue Service in San Francisco.

In the course of nearly two decades of practicing tax and estate law, Mr. Anderson has helped solve the inflation/tax problems of clients in many states, including California, South Carolina, Nevada, Utah, Idaho, Oregon, Washington, Texas, and New York. He has also helped develop and has used extensively such successful inflation/tax planning strategies as equipment trusts, ancestor trusts, and a variety of family estate-freezing partnerships.

Mr. Anderson is a graduate of Brigham Young University with a degree in psychology and philosophy and a graduate of George Washington University Law School with a Doctor of Jurisprudence (law) degree. Currently the executive vice-president of Financial Planning Services, he lives with his wife and seven children in Mapleton, Utah.

NEW FROM WARNER BOOKS

POSITIONING: THE BATTLE FOR YOUR MIND
by Al Ries and Jack Trout (K30-041, $3.75)

"Positioning" is the first body of thought to come to grips with the problems of communicating in an overcommunicated (too many companies, too many products, too many media, too much marketing noise) society.

You will learn in detail some unique concepts which can help you master the media: climbing the product ladder; cherchez le creneau (look for the hole); repositioning the competition; avoiding the no-name trap; and avoiding the line-extension trap.

OFFICE POLITICS **Seizing Power, Wielding Clout**
by Marilyn Moats Kennedy (K93-718, $2.95)

Marilyn Moats Kennedy is the founder and director of Career Strategies, a unique workshop-style consulting firm teaching successful career planning and offering a mastery course in effective office politics. In this book, she shows you how to get to the top—and how to use preventive politics to stay there, how to recruit mentors, your friends upstairs, and how to use them. Above all, you'll learn how to define your career goals, set them, and achieve them.

THE ART OF JAPANESE MANAGEMENT
Applications for American Executives
By Richard Pascale & Anthony Athos (K30-366, $3.95)

After WWII, Japan borrowed and then adapted U.S. business methods. Today, in industry after industry, from radios to automobiles to microprocessing, the Japanese have become, or are rapidly becoming, more productive than the U.S.

Japan is doing something right. The authors of this provocative book assert that the biggest part of that "something" is managerial, and they explore the tools available to our managers for closing the gap between Japan and America.

INC. YOURSELF
How to Profit by Setting Up Your Own Corporation *(large format paperback)*
by Judith H. McQuown (K97-817, $4.95, U.S.A.)
(K97-855, $5.94, Canada)

In easy-to-understand terms, Judith H. McQuown, an expert in the field of money management, explains the dollars-and-cents advantages of incorporating yourself: getting "Free" life and disability insurance; setting up your own tax-sheltered pension and profit-sharing plans; obtaining greater benefits than you get through the Keogh plan; generating legitimate "cashless" tax deductions; and incorporate without a lawyer.

HELP YOURSELF AND YOUR CAREER

THE SUCCESS FACTOR
by Dr. Robert Sharpe & David King (K93-980, $2.95)

Dr. Sharpe's therapeutic principles encompass a broad program to harness your personal strengths. First, learn to pin-point and eliminate those habits and feelings that lead to failure. Then unlock those characteristics that will bring success into your social life, professional life, and sex life.

NETWORKING: The Great New Way For Women To Get Ahead
by Mary-Scott Welch (K93-578, $2.95)

At last! Women are getting together to get ahead. Ms. Welch explains how to turn the "old boy" network into a "new girl" network. Women now have the resources to use each other for help and support. Provided here is advice on how to form your own network and how to plug into those already in existence.

GAMES MOTHER NEVER TAUGHT YOU:
Corporate Gamesmanship For Women
by Betty Lehan Harragan (K36-135, $3.50)

In the first book of its kind, Ms. Harragan analyzes the rules and philosophies governing corporate politics by tracing their origins and development. She also defines the strategy, language and style necessary for you to play the game.

WORKING SMART
How to accomplish more in half the time.
by Michael LeBoeuf (K33-147, $2.95)

In his lively, humorous style, Michael LeBoeuf will teach you how to set specific goals on a daily, intermediate and lifetime basis and how to analyze and revise your present use of time accordingly.

**Put your new knowledge to work.
Let the world's greatest salesman,
JOE GIRARD,
show you how to become a success at
anything by selling yourself.**

HOW TO SELL ANYTHING TO ANYBODY
by Joe Girard   *A large-format quality paperback
(K97-719, $4.95)*

Joe Girard has shown millions of men and women involved or interested in selling exactly how they can adapt the same selling techniques that lifted Girard to the top of his profession. he tells you: how to develop a personal and very effective direct-mail program; how to size up the customer's wants, needs and what he can afford; how to get the customer to trust you and to recommend other customers; how honesty can turn a "no" into a "yes"; how to turn customer complaints into orders; and how to make a lifelong customer from the very first sale.

HOW TO SELL YOURSELF
by Joe Girard   *A large-format quality paperback
(K97-336, $4.95)*

Includes: building self-confidence and courage; developing positive attitudes; learning to listen; managing your memory; exercising enthusiasm; selling yourself without selling out; the power of a promise; the sensation of a smile; and the payoff of persistence. With an introduction by Dr. Norman Vincent Peale, HOW TO SELL YOURSELF is the tool to a better, happier, more successful life for every reader.

BESTSELLERS TO HELP YOU
GET TO THE TOP